Wakefield Press

Searching for the Spirit

Jill Roe, AO, 1940–2017, was born at Tumby Bay on South Australia's Eyre Peninsula. She was Professor Emerita in Modern History at Macquarie University, Sydney, where she was awarded a DLitt as a higher research degree for her work on Australian writer Miles Franklin, principally the Margarey Medal-winning *Stella Miles Franklin: A Biography*. Her many publications in Australian social and cultural history include numerous entries in the *Australian Dictionary of Biography* and *The Wakefield Companion to South Australian History*.

Annie Besant, c. 1897
(Library of Congress)

Searching for the Spirit

Theosophy in Australia, 1879–1939

JILL ROE

Wakefield Press

Wakefield Press
16 Rose Street
Mile End
South Australia 5031
wakefieldpress.com.au

First published as *Beyond Belief* in 1986 by New South Wales University Press,
Kensington, NSW
This Wakefield Press edition published 2020

Copyright © Jill Roe, 1986, 2020

All rights reserved. This book is copyright. Apart from
any fair dealing for the purposes of private study, research,
criticism or review, as permitted under the Copyright Act,
no part may be reproduced without written permission.
Enquiries should be addressed to the publisher.

Cover designed by Michael Deves, Wakefield Press
Edited by Marian Quartly
Typeset by Michael Deves, Wakefield Press

ISBN 978 1 74305 674 5

 A catalogue record for this book is available from the National Library of Australia

This publication has been assisted by
the History Trust of South Australia –
Wakefield Press History Initiative.

   Wakefield Press thanks Coriole Vineyards for continued support

In memoriam,

Jill Roe
1940–2017

Contents

Abbreviations	viii
Acknowledgements	xi
Preface	xiii
Introduction	1
1 The first fellows	8
2 Minds maddened by Protestantism	30
3 Legends of the nineties	57
4 'The Great Unsatisfied'	92
5 To the court of the Faerie Queene	136
6 Men, Mars and the millennium	176
7 The height of expectancy	213
8 To theosophise Australia	245
9 The end of an era	304
Notes	313
Appendix	349
Index	351

Abbreviations

AA	*Advance Australia*
ADB	Australian Dictionary of Biography
AFAL	All for Australia League
AH	*Australian Herald*
ALP	Australian Labor Party
ALS	Australian Literary Studies
ANU	Australian National University
AONSW	Archives Office of New South Wales
AOT	Archives Office of Tasmania
ARA	Australian Reform Association
ATNA	Australian Trained Nurses Association
ASA	Australasian Secularist Association
AT	*Austral Theosophist*
AWM	Australian War Memorial
BaL	Battye Library, Perth
BL	British Library
BUAV	British Union for Abolition of Vivisection
CUP	Cambridge University Press
DAB	*Dictionary of American Biography*
DLB	*Dictionary of Labour Biography*
DNB	*Dictionary of National Biography*
DT	*Daily Telegraph*
EB	*Encyclopaedia Britannica*
EN	*Evening News*
ES	Esoteric Section
FL	Fisher Library, University of Sydney
GR	General Reports of The Theosophical Society Harbinger of Light (Melbourne)
HS[ANZ]	*Historical Studies [of Australia and New Zealand]*
ITS	Independent Theosophical Society

ITYB	*International Theosophical Year Book*
JAmH	*Journal of American History*
JAS	*Journal of Australian Studies*
JCH	*Journal of Contemporary History*
JHI	*Journal of the History of Ideas*
JRH	*Journal of Religious History*
LCC	Liberal Catholic Church
LH	*Labour History*
ML	Mitchell Library, Sydney
MTS	Melbourne Theosophical Society
MUP	Melbourne University Press
NCW	National Council of Women
NLA	National Library of Australia
NSWPL	New South Wales Public Library
OCC	Old Catholic Church
OSE	Order of the Star in the East
QTS	Queensland Theosophical Society
RSPCA	Royal Society for the Prevention of Cruelty to Animals
SDF	Social Democratic Federation
SDV	Society for Debating Vivisection
SMH	*Sydney Morning Herald*
SLV	State Library of Victoria
Star	*Star in the East* (Australian Division)
TAT	*The Australian Theosophist*
TinA	*Theosophy in Australasia**
TLS	*Times Literary Supplement*
TPH	Theosophical Publishing House
TPS	Theosophical Publishing Society
TS	Theosophical Society
TSA	Theosophical Society Archives, Madras
TS-I	Theosophical Society International
TSL	Theosophical Society Library, North Sydney
TSLon	Theosophical Society Library, London
TT	*The Theosophist*
UAP	United Australia Party
UBTS	Universal Brotherhood and Theosophical Society

UQP	University of Queensland Press
VAPS	Victorian Association of Progressive Spiritualists
VS	Victorian Studies
WCTU	Women's Christian Temperance Union
WEA	Workers' Educational Association
WSG	Women's Service Guild

Note: The journal of the Theosophical Society in Australia was titled *Theosophy in Australasia* from its first issue in April 1895 to May 1921 when it was re-titled *Theosophy in Australia*. The title *The Australian Theosophist* was used July 1926–August 1933. The title *Theosophy in Australia* was resumed in June 1936 (during a brief hiatus from 1934 it appeared as *Notes and News*). The abbreviation *TinA* is used for the first and second titles, *TAT* for the third.

Acknowledgements

This book originated in research for a short entry in the *Australian Dictionary of Biography* on George Sydney Arundale, third world president of the Theosophical Society, in 1977. Further work was supported by Macquarie University, in particular by Associate Professor Bruce Harris. Along the way I received assistance from numerous and diverse theosophists, who courteously responded to inquiries and requests, and generally taught me a great deal. Much appreciated also has been reading space in theosophical libraries and archives. I would like to thank Elaine Murdoch, who was general secretary of the Theosophical Society in Australia when I began, especially for introductions to TS people. For information on the Universal Brotherhood and Theosophical Society, I am grateful to the Theosophical University Library, Altadena, California.

The flavour of this book would be quite different without interviews with Majorie Bull, Elliston Campbell, Dennis Glenny, Irene Greenwood, Helen Heney, Ian Hogbin, and Clare Thompson. I have tried to acknowledge at the appropriate place in notes all briefer but no less generous communications, likewise the many references and other aid received from colleagues. Some sources of inspiration are subliminal. A general thank you to all who have taken an interest in this book, and finer points thereof, seems most appropriate. Acknowledgement extends to members of the history honours seminar 'Themes in the history of European morals' at Macquarie, and to Michael Roberts for keeping up his TLS subscription.

Some of the ideas advanced in the text have had a preliminary run, beginning with papers to colleagues at Macquarie and to the Sydney History Group. For responses of the day, I thank audiences at *Meanjin*'s fortieth birthday seminar in Melbourne, November 1980, and the nationalism and class seminar organised by the Australian Studies Centre, University of Queensland, September 1982. In that year a version of Chapter 5 was read to the women's study staff seminar at the University of Sydney; and I was able to make a start on Marion Mahony Griffin for the Australian Historical

Association conference at the University of New South Wales. Except for a contribution to the centennial retrospect on Professor John Smith held in Sydney, October 1985, to be published in the *Journal and Proceedings of the Royal Society of New South Wales*, ensuing articles are cited in notes.

To my first readers, I express heartfelt thanks. Bruce Harris kindly commented on an incipient chapter. Marjorie Bull and Elliston Campbell attempted to save me from technical error at several points. Max Harcourt, Ken Inglis and Beverley Kingston found time to read the original typescript. I include here Venetia Nelson, who edited it. Of course, responsibility for the text rests entirely with me.

I thank the trustees and librarians of the following for permission to cite papers held: Australian Academy of Science, Australian War Memorial, Battye Library, British Library, Mitchell Library, National Library of Australia, Nuffield College, Oxford, University of Tasmania Library. I thank also archives authorities of New South Wales, Tasmania and the University of Sydney for access to sources in their custody. Permission to reproduce photographs has been granted by the Australian War Memorial, Battye Library, Mitchell Library and the National Library of Australia. Macquarie University Library inter-library loans service warrants a particular acknowledgement.

The manuscript was typed with skill and care by Jean Scott; Helen Edwards and Gwen Noble helped at difficult moments. The text was set by Sue and Kay Jones. Assistance with photography was provided by Macquarie University audiovisual services unit, in particular by Reece Scannell. I thank John Ingleson for steady progress to print.

Last but not least, the bulk of this book was written at Pearl Beach, NSW, where I found an unusually high proportion of people sympathetic to the problems of writers. Their interest and enthusiasm encouraged me and increased my appreciation of cultural traditions.

Postscript

The death of Krishnamurti was announced as this book went to press [in 1986]. I hope something of my own good fortune in getting to know the real story of this remarkable man's association with Australia will be conveyed to readers in the pages that follow.

Jill Roe, 1986

Preface

As Jill Roe has described in her Introduction to the first edition, at the time entitled *Beyond Belief*, the origins of this book lay in an entry on George Sydney Arundale, general secretary of the Theosophical Society in Australia from 1926 to 1928 that she was asked to prepare for the *Australian Dictionary of Biography* in the 1970s. F.B Smith who was first asked to write the Arundale entry had declined. It is not clear that Jill knew much about Arundale or theosophy when she began, however she was interested in intellectual history and in fringe religious groups. Brought up as a Methodist on Eyre Peninsula, she spent her Sundays while boarding in Adelaide as a schoolgirl attending different churches, curious about what they had to offer. She used to say that she was mostly interested in the morning teas or lunches she was invited to after church. But in March 1957, she was accepted by immersion into membership of the Flinders Street Baptist Church by the Rev. L.J. Gomm, known then as a charismatic preacher. Her choice may also have been influenced by one of her teachers at Unley High who was married to a former Baptist missionary and who had been helpful in practical ways such as by finding an old bicycle Jill could ride to school. Her church membership lapsed by non-attendance in 1966 and she was never again officially a member of any church though she maintained a keen intellectual interest in religious history and her research files on religious subjects were perhaps her most frequently consulted to answer the many inquiries she received.

Her honours thesis in history at Adelaide University had been on 'The Impact of Darwinism in South Australia in the latter half of the Nineteenth Century' (1962). After she moved to the ANU in Canberra to work with Manning Clark and DWA Baker for her MA she studied the intellectual life of

Melbourne between 1876 and 1886 (1965). That involved more of the debate between science and religion as well as Charles Strong's struggle with the fundamentalists at the Scots' Presbyterian Church that led him to found his own Australian Church. In 1967, Professor Bruce Mansfield chose her as one of his first appointments at Macquarie University in part because of her strong background in religious history. Bruce went on to establish the *Journal of Religious History* and to become a leading authority on Erasmus. And Jill became an early contributor to his new journal. She was thinking about further research on spiritualism in late nineteenth-century Australia when she was invited to write the entry on Arundale for the *Australian Dictionary of Biography*. The history of theosophy quickly took her back into her work on the intellectual life of late nineteenth-century Melbourne. And she had a continuing interest in Australia's links with India that she thought were underestimated and undervalued. As a student she often browsed in Mary Martin's Adelaide bookshop and was intrigued by its links to India. As well she retained an interest in Baptist missionary work in India through her sympathetic teacher at school. So it wasn't surprising that Arundale became more than a simple professional task and quickly took her seriously into the fascinating story of theosophy, its Indian connections, and its cast of influential characters in Australia. They included Alfred Deakin, Ernest Scott, professor of history at Melbourne University and son-in-law of Annie Besant, and later, the Bean family, especially journalist Charles Edwin Willoughby Bean, general editor of the Australian War Histories and leading advocate for the Australian War Memorial, and his brother Major Jack Bean Secretary General of Theosophy in Australia, also A.E. Bennett, theosophist, founder of Radio 2GB, a younger brother of Lieutenant-General Gordon Bennett.

She soon had enough material for the short entry required on Arundale, but there was much more to say about the history of theosophy in Australia so she persevered. Her research took her into theosophical archives in all the Australian capitals, also in London, the USA, and of course at Adyar outside Madras in India. Manning Clark had instilled in her the importance of seeing the places, but with the theosophists, it was their archives as well that she needed to study.

Theosophy filled an interesting niche in late nineteenth-century Australia. To a dominating Christian society it offered gentle respite or an escape for those who found the alternatives of atheism or agnosticism too harsh or definitive. It provided opportunities for spiritualism without dogma and was not without intellectual content, though it could hardly be said to be very rigorous. It also looked forward to a kind of internationalism, exploring questions that were about to become much more important in the wake of World War 1 and the decline of the British Empire, looking forward to the multiracial societies of the future, even devising a place for Aboriginal Australia as a source of ancient wisdom and knowledge. The people attracted to theosophy in Australia were thoughtful, questing refugees from orthodox Christianity. Many were women attracted to a female mystic in Madame Blavatsky and the preaching of Annie Besant who had already made her mark as a supporter of women's rights in her battles for contraception and better conditions for women workers in England. Though there were men such as Arundale and later Charles Leadbeater in important leadership roles in Theosophy there was no recognisable male hierarchy. That eventually found its place in the Liberal Catholic Church, an offshoot that emerged in England and Holland in the late nineteenth century. During the early years of twentieth century, the dominant figures in theosophy were a woman and a child: Annie Besant, and the young Indian boy chosen to become the future world teacher, Krishnamurti.

Annie Besant died in 1933 but Krishnamurti lived until 1986 having renounced his place as 'the new world teacher'. Jill was lucky enough to see and hear him preaching in a grove of large trees outside Santa Barbara in California where she had gone to visit theosophical archives in Pasadena and San Diego. In London she was able to meet Mary Lutyens, who as a girl had visited Sydney with her mother, a friend of Krishnamurti, at the time when he was about to be proclaimed as the new world teacher.

After a brief flowering in the 1920s and early '30s, theosophy in Australia fell away. Though its radio station 2GB prospered, in part because of its cultural programming (later to be supplied by the ABC) and because financially it had benefited from the bequests of some of its grateful widows, the place of religion in society was changing. By the 1960s, although the Theosophical Society still owned a bookshop in central Sydney and an office block in North Sydney best known for housing a well-regarded art cinema, the Society itself was barely known. The discovery of alternative lifestyles, alternative religions, the hippie trail, and flower power changed that. Jill's book came in time to contribute to interest, and understanding especially, of the tradition of alternative cultural movements in Western history. In the history of education, for example, interest in older forms of alternative ideas of education led to the re-discovery of Rudolph Steiner who had come out of a theosophical background. There was interest in earlier theosophical influences in the music of Scriabin, in art and architecture with the work of Mondrian and Kandisky, Sir Edwin Lutyens (designer of New Delhi and the Tomb of the Unknown Soldier in Westminster Abbey) and Mervyn Napier Waller who designed the War Memorial in Canberra. As well, the work of Walter Burley and Marion Mahony Griffin acquired added significance though they were more attracted to Rudolph Steiner's anthroposophy than Madame Blavatsky's theosophy.

While Jill was completing her manuscript, the History Department at the University of New South Wales acquired a new computer system with the latest in word processing capacity. It seemed a good idea to use this excess capacity to publish small numbers of worthwhile manuscripts or history theses for which there would not be a great demand but that would add usefully to the dissemination of research in history. The UNSW Press hitherto concerned largely with publishing and distributing huge volumes of course materials became a partner in this experiment of which *Beyond Belief* was a part. Computerised typesetting developed at an incredible rate and soon the production qualities of the Modern History Series had improved out of recognition. With content probably slightly ahead of its time, the primitive appearance of *Beyond Belief* almost certainly told against it too, yet it found a niche in Australian cultural (and religious) history. This modern revised edition, retitled *Searching for the Spirit*, will make it available once more to a wider readership and serve as a fitting memorial to the life and work of Jill Roe.

Beverley Kingston
Pearl Beach
April 2018

Introduction

Not much has been heard of theosophy in recent times. Neither theosophy nor theosophists are a familiar quantity; the theosophical presence has receded so far since the 1930s that many people have heard of neither. But, to mention the best-known people to be glimpsed in these pages, Alfred Deakin, Sir Ernest Scott, Christopher Brennan, Rose Scott, Dr C.E.W. Bean and Miles Franklin were all acquainted with either theosophy or theosophists. In some parts of Australia theosophy was once highly respectable, Perth for example. Elsewhere it was notorious, especially in Sydney, and attracted press attention. During lecture tours by the second president of the Theosophical Society, the renowned ex-Fabian socialist, Annie Besant, thousands flocked to hear it expounded. Interest and with it knowledge has declined greatly since World War II.

Reasons for forgetfulness and lack of interest are not hard to find. Theosophists have seldom been historically minded and there are aspects of theosophical history which survivors might reasonably hope to forget. The only accounts published from within are now more than a generation old: the anonymous documentation of *The Theosophical Movement 1875–1925* (1925), Josephine Ransom's compilation *A Short History of the Theosophical Society* (1938) and *How Theosophy came to Australia and New Zealand (1943)* by Mary Neff. Since then few outsiders have been attracted to the subject, apart from cultural historians pursuing other themes and students of communitarianism in southern California. Bruce Campbell's *Ancient Wisdom Revived* (1980) is an accessible American introduction, but the author is not much interested in the rest of the world or the broad span of theosophical history before the revival of 'alternative' religion in the 1960s. However there have been several excellent biographies of leading theosophical personalities: A.H. Nethercot's two-volume biography of Annie Besant, *The First Five Lives of Annie Besant* (1960) and *The Last Four Lives of Annie Besant* (1963), Mary Lutyens' two volumes on the life of Krishnamurti (1975 and 1983), Marion Meade's *Madame Blavatsky* (1980), and most recently *The Elder Brother. A biography of Charles Webster Leadbeater* (1982) by Gregory Tillett.

We live in a determinedly secular age. It is inevitable that little meaning now attaches to theosophy, which might easily be seen as an early version of do-it-yourself religion. The *Macquarie Dictionary* offers a nicely distanced definition. It refers to 'forms of philosophical or religious thought in which claim is made to a special insight into the divine nature or to a special divine revelation'. More elaborate definitions are to be found in historical dictionaries and in religious encyclopaedias. In Hastings' *Encyclopaedia of Religion and Ethics* the entry for the Theosophical Society is written by Annie Besant.

As a mode of religious thought theosophy has a long history, dating back to the third century BC. It seems that theosophy has impinged most on society at times of anxiety and reorientation, as during the Protestant Reformation in sixteenth-century Europe. The revival of theosophy in the late nineteenth century coincided with another such period, when the impact of Darwinism was first felt. *The Origin of Species* was published in 1859. Modern theosophy dates from the mid-1870s.

The heyday of the modern theosophical movement extended from the 1890s to the 1920s, during which time it gained a foothold in many countries, including Australia. Since the 1890s, the aims of the theosophical movement have been exceedingly clear. They have been to constitute a nucleus of universal brotherhood regardless of distinctions of caste, class, colour, creed or sex, on the basis of man's latent powers and truths said to be common to all religions. Modern theosophy struck a note of high idealism; and in an era when nationalism has been a leading preoccupation, it has remained self-consciously internationalist. At heart the movement has been primarily mystical and occult. The historical significance of such a movement is not readily discerned. It is obscured by the fact that in modern history theosophy has been very much a peripheral force. Theosophy played no obvious role in metropolitan, especially British, history where it has been regarded as at best an amiable eccentricity, and little is known of it in northern Europe (though it was apparently quite strong in Holland and it is said to have played a part in the construction of a German ideology in the early twentieth century). However it was more noticeable in archaic and oppressed cultures at the margins of European civilisation. It is no accident that prominent figures in the Celtic revival like the poets 'AE' and William Butler Yeats espoused theosophy, or that theosophical circles sprang up in St Petersburg before World War I. A theosophical contribution is also evident in cultures then young, notably in North America, as suggested by recent studies in the idealist tradition in Canada and utopian experiment in the United States. Most striking is the role played by theosophy in colonial contexts, where it could be quite important as a strengthener of nativist elites. In India and in Indonesia it provided a non-racist forum and was a catalyst for nationalist movements. Indeed as recently as 1977 an Indian theosophist, Mrs Rukmini Arundale, was seriously considered for the presidency. It is also interesting to note that President Sukarno's father was a lifelong theosophist, and that the Theosophical Society played a part in Sukarno's education. These instances suggest that although theosophy seems at first sight arcane, and an unlikely historical subject, yet it made sense to some people in some places under some circumstances, usually colonial places and oppressive circumstances.

A theosophical presence in Australia has not previously been noticed. This is not simply because theosophy appealed only to a minority. That was the case everywhere. It is also due to what Dorothy Green has called a reluctance to take religious ideas seriously, and more generally to the cultural immaturity characteristic of young countries. It is hard to detect the relevant cultural pattern in Australia's brief history.

Chronology helps. The rise of theosophy in Australia coincided almost exactly with the decline of empire and the rise of modern concepts of nationhood, and its heyday encompassed the construction of a national as distinct from an imperial culture. Not only was theosophy present at these transitions, but it made a particular contribution. With the theosophical movement a little of the Indian experience of empire and nationhood filtered through to White Australia.

Moreover a cultural pattern does exist, or at least it was in the making, and theosophy drew on some of its elements. The pattern emerged from the ruins of revealed religion. It begins, as Henry Mayer has shown in *Marx, Engels and Australia* (1964) in the 1870s, with the motley collection of radicals and spiritualists who joined the First International. A thread runs from the 1880s through ethical halfway houses like Charles Strong's Australian Church in Melbourne to more diffuse concern in the early twentieth century about 'soft' moral issues like peace and the environment. Other responses to secularisation may be traced across the period through the rise of 'the Religion of Socialism' and in the creation of a civic religion in Australia after World War I. Against the powerful forces of materialism and utilitarianism, and the countervailing moral authority of the Christian churches, an alternative cultural tradition was in the making in Australia.

Paradoxically the quickest way to situate theosophy in an alternative cultural pattern is to compare and contrast it with a later movement normally regarded as part of the opposing materialist tradition, international socialism. This may seem a little far-fetched, as far-fetched as key theosophical teachings have always seemed to a majority of Australians, but it is valid in the framework of intellectual and cultural history. The two movements had much in common, and their histories overlap. Like the communist movement, the theosophical movement constituted an internationalist minority and it mobilised indigenous idealism. It was to organised religion as communism was to the organised working class. Of course there are fundamental contrasts of values and composition, and whereas the theosophical movement reached its peak in the 1920s, the story of international socialism was just beginning: its strength lay ahead in the 1940s. For present purposes, perspective is provided by the fact that in the 1920s there were more paid-up theosophists than members of the Communist Party in Australia.

The story of a forgotten or superseded idealism is intrinsically interesting. It may also be of wider significance. Idealism has taken a terrible battering in the twentieth century. But, in fragmented form, it survives, a much-debated tradition and recurrent resource. Like most idealisms, theosophy has been riddled with ambiguity, mostly of its own making. The motto of the Theosophical Society, 'There is no religion higher than Truth', is a disturbing rather than reassuring formulation in the Age of Relativity, a forewarning of the goodly number of what Manning Clark calls spiritual bullies in the theosophical movement. And, as with many historical idealisms, theosophy has been Janus-faced, looking backwards more readily than forwards. But it meant to look forward, and its logic was progressive. Not surprisingly, by its own standards it did quite well in Australia.

This book represents a first foray into the history of theosophy in Australia. It charts the rise and comparatively speaking, the fall of theosophy, from 1879 when the Theosophical Society enrolled its first Australian member, to 1939 when its secular mission was well and truly exhausted. The onset of World War II marks the end of an era in both theosophical and cultural history. As devotees of theosophical bookshops will know, an organised theosophical presence is sustained in Australia to the present day; tolerance of non-Christian religious positions is much greater now, and theosophists still believe that history will vindicate them. But the theosophical movement has never regained the momentum lost in the 1930s.

From the 1890s to the 1920s, theosophy made the most of conditions specific to a small, rich, remote and dependent society, and it had a momentum of its own. Chapters 1 and 2 address the obvious questions 'What is theosophy?' and 'Who were the theosophists?' in the historical context of late Victorian religious unease and associated cultural ferment in the colonial cities. From Chapter 3 onwards the fortunes of theosophy are pursued through the legendary 1890s and the years of federation and of feminism to the Great War of 1914–1918 and into the turbulent, millenarian 1920s to which two chapters are devoted; and so to abrupt decline in the 1930s, not so coincidentally the years of the Great Depression.

Annie Besant once defined theosophy as the embodiment of the highest morality, an irony considering the difficulties theosophy was to encounter with morality narrowly defined. Nevertheless, in a narrative increasingly paced by the astonishing expectation of a coming World Teacher and plans for a World-Religion, many moral issues emerge. The list includes race, gender, species, progressive education, peace and plenty, high culture and music, quality broadcasting, and the spiritual in art. There is scarcely an issue today called trendy with which theosophists were not concerned three-quarters of a century ago, and at its broadest this book reflects on the making of modern morality.

Ever since the 1880s alternative or 'underground' ideas about religion as about economics have either challenged or enriched the status quo. At the very least, it will be argued, theosophical perspectives expose and exploit tensions in orthodox religious history and test the scope of cultural history. But theosophical perspectives offer more. During the Besant era theosophy oversaw some crucial cultural transitions, and as dynamic heterodoxy sought to control them. In the late 1920s, theosophists entered politics to preach the harmonies of class and culture which the movement always advocated. Furthermore, the presence of a theosophical movement casts idealism in Australia in a different light from that shed by the better-known bush proletarians. The urban middle class which flowed in and out of the theosophical movement bespeaks a different cultural pattern, not least because there were so many women.

In Australia as elsewhere, the theosophical movement suffered splits. In fact it was normally divided, and its divisions were undoubtedly damaging. Yet for some reason, probably because of relative size, the splits in Australia do not seem to have had the same drastic institutional effect as in America (nor to have generated substantial dissident records). In Australia, dissident forces were usually overshadowed by the Theosophical Society, which was the main and enduring body. As a history of theosophy and theosophists, this book includes dissidents as well as loyalists, sometimes at centre stage, and in later chapters extends as far as alternative theosophia to the anthroposophy of Walter Burley and Marion Mahony Griffin. That is, it is not simply the story of the Theosophical Society, though the story is woven around the main body. Neither is it an historical sociology of Australian theosophists, valuable as that would be. As much biographical and sociological evidence as possible is included, but overall it is uneven and fragmentary. What is attempted is a general cultural history of the theosophical movement which situates theosophy in the history of the 'thinking classes'. There is as yet no general history of the intelligentsia in Australia, but when it comes the heretical theosophists ought to be in it, not as original thinkers – how many of those will there be? – but as ardent eclectics and would-be innovators.

The theosophical mind-set may seem strange today. Theosophical objectives remain accessible, but the basic texts and seemingly endless adumbrations thereon are hardly compelling reading, at least to the outsider. They have been cited at crucial points, often at length, for flavour and fairness. The underlying message was meant to be challenging, especially by Annie Besant, the dominant and domineering figure in these pages. (No matter how hard one tries to tell the story 'from within' and 'from below' the big figures light it up; and in any case the later Annie Besant is a significant historical figure in her own right as one of labour's lost leaders and that considerable peculiarity in British history, a woman religious leader.) All revelatory challenges are open to both credulity and incredulity, and whatever the reader may conclude, it is not the business of the historian to improve upon them or to do what only the passage of time can do, that is adjudicate upon matters of belief. Not that the early and impatient theosophists would have agreed with such liberalism. They meant to get beyond belief to certainty.

1

The first fellows

On 8 September 1875, in New York, Helena Petrovna Blavatsky, Henry Steel Olcott and fourteen others formed a society to save Religion: to rescue it from its enemies, to revitalise its forms, to restore its authority. In a flash of inspiration, they called the project theosophy. 'Theosophy', from the Greek *theosophia* meaning wisdom about things divine, suited their purposes nicely: a secure word, but fresh and unfamiliar; an interesting word which took the mind both forwards and back into history; big, bold and versatile. The Theosophical Society, as it became, held its inaugural meeting later that year, on 17 November 1875. According to the preamble to its by-laws, 'The Title of the Theosophical Society explains the objects and desires of its founders: they "seek to obtain knowledge of the nature and attributes of the Supreme Power, and of the higher spirits *by the aid of physical processes*"'.[1] The new society would be known officially as The Theosophical Society. In time, to its members the Theosophical Society would become, simply, the TS.

The Theosophical Society has earned a place in history as the first effective populariser of the Wisdom of the East, and for its role in fostering Indian and other nationalisms. It also belongs to that history of social thought which takes as its starting point the corrosion of Christianity in the West in the middle of the nineteenth century and follows the path of secularisation into the twentieth. With roots deep in the turbulence of Victorian religion and its alternatives, the Theosophical Society sprang directly from dissatisfaction with spiritualism and from hope of the equally mid-Victorian occult revival. In the founders' words, latter-day theosophists hoped that 'by going deeper than modern science has hitherto done into the

Helena Petrovna Blavatsky, a co-founder of the Theosophical Society
along with Henry Steel Olcott (Campbell Collection)

esoteric philosophies of ancient times', they might 'attain for themselves and other investigators proof of the existence of an "unseen universe", the nature of its inhabitants if such there be, and the laws which govern their relationship with mankind'.[2]

The society spoke in the language of liberalism and secularism. Disclaiming any dogmatic intent it dissociated itself from all existing religions, and offered membership, or fellowship, to all genuine truth-seekers. It pinned its flag to freedom of thought.

Late Victorian culture was hospitable to, indeed saturated with, radical religious thought. Wherever its domain, theosophy could expect attention, though exactly when depended upon the speed with which ships could move the requisite people and publications. An audience existed in Australia, as elsewhere. The colonial intelligentsia followed debate in the great metropolitan journals, which by the 1870s took an interest in historical and comparative religion, and they contributed to it themselves in new and substantial quarterlies established in Melbourne and Sydney. In all it took about two years for theosophy to make its way so far. News came first from travellers' tales, and then in spiritualist papers. The reading public gleaned a little from accounts of the first modern theosophical treatise, H.P. Blavatsky's

Isis Unveiled. A Master-key to the Mysteries of Ancient and Modern Science and Theology, a vigorous work in two volumes which appeared in 1877 and sold astonishingly well. Not long after, the young Alfred Deakin read the book with enthusiasm, though it does not seem to have been reviewed by the leading Australian spiritualist journal, the Melbourne *Harbinger of Light*.[3]

The year 1878 brought first-hand information about the Theosophical Society, in the agreeable person of Emma Hardinge Britten, a touring trance lecturer from America, in whose New York drawing room the society first assembled. Then, in December 1879, the *Harbinger* noticed the first issue of a new theosophical monthly published in Bombay, *The Theosophist*, edited by the mysterious Madame Blavatsky herself. The Melbourne spiritualist and proprietor of the *Harbinger*, William H. Terry (1836–1913), remarked that its appearance 'throws some light on what was previously obscure, and enables us to recognise in the Theosophist, an intelligent worker in the field of spiritual science'. Terry announced himself pleased with theosophy. 'We infer from the articles in "The Theosophist" that the object of the association it represents is a philosophical study of the laws and forces of nature, as manifest in both the material and spiritual universe, and the utilisation of the knowledge discoverable by their researchers'. Evidently, theosophists were like-minded people, allies in the development of rational religion.[4]

Subsequently, attentive readers of the *Harbinger* learned that Terry had joined the society, presumably unaware of its hostility to mere spiritualism; also that they could order *The Theosophist*, at the moderate rate of 20/- per annum, through Terry, accredited agent for Victoria. With that development colonists attracted by the sound of theosophy immediately improved their chances. Now they might peruse theosophical literature for themselves, rather than rely on second-hand accounts, and, thanks to imperial sea lanes, within weeks of publication.[5]

In fact, the Theosophical Society gained its first Australian recruit before the arrangement with Terry. A Melburnian called Gilbert Elliott joined in December 1879. An otherwise shadowy figure with an interest in Indian religion, Elliott was, in theosophical terms, the first fellow of the Theosophical Society in Australia, and thereby entitled to add the credential FTS after his name.[6]

Not that better communications in the 1880s created a flood of fellows. In 1881 a study group formed in Brisbane. By 1883 there were perhaps two dozen theosophists in Australia. Several other study groups formed tentatively during the decade, including a small branch in Hobart in 1889, which survived to be the oldest continuous lodge (to use the later theosophical word) in Australian theosophy. By 1889 the Australian fellows registered at the society's headquarters in India made up a handful of earnest and advanced 'truth-seekers'.[7]

The 1880s represent the first, informal phase of theosophy in Australia. Those who joined the society did so as individuals. They belonged to the eastern division. When Colonel Olcott PTS (president of the Theosophical Society) attempted to organise theosophists in Australia into a separate division, or section, of the society in 1891, a new phase began, though as will be seen the movement was very weak. Even in its first modest phase, theosophy proved to be a volatile affair. However the first Australian fellows of the Theosophical Society approached it soberly, cautiously, using whatever literature lay to hand. The new journal *The Theosophist*, expansively subtitled *A Monthly Journal devoted to Oriental philosophy, art, literature and occultism: embracing mesmerism. spiritualism and other secret sciences*, was probably the most helpful source of answers to immediate questions, such as 'What is theosophy?' and 'Who are the theosophists?'.

The editor of *The Theosophist* stated plainly that theosophy was the ancient 'Wisdom-Religion' dating back to Ammonius Saccas and Plotinus of the Neo-Platonic School at Alexandria, and far beyond, as far back as the sacred Indian Vedas. It consisted of mystical and esoteric knowledge – brutally suppressed in the Christian era – about the 'single Supreme Essence, Unknown and Unknowable': 'Theosophy and Theosophists have existed ever since the first glimmering of nascent thought made man seek instinctively for the means of expressing his own independent opinions,' wrote Madame Blavatsky. Further, with 'that higher intuition acquired by *Theosophia*', and the 'exact science of psychology' known to the ancient schools, came illumination and the rescue of souls from current misuse and decay of spiritual powers. Recovery necessitated a pure life (at that stage active membership of the Theosophical Society involved initiation and ritual promotion through the Mysteries). 'Purity of deed and thought can alone raise us to an intercourse "with the gods" and attain for us the goal we desire.' The editorial stated that modern theosophy believed in 'transmigration (evolution) or a series o[f] changes in the soul'.

It was further explained that theosophists were misrepresented and persecuted on all sides. It had always been so. But the new society stood for tolerance, for free and fearless investigation; in effect a 'Republic of Conscience'. All but atheists and bigoted sectarians would find a place, though the insane dreamers of socialism and communism were surely anathema to true students of religion. Otherwise, all were welcome to join the society, 'as all work for one and the same object, namely, the disenthralment of human thought, the elimination of superstitions, and the discovery of truth, all are equally welcome'.[8]

Blavatsky stressed particularly the superior possibilities of theosophy as compared with spiritualism, now proven not only narrow, but dangerous to its practitioners, amateur manipulators of powerful unseen forces. The findings of spiritualism could be comprehended only if they were recognised as but feeble repetitions of what had already been seen and studied in former epochs, indicated by a formidable collection of references to ascetics, mystics, theurgists, prophets, ecstatics, astrologers, 'magicians' and 'sorcerers' in times past.

All this led straight back to Blavatsky's book, *Isis Unveiled*. Though the journal made good its promise of membership of a learned society implied by the initials FTS, journal articles by many hands offered only fragmentary insights into the wisdom religion. The serious student would want to lift the veil of Isis too. The very title excited the imagination, harnessing contemporary fascination with all things Egyptian. That a woman writer proposed to expound on Isis the pre-Christian fertility goddess added interest.[9]

The book, a theosophical classic which still sells well, proved to be a touch on the times in more substantial ways. Although critics today tend to dismiss *Isis Unveiled* as an incredible grab-bag and to deplore the failure of theosophists to rescue it from charges of plagiarism, it was a challenging work for the well-informed reader with its energetic references to the daily disputants in the continuing battle between 'Science' and 'Religion'. Madame Blavatsky's literary debut enjoyed a measure of attention because her book presented the underside of debate about the future of religion in the late 1870s.

It did so at a cracking pace. A brief preface, submitting the treatise to public judgement, identified likely opposition to an effort 'to detect the vital principles which underlie the philosophical systems of old': Christians, scientists, pseudo-scientists, liberals and 'the mercenaries and parasites of the press'. Taking her stand on adamantine Truth, and the future, she proclaimed the day of domineering over men with dogmas to have reached its gloaming:

> The contest now going on between the party of public conscience and the party of reaction, has already developed a healthier tone of thought. It will hardly fail to result ultimately in the overthrow of error and the triumph of Truth ... we are laboring for the brighter morrow. (p. viii)

It emerges from *Isis Unveiled* that prospects for a 'brighter morrow' rested on more than 'tall tales from the East', though these abound. Madame Blavatsky's knowledge of Eastern adepts and their science are here sincerely proffered, as she said in the preface. They rested also on an obscure historical perspective, the survival of the ancient wisdom religion. In so far as *theosophia*, the wisdom religion, had survived as a tradition or way of thought in the West in the Christian era, it did so as magical or mystical knowledge, preserved by masters of the occult, magi and the like, among initiates and brotherhoods suppressed or rejected. Recent historical research into renaissance science and philosophy, and new evidence of theosophic aspiration in the plebeian culture of the eighteenth century, have clarified Blavatsky's perspective. As her readers may have known, the occult revival of which *Isis Unveiled* is a part, caught the dying ebb of an older and rejected culture. It did so at a time when spiritualism and the study of psychic phenomena were most fashionable, and interest in Asian religions was rising.[10]

Over some 1300 pages, Blavatsky urged the merits of ancient wisdom. Her treatise, divided into two volumes, 'Science' and 'Theology', contained abundant illustration of vitality. There are, following Bruce Campbell's resume, chapters on spiritualism, modern science, psychism, mesmerism, the cabbala, ancient feats and other wonders (volume 1) and secret societies, esoteric Christianity and comparative religion (volume 2). Against the merits of ancient wisdom were ranged the follies of modern science and dogmatic theology, whose rival claims so perplexed thoughtful people in the 1870s.[11]

Basically, Blavatsky advanced ancient wisdom as antidote to Darwinism. She announced that the day of modern materialism was done. 'The mere life-principle itself presents an unsolvable enigma, upon the study of which materialism has vainly exhausted its intellectual powers.' (I, 336) Likewise a positive perspective was available, by simple inversion of Darwinian premises. The ancient wisdom taught that 'all things had their origin in spirit-evolution having originally begun from above and proceeded downward instead of the reverse, as taught in the Darwinian theory'. (I, 154) And on that, Blavatsky asserted mysteriously, 'the last word was pronounced ages ago' – hence the book's subtitle, 'A Master-key'. Repressive and disreputable theologies could be discarded.

Amid the profusion of clues, two main sources of illumination and progress stand out, not only lost knowledge, but also, more startling, direct tutelage. Whereas knowledge of the divine could be reconstructed from ancient sources said to be preserved by secret fraternities in both East and West, on historic sites as far apart as Central America and 'Nangkor Watt', and in the rituals of Eastern holy men, spiritual evolution could be achieved by the individual with the aid of living masters, said to be located in the recesses of Thibet – then closed to the West – and able to materialise in the cause of true religion. Madame Blavatsky claimed that Masters helped her write her book (though others have since found more mundane sources of inspiration, including the Rosicrucian novels of middle-ranking mid-Victorian Tory politician Bulwer-Lytton). Madame Blavatsky's Masters are envisaged as members of a Great White Brotherhood or occult hierarchy ruling the world, and guides for disciples or *chelas* on the upward path. With this Blavatsky touched upon the ancient mystical tradition of 'mastery'; and the Masters became a dominant theosophical teaching and selling point – nothing more than perfected men, said one convert, of which there are examples in every religious tradition; a spiritualist up-date, says a more recent student of the irrational in modern history.[12]

In this manner, Madame Blavatsky meant to pull the rug from under current debate on 'Religion versus Science'. Equipped with a spiritualised view of history and evolution, and various themes from the occult tradition, the new theosophy was being positioned to promote a grand new synthesis of religion and science. As Bruce Campbell has concluded, hope of synthesis accounts for the interested reception of *Isis Unveiled* and subsequent readership:

Its readership has been composed to a large extent of educated persons to whom religion is important but who have become estranged from established religious organisations ... The idea of a wisdom-religion, a universal and ageless occult knowledge derived from a civilisation in which there was a unity between science and religion, suggests a possible common ground between science and religion, and a way to integrate the insights of the various faiths into a grand synthesis.[13]

When the basic texts were first studied in Australia, and what the earliest theosophic students made of them, is unknown. Perhaps they were sustained at first by other texts, such as Sir Edwin Arnold's immensely popular rendition of the life and teachings of the Buddha, *The Light of Asia*, published in 1879; or, like an early New Zealand theosophist Edward Toronto Sturdy, by an eighteenth-century translation of the Hindu epic, the *Bhagavad Gita*. A known source of encouragement was Edward Maitland (1824–1897) whose self-imposed life work of re-establishing religion on the basis of 'first principles, necessary truths and self-evident propositions' began in Goulburn, New South Wales in the 1860s. Later, in London, in collaboration with the compelling anti-vivisectionist Dr Anna Kingsford, he wrote *The Perfect Way* (1881), which, along with the writings of the aristocratic utopian spiritualist Laurence Oliphant, served to encourage a tiny band of would-be theosophists in Melbourne. H.W. Hunt recalled that these works helped at a time when the teaching was difficult and obscure; it was 'a red-letter day' when a copy of *Isis Unveiled* arrived. Like another early adherent and stalwart, the young commercial traveller S.T. Studd, Hunt's own first inspiration came from two books published in London in the early 1880s: A.P. Sinnett's *The Occult World* (1881) and *Esoteric Buddhism* (1883). These books created a sensation and were widely reviewed because the author, previously editor of an important paper in India, the *Allahabad Pioneer*, discussed 'the Mahatma letters' which he claimed to have received from Madame Blavatsky's Masters, precipitated from the astral plane. Whatever the case, as *The Theosophist* said, interested persons could make further application to the society in Bombay.[14]

By 1880 the Theosophical Society was in its fifth year. It had been launched by a doubtful assemblage of marginal intellectuals, not all of them pillars of respectability. Of these, three proved of lasting importance: Madame Blavatsky, Colonel Olcott and William Quan Judge, at the time the least of the three, but in whom, it had to be conceded, some leadership qualities did reside. (Judge, a wily Irish attorney, led the first of many splits in the wisdom religion, in America, but that was yet twenty years away.)[15]

Of course, in terms of intellect and image, Madame Blavatsky was the most important. Helena Petrovna Blavatsky, nee von Hahn (1831–1891), a White Russian of superior lineage, had long since abandoned her native steppes and an unfortunate youthful marriage for goodness knows how many careers and affairs in more places than she was ever prepared to specify – as a circus-rider, medium, magician, shopkeeper, journalist, in the Levant, London, perhaps Central Asia – before arriving in New York in 1873, aged forty-two, without visible means of support; but a lady nonetheless, as the title 'Madame' signified. And then there was Henry Steel Olcott (1832-1907), who had been a colonel in the Northern army during the American Civil War. When Olcott met HPB – the customary affectionate abbreviation – he too was just into the treacherous forties, and had behind him a worthy career in agriculture, first as a young farmer out west in Ohio, later as an experimenter, educator and journalist, then in the army where he was responsible for clearing up supply rackets, and latterly in law. All these he abandoned as his long-lived interest in spiritualism grew, and Madame Blavatsky laid hold of his imagination in the early 1870s. Like Judge, he came from a sober nonconformist background; but he was amiable and worldly too; and, to the distress of his wife, he entered into a lifelong partnership with Helena Blavatsky. These two are always acknowledged the co-founders of the Theosophical Society.[16]

As initially constituted, the Theosophical Society had scant chance of survival. The original sixteen faltered and disagreed, in an abundance of words. After the initial novelty wore off, and ridicule abated following a short-lived and agreeable notoriety caused by their public cremation of an unexpectedly impecunious member called 'Baron de Palm', interest waned. Blavatsky embarked on *Isis Unveiled* to shore up the cause which, as envisaged from her New York apartment 'The Lamasery', was weakening the while. In July 1878 she became an American citizen; but for all the amazing exuberance of religious life in Victorian America, it was not after all the promised land, nor an hospitable environment for theosophy. Fortunately, at that point, the founders received support from an unexpected but plausible source, from India. The Arya Samaj, a reforming Hindu group in Bombay (with which the young Gandhi was associated) proposed they join forces.[17]

So Blavatsky and Olcott took their chance and embarked for India via London on 19 December 1878. In London, theosophical correspondents and circles of spiritualists formed in response to the flood of mediums from post bellum America proved hospitable. A London branch formed in January 1879, a 'fashionable dress-coat affair' according to secularist Annie Besant, later to be graced by such notable figures as William Butler Yeats, and Oscar and Constance Wilde.[18]

News of HPB's drawing-room performances even reached Australia. Enthusiastic spiritualist and ex-representative for Sandhurst (Bendigo), W.D.C. Denovan, published in Melbourne in 1882 a vast compilation of *The Evidences of Spiritualism*, which included a report of Blavatsky en route, of various phenomena performed by her, and a curious dinner-table facial transformation – which might well have happened, given HPB's addiction to hashish. The reminiscences of Victorian annalist James Bonwick include an undated encounter with Blavatsky, whom he found somewhat overpowering.[19] Anyway, the flight to India – for flight it was as far as Olcott's family were concerned – proved to be the making of them and their society, as well as a convenience for followers in far-off Australia.

They arrived in Bombay mid-February 1879. Things went badly at first, but worldly, adaptable and, in a curious way, committed, the pair survived. Their first initiative *The Theosophist* made its way with surprising ease. By 1880 the society was organised into eight branches, in three countries: feeble in America, lively in London, and most promising in India. Educated Indians were only too happy to discuss their religious inheritance with unpatronising Europeans. Madame Blavatsky remarked that India owed nothing to Christianity except the Mutiny.

By 1882 the two founders had gathered enough support to create a proper headquarters in India. For £600, mainly proffered by rich Indians, they acquired Huddlestone's Gardens, a spacious mansion on the banks of the Adyar River eight miles south of Madras, now deserted as its erstwhile occupants repaired by rail to summer at the hill station of Ootacamund. They renamed it Adyar. Set in twenty-eight acres of lush tropical estuarine land, the Adyar compound has served as headquarters of the Theosophical Society ever since.[20]

Again, the founders chose well. The mission to rescue religion had found an appropriate locale. Madras, capital of the southern presidency of the British Raj was, on the one hand, a well-established provincial centre of British power and influence, and on the other a gateway to southern India, with its antique religious traditions virtually intact, its inheritance visible in an abundance of decaying temples. From Madras, the lines of communication spread out into old India, and through its port, to the farthest reaches of the British Empire. It was almost like coming home for Blavatsky, bred on the margins of imperial Russia and nurtured on provincial administrative life. Despite intermittent fears that she was really a Russian spy, and for all that a dreadful notoriety soon attended her, in part because of her hostility to Christian missions, Blavatsky and her partner could relax, in a site self-contained and superb, with plentiful servants and native notabilities in attendance.

By 1883, the fortunes of theosophy and the Theosophical Society seemed set fair. The ever-practical Olcott, who had long since abandoned early efforts at trade (agencies for tiger skins, perfumes) for evangelism, turned to the sad state of Buddhism in nearby Ceylon and attended to reform in education, including girls' education, and in agriculture, for which efforts he is honoured there still. The society now boasted the issue of ninety-five charters for branches, predominantly in India, a flourishing journal, the beginnings of a priceless library, and a secure home. News of theosophic advance in India duly appeared in the Melbourne *Harbinger of Light*.[21]

The feats of modern aeronautics notwithstanding, India in the 1880s was much closer to Australia than it is today, geopolitically speaking. The subcontinent, finally subdued under British rule after the traumatic Mutiny of 1857, had recently been declared the brightest jewel in the British crown. The Australian colonists were strongly loyal to the crown, even in the 1870s which saw an eddy of republicanism, and communications from the edge to the heart of the empire improved dramatically in that decade (with the telegraphic cable to Europe, and the Suez Canal). Many Australians, perhaps proportionately as many as Britons, knew India well, as continuous contact through governors, traders and missionaries would surely testify. Ex-army officers and tea-planters often retired to Australia. (As will emerge, there was also a small but unregarded resident Indian population in Australia.) The copious cups of tea daily consumed by Australians came mainly from the subcontinent, and there were other economic links, the horse trade for example. Hence the constant movements of an imperial people created contacts now unusual: the route 'Home' touched India usually at Bombay, then 'the Venice of the East', also at Colombo, and sometimes Madras. Even before the founders of the Theosophical Society settled in Madras, when they were struggling for a foothold in Bombay, it was quite simple for interested people from Australia to do what *The Theosophist* advised – that is, apply direct to India.

An early convert to theosophy in Australia did just that. Professor John Smith (1821–1885), foundation professor of chemistry and experimental physics at the University of Sydney, travelling Home on study leave in January 1882, stopped off in Bombay. He joined the society on 14 January, the second New South Welshman to do so (being preceded by Gavin Pettigrew). Having met Madame Blavatsky and learned more about her Masters, he received personal messages from one, the Master M(orya), apparently materialised from the astral plane. The *Melbourne Harbinger* published Professor Smith's strange experiences, along with W.H. Terry's earlier claim to have communicated with the other main theosophical Master, Master Koot-Hoomi, through a clairvoyant 'of exceptionally good lucidity', an event which Madame Blavatsky refused to confirm or deny.[22]

It was otherwise with Professor Smith, instructed by the Master M. to '[w]ork for us in Australia, and we will not prove ungrateful, but will prove to you our actual existence'. Smith was puzzled but *The Theosophist* said that the 'osmosing' of letters was an example of Aryan Arhat science which showed 'the superior familiarity with and control over atomic relations among our Eastern Adepts as compared with Western modern men of science'. Professor Smith, nearing the end of an honourable career in New South Wales, was prevented by poor health from making further advances in the psychic world; but he remained confident of the existence of the Masters and their supernormal powers after his return to Australia in 1883. He died in 1885.[23]

A few bold and troubled souls took up the challenge of applying to India. For instance, C.W. Rohner, a Tyrolese medical man in rural Victoria who translated European occult literature for the Victorian spiritualists, corresponded with the editor of *The Theosophist*. He sought explanations for distressing personal experiences involving thought transference. (He also debated the significance of Madame Blavatsky's phenomena in the *Harbinger* with another immigrant, Christian Reimers of Adelaide, a student of theosophic spiritualism.)[24]

Direct contact with India dramatised theosophy, but it was exceptional. Even John Smith first learned of theosophy through the American emissary, Emma Hardinge Britten. Britten made a considerable impact in Australia in the late 1870s. Of the many itinerant lecturers on the Australian circuit, she stood out as a woman lecturer, and was said to be the greatest woman lecturer yet heard, though not, it was also said, of the first rank scientifically. One of many interesting lectures showed her to be very close to Blavatsky: 'The Lines of Demarcation between Occultism and Spiritualism' explained the latter as but one phase in the study of hidden things. In Sydney she befriended Mrs Smith. Perhaps the Smiths were among those who attended the inaugural meeting of the Psychological Society of New South Wales which Britten helped found in 1879.[25]

Most inquirers of necessity depended on local sources, the *Harbinger* and W.H. Terry's *Catalogue, comprising the Literature of Spiritualism, Mesmerism, Psychology, Phrenology, Dietetics, Physiology, Chromopathy, Social Science, Secularism and Free Religious Thought*, from which might be purchased the works of the most advanced thinkers of the day, English, American and Continental, among whom were listed Blavatsky, Olcott and Sinnett. The *Harbinger* was a major source for the passionate enthusiasm of the third Australian fellow of the Theosophical Society, botanist Carl Heinrich Hartmann (1834–1887), who occupies an important place in the history of Australian theosophy as founder of the Queensland study group. Presumably George Scammel Manns, fourth Australian fellow of the Theosophical Society, also learned of theosophy from this impeccable spiritualist source. Manns, a spiritualist and a co-operator, active in radical politics in Victoria as secretary of the group which affiliated with the First International, was a teacher, proprietor of the Fitzroy Secular Academy, who had served as an officer in the Indian army, sufficient reason perhaps to attend to news from Bombay of religious advance.[26]

The names of the first theosophists in Australia 1879–1883 listed by Mary Neff in her booklet *How Theosophy came to Australia and New Zealand*, headed by Gilbert Elliott, W.H. Terry, Carl Hartmann and G.S. Manns, include the name of only one woman, Margaret Woolley. Mrs Woolley, who joined the society in July 1883, appears as the twenty-fifth name on a chronologically arranged list of twenty-seven recruits to 1883. She was the widow of the well-loved Dr John Woolley, first professor of classics at the University of Sydney who was lost at sea in 1866, and much missed – by for example, the distinguished Judge William Charles Windeyer, a convinced spiritualist, who later claimed spiritual communications with Woolley. Taken along with that of Professor Smith, the name of Margaret Woolley suggests that the first responses to theosophy in Sydney came from the liberal intelligentsia of the 1870s. It also suggests that although the *Harbinger*, and the better organised world of religious heterodoxy in Melbourne, provided a natural channel for theosophy in Australia, it was not an essential channel. Mrs Woolley and her daughters had been long associated with religious liberalism, especially as friends of Edward Maitland during his sojourn in New South Wales. Maitland himself joined the Theosophical Society in London in 1883.[27]

Meanwhile *The Theosophist* made what it could of new contacts in the Antipodes. Amid a dense array of heterogeneous information, much of it on Indian religions, the journal carried such snippets as the papier mâché house at the Sydney Exhibition, sightings of Flemington racecourse through an 'electroscope' by scientific men in distant, darkened rooms, and the progress of the Melbourne Burial Reform Society. It was interested too in primitive religion and the work of early anthropologists, hence a review of Edward Tregear's *The Aryan Maori* (1885). Material from the *Harbinger* occasionally appeared. Perhaps Blavatsky foresaw that in the Australian colonies there were men capable of seeing the highest truth, as Edward Maitland had proposed to Alfred Deakin in 1878 after a review of Maitland's unsuccessful *England and Islam* (1877) in the *Harbinger*.[28]

Alfred Deakin certainly was one of those who aspired to the highest truth though he was not yet ready to join the Theosophical Society. By the mid-1880s a prominent and successful Victorian politician, he had put away his spiritualistic youth; but, in the privacy of his note books, continued the quest for spiritual truths, and noted as they arrived the latest contributions to theosophic literature. That quest for illumination was to bring him closer still to theosophy and, briefly, into the fold in 1895; but in the glow of the eighties, he lived easily enough with that lifelong conflict between preaching and politics first emphasised to him by none other than Emma Hardinge Britten. She 'repeatedly prophesied that I should become a Spiritual teacher

& preacher but apparently connected with my profession too'. So, it was irrigation and legislation by day, and Sinnett and Swedenborg by night for Deakin.[29]

Most of the first fellows found theosophy not by solitary reading but in groups. *The Theosophist* says two study groups formed in the early 1880s. On the first, the Leneva group, no further information is available. Perhaps it was a short-lived Melbourne group. Possibly it referred to a Sydney group. Ransom's history of the Theosophical Society notes an application from Sydney by E. Cyril Haviland in January 1881, adding, 'There is no further history of this'. By contrast, the second study group is well documented, being the branch formed by Hartmann and his friends in southern Queensland, variously described as located at Toowoomba and in Brisbane, and called the Brisbane branch, later the Queensland Theosophical Society.[30]

The majority of the first fellows belonged to this branch, having been recruited by Hartmann, including two members of his family. Of the twenty-seven names listed as the first Australian fellows by Mary Neff, twenty came from Queensland. Hartmann's group, formed from among the patrons of George Smith's Progressive Bookshop in Brisbane, which had earlier seen a short-lived Psychological Society, included such men as: Judge Paul; the merchant-councillor J.B.L. Isambert; Harry Burton, artist; Smith; Edward Wilmot Pechey, politician; Charles Berger, MD; and Gavin Pettigrew, enrolled as the first theosophist in New South Wales but probably a border resident. There were no women. In 1886 the branch was still thought to have prospects. Unfortunately the prime mover, Carl Hartmann, died in 1887 and the branch expired. Hartmann, a Saxon immigrant of the goldrush era who prospered as horticulturist and acclimatiser at his nursery near Toowoomba, died of fever contracted on a research trip to New Guinea; but he was, as Neff puts it proudly, the first president of 'the first Theosophical Society in the Southern Hemisphere'.[31]

Two other discussion groups formed in Australia in the 1880s. When the Russian-born Buddhist Mrs Elise Pickett arrived in Melbourne from New Zealand in 1890, she called a meeting to discuss theosophy which revived an almost defunct Gnostic Society founded by visiting American spiritualist lecturers (see Chapter 2). And in June 1889, Blavatsky and Olcott authorised W.H. Dawson, Edward Ivey, J.W. Beattie and associates to form a Hobart branch of 'The Theosophical Society and Universal Brotherhood'.[32]

Such was the commitment to *theosophia* in Australia in the beginning. It was a weak response, though not so weak as to suffer greatly in comparison with, say, the numbers attracted to what was then called 'the Religion of Socialism'. Everywhere, and for both initiatives, it was a matter of a marginal intelligentsia from the middling classes: of liberal and academic circles, isolated individuals like Deakin, and study groups on the edge of progressive thought, as in Brisbane. The composition of the Brisbane group appears to parallel that of the founding group in New York. The Brisbane theosophists were if anything more respectable, but they were nowhere near so respectable as the members of the London branch.

Some fell by the wayside. W.H. Terry, for example, became a councillor of the society in the same year that he joined – the member for Australia as it were – and four years later, in March 1884, the *Harbinger* expressed continued support, with reservations: 'Whilst differing in some very important points with the conclusions of the Occultists regarding the future state of man, we are in hearty accord with the general work of the Society and hope as occasion offers to further its work in Australia.' Through the 1880s the *Harbinger* kept its readers informed of the progress of the Theosophical Society, reviewed theosophical literature, and repeatedly called for co-operation in the name of the Higher Spiritualism. But Terry, after bobbing in and out of theosophical membership lists, finally returned to spiritualism, finding himself in disagreement with theosophical teaching on the afterlife. L. de Caux, who had been advertising his powers as a medical galvanist and magnetic healer in Surry Hills, Sydney, in 1880, joined the Queensland branch in 1881, and then disappeared from view. Not all of the Queenslanders reappeared when summoned by Colonel Olcott to reconstitute the Queensland branch in 1891.[33]

Nevertheless, because of developments within theosophy itself, and due to certain colonial conditions, numbers were replenished over the decade, by fellows as far apart as New Guinea and Tasmania, as well as from the colonial cities, and they improved somewhat in the late eighties. The diploma of the fiery W.T. Willans, who made his mark on Australian theosophy in the 1890s, was dated May 1889, for example. By 1890 it was possible to find a reasonably accurate account of theosophy and theosophists in the more enlightened corners of the local press:

The Theosophical Society, whose headquarters are New York and Madras, is now, it appears, a large body. Its aim is the foundation of a universal brotherhood, and the study specially of the religions and science of the East. Theosophy presupposes that beneath all the creeds and religions there lies a secret doctrine, which has been corrupted and lost sight of amid the materialism and unspiritualness of the religionists and the world. To restore to men this hidden treasure, and unite them on the basis of a universal religion (or Divine Wisdom) is the object of the theosophist. There are also, it is asserted, certain psychic powers in human nature, which have been allowed, through non-cultivation, to die out in most people, or which, in the hands of the ignorant or unscrupulous, have been abused and perverted to the ends of sorcery and black arts. These powers a section of theosophists seek to cultivate and to use for the good of their fellow-men. Mesmerism and hypnotism they affirm are only re-discoveries of certain natural powers, and anticipations of a power possessed by man far beyond what modern science even dreams of, but capable of being developed by study, practice and moral discipline, by which the tyranny of our sensuous nature is overcome.[34]

Considering what happened to theosophy in the mid-1880s it was feat enough to have maintained some contacts, kept alive some groups, in remote Australia. Professor Smith died in Sydney in 1885 with his confidence in Madame Blavatsky's Masters probably intact. But scandal was building up. First came controversy over Sinnett's 'Mahatma Letters' and the possibility that far from having been precipitated from the astral plane, they had been penned by Blavatsky herself. (The evidence is deposited in the British Library.) Then in 1884–1885 came what theosophists call the 'Coulomb Conspiracy'. The Coulombs, Blavatsky's housekeepers at Adyar, aided by angry Christian missionaries in Madras, drew attention to certain carpentry in her quarters which they said enabled the Madame's domestic performances and materialisations.

The high-minded and impeccably scholarly British Psychical Research Society carried out an inquiry into the phenomena, and a young man from Melbourne, a lawyer and friend of Alfred Deakin and Henry Bournes Higgins, undertook investigation in Madras. He was Richard Hodgson, BA (1855–1905), a protégé of the great scientist and psychical researcher Professor Henry Sidgwick. Hodgson died in America a convinced spiritualist, but the magical Madame proved too much for the severe young man. He disdained the partially reassembled carpentry, and pronounced Madame Blavatsky's manifestations a fraud. In eloquent prose, painful to theosophists ever since, and much quoted, the Psychical Research Society drew its conclusion:

> For our own part we regard her neither as the mouth-piece of hidden seers, nor as a mere vulgar adventuress; we think she has achieved a title to permanent remembrance as one of the most accomplished, ingenious, and interesting imposters in history.[35]

The results were reported in the *Harbinger* in April 1886, with the comment that Madame Blavatsky would have difficulty in answering Hodgson.

Meanwhile, in March 1885, Madame Blavatsky fled to Europe, never to return to India (Colonel Olcott actively discouraged that). She had a certain magnificence – 'it is all glamour – people think they see what they do not see', she once said to a visitor at Adyar[36] – but she never entirely recovered. Even without the verdict, it was hard to see how false-backed cupboards and letter-writing Masters advanced the cause espoused at the beginning and promoted by *The Theosophist*. Despite a strong though necessarily surreptitious occult revival, in France and Ireland to name two places of moment, to most metropolitan minds there seemed to be less to theosophy than first promised.

Two developments in the late 1880s saved the day. In 1888, after much tribulation, Madame Blavatsky's second book appeared. The other flowed from Olcott's efforts, and India.

First, Madame Blavatsky's magnum opus, *The Secret Doctrine*, offered 'the grand synthesis' in two volumes ('Cosmogenesis' and 'Anthropogenesis'), 1500 pages in all. Those patient theosophists who had been waiting almost a decade for a sequel to *Isis Unveiled* rejoiced. The press, on the other hand, received it unkindly, as evidence of further humbug. Blavatsky's most recent biographer Marion Meade states that the book is 'an account of how the universe is created, where it came from and where it is going, what force fashioned it, and what it all means'. Equipped with this generalisation, it can be seen that the first book, organised around seven stanzas from a supposed lost Book of Dzyan, describes world formation from 'the Great Breath' to the descent of life, the appearance of humans, at the beginning of the fourth evolutionary round: 'cosmogenesis'. The second book, 'Anthropogenesis', outlines the evolution of humanity by round and root-race to the present, fifth root-race.[37]

The Secret Doctrine provided theosophy with an elaborate, poetic (not to say fanciful) and comprehensive cosmology, strongly anti-Darwinian, and a highly impersonal teaching. It reads as if reality is beyond human understanding, in a universe governed by ceaseless motion, the individual identified with it, through endless incarnations. Written at speed and under trying circumstances, *The Secret Doctrine* remains an occult classic, for all its opaqueness.

One invaluable spin-off from *The Secret Doctrine* was *The Key to Theosophy*, Madame Blavatsky's last and most accessible book completed in London in 1889. By simple question and – answer technique, the book summarised fundamental teachings and the grounds from which they sprang. It also shaped the theosophical message in a self-consciously post Christian way, and thereby serves as a sign post to the future of the theosophical movement.

Thus, the new theosophy was not to be dismissed as 'a new-fangled religion' or a mere extension of spiritualism. In place of revelation and wonders, it offered archaic knowledge, unveiled by altruistic occultists, a Divine Wisdom wide enough for modern needs. Instead of sin, suffering and death, it proposed spiritual evolution; there would be no need for anthropomorphic deities, demeaning supplications or an historical atonement; the constraints of creedal Christianity belonged in a painful past unredeemed by the wisdom of the East and of the ancients. The new theosophy, based on Universal Divine Principle, a kind of esoteric pantheism, offered psychospiritual science and knowledge of the laws regulating the life cycle – specifically, karma, the moral law of cause and effect – and reincarnation. 'The spiritual pilgrim is eternal,' she wrote.

Reincarnation, 'the most difficult of our tenets', had not always been a fundamental teaching. Its increased prominence may be explained in part as social theory, previously inconspicuous among if not altogether absent from theosophical preoccupations. It provided the key to practical theosophy, being the most reasonable and progressive explanation of human unhappiness. A guilt-free teaching, it allowed for self-improvement and for social amelioration by philanthropic brotherhood and cooperation: 'altruism is an integral part of self-development'.[38]

In this her last statement Madame Blavatsky remained optimistic. Her prognosis was that theosophy would benefit from distrust of conventional religions and their complete failure to preserve morals and purify society. The Theosophical Society was admittedly far from perfect, but it served as a focus and a channel of idealism. In a refurbished vision of Harmony and Progress, Blavatsky predicted that if the Theosophical Society survived into the twentieth century, it would have a leavening effect:

> It will gradually leaven and permeate the great mass of thinking and intelligent people with its large-minded and noble ideas of Religion, Duty and Philanthropy. Slowly it will burst asunder the iron fetters of creeds and dogmas, of social and caste prejudices; it will break down racial and national antipathies and barriers, and will open the way to the practical realisation of the Brotherhood of all men. Through its teaching ... the West will learn to understand and appreciate the East at its true value. Further, the development of the psychic powers and faculties, the premonitory symptoms of which are already visible in America, will proceed healthily and normally ... Man's mental and psychic growth will proceed in harmony with his moral improvement, while his material surroundings will reflect the peace and fraternal goodwill which will reign in his mind, instead of the discord and strife which is everywhere apparent around us today.[39]

Compared with Blavatsky's writings, the second saving development operated imperceptibly. In the eighties the Theosophical Society gradually adapted its aims to India and internationalism. The society which began as a secret society or brotherhood became a society to uphold Brotherhood. Convention by convention, it reworked its objects and the rules so that by 1890 the priorities of 1875 had been virtually reversed. In the beginning 'the psychic self ' came first; materialism in science and theology were to be opposed, Oriental religion advanced as against Christianity, and by a brotherhood. In 1881, the order was reversed to read, more tactfully:

1. To form the Nucleus of a Universal Brotherhood of Humanity.
2. To study Aryan literature, religion and science.
3. To vindicate the importance of this enquiry and correct misrepresentations with which it has been clouded.
4. To explore the hidden mysteries of Nature and the latent powers of Man, on which the Founders believe that Oriental Philosophy is in a position to throw light.

In 1886, after rules about initiation and secrecy had been deleted, the important rejections of racist, creedal and chauvinist distinctions were written in, and in 1888, of sex and caste, all incorporated in the first object. Though the idea of a brotherhood did not disappear completely from the rubric until 1896, after which theosophists might consider themselves merely part of a, not the, nucleus for Brotherhood, by 1890 the objects had assumed something like their present rather bland form. Triune, they then read:

1. To form the nucleus of a Universal Brotherhood of Humanity, without distinction of race, creed, sex, caste or colour.
2. To promote the study of Aryan and other Eastern literatures, religions, philosophies, and sciences, and to demonstrate their importance to Humanity.
3. To investigate unexplored laws of Nature and the psychic powers latent in man.

Taking into account revisions in 1896, and minor emendations since, it can be seen that only a few refinements were necessary to produce today's wording. By the late 1970s, the three declared objects of the Theosophical Society were:

First – To form a nucleus of the Universal Brotherhood of Humanity, without distinction of race, creed, sex, caste or colour.
Second – To encourage the study of comparative Religion, Philosophy and Science.
Third – To investigate unexplained laws of Nature and the powers latent in man.[40]

There were other, and more disturbing, internal developments in the late 1880s. In 1888 Madame Blavatsky was allowed to set up an inner, Esoteric Section of the society devoted solely to its third object and still subject to the older rules and rituals of secrecy and authority. The Esoteric Section, source of much friction later, was explained constitutionally as 'a distinct private division of the Society under the direction of the Corresponding Secretary'. Historian Ransom remarks drily that the ES had 'rather drastic Rules, which had later to be modified'.[41]

Although the reading public had long since rejected Madame Blavatsky's phenomena, there she was ensconced in London in another circle at the end of the 1880s, with her new books attracting fresh attention. Meanwhile, the public face of the Theosophical Society had been cleansed of its disreputable and conspiratorial features, and with an increasing membership, branches organised in three sections (as they were now called) in America, India and England, there had been 'expansion in East and West'. The theosophists had come a long way since 1875, as had the idea of theosophy.

At this point in religious histories it is not unusual to settle down into a triumphal tale. The early days are often the most exciting, as heroic leaders struggle to convey their message to an uncomprehending world and are pilloried by all but an enlightened few, whose fidelity to the original vision ultimately secures a new church or movement. The story of modern theosophy could be and has been told in that way, but it makes better history to admit at its beginning that this is not a triumphal tale, nor does it ever really settle down. In the first phase a heady brew was prepared by colourful leaders, and some dramatic shifts occurred: from spiritualism to *The Secret Doctrine*; from America to India; and from a brotherhood to Brotherhood. In the remote Australian colonies, a few of the enlightened ones were attracted to the cause. Why they were attracted is the next question.

2

Minds maddened by Protestantism

A curiously flickering light is cast over the making of a post-Christian society in Australia by the appearance of the wisdom religion in the 1880s. Theosophy might easily have passed into oblivion like the forgotten fad for phrenology in the 1840s or, a century later, the moral rearmament movement.[1]

Yet in this Christianised country it survived. Two new branches in Hobart and Melbourne by 1890 showed renewed interest. Others picked up the baton dropped by the first fellows: Swedish-born administrator E.G. Edelfelt stationed in New Guinea, W.T. Willans in Sydney, Elise Pickett in Melbourne.[2]

Although the theosophical movement had not yet gained its 1890s momentum, theosophical ideas remained alive in the colonial culture. In so far as the forces which kept them alive also shaped the moral mainstream theosophy was indeed quite important. At least in the formative eighties its very presence foreshadowed a strategic significance in Australian culture – disdainful as the theosophically minded were of all such notions of a mainstream in unreconstructed Christian societies – as well as its own survival.

What kept theosophy alive across the 1880s is a question easier asked than answered. Sociologically speaking, theosophy found the space for alternative religion. According to much religious sociology, there will be in any society a minority willing to entertain unorthodox religious ideas. Thus theosophists led the way into *Other Temples, Other Gods* (the title of a recent survey of the occult in Australia); and, it is true, the Theosophical Society did become a major marketer of alternatives to Christian orthodoxy.[3] The fact remains, however, that the first theosophists did not see themselves as purveyors of alternative religion, but as torchbearers of true religion. As the great seventeenth-century Puritan poet John Milton put it, 'the mind is its own place'.

The first theosophists were men and women adrift from orthodoxy, as was Blavatsky herself. When she offered a counter to what she called 'the maddening effect of Protestantism', she threw out a wild, bitter but largely accurate historical diagnosis.[4] The mental distress of late Victorians unable either to retain or relinquish religious faith is well attested. Just as she had wandered far from the splendours and rigours of the Russian Orthodox Church, so her Western followers had abandoned their own usually Protestant orthodoxies.[5] Blavatsky knew they hungered for another. They hungered especially for a spiritual order free from the constraints of nineteenth-century Christianity, Protestantism in its evangelical and fundamentalist forms or Catholicism in its puritanical Jansenist form – residues of which were indeed to be observed in the lunatic asylums of the period.[6]

The new mind-doctors declared such people mad – victims of chronic delusion: '[they] exist entirely as parasites and are utterly unreliable … lack self-control … The paranoid and mattoid revel in spiritualism, theosophy, christian science and other occult nonsense.'[7] However, those first theosophists were not candidates for state asylums. They were, rather, participants in frenzied debate about religion and society, which continued unabated through the eighties into the early twentieth century.

In Australia there has always been a reluctance to take religious ideas seriously, as Dorothy Green wisely remarks in a rare account of one late Victorian Australian's spiritual odyssey, *Ulysses Bound. Henry Handel Richardson and Her Fiction* (1973). Rampant anti-intellectualism in colonial society discouraged the confession of unorthodox beliefs; no accident that Deakin tried to play down his spiritualistic youth, that both Alfred Deakin and Justice Windeyer recorded their spiritualist experiences in privacy for posterity, or that it seems impossible to establish when Bessie Rischbieth actually joined the Theosophical Society. Such things were only too likely to create a sensation, or worse, in a fierce world accustomed to deride the opportunistic edge of orthodoxy – rip-off lecturers, commercial mediums (seances, private, Tuesday and Saturday, 1/- a head, no guarantees), and 'nerve' doctors.

The contrast between the public and the private sphere is quite marked. Bourgeois culture flourished in the 1880s, and there were many distinguished contributors to the continuing debate 'Religion versus Science', but few individuals left records of personal turmoil and quest.[8] Unlike Britain, it was never the case of 'the experience of members of a small intelligentsia whose spiritual pilgrimages were recorded in some detail' (an approach which in any case neglects the social and moral sources of popular disaffection with Protestant Christianity).[9] It does not follow, however, that the passage to unbelief in Australia was simply a sloughing off of Old World superstitions, the inarticulate passage so graphically conveyed by Manning Clark as *fin de siècle*:

> The priests and the clergy grieved over a lost generation, but their warnings, their threats, had lost their sting. Heaven and Hell, it is said, were priests' inventions: Australia could not believe in such places. Raymond Bedford ... gave up the religion of darkness, and walked out into the bright light of the Australian sun. His name was legion.[10]

More likely, thoughts remained *Unspoken Thoughts*, as was the case for parson's wife Ada Cambridge. Her rebellious poems published in 1887 distressed the parson, and were withdrawn from the market immediately, never to be republished.[11]

Collections like *Unspoken Thoughts* suggest the territory such minds traversed, though there is as yet no clear map of it. The cultural context of the 1880s is not as well understood as the preceding decade, which saw the first dramatic impact of Darwinism. The intellectual ferment of the eighties has attracted less attention, perhaps because the big issues had already been worked through, while new ones had yet to be marshalled. Older, religion-based world views were in dissolution. New constructs were still in the making, as recent histories of psychology and sociology disconcertingly reveal. Owen Chadwick in *The Secularization of the European Mind in the Nineteenth Century* (1975) makes the general point: 'In the 1880s passed over Western Europe one of those movements of mind that history perceives but cannot easily analyse or define.'[12] 'Movements of mind' included a new sense of the reality of non-Christian religions, particularly the great Indian religions, part of the flood-tide of imperialism.[13]

By and large, the British discounted Indian religion until the mid-nineteenth century when scholars like German philologist Max Müller at Oxford kindled interest: 'a generation ago', wrote Sir Edwin Arnold, introducing *The Light of Asia* in 1879, 'little or nothing was known of this great faith of Asia.'[14] By the last quarter of the nineteenth century, intellectuals increasingly sought to focus 'the light of Asia' upon their own dilemmas. Some, like communitarian socialist Edward Carpenter, went so far as to consult a guru in Ceylon, attaining thereby release from past distress.[15] Gilbert Elliott, FTS, reviewing Sinnett's *Esoteric Buddhism* in 1883, while defending the TS and expressing guarded hope of the Mahatma letters on which *Esoteric Buddhism* was based, remarked that 'the real constitution of man is hardly at all understood by Europeans'.[16]

Consider, too, some of the more curious fashions of the day: for Japanese furnishings and for all things Russian (a mood which undoubtedly benefited Madame Blavatsky). In the new enthusiasm for Russian literature, Chadwick notes the ache of revolution.[17] And to some, the late 1880s did seem to be the dawn of long-awaited revolution. At the heart of the British Empire, radical and working-class 'free speech' demonstrations in London in 1886 and 1887 were the largest since the days of the Chartists in the 1840s. In New South Wales in 1887 Henry Parkes abruptly closed facilities for Sunday lectures and public meetings for fear of disloyalties fomented by rag-tag and bob-tail radicals in the year of Queen Victoria's Jubilee. The *Liberator* called him 'Czar' Parkes; bookseller McNamara wrote that the revolution was at hand.[18] The last one, political, occurred a century ago in France; the next, with 1889 in sight, would be a revolution of minds and hearts. The revolution of the mind would see a great surge of radicalism and democracy. The revolution of the heart, more problematic, would be recovery from a cold materialism.

By the 1890s the leaning towards the wisdom of the East surfaced in political literature, in such places as William Lane's political novel *The Workingman's Paradise*, published in Sydney in 1892. In a scene set in the home of sympathetic intellectuals in the eastern suburbs of Sydney, working girl Nellie says scornfully, 'There is no God. How can there be?' But the mysterious socialist Geisner rebukes her in words straight from *The Secret Doctrine*. There is at least 'the imperishable breath of the universe'. The young Queensland unionist Ned listens to Geisner puzzle about purpose:

> To me the Purpose of Life is self-consciousness, the total Purpose I mean. God seeking to know God. Eternal Force one immeasurable Thought. Humanity the developing consciousness of the little fragment of the universe within our ken.[19]

When Nellie says it sounded a barren faith, Geisner replies it is better than utter negation. Later he says that some such faith will be essential for the revolution:

> Socialism is not a thing which can be glued like a piece of veneering over this rotten social system of ours ... [B]efore action must come the dominant thought ... [Y]ear after year, the number of men and women who hold Socialism as a religion is growing. And when they are enough you will see this Old Order melt away like a dream and the New Order replace it.[20]

Subsequently Lane traversed the whole field of faith, and after the collapse of the utopian New Australia colony in Paraguay, finished up as a Tory imperialist editor in Auckland, New Zealand.[21] Perhaps, like Rudyard Kipling, the restless Lane had been touched by theosophy in his youth.[22]

One reason the ferment of the eighties has remained confusing is that history did not vindicate the radical optimists. Historians have been inclined to see that ferment in the shadow of the 1890s, as the death throes of bourgeois civilisation, the end of old-style radicalism, the beginning of class-divided society. It is, however, essential to catch the apocalyptic note. The turning point had not yet come. There were class differences of perception, and no balance between optimism and pessimism existed in the world of ideology – quite the opposite, according to one well-placed observer of religious life, both metropolitan and colonial.

Moncure Conway, the American-born incumbent of the pulpit of the renowned South Place ethical church in London, recalled a congress of so-called liberal thinkers in London in 1878 amid reaction and confusion:

> Wonderful London! At the very moment when our assembly was probing the foundations of religion and theoretically abolishing superstition, around us was the recrudescence of the wildest fanaticism ... If London in the early seventies was a Mars Hill, towards the close of that decade a Babel in fragments appeared on the top of it.[23]

Five years later, in Australia, passions of religious life in both Sydney and Melbourne appalled the preacher. 'The whole population seemed to have their eyes set inviolably on the future life.' Colonial behaviour made a rational man disconsolate: 'The majority of mankind find that life is hardly worth attending to, or even worth living, unless it be the vestibule to a world in which their ideals are realised.'[24]

It was Conway's misfortune to visit Australia at a peak of religious passion. In the course of a *Pilgrimage to the Wise Men of the East*, which included an amusing interview with Madame Blavatsky in Madras, Conway took in Sydney and Melbourne, arriving in the middle of the Strong case. The Strong case, *cause célèbre* of late-nineteenth-century Australian religious history, was in effect a heresy charge mounted against the outstanding and outspoken liberal minister of Scots Church Melbourne, the Reverend Charles Strong, by the conservative evangelical forces which dominated Victorian Presbyterianism.

The case provoked fierce controversy and pushed Strong and most of his well-heeled congregation out of Presbyterianism altogether to found the native ethical church, the Australian Church, in 1885.[25] Conway found that his soothing words did nothing to allay conflict. Then in Sydney he experienced sectarian assault. 'The Fates,' he recalled, 'during my first week in Sydney were ugly as Furies.' With Henry Parkes amongst a respectful audience assembled to hear him lecture on such subjects as 'The Pre-Darwinite and Post-Darwinite World', hymn-singing salvationists invaded the theatre to break the lectures up. They called Conway a religious larrikin. He was appalled at press misrepresentation. His hurts were healed in the homes of the ladies Windeyer and Heron, a liberal minority, who nevertheless disdained to defend him: 'Why reason with people who do not know the meaning of reason?' Was an immigrant population especially prone to religious madness, he wondered.[26]

The colonial culture certainly was agitated about religion in the 1880s. The place to start on the road to unbelief is where they all started, with the churches, now in deep trouble. Especially in New South Wales, churchmen began that long struggle to defend 'a Christian country" against secular and radical alternatives vigorously fostered by a lively intelligentsia. However, if there was a colonial religion as distinct from religion in the colonies, it was to be a religion without churches and churchmen: 'What I detest is not religion but *priestcraft* and *dogma* and *intolerance*,' wrote Alfred Deakin in 1880.[27] Australia may have been a Christian country according to late nineteenth-century statistics, but the emergent Australian legend of a free and equal society had no room for parsons. 'A Tolerant Man', as in Henry Lawson's poem, could stomach anything but!

In the third quarter of the nineteenth century, the churches, especially the Protestant churches, were increasingly on the defensive, challenged by the accumulated criticisms of Christian teaching by scientific and historical knowledge. By the last quarter of the century the old founts of authority were themselves under attack both from within and without: the Bible, the historic creeds and confessions, the clergy. Although there is no evidence that the churches in Australia were undermined by such attacks, the prestige of Christianity suffered and sectarian divisions within Christianity appeared the more obvious and objectionable. Thus Henry Lawson's view of religion originated in distaste for intolerance, imbibed in Mudgee primary schools.[28]

Meanwhile the radical and freethought tradition dating from the French Revolution and the writings of Thomas Paine had recovered its vitality in the 1860s. In the late 1870s secularism, as it was now called, took on the dimensions of a popular crusade in Britain. Secularists drawn from the lower middle and working classes aimed to discredit Christianity and to expose its institutional outworks. In Edward Royle's crisp and illuminating resume, they sought 'a radical restructuring of society by peaceful means', on the premise that the problems of society sprang from the baneful effects of religion. The mission reached its climax in the early 1880s when secularist leader Charles Bradlaugh battled to take his seat in the House of Commons as the duly elected member for Northampton by secular affirmation of loyalty instead of religious oath. Secular affirmation being unheard of constitutionally speaking, it took four gruelling elections to win through. Radical and working-class Australia thrilled to these momentous struggles against church and state.[29]

Indigenous secularism also dates from the 1860s in Sydney and Newcastle. Its heyday came in the 1880s in response to illiberal and anti-democratic forces seeking to control the lower orders. In the 1870s freethought and discussion groups formed in most of the colonial cities – even Adelaide secularists managed a monthly meeting of thirty souls from 1877, and a

Review which lasted over a year from March 1878 to April 1879, a sign, it was said, that '[f]ree thought is steadily progressing in defiance of every obstacle'. Then in July 1882 Melbourne secularists, led by ex-spiritualist lecturer Thomas Walker, founded the Australasian Secularist Association (ASA) to oppose renewed sabbatarianism in Melbourne. The ASA called an intercolonial conference in 1883; and in 1884, when Charles Bradlaugh's own nominee Joseph Symes came to replace Thomas Walker as leader, the ASA had over 1000 members in Melbourne, Sydney and Newcastle. Symes started the *Liberator*, which appeared for the next twenty years as the voice of Australian secularism (from 1884 to 1904), and in the late 1880s it claimed a circulation of 20,000. In Sydney William Whitehouse Collins and freethought bookseller William Willis successfully defended a free press and published their own journals to promote the cause, *The Freethinker and New South Wales Reformer* (1886) and *Freedom* (1889).[30]

In 1887 'the heretical company' of Sydney secularists at last managed to open a fund to build a freethought hall. They envisaged a building devoted 'to teaching the highest of all religions – the Religion of Humanity'. Children in the Sydney Lyceum, a hundred-strong secularist Sunday school, helped raise the money, and when the foundation stone was laid on 26 January 1890 they formed an ASA choir to sing 'Our Southern Home', composed for the occasion. All the great traditions of Sydney secularism were recalled and it was hoped that the hall on Campbell Street would be a force for unity and against inertia. At least the fractious Sydney secularists had proved Joseph Symes wrong when he said bitterly that there were five times as many secularists in Sydney as in Melbourne but they couldn't even manage a hall of science. But by 1890 the effort came too late. Like the Melbourne Hall of Science, the Sydney building did not suffice to consolidate or institutionalise secularism in a land acclimatised to anticlericalism. It was noted in 1892 that in addition to apathy and commercial depression the old approach had ceased to appeal, given 'the undoubted tendency of modern thought ... to attach increasing importance to social and economic questions, and relegate to a subordinate rank questions of a theological, or anti-theological, character'. And, as times changed, secularists divided over those social and economic questions.[31]

As Peter Coleman correctly judged in his history of censorship in Australia, the freethinkers mattered in the long run in that they belonged in the ideological mainstream and advanced the dominant approach of colonial intellectuals, which was rationalist, secular and republican. They mattered in the short run too, because the radical free thought tradition contained the crucial continuities of experience across the period. Freethinkers experienced the transition from optimism to pessimism. But what happened to the people for whom secularism failed?

Some were permanently preoccupied with intellectual and ethical objections to the Bible which they had discovered as young Methodists and Baptists. (A high proportion of secularists came from those denominations.) Not many actually went mad like Symes, who returned to England to die in pained obscurity in 1906. A few even attained political respectability, like the immigrant leaders Thomas Walker in Western Australia and W.W. Collins in New Zealand. Amongst the native-born there were dislocations, if the subsequent careers of two young Melbourne secularists are any guide. Both Montague Miller and the poet Bernard O'Dowd reappeared in the 1890s on spiritualist platforms, urging a larger view; both were aware of the claims of theosophy, and O'Dowd, who had studied Indian texts in the 1880s, was quite sympathetic. Thus, although the question of what happened next for freethinkers cannot be answered definitively here, and probably there is no one answer since they went in every direction, one point emerges. It is that the agitated free thought tradition was one element in the survival of theosophy across the 1880s.[32]

Recent studies of unbelievers in late Victorian Britain show that secularists inhabited a mirror world to the churches they opposed, emotionally, intellectually and institutionally; they exhibited a negative passion for the Christian religion. Moreover, they had suffered for their stance. At the foundation stone ceremony in Sydney in 1890 it was said that secularists were moral people. So they were earnest representatives of Victorian culture. But they were often labelled immoral as well as mad. The old charge of immorality surfaced in the 1880s, fed perhaps by Joseph Symes's successful but notorious pamphlet, 'Ancient and Modern Phallic or Sex Worship' (1887).[33] The frightful effects of unbelief were portrayed in one prize-winning essay in defence of Christianity. According to the Reverend James Milne of Bega, NSW, in 1887, agnosticism produced 'rude men, with nothing to work for, degraded women with nothing to live for, and a diminishing population'.[34]

As the first self-consciously de-Christianised generation, they had experienced losses as well as the one great gain, and the loss of a stable psychological frame – however gruesome and unacceptable its parts – took its toll on individuals, who suffered loneliness and isolation. Like some of today's liberated people, true freethinkers and atheists in particular suffered not merely loss of social esteem but sometimes livelihood as well. South Australian freethinker Wilton Hack, ex-Baptist minister and missionary in Japan, found that when he returned to Adelaide with £5 in his pocket he was no longer welcome as a preacher: 'His old Christian friends shut their doors in his face', and he took to teaching, without much success and with no money. Later he joined the Theosophical Society and became a co-operator in the Flinders Ranges.[35]

Equally important for the theosophical impulse were the associated movements to reform religion. If unbelievers hoped to dish the churches, only the wildest few hoped to see an end to religion. Many more hoped to salvage what was valuable in the old religion. For that minority it was unthinkable that religion could or should disappear as the organising force in personal and social life. The view that religion provided the essential significance, sanction and cohesion in civil society died harder and much more slowly than that. It was not undermined intellectually until Marxism made its way, well after Marx's death in 1881. Even then it was largely through 'the Religion of Socialism' (a few oldsters answered 'socialist' to the question on religious adherence in the Australian census up to 1933). In a harsh and uncertain world, most of the disaffected found solace in the array of spiritual and ethical 'halfway' houses built by critics of Christianity on either side of the Atlantic over the preceding century, in such liberal alternatives to the maddening orthodoxies as unitarianism, transcendentalism and spiritualism.

Of these the most important to *theosophia* was spiritualism. A spiritually distressed Louisa Lawson learned 'Zooistic Science, Free Thought, Spiritualism and Harmonial Philosophy' all together from a spiritualist organisation in Sydney during the 'freethought craze' of the 1880s.[36] Spiritualism in Australia became quite vigorous in the later Victorian years and since theosophy originated among dissatisfied spiritualists in New York, it is only to be expected that the spiritualist movement generated a constituency for theosophy in Australia. A sketch of Australian spiritualism – there is no general history – in Sydney and Melbourne strengthens the impression already gained from a view of secularism in the two main cities, that there were slight but significant differences in the two urban cultures, shaping channels of differing depth for the currents which carried theosophy through the eighties.[37]

Spiritualism, which rested on the twin ideas that it was possible to communicate directly with the dead and that individuals could address spiritual forces, began in America in the 'burnt out' districts beyond New York in the late 1840s.[38] Best remembered in caricature as a drawing-room fad, spiritualism was originally more plebeian. Like secularism it had its own mission, being 'the first popular attempt to rebuild the temple of belief upon the rubble of broken dogma'.[39] As compared with the churches, it too was radical, or at least liberal, and also democratic in its forms, without benefit of clergy.[40] It spread to Australia in the 1850s, its heyday coinciding with that of secularism in the two decades between 1870 and 1890. It coincided too with attempts at theological liberalism in the two cities of which Strong's nativist ethical Australian Church was a rare enduring outcome.

It is impossible to estimate the extent of spiritualist practice in the colonies after the goldrushes, but it gradually attracted a following. In 1869, in Melbourne, W.H. Terry and friends formed the Victorian Association of Progressive Spiritualists (VAPS). Terry launched the main spiritualist journal, the previously mentioned *Harbinger of Light*, which disseminated theosophical literature. In 1872 the VAPS established the first lyceum as a spiritualist Sunday school. With some wealthy members, notably T.W. Stanford, brother of the American railroad king and fortunate possessor of the Australian franchise for Singer sewing machines, the Victorian spiritualists were able to organise Australian lecture tours of eminent spiritualists, mainly from America but also from Britain.[41] By that time spiritualism attracted professional people, the 'doctors, lawyers, merchants and men of eminence' mentioned by lecturer Emma Hardinge Britten in her two chapters on Australian spiritualism in *Nineteenth Century Miracles* (1884). Britten, whose optimistic eye perforce rested upon the biggest names and incidents, had noticed that gap between private practice and public confession remarked upon at the beginning of this chapter, and it is a pity that the claims of the cause forced her to pass over the popular spiritualism of the country towns and mining districts which preceded organisation in Victoria, omitting 'the hundreds of accounts of personal experiences and home circles, [the] ream upon ream of alleged Spirit communication ... tendered for insertion', and that she refrained from speculating upon the 'many features of interest' in Aboriginal spiritualism. Still she felt that the stream of public sentiment was leaving the dull platitudes of the old theology far in the rear.[42]

In Sydney 'many converts of rank and influence' appeared upon the scene. Sydney, older and in some ways more staid, had its own prior culture, as shown in the Stenhouse circle, and the friends of the Garran family, which included the homeopathic medico Dr John Le Gay Brereton, who was also a Swedenborgian.[43] J.M. Peebles, one of the first travelling spiritualist lecturers, found Australia an uninviting country for 'angel-ministry' and Sydney 'conservative, opinionated and gold-clutching', though housing some good men, candid investigators and true believers, like John Bowie Wilson.[44] Other lecturers made significant converts in Sydney, like the automatic slate-writer Henry Slade who converted E. Cyril Haviland in Sydney in 1879 by producing messages from his dead wife. The poetic Haviland, along with John Bowie Wilson, was the mainstay of Sydney spiritualism, if his editorial efforts are any guide: *Free Thought* (1880), *Rainbow, or the Sydney Progressive Lyceum News* (1883–1884), and the *Australian: A Monthly Magazine* (1879–1881).[45] It was Haviland who inquired about forming a branch of the Theosophical Society in Sydney in 1881.

On the scattered evidence to hand, the peak of Sydney spiritualism came in the early eighties, its demise towards the end of the same decade. Three levels of activity show up, the first being the Psychological Society formed in 1879 when Emma Britten was in town. The Psychological Society attracted 150 people to its first meeting, 'some of the most accomplished writers and thinkers of the city' according to Britten. From its first executive it must have been a middle-class initiative, with Bowie Wilson president, Edward Greville, MP, vice-president, E. Cyril Haviland secretary. The *Harbinger* reported that 'the Upper Ten' kept aloof, a reference to another level and more private practice, probably the Woolley–Windeyer circle[46] (Another instance of private practice was Mrs Annie Pillars, widow of the forceful and renegade Sydney unitarian preacher the Reverend James Pillars, and soon to remarry Charles Bright, spiritualist lecturer and insurance agent.[47]) Then there was the third popular level, the level of wonders, the lecture circuit.

During the late nineteenth century the public lecture was an established form of entertainment. The colonial cities offered platforms for a continuous procession of travelling lecturers trying their luck on the colonial circuit. Men (few women) crowded inner-city halls for amusement and instruction on literary, political and religious subjects.[48] A lively self-improving culture flourished in the freethought halls, temperance halls, the halls of self-improvement in the schools of art and academies of music, brotherhood halls owned by the Oddfellows and the Freemasons, and the ethnic and denominational halls like Concordia Hall next to the German Club and the Methodist Centenary Hall in Sydney, not to mention municipal and public halls, buildings once integral to the urban fabric but now either demolished or dwarfed by commerce.[49] The halls were the venue for the evening, especially the Sunday evening, component of the popular culture. In an era when the 'British Sunday' cast gloom over the colonial cities and there were no Sunday papers or cinemas, the lecturers in the halls offered a cheap and pleasing alternative to hard pews.

The public lecture culture remained alive until well into the twentieth century. By the time the Melbourne entrepreneur R.S. Smythe organised the most significant theosophical tour in the early 1890s, he had over a decade's experience in its vagaries. In the 1880s, it spread the seed of theosophy, especially among spiritualists. Thanks largely to the VAPS, the colonial cities witnessed a continuous procession of visiting spiritualist lecturers. Some were mere charlatans, mercenary entertainers and tricksters. Others were admired for their sincerity, like William Denton, author of *Commonsense Thoughts on the Bible* (1880), genuinely mourned when he died in New Guinea on a scientific expedition. By the 1880s the most cerebral of these emissaries of 'advanced thought' knew of theosophy, and two of them, the American Professor W.H. Chainey and his wife, established a small study group in Melbourne, the Gnostic Society, in 1886. (The group barely survived the Chaineys' departure in 1887; as the *Harbinger* primly remarked, Chainey's influence as a religious teacher was diminished when in 1889 he was converted to Christian Science).[50]

It is interesting that the two main local performers in Sydney over the period went mad and theosophical respectively. John Tyerman, once an Anglican clergyman at Kangaroo Flat in Victoria, took up spiritualism and, after bitter experiences with his bishop, determined to devote himself to popular advocacy. A committee of gentlemen invited him to Sydney in 1874.

Tyerman's Sunday lectures are said to have attracted audiences of up to 2000. But his health collapsed. He died insane in 1880.[51] Meanwhile Charles Bright was already performing remarkably well in Sydney. In 1880 he advertised himself as speaking from the freethought platform on Sundays in the Theatre Royal on 'Free Thought, Social Reform and Spiritual Philosophy' – a heady brew. The brew strengthened with his marriage in 1883 to Annie Pillars, who became 'a formidable spiritualist, feminist and editress', in the words of the *Australian Dictionary of Biography*. By the mid eighties, when organised spiritualism in Sydney ran into the sands, they had established their own Australasian lecture circuit. Later still, the Brights, especially Annie, viewed theosophy sympathetically.[52]

Whereas Victorian spiritualism proceeded in the 1880s in a fairly orderly manner under the eye of Terry and the auspices of the VAPS, no such order or continuity is apparent in Sydney spiritualism. No one organisation persisted and no one individual dominated an organisation. The tiny world of radical and spiritualist religion in Sydney awaits closer study. Undoubtedly, it was volatile and fractious and there were some queer developments, such as the one reported by Moncure Conway in the early eighties: a fusion of freethinkers, spiritualists and theosophists. This coalition, he heard, had almost swallowed up Unitarianism.[53]

Even Unitarianism in Sydney led a bumpy life compared with its steadier and impressively respectable counterparts in Melbourne and Adelaide. Sydney Unitarianism attracted to its pulpit some very agitated men who were conduits of ever more radical religiosity and whose passions made the history of late nineteenth-century Unitarianism incredibly chequered. The two most dynamic were Pillars, incumbent 1864–1875, and the ex-Australian Churchman from Melbourne the Reverend George Walters (1888–1898, 1902–1926). Both, at various points, led their congregations out of Unitarianism in search of more liberal religion. The volatile Walters in the 1890s passed over theosophy to form a NSW branch of Strong's Australian Church, and finally returned to Unitarianism. In Melbourne they built a fine new church and all the liberal churchmen spoke at its opening. In Sydney, from time to time, Unitarians were to find themselves homeless in one sense or another.[54]

The fact is that liberal religion never found a home in Sydney. No such dramatic challenge to the churches as the Strong case occurred, but the case was much remarked upon; and, partly in response to the ructions in Victoria, a Sydney Liberal Association was founded in 1881. In 1883 Wilson, Bright and others in the Liberal Association produced a journal, *The Liberal*. *The Liberal* stood for universal brotherhood, freedom of thought and expression, maintenance of liberty, fidelity to knowledge, aspiration to the highest morality, respect for known worth, sanctity of truth, the emancipation of women, the right to the product of one's own labour, and a secularised state. It covered a range from freethought, Unitarianism and liberal Christianity (including news of the Reverend Charles Strong) to theosophy in India, and even noticed the death of Karl Marx. Its first editor was George Lacy, quickly supplanted by Charles Bright. It lasted less than two years. A similar fate over took Haviland's *Free Thought*, 'A Monthly Journal of Free and Advanced Thought, Psychology, Metaphysics and Spiritualism etc.'. H.W.H. Stephen laid down in the third issue that it stood for the promulgation of truth and the confusion of error, and that it should show that 'Freethinkers and Spiritualists do not fear to court enquiry'. It lasted less than a year, in 1880. The journals did not survive either because of internal conflicts and editorial clashes, or because they represented temporary coalitions.[55]

Overall it seems that Melbourne had the stronger organisations, Sydney the freer market, for heterodoxy. The longstanding impression that in the late nineteenth century Melbourne was the focus of radical thought, including radical religious thought, is attributable in part to the simple fact that that was where the money was. However there could be no monopoly on ideas among the liberal bourgeoisie in the age of free trade, and at one level interdependence is striking. The wild ones needed one another to support journals, write articles, make up a lecture circuit, maintain confidence. There is plenty of evidence of shared experience, despite the distance and rivalry between the two cities. Thus Windeyer's record of spiritualist illumination contains experiences in Melbourne as well as Sydney, and it was only natural that Charles Bright read papers in Sydney on 'Magnetic Education' which he had received from a medium in Melbourne.[56]

At another level, of impact rather than input, differences are more obvious. The particular harshness of Melbourne's cultural life and response was that the dominant forces of Protestant nonconformity met the challenge of radical and secular thought head on, maddening some like Joseph Symes, discrediting others like Thomas Walker and marginalising more, the fate of the Australian Church members. The harshness of the Sydney response came from a different source. It seemed to come not so much from the churches but from the intellectual marketplace itself, where new prescriptions were promoted and abandoned again, dropping into a sea of incredulity. Beyond the market place lay apathy, and forces experienced in evasion. Sydney spiritualists bewailed 'an extreme secularising tendency', thought to be even more inimical than Melbourne's 'creedal bigotry'.[57]

Theosophy in Australia was not simply a tale of two cities, but the comparison between Sydney and Melbourne has a bearing on its survival in the 1880s and afterwards. The message came to rest in different places because the people who were working for a world free of churches faced differing forces in the two main urban cultures. It was a question of liberalism. In Melbourne the battle for liberal thought continued unhappily until, through the Australian Church, it commanded a space of its own. Theosophy gained a hearing in Melbourne at the Religious Science Club of the Australian Church – a cult on the edge of heresy.[58] In Sydney the battle for liberal thought raged in the eighties too, but it never found a resting place. There the first theosophists met in hired room, quite outside the churches.

Ironically, there was more need of liberalism in Sydney. In New South Wales the old 'state' churches held sway, with nearly three-quarters of the population either Anglican or Roman Catholic, the highest proportion in any colony. With less than one in four adhering to either old or new forms of Protestant dissent, New South Wales stood in sharp contrast with neighbouring Victoria, where the goldrush generation and its offspring, plus a big flow of immigration in the 1880s, combined to strengthen Protestantism. The Protestant preponderance of the younger southern settlements showed up in extreme form in South Australia; every second South Australian, just over 50 percent of the population, adhered to Christian churches other than the churches of England and Rome.[59] The situation in New South Wales led to nominalism and a notorious sectarianism. The cry for liberal religion remained unsatisfied.

It can be argued that the cry intensified as radical and working-class organisation in New South Wales brought the Irish-Catholic working class into politics. By the turn of the century sectarianism was institutionalised in the new party-cum-class politics.[60] It appears that there was an inverse relationship between liberalism and theosophy. In the space between contending religious and political forces, all the 'reform' movements huddled together and made their way together in the marketplace. So it was that Sydney would usually be the better locale for theosophy than Melbourne or anywhere else in Australia, though Perth and Brisbane held promise. So it was too that the field for theosophy lay with disappointed secularists, disgruntled spiritualists, and people even further out of the orbit of the churches, Swedenborgians or, nearer the secular edge, Freemasons. Wherever there was room for socioreligious radicalism there was room for theosophy.

Socioreligious radicalism included feminism, an important tension virtually immune to geographical variation. Given the claims of evangelical religion upon late Victorian women, and the pressures fundamentalist theology placed on the female psyche, it would be amazing if the liberalising strain did not affect women as well as men. As both Louisa Lawson and Annie Bright could testify, colonial women suffered spiritual turmoil too, and they had much to suffer and endure in a world which knew sudden death only too well. Moncure Conway deplored religious mania in the colonies and wondered that colonial mankind peered so strenuously into the glass of time to see a world where their ideals would be realised. Womankind, too, struggled to realise ideals.[61]

Annie Bright took to the platform, testifying to the fearful enslavement of womankind by Christianity and the way little children were terrorised by tales of Hell. Addressing an audience in Dunedin, New Zealand, in 1884 on 'The Emancipating Influence of Spiritualism', she explained how spiritualism made her a more ardent secular worker as well as a stronger spirit. In an autobiography more typical than she knew, she described her distress when her first husband disappeared inexplicably at a Sunday school picnic in 1879. Unitarianism proved a barren and comfortless creed, and she only slowly recovered from sorrow and loss by reading Conway's transcendentalist sermons and spiritualist testimony by the Melbourne writer H. Junor Browne, and by abandoning an anthropomorphic God for the freedom of the spirit world and a seventh sense. In her own mind she had moved an enormous distance:

> I thought I was a Radical and a Freethinker before I became a Spiritualist, but I find I was more conservative than radical, more of a dogmatist than a

Freethinker ... I presumed to limit the capabilities of man's nature ...[and] knowledge of this speck of earth of ours ... I have also become a more ardent secular worker.[62]

The Australian record of such experiences is abysmally thin, and women like Annie Bright stand out so far as to suggest that they are unrepresentative. However, there is no reason to suppose that women in Australia reacted so very differently from American women, where in the mid-Victorian period radical feminists increasingly withdrew allegiance to established religion. It is no surprise to find reports of the Victorian Women's Suffrage Society in the *Harbinger* (which also contains a fair amount of evidence of women lecturers and women's seances). As well as any other women, colonial women could see 'The Necessity of Progressive Thought', the title of an address delivered by Miss M.A. Finlayson at the Castlemaine Lyceum in 1884, where she advocated partnership between theosophy and spiritualism while reserving for the former 'the highest place in the spiritual ladder'.[63] By the 1880s in Australia outspoken women were to be found in all the radical alternatives to Protestantism, not only in spiritualism but also in the Unitarian pulpits of Adelaide and Melbourne and on the freethought platform advocating birth control.[64] The chances are that in a society as male-dominated as Australia women took to such alternatives with enthusiasm.[65] After all, it is hard to see how organised spiritualism could have been sustained without the enormous input from predominantly female mediums. Madame Blavatsky spoke forcibly on the psychological damage of mediumship but it remained popular with women who willingly endured the exposure and frequent indignity for the sake of the freer life it offered. Furthermore, the spirits were frequently ardent feminists.[66]

At which point enter 'Red Annie': Annie Besant, secularist and socialist, organiser for the first match-girls' strike in London in 1888. In 1889 she read *The Secret Doctrine* and declared herself converted. Annie Besant's conversion is well documented, though typically from public rather than private records; and while she would never have admitted it, she was a case par excellence of a 'mind maddened by Protestantism'. And there is more to it than that. Besant's espousal of theosophy adds another dimension to the progress of the wisdom religion in the 1880s, a dimension now totally lost, but important at the time, probably more important than the lure of Indian religions. It effectively linked theosophy to the intellectual and political as well as the religious eddies of the day.

Born in London of Anglo-Irish stock in 1847 to comfortable circumstances, privately educated in an intense Anglican evangelicalism, at twenty Annie Wood married a curate, the Reverend Frank Besant. After tribulations in a remote Lincolnshire rectory, she abandoned the marriage and one of her two young children and escaped to London. She also abandoned that early devout evangelicalism, arguing her way through liberal Christianity to secularism. In 1874 she joined the National Secular Society and soon became a leading secularist lecturer, vice-president of the society, Charles Bradlaugh's right hand. Besant became famous in the secularists' battle against censorship of birth control literature, and in another terrible battle with the Reverend Frank over custody of her daughter Mabel in the late 1870s. Having successfully studied for a science degree at the University of London, South Kensington, she found herself denied the degree by an egregious but intangible sexism. In the early 1880s she took up socialism, despite Bradlaugh's antipathy to socialism as 'foreign mischief in our English labour struggle', trying out the many varieties which surfaced in this, the revival of socialism in England. In 1885 she finally joined the Fabian Society, a very British moderation of the doctrines of revolutionary class struggle, being gradualist, evolutionary and non-dialectic. While retaining her position as freethought lecturer in the radical and working-class clubs, she became a socialist organiser and intellectual, in 1888 a member of the Marxist Social Democratic Federation as well. Her radical and socialist friends were flabbergasted when, in 1889, she turned to theosophy, which proved to be the resting point of a radical life. She became protector to the ailing Blavatsky, now living in London, and ultimately, in 1907, succeeded Colonel Olcott as second president of the Theosophical Society.[67]

Annie Besant was theosophy's most famous convert, and a crucial one. It is doubtful that theosophy would have emerged from the eighties without her formidable skills as a publicist. The society may have done so in India, where it played an early (though small) part in liberating middle-class Indians from the thrall of British civilisation. It had a similar opportunity in other colonial contexts, like the Dutch East Indies where its rejection of racism again offered encouragement and education to native intellectuals. In Europe, as part of the occult revival, theosophy gave a boost to unhappy representatives of archaic and repressed cultures on the margins, such as aristocratic Polish emigres in Paris and the rebellious intelligentsia of Dublin, poets 'AE' and William Butler Yeats being the best-known Irish theosophists. But the declining Blavatsky could hardly have recharged the cause at the centre of western culture without fresh support. In fact she had been fishing for freethought support for years in *The Theosophist*. Her delight when at last she landed Annie Besant was totally justified, though restrained in its expression: 'My dear Mrs Besant, if you would only come among us.' Not only had she ensured a successor but she had finally tied theosophy to progressive culture.[68]

By common consent Annie Besant was the greatest woman orator of her day. Words were her life's blood. When she discovered her voice – in her husband's pulpit one sleepy day in Sibsey – she discovered herself, and her livelihood. Ever after she lived an unremitting life in the public eye, as lecturer, journalist, editor, increasingly an activist. She became, in the words of Edward Carpenter, 'the exponent in succession of large and important blocks of modern thought'.[69] Basically she moved from materialism to idealism, and, ultimately, again in Carpenter's words, completed 'a quaint circle' from evangelicalism to theosophy. Every major step she took occasioned a public apologia, published (of course) on freethought presses. Thus, in 1877, *My Path to Atheism*; then, in 1886, *'Why I am a Socialist'*; and, in 1889, *Why I became a Theosophist*. The last step, outlined to her old freethought constituency assembled in the London Hall of Science, she presented as natural and logical.[70]

Outlining her progression from Christianity through atheism to pantheism, she argued that her scientific studies had brought her to face questions they could not answer: 'What is Life? What is thought?' The riddles of emergent psychology proved particularly vexing to an avowed materialist. She listed normal phenomena like memory and many abnormal ones, problems of perception evidenced by clairvoyance, clairaudience and thought-transference, referring also to hypnosis, hallucination, dreams and prodigies of various kinds. Finally, having berated her freethought critics for circumscribing the grand old freethought platform and equating fossilisation of the mind with mental strength, she upheld the Theosophical Society as a society of mental scientists, which also aspired to true brotherhood: 'There is sore need, it seems to me, in our unbrotherly, anti-social civilisation, of this distinct affirmation of a brotherhood as broad as Humanity itself.'[71]

It is a pity that no personal papers have survived. The biographers of Annie Besant have been at once weighed down by the public evidence and deprived of a crucial dimension.[72] That Besant's most recent biographer, A.H. Nethercot, had difficulty in identifying the momentum of her life is reflected in the titles of an impressive two-volume biography, *The First Five Lives of Annie Besant* (the English phase, to 1893) and *The Last Four Lives of Annie Besant* (the Indian phase, to her death in 1933). The notion of the nine lives of Annie Besant carries the unfortunate inference that she was more animal than divine.

The last word has yet to be said on Annie Besant. It may come from the full flowering of feminist historiography. But a gifted American journalist, Gertrude Marvin Williams, who studied Besant in India in her old age, comes closest to explaining the conversion. In *The Passionate Pilgrim* (1931) Williams explains it as a development rather than a disavowal of Besant's previous materialist position, which had rejected religious authority in the name of free, rational and independent inquiry. According to Williams, theosophy was a delusion which became for Besant increasingly self-delusion. One of Williams's reviewers thought her too harsh: Besant was a mystic, 'a relentless searcher after truth', endowed with an 'amazingly plastic mind' and tormented by 'a brain that could not be appeased'. By contrast, Carpenter expressed the view that she failed to penetrate the spiritual worlds she espoused.[73]

None of these judgements takes sufficient account of Besant's intellectual environment, however. The range of ideas and experience which passed under Annie Besant's editorial eye in the monthly magazine *Our Corner*, published in London during the 1880s, shows her to have become the very cynosure of intellectual fashion. *Our Corner* contained not merely entertainments and information, regular contributions on science, art, politics, gardening and chess, and tales of freethought heroes like Giordano Bruno and Benjamin Franklin, but also European literature in translation, essays on topical political issues and up-to-date book reviews. The magazine noticed books on tsarism, vivisection, the emancipation of women, and socialism, for example. Annie, as well as being general editor and science correspondent, was herself a regular contributor and reviewer. At the time en route to Fabian socialism, she published in *Our Corner* some of her most important sociological lectures, 'The Redistribution of Political Power' (March 1885), 'The Evolution of Society' (July 1885), 'Modern Socialism' (February 1886), and the first of several versions of her autobiography, 'Autobiographical Sketches' (from January 1884). Beginning as a literary entertainment, *Our Corner* became increasingly preoccupied with tensions in politics and religion. In the issue for November 1886, Besant asked 'Who shall be the Radical Leader?'; the issue also contained articles on the Russian nihilists, evictions in Ireland, 'Radicalism and Socialism', 'Secular versus Christian Morality', and 'Christian Evidences'.[74]

'Autobiographical Sketches' made 1886 the passionate pilgrim's turning point. Amid disputes over socialism with Bradlaugh, and increasing commitment to Fabianism, she was secretly pursuing spiritualistic experiments, a fact uncovered by Nethercot. Unknown to her comrades, who saw only Red Annie, she experienced increasing confusion and anxiety, which she clothed in the language of socialism. In the series 'Why I do not believe in God', published in early 1887, Besant concluded with considerable passion:

> My mind finds no grounds on which to build up a reasonable faith. My heart revolts against the spectre of an Almighty Indifference to the pain of sentient beings. My conscience rebels against the injustice, the cruelty, the inequality which surrounds me on every side. But I believe in Man. In man's redeeming power; in man's remoulding energy; in man's approaching triumph, through knowledge, love and work.[75]

Hinduism, she noted, did not require belief in God.

Hard on the heels of doubt came disillusion in the political field. The revolution failed to happen. Despite scenes in the streets of London's West End which scared comfortable clubmen, rallies of the unemployed in Trafalgar Square culminating on 'Bloody Sunday', 13 November 1887, proved to have been over-orchestrated, provoking fierce police reaction. One man died. There were great processions and a funeral, but there it all ended. The rest was played out in the courts.[76]

In the immediate aftermath, Besant and the crusading journalist W.T. Stead formed a Law and Liberty League to defend the liberties of the people. Thinking to marshal a larger movement still, and the 'older heroism' of Oliver Cromwell, they envisaged 'The Army of the Commonweal' (the vigilante groups proposed reminded Gertrude Williams of the Klu Klux Klan). The league amounted to very little, as the scene soon shifted from the unemployed in the streets to the demands of unskilled labour in the workplace and New Unionism. Neither did the league's half penny journal *The Link*, subtitled 'A Journal for the Servants of Man' and replete with motto from Victor Hugo, himself a symbol of political oppression in France: 'The people are silence ... I will be the Word of the People. I will be the bleeding mouth whence the gag is snatched out. I will say everything.'[77] Neither the league nor *The Link* survived to celebrate the centenary of the French Revolution in 1889.

That failure clarifies the point at which radical Annie had arrived by the late 1880s. It emerged that *The Link* sought to redeem hope by mass spiritual recovery, restoring altruism:

> The decay of an active faith in the reality of the other world has, no doubt, paralysed the spring of much human endeavour, and often it has left a great expanse of humanity practically waste, so far as relates to the practical cultivation of the self-sacrificing virtues. We go into this waste land to possess it. It is capable of being made to flourish as of old.[78]

Simultaneously, *Our Corner* spoke of a church of the future: 'The teaching of social Duty, the upholding of social Righteousness, the establishment of Justice, the building of a true Commonweal, such would be among the aims of the Church of the Future.'[79] Herbert Burrows, a member of the Social Democratic Federation who accompanied Annie Besant into the Theosophical Society, called for the development of corporate ethical consciousness led by a purified vanguard.[80] It emerged that the leaguers wanted 'a realisable Social Ideal'. That meant not only free libraries, peoples' palaces, school meals and an end to the white-slave traffic and sweated labour, but also 'the effacement of class': 'The ideal of the Social Reformer is the effacement of class ... all that tends to soften class distinctions by assimilating class surroundings is useful Service of Man.'[81] 1888, the year of Annie Besant's greatest political successes on the London School Board and with the match-girls at Bryant & May, saw her set her face towards the Apocalypse. Over the next two years her name disappeared from the lists of the Fabian Society, her editorial contributions to the SDF paper *Justice* ceased, and she passed out of the eye of the London working class.[82]

In 1889 Annie Besant was forty-two years old. She had experienced in her thirties personal travail, both with regard to her children and the men in her life: the feckless Edward Aveling who later drove Eleanor Marx to suicide; the whimsical and unmanageable George Bernard Shaw, a man on the make; and Charles Bradlaugh, with whom she had once a chaste and brilliant partnership but from whom she was now estranged. She had made her way in the metropolitan culture as a publicist. And in the fifteen years since she eschewed evangelical Protestantism, she had covered vast intellectual distances, from atheism to socialism, even to the edge of spiritualism. Then, amid socialist upsurge, her voice failed to command the streets, and the many comrades from the radical and socialist clubs who rallied to the league faded away. As Williams wrote perceptively, she had reached the dangerous years, a stormy petrel of sweeping social changes. As early as 1887, Beatrice Webb (or Potter, as she was then) recognised the signs. Herself a passionate pilgrim who was capable of envisaging the coming woman as a saviour of humanity, Webb noted Besant's spiritualist interests, and feared that she would be victim of 'antagonistic currents' in the socialist movement, of hostility to leadership and jealousy of women who assume leadership.[83]

In retrospect four things stand out in Annie Besant's passage from materialism to idealism: the romantic promise of the period, the challenge of 'psychology' to mechanistic science, the failure of street radicalism, and the frustration of a strong female leader. Her resting point is clear evidence of the mood which Chadwick argues could be found everywhere in the 1880s and after:

> That mood was anxious, doubtful of progress, seeing the physical sciences withdraw into their proper field and cease the claim to order all the affairs of men, concerned over the moral ordering of society, positivist by instinct and discontented with positivism, part-sure that the churches had little to offer, and part-eager to reconcile the new intelligence with an ancient inheritance in religious apprehension.[84]

When she read *The Secret Doctrine* it was as if she had had a brainstorm. Madame Blavatsky had brought her 'to the very threshold of knowledge' and an entirely fresh perspective on evolution. Cautious at first, Besant was soon to see in the book the promise of powerful new knowledge 'for those who have learned the lesson of love'. Out of the aridities of freethought and the impasse of politics, Besant saw in Blavatsky's elaborate cosmology a key giving 'into the hands of the selfless the control of those natural forces which misused would wreck society'. By 'natural forces' the secular Annie probably meant something intractable, similar to what Christians call original sin.[85]

Henry Steel Olcott, president of the Theosophical Society, hastened to welcome so conspicuous a convert, 'one of the most intellectual and best educated women speakers and writers of our epoch ... conspicuous for courageous devotion to any cause with which she identifies herself'. He tried to reassure a gravely alarmed Bradlaugh too, and capitalise the great gain, stating that theosophy was the natural home for materialists and spiritualists: 'It is more materialistic in its philosophy than the most confirmed Materialist of the schools, and yet it is at the same time more spiritual than the most spiritual of religions.'[86] Readers of *The Theosophist*, many of them equally alarmed but for different reasons, were reminded that Annie Besant was a woman remarkable for purity of life and for unselfish motives.

Looking back on the storm which enveloped her in the late 1880s, Besant wryly remembered 'a beatific vision'. What it amounted to was a reclamation of religion as the only cement sufficiently strong to secure drastic social change. She put her dawning perception in the following way:

> Ever more and more had been growing on me the feeling that something more than I had was needed for the cure of social ills ... [W]here to gain the inspiration, the motive, which should lead to the realisation of the Brotherhood of Man?[87]

Likewise, the Law and Liberty League had spoken of 'a realisable Social Ideal' and 'the effacement of class'. The modern reader, sensitised by a century of critical Marxist analysis, might well fail to discern ambiguity in the strained idealism of such phrases, which could easily be read as reactionary, the outcome of a taste of class conflict. Bernard Shaw thought so, seeing disaffection with democracy in the transition. Yet ambiguity there was, partly inherited from the radical past, partly enlivened by the idealistic 'Religion of Socialism', and partly as a dim foreshadowing of the future which saw dreams shattered upon unacknowledged social and moral divisions. In the ambiguities of late Victorian idealism experienced by Annie Besant lay the seeds of theosophy's survival. So this lengthy account of her conversion and its cultural context is essential to the tale. Furthermore, it was Annie Besant who put theosophy on a firm footing in Australia. *The Harbinger*, noticing Mrs Besant's unexpected conversion to theosophy in September 1889 as 'a natural sequence of the action of progressive ideas', correctly predicted that her admirers would examine the ground she now stood on: 'not a few, we think, will be likely to follow her.'

The history of religion and the rise of capitalism is well known, if still contested. To relate religion and the decline of capitalism is to enter uncharted territory. Nevertheless, the survival of theosophy across the 1880s is best understood in the context of long-predicted crises in both religion and capitalism during the decade. The 1880s saw the end of mid-Victorian faith in progress and prosperity, and the beginnings of liberal malaise. Hence the collapse of old prescriptions and the rise of new ones – the demise of secularism, the decline of spiritualism and the revival of socialism – along with many intimations of an unstable order. Theosophy was part of 'a chaotic cultural milieu' extending into the 1890s. As Stanley Pierson has observed:

> The eighties and the nineties witnessed a proliferation of cults and movements which promised to re-order a fragmented existence. Positivists and Socialists, theosophists and Spiritualists, Whitmanites and Swedenborgians, the Fellowship of the New Life and the Ethical Societies, even the more extreme adherents of vegetarianism and anti-vivisectionism, were participating in a common quest for a new unity amid the bewildering changes of modern life.[88]

In America comparable crises produced an 'authoritarian socialism', clearly aligned with theosophy. Similar ferment is evident in the urban subcultures of Australia during the late Victorian period, and they proved at least as hospitable to theosophy as were metropolitan cultures.[89]

Plainly theosophy was but one of many options assuaging the unease of 'the thinking classes'.[90] But it did endorse a world free of churches and churchmen – no clergy, no creeds, not even a deity. And it did address many of the critical issues, as the exemplary conversion of Annie Besant illustrates, issues of class, culture and empire. It envisaged, as worthy work for basically religious people, the reconstitution of religious experience and authority. Alongside instant dismissals of 'this latest craze of weak, sentimental, morbid men and women' stands Joseph Furphy's expectation that theosophy would prove to be a sound and serviceable approach to 'the religion taught by Christ' as it preserved the one thing needful, fidelity to the better self: 'it seems to serve the purpose of a religion better than any other scheme I have met with.'[91] For those who feared that a wrong turning might be taken by the new prescriptions and new politics, the wisdom religion had a good deal to offer. 'We do not believe that forces of Evolution are exhausted,' said Annie Besant.[92]

Neither did most Australians. In Australia the ground was tilled through the periodical press, the lecture platform, and the clubs. If not exactly ripe for the harvest, it produced enough anguished secularists, disgruntled spiritualists and other infidels, people even further out in freemasonry, the occult and non-Christian religions, plus a political edge of idealistic socialists and philanthropists, to assure oncoming theosophical messengers of the 1890s a hearing.

3

Legends of the nineties

Early in 1891 Henry Steel Olcott, PTS, spent several months lecturing in Australia. Departing Adelaide on 27 May 1891, he authorised an Australasian section of the Theosophical Society. The section consisted of seven branches, three newly organised in Sydney, Adelaide and Toowoomba, the three already functioning in Melbourne, Hobart, and Wellington, New Zealand, and one revived in Brisbane. The Australasian section soon collapsed, but Olcott's tour marked the beginning of organised theosophy in Australia. Three years later when Annie Besant toured Australasia she had no difficulty in resuscitating the section. It continues, in modified form, to the present day. In the short span between 1891 and 1894, theosophy gained an effective foothold in Australia.

At first glance the improving prospect owed little to the merits of theosophy. Colonel Olcott's visit arose from an unexpected exigency. Unlike most itinerant lecturers, Olcott came to divest himself of money, not to make it. He came to deal with the Hartmann bequest. When founding theosophist Carl Hartmann died in Brisbane in 1887 of fever contracted in New Guinea, his family were appalled to discover that he had willed his whole estate, some £5000 worth of flourishing nursery near Toowoomba and other assets, to the Theosophical Society. It was a windfall for the society, but the council of the society in Madras soon learned of 'difficulties'. So, characteristically, President Olcott determined to deal with them himself.[1]

His decision heartened the faithful. Coincidentally, the presidential presence ensured the attention of the thinking classes, now badly distracted by economic depression and agitated by the continuing clashes between capital and labour. Olcott travelled the eastern seaboard in the months

Olcott Hall, Russell Street, Toowoomba, Queensland (*TinA*)

of the shearers' strike, when news of armed camps in remote Queensland aroused fear and anger in liberal breasts, and it seemed to Henry Lawson as if there would soon be 'blood on the wattle'. Just as theosophy had survived as an eddy in the ferment of the eighties so its message of remoralisation had a bearing on the painful realities of the early nineties, a watershed in Australian history. The amiable and idealistic Olcott may have entered fortuitously upon the scene, but there was a hearing for theosophical optimism. Amid confusion and uncertainties, theosophists were to add something to the making of legends.

Olcott arrived in Melbourne from Madras in March 1891, and was greeted by a small, excited band of theosophists and entertained at Mrs Pickett's house in Kew. W.H. Terry interviewed him for the *Harbinger*. Making his way north with due speed, he stopped in Sydney for a garden party and dinner at Government House with Earl and Lady Jersey, acquaintances from their former days in India. On 27 March the steamer *Barcoo* delivered him in Brisbane and he repaired straightway to the office of the *Courier*, which obligingly announced his arrival next day. In the Japanese-decorated home of Judge Paul, he then approached the ticklish issue of the Hartmann legacy.

Olcott improved the image of theosophy mightily by offering to share the bequest with the aggrieved family, reserving his own travel and legal costs and retaining £1,000 for the society: 'I was amused to see the instantaneous change in public opinion towards the Society and myself.'[2]

Business completed, Olcott turned to proselytising, lecturing in Toowoomba on 'Theosophy and Buddhism'. The Hartmann family joined the Theosophical Society. Having chartered a branch in Toowoomba – later theosophists built Olcott Hall there on Russell Street – he departed for Brisbane. In Brisbane on 24 April he chaired a meeting held in rooms on elegant Wickham Terrace which established the Queensland Theosophical Society (QTS), forerunner of Brisbane lodge, and twenty-seven of the twenty-eight men and six women present became members. Some of the men of the eighties, from George Smith's Progressive Book Depot circle, reappeared, Gavin Pettigrew for one.[3]

A record of this meeting survives in the TS Archive Adyar, the only complete list of attendance at an inaugural branch meeting in Australia to do so. Along with records preserved by Brisbane lodge, it serves to show that the first theosophists were professional and commercial people: a judge, two doctors, two sharebrokers, two lawyers, a clergyman with the pleasing name of Manly Power, two booksellers, four public servants (a meteorologist, an entomologist, the taxing officer at the Supreme Court, and Francis Kenna of the Electric Telegraph Department), a draper, and three names well known in Queensland politics, Gavin Pettigrew, J.B.L. Isambert and Rowland Macansh (or Maccansh) of the Queensland Mercantile Co. Their number was soon augmented by similarly placed men in country towns, like Edelfelt, now a dentist at Rockhampton, and Frederick Charlton, a Maryborough surveyor. The first members of the QTS came from good city addresses, the better suburbs like Kangaroo Point, and rural outskirts and outposts of Brisbane such as Rosalie, Sherwood and Southport.[4]

All the six women present were married, but Miss Pattison (or Patterson) from South Brisbane joined Mrs Mallison, Mrs Mary Given, Mrs Rhoda Lyons, Mrs Neill and Mesdames Taylor and Woodcock next month. Of these seven women information is available for only one. Mrs Mallison of Wickham Terrace had been a member of an 'Esoteric School' conducted by 'Professor' Theodore Wright (as had Dr Edelfelt who joined the TS in 1888 and appeared on the QTS roll in June 1891).[5]

Annie Besant with her daughter and granddaughter, 1894 (*Cosmos*)

Though few, it seems that women had kept up their commitment better than the men; and women were attracted increasingly to theosophy. By the time the QTS disbanded, to reform immediately in April 1895 – again a list survives – not many of the respondents to Olcott's call reappeared. Of the eight surviving from 1891, three were women, Mrs Given, Mrs Mallison and Mrs Taylor, along with Dr Taylor (chair), Baines, Macansh, Henry Tryon and Wishart the draper. Eight of the twenty-five who met in April 1895 were women; this number included Isabelle Edelfelt, now widowed. Present also were H.A. Wilson and the accountant W.G. John, who joined the QTS in 1893 and in 1902 became general secretary of the Australian section, as it became

A young Annie Besant

subsequently (see Chapter 4). All three became stalwarts. Otherwise there are few clues to the new recruits of 1895; but Henry Sleath, musical instrument maker, and Alex Morgan, possibly a printer of Red Hill, suggest less elevated circles of society and a change in the theosophical movement in the wake of Annie Besant.[6]

The Queensland Theosophical Society held monthly meetings through 1891 in various chambers to discuss theosophy and hear papers on, for instance, 'Animal Magnetism'. It invested in a small library, Bulwer-Lytton's *Zanoni*, Anna Kingsford's *The Perfect Way and Light on the Path*, and books on mesmerism and the occult. But it could not afford back numbers of *The Theosophist*, and it failed to find a permanent home. Attendances dwindled. Limping into 1893, the QTS adjourned *sine die*, to be revived a year later at news of another theosophical lecturer, Mrs Cooper-Oakley from London.[7]

Meanwhile Colonel Olcott was well pleased with Brisbane, where he felt at home. His hotel rooms were 'thronged with ladies and gentlemen of the highest social position, anxious to question me and join the Society'. The turnout reflected uncertainties within the small urban bourgeoisie in the wake of the boom of the 1880s. Theosophy offered a new haven from an aggressive climate of opinion, and from the anti-intellectualism of an urban outpost of empire. Brisbane intellectual life was already scarred by religious rivalries, not to mention the clashes of class and race now focused by the labour movement. Religious journals had poured scorn on advanced thought, being 'tolerantly critical of phrenology and astrology whilst pouring vitriolic contempt upon movements of rationalism, freethought and other manifestations of an age of "mealy-mouthed agnosticism".'[8]

By the 1890s the churches had identified 'a puzzling social secularism'. If there was more to it than simple evangelicalism and primitive rationalism, it was the weakness of liberal Protestantism, especially Anglicanism; this despite the fact that in 1891, 60 percent of the Queensland population adhered to either the churches of England or Rome. The number of places in which the liberal-minded could feel comfortable in Brisbane was small. Olcott's impression was only slightly askew: in Brisbane, as elsewhere, liberal opinion heard him out, and members of the thinking classes rather than the highest circles joined the Theosophical Society.

Returned to Sydney by early May, Olcott lectured at the Protestant Hall, introduced by Edmund Barton, MLC (subsequently first prime minister of Australia), with Drs Garran and O'Neill on the platform. *The Sydney Morning Herald*, previously edited by Dr Garran, reported him well received. Lady Jersey wrote that he 'excited considerable interest'. The main aim of theosophy, said Olcott, was to secure liberty of thought and open up the sources of Eastern philosophy; the time had come 'to strip off courageously every veil' between conscience and truth so that man might stand out in all his majesty. He testified to the existence of a secret doctrine and adepts: Masters, not miraculous but examples of man's divine nature – man fully evolved. The society opposed materialism and aimed to help suffering humanity. He outlined the scope of practical theosophy and mentioned his own work in Ceylon in women's education (he might have added agriculture). Mr Copeland, MP, seconded Garran's vote of thanks. The *Daily Telegraph* contented itself with noting that theosophy opposed dogmatism and intolerance, while the *Bulletin* amiably refrained from calling Olcott a fool or a charlatan, recalling him in 1894 as a blinking John the Baptist.[9]

William Turner, a member of the Australian Church in Melbourne, heard the lecture. Addressing the Religious Science Club some years later he recalled a bland message, and his own reaction, that there was no need for the Theosophical Society, as it was 'nothing more or less than Christianity as understood and held by me'. Adverse press comment in Sydney and subsequent study caused him to change his mind – theosophical writings were full of 'repellent matter', all rubbish really. However, Charles Strong did not endorse the churchman's view entirely; his *Australian Herald* agreed that theosophy lacked system, but as a response to crushing orthodoxy and a blighting materialism it had some strength, spiritually and morally. Perhaps Strong recalled that the Australian Church had failed in Sydney at about that time.[10]

Theosophy did better. Expectations of a strong Sydney branch were fulfilled instantly. On 8 May 1891, Olcott chartered a Sydney lodge of twenty-three members, Dr O'Neill being the first president. Dr Alan Carroll the anthropologist joined, and stockbroker Thomas Hammond Martyn, also a wilder one, W.T. Willans, all of whom became significant figures in the history of Australian theosophy. A full record of members has not survived, only a draft of the by-laws of the Sydney Theosophical Society dated 20 May 1891, which set the subscription at 2/– quarterly in advance, and laid down that candidates must be recommended by two fellows and vetted by the executive. The society, said the *Herald,* would encourage scientific research and spread knowledge of higher forms of philosophic thought.[11]

Two days later in Sydney Olcott heard of Madame Blavatsky's death in London on 8 May 1891. He cut short his Australian tour, excising New Zealand and Tasmania from the itinerary altogether, and restricted himself to Melbourne and Adelaide, whence he left for London on 27 May.[12]

In less-than-Marvellous Melbourne by 12 May, Olcott spoke at the Freemasons' Hall with reminiscences of HPB, John Ross in the chair. His second lecture on Buddhism was chaired by Alfred Deakin, a recent investigator of irrigation and religion in India. Again stressing theosophy's opposition to sectarianism, and hope of a true religious sense, Olcott lured 'leading thinkers' who heard that Buddhism was a religion that freethinkers could make their own. A religion professed by one-third of the earth's population must have especially attractive features, such as the law of ethical causation called karma, a science of psychology, and a practical morality: 'a good man should be respected ... unmerited misfortune should be relieved, and the bad man should be punished.'[13]

In Melbourne the press paid close attention to 'psychism', and fraud. An *Age* editorial of 16 May surveyed Olcott's passage from spiritualism to theosophy, adding an account of the findings of Hodgson and the Society for Psychical Research at Adyar in 1885. Madame Blavatsky, it said, was a 'wonder-monger'. Nevertheless, in an age of transition when inductive modes of thought were under challenge, Westerners might learn something from Eastern sages. At least Olcott agreed that mesmerism was a form of hypnosis. Olcott responded irritably that the *Age* was not well informed about new psychical sciences, nor the ardent discipline of yoga, and that he knew Himalayan masters personally.[14]

There was a further point. Olcott wrote to the *Argus* (which took a more disdainful view than Syme's *Age*) seeking donations for the work of the Women's Education Society of Ceylon. No one responded. The wealthy Melburnians, themselves advanced educators of girls, ignored the request, perhaps because Olcott had been at pains to stress that these were not missionary schools which destroyed native self-respect. Unfortunately the ungenerous were vindicated. Mrs Pickett's daughter Kate volunteered for the work but she drowned in a well on school grounds a fortnight after her arrival, a mystery the experienced investigator Olcott was unable to unravel. The *Australian Herald* noticed the death of an occasional contributor.[15]

It seems that the space which theosophy might hope to enter in Melbourne was already occupied by the radically eclectic Australian Church, an 'influential centre of broad religious thought' and in that sense itself 'theosophic'. Bishop Moorhouse in the mid-eighties had made space for liberalism within Anglicanism too.[16]

From the very beginning in Melbourne in the late eighties, theosophy assumed a low profile. The clandestine circle mothered by Mrs Pickett, who founded the Melbourne lodge in December 1890, had already found Melbourne unpromising. They met with ridicule, hostility and ostracism, and their Sunday evening lectures at the Hibernian Hall were broken up by stump orators. After as before Olcott's visit, the Australian Church and its paper the *Australian Herald* were virtually the only places theosophy got a sympathetic hearing. Melbourne was the burnt core of organised freethought and spiritualism, but those who made their way to new positions in the 1890s kept their heads down, for instance Alfred Deakin whose interest was far from exhausted. One convert to follow from Olcott's efforts was H.B. Leader, secretary of Melbourne branch 1892–93.[17]

In Adelaide, Olcott gained a further handful of converts. No respectable citizen chaired the lectures in this paradise of dissent but he attracted reasonable audiences, first in the Spiritualistic Society's rooms, then at the Trades Council hall at the Selborne Hotel. As usual he urged that the TS filled a need, and that Buddhism was a rational religion. From the *Adelaide Advertiser's* report, listeners included both enthusiastic freethinkers who cheered to hear that the Theosophical Society was a standard-bearer of truth, and hostile questioners who wanted to know how living beings could have spiritual counterparts. The outcome was a new branch of seven members.[18]

The first theosophists in Adelaide included people of similar station to the members of the Queensland Theosophical Society: an accountant with a mansion in Burnside, an astronomer, a professorial wife and a person with close links to the musical world. The group also numbered the sister-in-law of A.P. Sinnett, author of *Esoteric Buddhism*, possibly the widow of Frederick Sinnett, journalist and litterateur. The branch, which grew a little larger over the year, met fortnightly on Sunday mornings in rooms off Victoria Square, embarking upon a systematic study of theosophy with whatever materials it could command. In late 1891 six men and eight women made up the Adelaide branch. They were strengthened by the arrival of Mrs Pickett from Melbourne, and stable characters took over the executive, accountant Nathaniel Knox replacing A.W. Dobbie as president (1893–1907), Kate Castle taking over from Mrs Pickett as secretary (1895–1909). Among the recruits were Professor MacCully, treasurer in 1894, and Leonora Gmeiner, a teacher at the Model School, Lefevre Peninsula. Harold George Oliphant (1876–1963), the father of Sir Mark Oliphant, public servant and leading Anglo-Catholic layman – a wonderfully unwordly man – joined later, in 1895, his commitment to theosophy lasting until his resignation in 1925 after seventeen years as president of Adelaide lodge.[19]

Before leaving Adelaide, Olcott authorised the formation of an Australasian section of the Theosophical Society under the revised constitution of 1890. The seven constituent branches were to be federated from Sydney, and Olcott duly appointed two Sydney men as officers, an act which it may be guessed Melbourne theosophists never quite understood: 'I appoint Dr A. Carroll, AM, MD, FTS, Sydney, *pro tem* General Secretary and W.T. Williams Esq., FTS, *pro tem* Assistant General Secretary of the Australasian Section ...' However, the president had taken the forward-looking Pacific view, a view which accorded well with that of at least one of the Australian branches, the tiny but steady Hobart branch formed in 1889.

Records preserved by Hobart lodge and now deposited in the Tasmanian archives include minutes of general meetings dating from Olcott's Australian tour. These cover the period June 1891–April 1903, and reveal regular, usually monthly, meetings to 1898, when meetings became less frequent. (The 'palmy days' of Hobart Theosophical Society were yet come, in the Edwardian years.) Attendance was never impressive in the 1890s. But Hobart theosophists were encouraged in the early days by attentions from ardent mainlanders like Mrs Pickett and the branch had surprisingly good links with the wider theosophical world, receiving reports, papers and correspondence from England, India and also from America.[20]

When President Olcott returned to Adyar, he expressed optimism for the coming federation of Australian colonies, and the evolving Australian temperament. Australia was rich and zealous like America:

> Our race is building at the Antipodes an empire or a republic that will become in time one of the greatest on earth ... And I find another – to us, a much more important – thing out there: the Australian temperament is evolving, like the North American, mystical tendencies and capabilities ... A coarse vagabond brutality is being also evolved, it is true; but this mystical quality is already showing itself.[21]

He opined that fifty years hence theosophy might have its strongest foothold among 'the dear good people who were so kind to me throughout my recent tour'. The interest of Olcott's observations lies in the unselfconscious expression of evolutionary optimism and idealism. It was premature to be outward looking, but American models and an Asian outlook carried increasing weight as against imperial sentiment in advanced thought.

On 19 June 1891, Dr Alan Carroll, MA, MD, delivered the presidential address to the first general meeting of the Sydney Theosophical Society at 69 Hunter Street. Presumably the founding president Dr O'Neill had stood aside. If so, he did wisely, for Carroll was especially well equipped to convey theosophical ideas.

Alan Carroll (18??-1911) was a physician trained in London, Paris and Berlin. In Paris he worked with the psychological experimenter Charcot who so impressed theosophists like Besant and Olcott, and who influenced

Sigmund Freud. He became interested in anthropology but found that 'no certain knowledge' could be attained in Europe, so he took to the field in the Pacific, first in New Zealand and possibly New Caledonia, and then Sydney, where he settled. In letters to missionaries and men of science written during what may have been a preliminary visit to Sydney in 1886, Carroll said he planned a work 'On the races that inhabit the Pacific', and expressed concern for the protection of Aborigines. To the Reverend Lorimer Fison he wrote, 'I wish to bring out the truth as to who and what the Polynesians, Melanesians, Micronesians and Australians where [sic] and whom they came from'. It seems the truth Carroll most wished to establish was a common middle-eastern origin of mankind: that is, by means of that indomitable empiricism so typical of nineteenth-century gentlemen scientists, he hoped to harmonise evolutionary and creationist theory. Evidently he agreed with Olcott that Sydney was the centre of 'this wide Austral region'.[22]

From Sydney Dr Carroll published findings in several articles in the early 1890s. One appeared in *The Theosophist* in September 1891, on the relationship between Australians and Indians in religion and race, stating that there was no one Aboriginal race peculiar to Australia but rather several waves of migration, beyond even the Dravidians, traces of whose religion survived in the Tasmanians. Two further articles in the Sydney *Quarterly Magazine* in 1892 discussed 'The Black Races of Australia' and 'The Australian Blacks as Known to Science'. Carroll advocated an anthropological institute and in 1893 founded the Anthropological Institute of Australasia (later the Royal Anthropological Society of Australasia), and was first editor of its journal, *Science of Man*.

Dr Carroll was not a young man when he came to Sydney. However, he was vigorous in several fields of social reform. He established a public health clinic and earned a reputation as a philanthropist, also as a rather cranky health reformer, being a vegetarian and antivivisectionist with his own cures and company producing dietary products. (While eccentric in some respects, his methods were within the limits of orthodoxy in the judgement of medical historian Dr Bryan Gandevia, and his therapeutic influence beneficial.) In 1898 he founded a Child Study Association, an American-inspired move towards child psychology which foreshadowed his interest in eugenics, quickly taken over by educators bent on enhanced professional status; and in 1904, the Child Study and Adult Health Association, which attracted the support of prominent Sydney doctors such as Dr C.P.H. Clubbe. As his articles on the Aborigines show, Carroll was a typical 'reform' Darwinist, that is, one who thought in terms of progressive social evolution. Given his interest in mental science and racial anthropology it is easy to see why theosophy appealed to him, especially the version advanced in *The Secret Doctrine*, with its cycle of races and continents.[23]

The scope of Carroll's theosophy has amazed later theosophists. His presidential lecture defended the society against 'mysticism' as levelled by mean journalists and 'the most bigoted and ignorant' of the priestly population. It outlined with some eloquence and skill the geological assault on the Old Testament version of creation. Anthropology and linguistics led to his view of racial evolution; he referred to the British occupation of India as promoting knowledge of Aryan origins and the ancient history of the subcontinent. The first competent teachers of religion, he said, were the Kush, or Aethiopians, whose record theosophists should study.

Then Carroll outlined the 'social benevolent and fraternal portions' of theosophy. In an age of so-called civilisation, where was Brotherhood? Everywhere lay evidence of enmity, unrest, disorder: at home, gambling and speculation, and thousands of Nihilists, Anarchists and Disrupters of Society; abroad Russians persecuted Jews, the Chinese burned trading posts, Boers were trekking into Mashonaland and there were atrocities in the Congo. 'In all countries the same absence of fraternity and liberality is to be seen.' As for the bold and ambitious who glibly proposed the reconstruction of society, they might leave the overpopulated cities and, in New South Wales, till the undercultivated lands to contribute to recovery.

The work of Sydney lodge, he announced, would be tenfold: to examine ancient languages, religions, and anthropology, especially of the Australasian races; to study matter, the forces of nature, crystallography, life – vegetable animal, etc. – and mental phenomena, also ancient and modern science; and to advance theosophy. An open university no less!

Finally, Australians must not linger slothfully on the verge of progress. There must be more practical toleration, independent thought and advancement of women:

> While the temples or churches have kept women from their highest offices,
> Theosophy welcomes them to participate in its highest achievements,

holding that the mothers, sisters, wives and daughters are as competent as the men to reach as correct a knowledge of spiritual things, and then to apply them wisely for the good of society and the happiness of the world.[24]

The intellectually ambitious presidential address contained more than a hint of impatience and authoritarianism. Perhaps it was to counter aggressive individuality among the uneasy men attracted to theosophy that it stated that topics for discussion be cleared with the executive first so as to avoid 'unpleasantness for all'. Howsoever, Carroll succeeded in catching up themes of the early nineties – lost knowledge, moral reform, feminism – for the promotion of brotherhood and the avoidance of conflict.

Carroll's career as a spokesman ended there. But for a report in *The Theosophist* in 1893 of studies of Easter Island inscriptions, he disappeared from the record almost immediately, replaced as president of the Sydney Theosophical Society in 1892 by George Peell, an officer in the NSW Lands Department. A man of 'angularities', Peell nevertheless found a home in Sydney theosophy after ten years as secretary of the Unitarian Society, and remained president until his death in 1904.[25]

As for Olcott's proposed section, it was scarcely Carroll's fault that nothing came of it. Rationalistic theosophists were especially keen on forms and titles, and like many another small weak association, prone to inflating themselves. Federalism was a new idea everywhere; and none of the new groups had sufficient resources to sustain it. Brisbane branch expressed willingness to co-operate but could not even afford to contribute to a Blavatsky memorial fund. Olcott realistically cancelled the authorisation in 1892, remarking that individuals advanced the cause untiringly in the Antipodes and that the movement was gaining ground everywhere, due to Annie Besant's advocacy. Actually the Australian lodges – as they came to be called – gained ground too. In 1894 there were seven: although the two Queensland lodges faltered, several new ones formed after 1891. Sufficient foothold had been secured to attract Besant herself. A prior tour in 1893 by Mrs Isabel Cooper-Oakley paved the way.

With only four of the six branches chartered in 1891 functioning properly in the early 1890s news of new branches was good news. Signs of resurgence in Queensland were particularly heartening. They came not from Brisbane but the coastal towns, ever after a source of hopefulness to theosophists.

Capricornia lodge, founded by Dr Edelfelt in 1893, met at the School of Arts Rockhampton and reported fair attendances. Bundaberg lodge began in 1894, and a start further north in Cairns seemed likely (but not until 1896 a reality). In Melbourne in 1892 the indefatigable Pickett founded another group called Maybank at Fitzgerald Street South Yarra (on the poorer, Prahran side of the tracks), a study group, in effect a family affair and discomforting adjunct to the Melbourne branch whose sixteen or so members met in the Eastern Arcade. Most interesting was the short-lived breakaway Lemurian branch in Sydney, formed by W.T. Willans and friends.[26]

The general report of the Theosophical Society for 1892 states that the Lemurian branch aimed to 'spread theosophy among the people rather than induce membership of the TS'. The new branch spoke in populist terms, therefore, and hoped for an 'Australian' theosophy. In the years between Olcott and Besant, interim years institutionally speaking, it raised the issue of self-reliance. Unfortunately in theosophy as in all else the ruling ideas are the ideas of the ruling class: dependence on imported ideas and the big names proved to be a feature of the rise of theosophy in Australia. But in the early nineties the alternative received a first airing, albeit in a typically obscure fashion, in the first theosophical journal in Australia, produced by the Lemurians.

'Lemuria' is not a word which appears in the *Oxford English Dictionary*, or as a place in any atlas. Unlike the comparable concept of Atlantis, Lemuria has but attenuated life left in it today, except perhaps in geological debate about continental drift. It could however be assumed familiar to 'the cultured reader' by Madame Blavatsky; and she made good use of it. Coined by a mid-century naturalist to describe the habitat of the lemur from Madagascar to Malaya, and taken up by Ernst Haeckel as the cradle of the human race, Lemuria became associated with the Greek myth of Atlantis, largely due to Madame Blavatsky's efforts. She had appended a hasty note to *Isis Unveiled* in 1877 incorporating Louis Jacolliott's evidence for a further lost continent in Polynesia. In the fullness of time came the reason for her interest in 'submergence of continents in prehistoric days'. Lemuria became a legend of the nineties.[27]

The *Secret Doctrine* mapped Lemuria as a mega-continent:

> It covered the whole area of space from the foot of the Himalayas, which separated it from the inland sea rolling its waves over what is now Tibet,

Mongolia, and the great desert of Schamo (Gobi); from Chittagong, westward to Hardwar, and eastward to Assam. From thence, it stretched South across what is known to us as Southern India, Ceylon, and Sumatra; then embracing on its way, as we go South, Madagascar on its right hand and Australia and Tasmania on its left, it ran down to within a few degrees of the Antarctic Circle; when, from Australia, an inland region on the Mother Continent in those ages, it extended far beyond into the Pacific Ocean, not only beyond Rapa-nui (Teapy, or Easter Island) ...[28]

Nor was that all. It had once extended as far as Greenland and far Kamschatka. In horseshoe fashion the two ends were united by the coastal fringe of Siberia. But 'this broke asunder and disappeared. In the early part of the Third Race – Lemuria was formed'.

It is stated that of the five root-races the Lemurians remain most mysterious; although complete records of the Lemurian civilisation exist in secret annals, the annals are written in symbolic code, virtually impenetrable in the age of materialism. Degraded Lemurian remnants survived in Australia, but the Tasmanians became sterile, and 'flat headed' Aborigines suffered 'the curse of retardation':

> It has been suggested by many geologists that the Australian native – co-existing as he does with archaic flora and fauna – must date back to an enormous antiquity. The whole environment of this mysterious race, about whose origin ethnology is silent, is testimony to the truth of the esoteric position.[29]

In lieu of the evidence which might still be collected in Australia and places like Easter Island, Blavatsky relied on Science, and 'UNIVERSAL tradition'.

The androgynous Lemurians are sometimes portrayed as giants and hairy, but in Blavatsky's book they had the best of things, a golden age of elemental religion. And as precursors of the most ancient people and wisdom of India and the Levant, they played an essential role in evolution:

> Had they not their bright gods of the elements around them, and even within themselves? Was not their childhood passed with, nursed and tendered [sic] by those who had given them life and called them forth to intelligent, conscious life? We are assured it was so, and we believe it. For the Evolution

of Spirit into matter could never have been achieved; nor would it have received its first impulse, had not the bright Spirits sacrificed their own respective super-ethereal essences to animate the man of clay ... It was the 'Golden Age' in those days of old ...[30]

Paradoxically, the mythic Lemurians also set the scene for a theosophical version of the Fall which came in the next, Atlantean, phase. From the 'Book of Dzyan' upon which *The Secret Doctrine* is extended commentary, stanza X announces: 'Then the third and fourth (races) became tall with pride. We are the kings, we are the gods.'

In the theosophical version of Lemuria, volcanic action submerged the antique continent almost entirely. As Dr Carroll obviously realised, more research was needed. Some creative writers in Queensland and Western Australia seized the Lemurian hypothesis to locate Australian themes and enrich romance and adventure stories, George Firth Scott's gothic tale of the Centre, *The Last Lemurian* (1899), being a telling example. Most were merely exploiting it, though as a spiritualist in London, Rosa Campbell Praed took it very seriously. It goes too far to posit a 'Lemurian nineties' in Australian literary history, but the legend of Lemuria provided one new perspective and gathered in suggestive fragments of natural and social science which in one form or another have retained their romantic and historic appeal in Australia.[31]

In theosophical circles Lemuria lured only a minority too. Perhaps the thought of Australia as site of a golden age spurred the Sydney rebels on. Although Blavatsky's cosmology bore painfully upon Black Australia, her spiritualised Darwinian perspectives fed white hopes: 'Australia is one of the oldest lands now above the waters, and in the senile decrepitude of old age, its 'virgin soil' notwithstanding. It can produce no new forms, unless helped by new and fresh races, and artificial cultivation and breeding.'[32]

The Sydney Lemurians lasted less than a year, but they went on the offensive. Whereas the Adelaide theosophists gave papers in private on subjects like 'The best answer to give materialists', the Lemurians hired the Freethought Hall for public debates and approached the press. Brother Hewison, it was claimed, inserted theosophical paragraphs in the *Workman*. The *Daily Telegraph* reported that one of the regular lectures for inquirers on reincarnation was an interesting and instructive session. The executive also suggested a livelier, more cosmopolitan drive, with Dr Clive Belisario, president, Geza Kvanka, an American socialist lecturer vainly seeking a cure for TB in Australia, and George de Cairos Rego, plus F.E.S. Hewison, an enthusiastic Sydney spiritualist since 1878, and the fiery Willans (FTS, 1889), secretary.[33]

Their magazine *Upadhi*, subtitled 'An Australian Monthly Theosophical Publication of News and Opinion', edited by Willans and Rego, had as its motto, 'Believe only that which appeals to your reason'. It tried to act as focus of the Australian branches and to assert independence: 'The ablest exponents of the Esoteric Philosophy are unanimous in expressing their opinion that the only help we can expect in finding the Path is through the development of ourselves on the lines of the fundamental laws of our being.'[34] Reading in the London journal *Lucifer* that there had been a cry for help from Australia, Willans reacted angrily. Australian theosophists were already fortunate with access to so much literature. He mentioned *The New Californian*, a journal from a vital late-nineteenth-century centre of radical and utopian thought.[35]

But the small Lemurian branch could not sustain itself. By 1894 its members had returned beaten but not broken to the Sydney Theosophical Society.[36] Soon Willans and his friends were completely upstaged in taking theosophy to the people by Annie Besant.

Nor had *Upadhi* gone to the people. At 2/- a copy it was expensive and distribution was scarcely attempted (though a copy did reach Hobart). Eight typescript issues were produced between 1892 and May 1893, but readers had to write in for copies. It does show that the Current questions were mostly 'doctrinal' – what is theosophy, where does the soul originate, what is the second logos? Many were spiritualistic – is communication with the dead taught, what is the relationship between theosophy and spiritualism? Answers stressed the voluminous proof of reincarnation, and that brotherhood was an affair of the heart.

Just as would-be Lemurians gave way in Sydney, Mrs Cooper-Oakley arrived in Melbourne on a private visit. She remained in Australia for six months in 1893 and proved a good organiser and forthright. Melbourne, she said, had a need of utopian objects after the land boom; and Sydneysiders should contemplate the theosophical fact that if they allowed slums they would very likely have to live in them themselves next time around. She certainly was a lady, said the *Argus*, impressed perhaps that she had been a successful businesswoman in London where she had run a dress agency on Bond Street and 'Dorothy' restaurants for working girls in the West End.[37]

Of northern English extraction, Isabel Cooper-Oakley was born in Amritsar, India, in 1854; her father was Commissioner of Lahore. She spent much of her girlhood in Europe and enrolled at Girton College Cambridge, but ill-health prevented her from completing a degree. An early convert to theosophy, she was at Adyar during Hodgson's investigations and later lived in Annie Besant's commune at St John's Wood London where Madame Blavatsky died. In that she had seen HPB more recently than Colonel Olcott, Mrs Cooper-Oakley was a welcome emissary to remote places.[38]

The cry for help reported in *Lucifer* which so irritated Willans probably came from Annie Besant's daughter Mabel. Mabel had married a young London journalist, Ernest Scott from Northampton, in July 1892; the couple, who adopted the surname Besant-Scott at Mabel's insistence, left a week later for Melbourne. Cooper-Oakley stayed with the Besant-Scotts in Jolimont. Her first move from Jolimont was the Victorian Theosophic League to unite the Melbourne lodge and Mrs Pickett's Maybank group. In April 1893 she told the press:

> Here my success has already been greater than I anticipated, and while not losing sight of our first aim to co-operate for a higher moral standard and just social conditions, I hope also to create an interest in the serious and earnest study of the underlying laws governing mind and matter.[39]

Mrs Cooper-Oakley spoke favourably of Melbourne. She found the place better for psychic tendencies than anywhere but America, with many thoughtful men seeking a scientific base for religion, which she attributed to 'mixtures of blood', and North Country stock. It is true that prerational religious practices did survive in the north and on the Celtic fringe of the British Isles, though the 'mixture of blood' in Melbourne is an impression to be wondered at.[40]

As well as presiding over the Theosophic League, Cooper-Oakley ran afternoon soirees, said to attract 300 people, with forty ladies among the 'intellectually unconventional' men. In Sydney at another crowded gathering the ratio of the sexes was reversed, probably because the meeting was convened in the Women's Literary Society rooms by well-known feminist and educationist Maybanke Wolstenholme (later Anderson): a room full of ladies except for a learned judge and a literary labour man, with 'no butterflies', rather, 'all that is practical and admirable'. But theosophy was 'all -isms and -isis's' to the down-to-earth reporter who naively inquired as to the ultimate destination of the soul under theosophy.[41]

Like many of the radical religious, Cooper-Oakley proved to be a strong woman suffragist. Rose Scott invited her to address the Woman's Suffrage League of New South Wales, and when some of the members protested, fearing they would be linked with theosophy, she agreed to speak without reference to it. However, she did begin with the proposition that theosophy was 'a woman's cycle', and an attack on dogmatic theology and the priesthood, which weakened women – 'The priesthood had never been a friend of women' – before moving to the apathetic state of the movement in Britain. Labour women, she predicted, would be the best help in gaining the vote. Lady Windeyer chaired the meeting.[42]

The visitor showed her mettle on the public platform. In addition to women's meetings and addresses to Unitarians and the socialists, she gave four public lectures in Sydney and established another theosophic league. The public lectures, chaired by cremationist Dr John Creed MLC, attracted improving audiences, reaching 400 by the last. Her subjects included 'Life of Man – the seven principles, Reincarnation, Karma', and she stressed the role of theosophy in promoting rational evolution. Some thought her teachings fatalistic, others incredible (what of the proliferation of population which must occur with reincarnation?); and others dismissed her either as unsexed or fraudulent. The *Sydney Morning Herald* editorialised with wearied liberalism that theosophy was 'a manifestation of the restlessness of modern thought'. Perhaps it was still a force to be reckoned with: where some saw charlatans, others saw the hope of the race. Even if it was tiresome to winnow the wheat from the chaff, the appeal of theosophy undoubtedly lay in its many mysteries, and worked for those 'who prefer to shape their religious systems for themselves'. Restlessness, impatience, inquiry filled the air, and Madame Blavatsky could be credited with extracting 'something suitable for her times'.[43]

When Cooper-Oakley launched a Sydney Theosophic League, she organised the work into thirteen departments. Whether or not Sydney theosophists had the capacity to run them, they indicate what was thought to be effective activism:

branch organisation; press correspondence; elocution; social evenings; leaflet distribution; Secret Doctrine classes; public lectures; a debating club; theosophical reading groups; concerts; clothing for the destitute; classes for children; scientific and psychological research.[44]

The organisational effort included encouraging theosophical libraries. When she left Melbourne, the lodge boasted a first-class library. Later it was claimed to be the largest occult library in the southern hemisphere, due to the generosity of founding member Miss Minet.[45]

Mrs Cooper-Oakley may not have been the warmest of personalities – when questioned about the carpentry in Madame Blavatsky's rooms at Adyar which so upset Hodgson, she asked sharply if the questioner took the word of dismissed servants – but in six months she created order among the fractious and fragile theosophists of Melbourne and Sydney, kept theosophy in the public eye, and prepared the way for Annie Besant. In Melbourne in early 1894 the Theosophic League held a musical soiree for 200 people to celebrate 'Reunion'. Public lectures continued on the broadened platform, from that evergreen of Melbourne journalism, the advocate of the Higher Spiritualism, James Smith, from Ernest Besant-Scott, and from H.W. Hunt, now president of Melbourne branch. If by August numbers diminished and opposition from the churches was discouraging, classes on sunken continents and the Mahatmas kept up. The emissary departed for the World's Fair in Chicago in September 1893, where she represented Australasian theosophists at the Parliament of Religions, her credentials signed by H.W. Hunt and H.B. Leader of Melbourne.[46]

From an historian's point of view, Mrs Cooper-Oakley's most significant achievement was to encourage the *Austral Theosophist*, immediate predecessor of the sectional journal known today as *Theosophy in Australia*. Although the editor remained anonymous, it was undoubtedly Ernest Besant-Scott, later Professor Sir Ernest Scott (1867–1939), Professor of History at the University of Melbourne 1914–36, a distinguished Australian historian who counted among his friends Alfred Deakin and Charles Strong. Scott, previously a Roman Catholic, does not seem to have referred very often to theosophical sympathies in early manhood, but they dated back into the ferment of the eighties, especially the Bradlaugh–Besant campaigns in his native Northampton. When his marriage dissolved in the mid-1890s

T.H. Martyn, a Sydney stockbroker and stalwart fo the Theosophical Society for thirty years (*Path*, 1927)

he abandoned the hyphenated name by which he was known when he first arrived in Melbourne; and seemingly theosophy also. In the early nineties, however, the young journalist served the cause and brought it closer to the main stream of intellectual life.[47]

Mrs Cooper-Oakley's main achievement in Sydney was of a comparable character. She brought T.H. Martyn to the fore as president of the Sydney Theosophic League. The league flourished, and Martyn emerged as pivotal figure in the history of Australian theosophy until his sudden death in 1924. Born in Finchley, London, in 1860 of a Cornish family, Thomas Hammond Martyn emigrated to New South Wales in 1884, starting in a small way at Goulburn where he married Alice Furner, possibly daughter of a leading Goulburn storekeeper. They shifted to Sydney in 1887. He intended to study law but amid a minerals boom became a successful investor instead, registering with the Sydney stock exchange in 1889. In 1890 he took chambers as a stockbroker in Pitt Street. He prospered greatly and later moved his private residence from Randwick to the more theosophical or perhaps

Cornish-sounding address of 'St Michael's' in Raymond Road, Neutral Bay. After his first wife's death in 1899 he remarried in 1901.[48]

Martyn had sympathised with land reformer Henry George and taken an interest in politics on the free-trade side in the 1880s. In 1891 he was recruited by Olcott and thereafter devoted himself to theosophy, becoming prominent by 1894. His 1894 lectures entitled 'Theosophy and Spiritualism' increased league attendances. The league consolidated its position in the city when it moved to new quarters in Margaret Street, meeting place of Sydney theosophists until 1907. The public lectures which had been held in the Oddfellows Hall were now held at Margaret Street, and in 1894 theosophical feminists and socialists as well as theosophists held forth: Mrs Wolstenholme, FTS, on the education question and 'Theosophy in Common Life', and T. Soderberg on 'Socialism and Theosophy'. In harmony with Mrs Cooper-Oakley's prescriptions, a lunch club and a ladies' sewing club for the poor were instituted, and a Sunday reading class. The successes of the Theosophic League marked the beginnings of a Sydney bias in Australian theosophy; and subsequent dominance by Sydney lodge owed a good deal to T.H. Martyn. Under his leadership in the early twentieth century, Sydney lodge was to become the largest and richest theosophical lodge in the world. In 1894 he served as Annie Besant's 'Chief of Staff'.[49]

The new Melbourne magazine offered the invigorated and expectant groups a means of co-operation. The *Austral Theosophist* stated that its first aim was to link theosophists, said to be 'a numerous body' (there were perhaps 200). Its second aim was to lift the level of debate and dispel misconceptions: 'Up to the present ... the criticism of Theosophy in Australia has for the most part commenced with a slander and ended with a sneer.' In language redolent of early Victorian improvement societies, it announced itself A Magazine devoted to the Diffusion of Knowledge on the Esoteric Philosophy and kindred subjects. The sixpenny monthly laboured to fulfil those aims in fourteen monthly issues throughout 1894 until February 1895. It is therefore a source of information about not only leagues and branches and breakaways, but also the mental world which Annie Besant was soon to enter so easily.

There was very little of the Lemurian in the *Austral Theosophist*, very few articles on ethnology – one on 'Maori Mysticism', some reviews of books on Aboriginal religion. Contributors dealt mainly in *theosophia*:

theosophy, the Theosophical Society and its objects; the main teachings, reincarnation, karma and the Masters (Mrs Cooper-Oakley advised that the Masters be emphasised as 'a necessity of 'evolution', advice not followed); and, theosophical mainstays, psychic phenomena such as mesmerism, psychometry, hypnosis and magic.

Mostly the contributors were locals like Hunt, Edelfelt, Nathaniel Knox, Wilton Hack. There were some women contributors: Emma Richmond, Lilian Edger, MA, a valuable New Zealand recruit, and Mabel Besant-Scott, who provided reminiscences of the distant great ones and tried her hand at 'Eastern Knowledge and Eastern Investigation'. The fare was supplemented with reprinted material, Blavatsky on 'Lodges of Magic', and Londoner Herbert Coryn on 'Heredity and Occultism'. Such papers, along with accounts of phenomena, lost Tibetan manuscripts and numerology, served the study groups, as did Edger's series on *The Secret Doctrine*.

The distinctive feature of the Melbourne journal was its metropolitan ambience. That was apparent not so much in references to awful Melbourne meat shops, stinking cemeteries and vivisection, or articles on vegetarianism, cremation and education: those were stock-in-trade of theosophical and radical journals alike dating back to the 1880s. Nor were the aphorisms and excerpts from key nineteenth-century cultural figures like Ruskin and Emerson noteworthy flourishes. But articles such as 'Tolstoi on Proselytising', 'The Religion of a Literary Man' (Richard Le Gallienne) and 'The Gospel of Anarchy' referred to the liveliest point of 1890s communitarianism. All unattributed, these brief up-to-the-minute and well-written pieces suggest the hand of the editor, and his sympathies.[50]

Conspicuous by its absence in the earnest *Austral Theosophist* is evidence of religious passions, or tension, among individuals. There is no intimation, for example, of experiences like those of the young Christopher Brennan, returned to Sydney from post graduate study in Germany in 1894. Brennan's biographer Axel Clark has outlined the poet's recourse to esoteric systems of thought, especially gnosticism, at this time, and his affinity with Yeats, then far advanced into the occult. Alongside Brennan's quest, the mental and spiritual world of accredited theosophists seem drained, drab and middle-aged. Only the occasional glimpse of personal faith and hope emerges from the well-produced pages of the *Austral Theosophist*.[51]

Ernest Scott's own view in 1894 has to be deduced from an article 'The

Spectrum of Truth', first delivered to the Victorian Theosophic League. It described a rather abstract ecumenical position, with yearnings perhaps but no sign of ferment or the wildness of literary men. Citing Blavatsky to the effect that theosophy was like the white ray of the spectrum, and the religions the prismatic colours, he argued that the direction of modern thought was theosophical, that true thinkers everywhere had shaken free of mere creeds, and that the pure white light of religious truth would soon shine forth. Referring to recent scholarship pertaining to Islam and Buddhism, he emphasised the contribution of Max Müller in the noble work of religious reconstruction, regretting that the great Sanskrit scholar's recent lectures *Theosophy or Psychological Religion* attacked the work of the Theosophical Society. From such theosophical leavenings, Scott's conclusion anticipated 'a time to come when the barriers of creed shall be broken down, and, with vision undimmed by mists of prejudice, men shall gaze, inspired and aspiring, upon the pure white light that is concentrated in the spectrum of truth'.[52] What residual effects this may have had on the approach of one of the first significant Australian historians is not a relevant question here; but the hope of future harmony it expresses bears upon the radical optimism which many have noticed in the legendary nineties.

The Austral Theosophist shows that its readers were aware of the older radical culture but ambivalent about it. A few single-taxers, co-operators and socialists contributed. As in America, state socialism found theosophical advocates, F.E.S. Hewison, FTS and socialist of Arncliffe, for instance: 'I want to see, as I am sure all true theosophists must also wish to see, an end to wage slavery.'[53] But the correspondents could agree only on the higher idealisms. The interests of theosophists and single-taxers could not be assumed to run parallel. Co-operation was admirable but unrealistic in the present state of evolution – and so Wilton Hack left the society soon after. It was understood that there was something profoundly wrong with social organisation, yet radical reform was impossible without radical reconstruction of the individual. In general, the magazine suggests that theosophists in the early nineties were wordly but not primarily interested in this world. Encouraged by Ernest Scott, they came closer to it than usual. But collectively they stood back from the radical culture. The way forward was yet more taxing:

Everyone knows the great effort that it takes to lift oneself out of a particular groove, be it orthodoxy or materialism. The uprooting of one's prejudices is in itself a sufficiently difficult task, and when those prejudices are supported by self-interest – when to turn our back on our own preconceived notions is to incur the ridicule of a servile press, and to earn the disrespect of a large majority of the public, the way must indeed be hard.[54]

A last point from the *Austral Theosophist*. Its pages referred with increasing frequency to the impending tour of Annie Besant, an advent viewed with uncertainty by the older theosophists, who sensed a turning point. Knox of Adelaide wrote:

I cannot but think that the advent of Annie Besant to Australia is no common incident in the career of the Society, but is fraught with important results ... to Theosophy generally. Even from what little we know of her great character and her literary and other work for the benefit and advancement of humanity, we cannot feel otherwise than proud that so noble a woman has become so prominent a member of the Society.[55]

So noble a woman. Yet, as Knox hinted, there might be more to the tour than the uplift. For Annie there was indeed an important result to be achieved in the Antipodes, along with encouraging the cause and seeing Mabel. Her motives were mixed, typically Besantine.

From time to time the gentle journal referred obliquely to trouble. It had acknowledged another harmful attack on Madame Blavatsky in the London press, but merely as 'a rechauffer of the Coulomb and Hodgson libels'. Now another battle approached its unpleasant climax. Annie Besant charged William Quan Judge with forging messages from the Masters, using Madame Blavatsky's seal. The messages proclaimed that Judge, not Annie, should be head of Blavatsky's inner group, the Esoteric Section of the TS. The matter was subject to internal inquiry and shortly to come before the council of the society. Under the society's constitution, representation on council was by territorial section. Thus the tiny antipodean branches, if properly constituted, represented another vote, and if organised by Annie, probably a vote for her. So the trip did bear on the future of theosophy, as implied by Knox, and as will be seen in greater detail in the next chapter. Not of course that such crudities were ever stated; but the leonine lady of the radical clubs understood the force of numbers. There were only a few branches in Australasia, compared with America's eighty-six or India's 175, but it was clearly a territory and, since 1891, virtually a section.[56]

The issue had to be treated gingerly because of strong American sympathies among members like Willans. Some lodges preferred American theosophical literature to any other; Sydney lodge in 1894 was studying Judge's *Ocean of Theosophy* for example. It was hoped to attract American lecturers. Co-operation did not come so easily, no more guaranteed by literary effort than by Colonel Olcott's optimistic constitutionalism back in 1891. Not until the section was actually reconstituted and a vote taken could the real balance of feeling be tested. By then, of course, Annie Besant had swept through.

Besant's Australian tour, though not more than an incident in an eventful life, took five months. She left London in late July 1894, sailing via Colombo and arriving in Melbourne on 3 September; then, after a fortnight, on for another in Sydney and to New Zealand in October, returning in November to depart via Melbourne and Adelaide on 5 December for Christmas at Adyar. Western Australia, Tasmania and Queensland were not included in the itinerary, though she found time to send word of encouragement to Bundaberg branch.[57]

The tour was a personal triumph. 'She is consecrated,' breathed the *Austral Theosophist*, confident of improvement in the status of theosophy and clear teaching at last. The tour was also an interesting event in the history of colonial culture, evidence not so much of the colonial cringe, though there were elements of that, but of colonial aspirations and affinities, anxieties and aggressions. Thus Henry Parkes, chairing her second Sydney lecture, introduced her as unexcelled in courage, devotion and independence.[58] Besant's credentials could hardly have been bettered personally, politically, culturally; and she came refurbished with novel teaching. During her first week in Melbourne Besant gave five lectures and announced another series to be delivered on return from New Zealand. She conducted a daily flow of interviews and classes, the latter of up to twenty at a time in the Theosophic League's rooms. One inquirer, by private arrangement, was Alfred Deakin. In Sydney from 18 September to 1 October she lectured nightly, giving ten lectures in all, the set of five and a further five 'by popular demand '. Later in Adelaide for six days between 29 November and 5 December, she spoke three times to theosophists and conducted interviews over three days while delivering the set five lectures at Adelaide Town Hall. The unexpected rigours of the Australian climate notwithstanding, Mrs Besant was a demon for public work.

At first the press fumbled. 'Eloquent and energetic,' said the *Age*, but had she reached the end of a doughty pilgrimage? 'A dignified dame,' was the *Bulletin*'s first response. The *Sydney Morning Herald* made do with 'Woman of Today'. Thyra Gebinn, enthusing in *Cosmos*, confessed to chill and disappointment close up but then was astonished and delighted by the lectures. 'Sappho Smith' (Ina Wildman) of *Bulletin* fame found Mrs Besant amazingly natural: 'I never heard anyone talk so well as Mrs Besant'.[59]

After the first lecture in Melbourne copywriters had something to go on. 'MOST ENTHUSIASTIC RECEPTION by a Cultured, Crowded and Fashionable Audience of the FOREMOST WOMAN OF THE AGE The Universal Verdict'. The *Bulletin* reporting the debut was impressed by the audience. There in serried ranks were the 'deep philosophers' in blue spectacles, the cheerful agnostics with l/- buttonholes and scarce a bald-headed Presbyterian in sight. Middle-aged women 'not strikingly odd' came on their own. By the fourth lecture, 'the most eloquent address ever delivered from a platform in this city', the large audience was visibly affected. They neither coughed nor sneezed nor whispered and no one left for a drink midway. Few sat upright. Most strained forward to the stage like 'a plot of sunflowers with their faces turned towards the sun'.[60]

It was not just because colonial theatres tended to be gloomy, ill-lit. It was also the spectacle – the oratory – the experience. There she stood, a woman in her prime, in a white flowing gown, floor-length, satin dressed with brown lace fichu, her firm face shaped by short white hair, straight as a bulrush, short but impressive. With white gloves removed, strongly sinewed hands calmly folded in front, formalities complete, she would talk for an hour in a melodious voice, without a note, without a smile and scarcely a gesture, diction and organisation so clear the words could be copied down verbatim in orderly prose.

Many have tried to distil the essence of the oratory of Annie Besant. The young theosophical lecturer Clara Codd compared her with that great practitioner William Ewart Gladstone, whose peculiar capacity, it has been suggested, was to treat the individual and the mass as one, thereby sealing the compact between aristocratic government and democratic politics. Hers was the old oratory, 'full of magnificent gestures and flowing periods', the more impressive from a woman. Beatrice Webb, who could not admit the propriety of public speech by women, and shuddered to see her speaking, thought Besant unique: 'I heard her speak, the only woman I have ever known who is a real orator, who has the gift of public persuasion', she recorded in her diary in 1887. According to Clara Codd, Annie Besant held audiences spell-bound by 'a flawless sincerity'; they were fixed in the eye of a 'noble child'.[61]

Mrs Besant never shouted. She had no need to. She could modulate her voice to suit the size of the audience, easily heard by 10,000 in the open air or pitched at the edge of audibility in confidential conversation. The Indian politician Sri Prakasa who first heard Mrs Besant as a boy at Adyar in the late 1890s, forty years later remembered that, and other aspects of a relentless professionalism. He recalled meticulously prepared lectures which filled the allotted time exactly, and close attention to detail, seating for example, the agenda, and her own dress. Mrs Besant disliked central-aisle seating arrangements in halls. Announcements afterwards irritated her. On shared platforms she preferred to speak last and to leave when she had done – 'She just finished off at the very height of her eloquence, and sat down or departed from the rostrum, leaving her audience spellbound to applaud or demonstrate as they liked'. She always wore white, a colour not worn by men or women in public even by the 1940s. (One of Annie Besant's lecturing gowns is lovingly preserved at 'Ou-rata', a proud old theosophical estate owned by the Radcliffe family at Klemzig, Adelaide, now the property of the Theosophical Society).[62]

Perhaps her admirers exaggerated, but more likely Prakasa did catch the essence when he portrayed a master of lost art:

> She was a great artist in words, which in her mouth were like music, and her voice rose and fell as the waves of the sea when she spoke. It is a matter of deep satisfaction that microphones, loudspeakers, and amplifiers had not come into existence in her younger days. The contemporary world would otherwise have lost the virgin beauty of her eloquence.[63]

Agreeing on the impact, the *Age* questioned the content of Mrs Besant's lectures. It 'appeared to have a greater effect upon the audience than would have been the case had [it] come from a less eloquent person'. In a hostile retrospect, the Sydney *Bulletin* complained at skilled advocacy of an unacceptable message; her argument was all holes and no ladder. Nevertheless, audiences appreciated eloquence: at her last Sydney lecture at the Opera House on 'Politics: What they can do and What they cannot', '... with most impetuous and poetic eloquence, Mrs Besant urged her hearers to make Australia a nation of great thinkers and workers, all labouring together for the common good'.[64] There were prolonged cheers when she concluded everyone should serve. The crowd was 'unusually demonstrative'.

Australians learned that her name should be pronounced 'Bezant' to rhyme with 'pleasant', or at least that was what she preferred. They filled the theatres and halls. And the promoters became ever more emphatic in the entertainment columns. Beginning by announcing the MOST CELEBRATED ENGLISHWOMAN that ever visited the colonies, the FOREMOST THINKER and the FINEST SPEAKER, and leader of the EMANCIPATION OF WOMEN, the billing moved to the FOREMOST WOMAN OF THE AGE, MOST WONDERFUL ORATOR and the APOSTLE OF THE BROTHERHOOD OF MAN, and ended up after a week in Melbourne with GREAT GENIUS, Apostle of the LARGER HOPE.[65]

But criticism increased too. The critics said that you came out none the wiser about the new gospel of theosophy, that Mrs Besant failed to make her teachings 'intelligible to the average intellect', or alternatively of the first lecture, 'The Dangers that Threaten Society', that it was shallow and elementary. There were no tricks to watch either. 'Sappho Smith' had the temerity to criticise Mrs Besant's personal presentation, especially her spook-like jewellery – probably Madame Blavatsky's ring, which she always wore – and warned women that here was 'quite a little "East Lynne" on wheels'. Male journalists did less well with deflationary phrases. Elsewhere the *Bulletin* remarked quite gratuitously that the Mahatmas seemed to discourage the corset, while in the same breath asserting that local lady haranguers could learn a thing or two. When she first arrived in Sydney, the *Bulletin* judged her creed trivial, but admired the altruism of a good woman. After all, 'the intellectual belief of a good woman is of comparatively slight importance', a remark on a par with the observation that most of her audiences wore spectacles. The *Argus* in Melbourne did best: surprised at the fluency and force, it hazarded that Mrs Besant learned it all from her benighted clerical husband the Reverend Frank.[66]

Whether or not press interest lasted (it did in Sydney but not so well in Melbourne) and despite the disappointed, disaffected and downright disagreers, those who lasted the distance thought that she got better and better. New listeners came forward, respectable people who had at first been uncertain, or put off by theatrical venues. Announcing that the second series in Melbourne would be transferred from the Bijou Theatre to the Athenaeum Hall, the organisers explained that it would be 'for the convenience of clergymen and others who prefer to avoid the associations of a theatre'. True friends of religion would hear little to complain of. So were summoned:

> Christians and unbelievers – Bishops and curates and All Congregations ... Professors and Preachers – Moderators, Ministers, Rabbis – Advocates of Bible-reading in State Schools, Advocates of Science Teaching in State Schools – Believers in Moses, Disciples of Darwin – Statesmen and Politicians – Liberals and Conservatives.[67]

Theosophical sources asserted, as usual, that audiences increased. It was only to be expected in Sydney. But in Melbourne too theosophists glowed at audiences said to contain 'the flower of the intellectual life of the community'. To the *Austral Theosophist*, Annie Besant was simply the grandest and noblest woman of the day.[68] En route she gave theosophists a lesson in propaganda. Addressing members of the Esoteric Section in the newly formed 'Ibis' branch in Toorak, Melbourne, the branch founded in her honour which had as its first secretary Alfred Deakin with ex-British labour leader H.H. Champion a founding member, she illustrated some of the principles which made lecturing effective. First, lectures should be expansive – open-minded, and encompassing all movements directed at Brotherhood. Second, they must be positive: inquirers needed attracting thoughts, not bullying. Third, they should abandon the fashion for complexity, remembering the importance of simplicity in life. When she wrote sharply that Eastern teaching was inaccessible to Western minds and that Sanskrit terms were gibberish to most people, she spoke with authority, having spent her travelling time to Australasia translating the *Bhagavad Gita*. Finally, theosophists must keep up; they should be ready to adapt the latest findings in chemistry, archaeology, psychology. (It was an article of faith that the twentieth century would vindicate Madame Blavatsky.)[69]

In short, as a lecturer with twenty years' experience on the freethought platform in Britain, the only Fabian socialist to command attention in the radical and working men's' clubs of England as well as command rallies in Trafalgar Square, with material honed in a thousand theosophical drawing rooms and on the American lecture circuit, Annie Besant found herself comfortable on the colonial stage. The halls filled and so did the coffers. With dress circle seats at the Bijou at 3/-, family circle 2/-, and the gallery l/-, minor irritants could be overlooked. Mrs Besant received 50 percent of the proceeds, probably a reasonable gloss on the advertised claim that the profits would go on the 'objects of The Theosophical Society'. Even at 3/-, it was not too much to pay. She said what must be said in straitened times to guilty, gullible mankind, and was perhaps a godsend to the Turner coalition in Victoria, then in the midst of a depressing election campaign: 'Let your national ideals have [their] keynote in the higher part of Man ... Turn from the struggle for wealth; simplify your life; have fewer physical wants; ask more from the spiritual',[70] and, in an unusually poetic phrase, 'material joy is like the cut flower'. The cut flowers of the Melbourne land boom were at that moment wilting in the bankruptcy courts. 'We are having bad times here just now,' confessed Alfred Deakin, 'after our period of speculation which has stripped me with many others of all we had.'[71]

Eloquence is never enough. What was said mattered most. Just as she had expounded the freethought program so now a new prescription applied. Having traversed all conceivable ground, she had come through. Hers was an extreme solution, but it had authority and was softened by skilful development of subject matter over the lecture series, which proceeded, as in the old adage, from the known to the unknown. Starting from social pathologies, it proceeded to psychic remedies, and the call to remoralise society. As copied and arranged by an anonymous devotee, the lectures began with 'The Dangers that Threaten Society', then dealt with 'The Evolution of Man', 'Theosophy and its Teachings', 'Hypnotism and Mesmerism', concluding with 'Reincarnation'.[72] There were variations, and additions, but the message remained constant.[73] Discontents both legitimate and artificial threatened progress; advance was impossible under present competitive and morally enfeebled arrangements; the best minds were in revolt; while the churches continued to preach the blasphemy of original sin mainly to women and children, all cried out for new ideals, ideals which were rational and cohesive. By taking hold of latent spiritual powers, the track of evolution could be recovered. Eastern teachings offered a viable model of the necessary mental evolution. Reincarnation, she claimed, could revolutionise social thought: '(If true] it must alter our whole conception of human life and give a new basis to our thoughts of human duty.'[74] The *Sydney Morning Herald* reporter found this lecture not only well-organised but in some respects the most interesting of the series.

The message bore elaboration: on 'Death and the Life after Death', on 'The Mahatmas as Facts and Ideals', and the problems of spiritualism. It was not simply the Higher Spiritualism as W.H. Terry rushed to assert. It was not a higher fatalism either. The powers, the force, the ideal Men existed. She testified to all of it. The *Bulletin* decided the message was vague and threatening – 'believe, or Karma will catch you' – but trivial too, and in some respects as deluded as poor millenarian Joanna Southcott eighty years ago who believed that she, a domestic servant, was a woman 'clothed with the sun' and mother of the Messiah. It was cruel comparison for so good and respectable woman as Annie, but the *Bulletin* went further: her message was immoral. Forgetting that her 'brightest point' had seemed to be her opposition to the churches' teachings on the depravity of man, the *Bulletin* was not taken in by her optimistic tone. 'The good woman is a pessimist,' it declared.[75]

What she actually said was:

> If in this city you wish to raise the public morality; if you wish to see social and political reforms introduced, you must direct your thoughts to the desire that those ends should be accomplished ... By nobly thinking every one of you becomes a great force in society.[76]

Her strengths are most evident from the lecture on the possibilities of politics, which explained the spring of progress via state intervention – a sequence of great ideas, their practical dissemination and political application – as in the socialist progression to a co-operative commonwealth. After 'a very brilliant description of the horrors of the London slums', she predicted confiscation. She then moved her argument from Bellamyite state socialism to theosophy: confiscation would be justifiable on the basis of reincarnation. Slums attracted the least developed souls, the souls of savages and criminals and the idle rich. Slum clearance was not just a sectional demand, but a psychic necessity. Reincarnation offered a base for brotherhood.[77] The lecture's references fitted the mould of colonial reformism, even if its reasoning was abstruse. And it was bold, as were her more manageable and equally vigorous proclamations about national ideals. When the foundation of a nation was being laid, concern should be shown for 'the best conditions ... for that long evolution in which all that is noble in the human race may find consummation', for developed individuality, for greater harmony than existed in Britain where the balance of classes suited none. 'The Australia of the future is building in the minds of today.'[78]

To summarise press reports is to heighten the conservative effect while diminishing the field of play of Besant's rhetoric. Her impact depended upon the latter, which stretched from the authoritarian socialism of the Bellamyites across feminism to the spiritualised Darwinism of Madame Blavatsky. Framed by contemporary discourse, illustrated by current realities and anxieties, and pitched to the heights of late-nineteenth-century idealism, the whole resounded, as one person thought, like an 'almighty fugue'. It would be brash to say she was a raving lunatic; though that must be the ultimate outcome for followers of the Masters, said the *Bulletin*. At least she had more novel things to say than that other visiting preacher, the Rev. John McNeil, known as the 'Scottish Spurgeon' because of his forceful fundamentalist preaching style, who attacked colonial failings – betting, beer and ballroom dress. Dr Strong, who did not hold with theosophy; noted that though the churches would have none of her, she had probably had a good influence, as a 'good and earnest teacher is to be welcomed in our dead city'. Some even saw Mrs B. as a messenger from God, and wanted a 'Conference of Religions' as in Chicago. She represented the higher evangelism attuned to the 1890s.[79]

Meanwhile others found it refreshing merely to have Mrs Besant in town, like the delegation from the newly founded NSW Vegetarian Society led by Mr Gatchell and W.D. Campbell, FGS. She explained her diet. On tour she ate mainly lentils, for ease of carriage. With considerable foresight, she extolled the benefits of vegetarianism in an increasingly sedentary society, while pointing out the present horrors of meat-eating, best exemplified by the charnel-house of Chicago, which was at that time undoubtedly one of the most shocking cities in the world.[80] Her preference meant an unconventional dinner for Justice Windeyer though, when she invited him for a pre-lecture snack in Sydney in acknowledgement of his important judgement on *The Law of Population* in 1888.[81]

Amid high seriousness, there were also moments of farce. Fortunately for her, Mrs Besant had left Sydney when the laughter broke out. A splendid spiritualist scandal occurred, which she had in effect created, not just by adding a lecture on spiritualism in Sydney but by taking a personal interest in Sydney spiritualism. She attended a materialisation achieved by the celebrated medium Mrs Annie Mellon, pride of Sydney spiritualism since her arrival from the north of England some three years earlier. It was partly because of the Mellon affair, 'the talk of the town', that the *Bulletin* could refer to 'Annabai' in Spookland.[82]

Reports vary as to Besant's view of 'Geordie' and 'Sissie', Mrs Mellon's materialisations. But she certainly saw them when she attended the select but well-publicised gathering at the home of Dr Charles MacCarthy in Elizabeth Street, Hyde Park. Dr MacCarthy published photographic evidence in *Cosmos*. The press besieged Mrs Mellon, and the Victorian Society for Psychical Research, founded late 1893, wanted to conduct tests. According to *This World and the Next*, the medium resisted all such blandishments on health grounds and for fear of press bias. Then on 12 October 1894, at a séance at Mrs Mellon's own home in Woollahra, architect and self-confessed sympathiser with spiritualism T. Shekleton Henry proved unable to restrain himself any longer. Abandoning customary propriety, he leapt from his carefully positioned chair a short distance across the darkened room and did loud battle on the floor with an all-too physical manifestation near the medium's cabinet.[83]

Not all present thought this quite fair. Testimony was confused. Unitarian minister the Reverend George Walters was one of those who refused to renege on spiritualism and Mrs Mellon, though Henry claimed a 'complete and irrefutable' exposure of fraud. For those present the matter was never resolved, as subsequent tests had to be abandoned because of the medium's poor health. The tests were conducted by public-spirited citizens, a committee headed by Justice Windeyer and including J.M. Creed, Edward Greville, Henry Copeland and Annie Bright. It was at about this time that Rose Scott attended seances at the Windeyers' and Alfred Deakin recorded his spiritualist experiences for posterity, including one in Sydney with Mrs Mellon after the expose, which he found reassuring.[84]

The Melbourne Society for Psychical Research fell into some disarray too, despite its weighty committee, two professors, several medicos and a respected editor A.L. Windsor, plus the Reverend Dr Strong, James Smith and veteran theosophist H.W. Hunt; the president, Professor Laurie, ceased to hold office. No matter, said the *Australian Herald*, it was wrong to exploit people's deepest longings, as the abyss to which the Mammon worshippers had brought Melbourne showed. The *Austral Theosophist* tried to be even-handed in the face of a possible recrudesence of vulgar spiritualism.[85]

The Mellon affair exposed that section of society which stood closest to Annie Besant, the hopeful séance-sitters, would-be psychical researchers and other seekers of religious renewal. They represented the respectable top of a more diffuse audience at the lectures. That audience, now confused, guilty and anxious, still seeking the larger, if not the Lemurian, hope, recognised that Annie Besant, like Conrad's *Lord Jim*, was 'one of us'. They helped make 'the legend of the nineties'. Annie Besant – 'She tried to follow Truth' – was a legend herself. Only to the most brazen, and in an extended historical perspective, was it clear that she was also representative of a dying culture, idealist, elitist, imperial.

The Theosophical Society in Australia, which she effectively founded in 1894, kept her legend alive. Her earliest followers were recruits from the thinking classes, respectable people but not of the first rank, men and women at the margins of intellectual life, whose activities are recorded only in such obscure sources as *Uphadi*, the *Austral Theosophist* and *This World and the Next*. They sought an authoritative and progressive centre. Sometimes, as with Annie Besant, they felt themselves somewhere near it.

4

'The Great Unsatisfied'

Writing back to Adyar from Dunedin, New Zealand, in late October 1894, Annie Besant informed President Olcott that she had successfully re-formed the Australasian section of the Theosophical Society. The Australasian section, which came into existence on 1 January 1895, consisted of five branches in Australia and four in New Zealand – a short-lived arrangement since New Zealanders formed the seven branches requisite for separate existence in 1896 and an Australian section emerged. The new Australasian section would be run from Sydney by Besant's nominee, English theosophist John C. Staples, as general secretary.[1]

When he stepped off the boat in Melbourne, Staples told the *Age* that a new stage in theosophy had begun. One theosophist proclaimed the beginnings of a great work:

> in Australia, where the old orthodox Christianity has but little hold on the real colonial mind, being like so many other of our institutions, neither belonging to the country nor yet adapted to its peculiar requirements ... a faint shadow, or a reflection of a shadow ... the Theosophical Society has great work to do.[2]

Another idealist extolled a new sense of community and fellowship:

> We have joined our hands with the fellowship of the great unsatisfied ... those for whom the church altars are not high enough, creeds are not deep enough, and for whom the good that is being done is not good enough, and the life to do it in not long enough.[3]

Some of 'the great unsatisfied' were already inside the theosophical movement in 1895; and more important, the movement itself broke in two in the very first year of its corporate existence in Australia. It fragmented further before World War I in America and in Germany, though with fewer long-term repercussions for Australian theosophy.[4]

Fracture followed in the wake of the so-called 'Judge affair'. The anticipated inquiry in London in July 1894 proved unable to assess the charge, formulated by Besant, that Judge had fabricated letters from the Masters to sustain his claim to be the true inheritor of HPB's powers: Judge refused to confess and the alternatives involved assessing the Masters themselves. Who was to say that they could not have written such letters as in days of yore? The London papers, especially the *Westminster Gazette*, delighted in exposing such 'theosophistry', as Annie Besant learned in New Zealand. Back at Adyar after the debacle of the inquiry, the next step followed. The sections must vote, on three options, requiring that Vice-President Judge either resign, or explain, or be expelled.[5]

The fledgling Australasian section returned a loyalist verdict, two-thirds voting against Judge, with a group in Sydney branch led by ex-Lemurian Willans dissenting. As recounted in the *Irish Theosophist*, Willans raged against Annie Besant, and all British overlords, pious, immaculate and authoritarian: 'Australia claims to have a say ... at least those who have found voices to speak in this country.' He ranged 'Australia' with the dissident Americans and Irish (Judge was American-Irish). On these freer shores, he said, 'the evolutionary tendencies of a grander and better race are helping us; with a crop of Irish elementals to aid us also in acknowledging no authority that does not pass the counter-sign to our own hearts'.[6]

Meanwhile the American theosophists declared independence. In April 1895 they formed a Theosophical Society in America, proclaiming not merely autonomy but primacy. Their claim to be the one true theosophical society was not sustainable legally, and later the new organisation adopted the title Universal Brotherhood and Theosophical Society.[7]

Twenty-six Sydney dissidents followed suit, and applied to the new organisation for affiliation by charter, which Judge granted on 23 August 1895. They formed a New South Wales Centre of the Theosophical Society in America, drew up a new constitution and declared William Q. Judge president of an autonomous Theosophical Society in Australasia. Its executive contained some familiar names of early theosophy in Sydney, Brother Willans president, A.A. Smith of Gordon secretary, and Mr and Mrs

Minchen. They held a convention in December 1895, and the preamble of its report stated that freedom of opinion and toleration had been assailed 'by an attempted official authority'.[8]

Then, unexpectedly, Judge died in early 1896. He was succeeded by Katherine Tingley, a minor but colourful figure in American social reform, who immediately embarked on a world crusade to emphasise her claims and organisation, also to collect funds for a School for the Revival of the Lost Mysteries of Antiquity, soon to become a reality at Point Loma on the outskirts of San Diego in southern California. The Purple Mother, as she was called because of her preference for garments in that shade, included Australia in her itinerary, giving the ex-Lemurians a further boost.[9]

The scant surviving evidence suggests that the rebels shared Judge's distaste for the 'Indianisation' of theosophy, and that they laid greatest stress on theosophy's third object, the latent powers of man, as remedy for the ills of Western society. The Mitchell Library in Sydney holds three issues of Willans's second attempt at a theosophic magazine, *Magic*, which appeared October–December 1896, the months before Tingley's arrival in Australia in January 1897; also an undated leaflet, *Winged Seed* (both sources are stamped with the name John Dwyer).

Magic, 'Devoted to Universal Brotherhood, Theosophy and Archaic Science', nailed its colours to the new mast by hailing the New Day, and the continuity of theosophy from Blavatsky through Judge and Tingley; America as the first-born child of the Future Race; and the Destiny of Australia. Willans stressed magical powers in a blend of alchemical and Darwinian rhetoric: 'We hold ... that the powers of the Soul are magical: that their exercise is fraught with the practical and intelligent transmutations of latent good ... At the core of the heart of man lies this potent power to regenerate himself, a family, a nation or a race.'[10] Theosophy brought to the fore the great truths concerning origin, evolution and destiny; karma and reincarnation offered keys to brotherhood ('We have strayed far away from the equilibrating point with our abnormal development of selfishness and greed'); it was the great remedy for all conflicts. Magic, it seems, was another word for divine wisdom, latent powers, and the new Tingleyite teaching of Raja Yoga, representing a higher path. The forces of white magic would be deployed against black. The editorialist went on: 'Without this base, religion becomes emotional and approved of only by credulous minds ... [It is] easily made the tool of destructive forces and intelligences and dashed on the rocks of scepticism and doubt.'[11] *Winged Seed: Theosophy* stated that 'selfishness, indifference and brutality can never be the normal state' of man, and called for social improvement, self-abnegation and labour for the poor. The far echoes of radical and utopian sentiments are here heard in the passive voice, interwoven with magical prescriptions.

The crusade, however, failed. Madame Tingley and her entourage attracted little attention, and what there was in the press was largely hostile to the public display of rifts in theosophy and such Tingleyesque flourishes as a huge purple standard with gold tassels. Neither the special role allotted to Americans in racial evolution nor the summoning of the arcane mysteries struck a chord. The Adyar loyalists in what was by then an Australian section breathed a sigh of relief at the meagre response, and ceased counter-attacks on the rival organisation and its proposed school as a manifestation of clericalism, in the hands of a professional medium to boot.[12]

Stalwarts like Willans are credited by their heirs with saving theosophy from 'psychism', a reference to developments fostered by Annie Besant and her latest offsider C.W. Leadbeater; and Willans survived to see another generation of dissidents.[13] But the flurry of the mid-1890s failed to divert the mainstream. In any case it would have been difficult to build on the crusade, since Tingely concentrated effort on 'the white city in the east', and made no effort to foster a branch network. The Sydney affiliate faded away, though there is evidence of continued effort in the late 1890s (for example in papers which preserve a copy of a Brotherhood publication, *The New Century*, for April 1899, listing No 1 Universal Brotherhood lodge Sunday lectures at 113 Pitt Street, Sydney), and as far on as 1905.[14] The Universal Brotherhood and Theosophical Society has a fascinating history of its own in the context of Californian communitarianism; but in Australia it served mainly as a counterpoint to the rise and fall of a theosophical movement dominated by the Adyar-based organisation. It had its chief influence later, in the 1920s. As will be seen, Madame Tingley proved to be a wily opponent of Adyar and Annie.

Momentous events notwithstanding, loyal Adyarites in Australia felt themselves to be on improving ground. They put their faith in organisation. John Staples, a cultured English gentleman previously a black-and-white artist, saw the next step as systematic teaching and branch-building: 'The

Charles Leadbeater

influence exerted by our respected Sister Annie Besant, I am assured, lies deep in many hearts, and only needs the facilities which the establishment of this Section affords to take root and spring into active life.'[15] In Sydney by March 1895 Staples organised the first annual convention and produced the first issue of *Theosophy in Australasia* only two months after the last issue of the *Austral Theosophist*. Noting that the general public declined to associate itself with theosophy – a reference to exposé of the leadership struggle in the *Westminster Gazette*, among other difficulties – he nevertheless expressed the customary theosophical optimism. As a result of Besant's tour, 'there is hardly a country hamlet or town where at least one member or associate or correspondent of the Theosophical Society does not reside' (a very considerable exaggeration since the first available statistics show 267 theosophists in all Australia).[16] Responding to the challenge of the Antipodes, and 'pressing invitations', Staples was soon lecturing in outlying districts such as Bega and Maitland, and visiting other branches.[17]

Through 1895 Staples' labours were supported by another visitor, the ageing Blavatskian intimate, the Countess Wachtmeister (or de Poma). Her drawing room talks were no great success. She attracted only a fair attendance of questioners to Brisbane meetings in October, likewise in Hobart; but there were hopes that a new recruit, Heinrich Kessal, would establish a branch in Mount Gambier, South Australia, and she also helped bring the New Zealand section into existence by April 1896. In Sydney the countess stayed at the Hotel Metropole at the expense of Mrs Gooder Gunter, and her presence added cachet to a post-burial ceremony performed by the unitarian minister George Walters at Waverley Cemetery to the accompaniment of cheerful Australian verses.[18] She opened a new branch in Sydney called Dayspring, formed by theosophic temperance workers led by Lorimer E. Harcus and G.W. Marks, the society's printer. The countess was pleased to find pioneers of social improvement united in theosophy, the real spiritual basis upon which such practical endeavours must surely be based. The eleven members of Dayspring discussed 'knotty problems' in a Congregational schoolroom in Surry Hills, the syllabus enlivened occasionally by moonlight ferry trips to Manly. Dayspring branch was the newest of ten branches to appear on a listing of Australasian branches in May 1896.[19]

Of 267 fellows of the Theosophical Society in Australia in 1896, a majority lived in the capitals of the eastern seaboard: ninety-two in Melbourne, sixty-one in Sydney. *Theosophia* scarcely made a showing in Adelaide (twenty fellows), or remote Tasmania (fourteen in Hobart), while a branch in Western Australia was yet to be secured. The best opening still appeared to be Queensland, with eighty members in three branches.[20]

Queensland offered most hope for several reasons. The first branch had been formed in Queensland, and throughout the 1890s there were more branches formed in Queensland than anywhere, and more accredited theosophists than anywhere except Melbourne. The tropical environment reminded theosophists of India and other colonial contexts where theosophy concurrently enjoyed some success. Third, conditions in Queensland accorded best with the theosophical view of racial evolution.

Mention has already been made of Blavatsky's complicated cosmology in *The Secret Doctrine* which envisaged an upward evolutionary cycle through the rise and fall of dominant civilisations such as Lemuria and Atlantis. It further taught that each civilisation represented the work of a root-race and produced a perfected racial type. Each root-race spawned many sub-races, and successive root-races emerged from the most advanced of existing sub-races. The late-nineteenth-century world stood at the end of the fifth cycle of civilisation (or Mantanvara), with the work of the fifth root-race, the Aryan, already done and in decay. The sixth root-race would bring with it the requisite spiritual refreshment and advance, and was already in the making, evolving from sub-races thrown off from the Aryan round. The sixth round men would be an entirely new breed: 'Every "Round" brings about a new development and even an entire change in the mental, psychic, spiritual, and physical constitution of man, all these principles evoluting on an ever ascending scale.'[21] Progress now depended on the next race round.

The late-nineteenth-century reading public was unlikely to be appalled by the fantastic complexity of this application of evolutionary imperatives to conventional racist thought. The principles of Darwinism had been thoroughly disseminated in Australia, the source incidentally of extensive evidence pertaining to the Darwinian hypothesis. Social Darwinist perspectives strengthened as the first anthropologists set to work. And the long gap between Darwin and Mendel left plenty of room for speculation. Do-it-yourself Darwinism flourished in a culture predisposed to ideas of spiritual evolution and, increasingly hospitable to the prospect of social evolution, a liberal Darwinism. By the late 1890s the Australian political culture was saturated with liberal Darwinism: the land of the 'social laboratory' grew accustomed to 'experiments' in the name of progress, harmony and community. Conceivably it would teach an evolutionary lesson in the near future.[22]

Theosophists expected the sixth round to start in California, not Australia. What they saw in Queensland was only a tendency, an emergent contributory sub-race. They believed that Queensland's climate was especially conducive to the New Race type, and that the mix of its people encouraged its evolution. The promising mix included British, German, Italian and even Chinese people (but not the Aborigines, that unfortunate Lemurian remnant). Mention is often made of the efforts of Piedmontese theosophist Chiaffredo Venerano Fraire who brought the first shipload of Italians to Townsville in the 1890s, a practical contribution to the New Race. To the eye with a theosophic squint, Queenslanders look like a key sub-race.[23]

Furthermore, Queensland at this time presented a milieu in which theosophy might be expected to flourish – muddled, tense, volatile, futuristic. It was Queensland in 1899 which gave the world its first brief glimpse of a Labour government, as it had been Queensland which saw protracted class conflict in the early 1890s and spawned the utopian disillusion which led William Lane to Paraguay. Assisted immigration from Britain continued longer in Queensland than elsewhere in Australia, which meant more new arrivals with up-to-date ideologies; labour followed capital from the south, especially the far-flung pastoral industry; after 1860, mining booms punctuated the development of the farthest north (in some versions of Australian history that alone bespeaks a more alert population); and, as is sometimes said there never was and never will be a White Australia north of the Tropic of Capricorn.

Later, thirty years on, theosophists would anticipate a Pacific rim view of the world, and make greater play with Australia as the home of an advanced sub-race. In the 1890s they concentrated on Queensland, and hoped to exploit its progressive image. Tensions in Queensland would surely increase the numbers of the great unsatisfied and enhance the claims of theosophy, just as cramped conditions among the thinking classes had encouraged a minority to attend to the message of President Olcott in Brisbane in 1891. The doctrine of the advanced sub-race simply focused common idealisations of 'The Coming Race' and 'The Coming Man', which had gathered strength in Australia since first advanced in the 1880s.[24]

That there was something special about the meeting of neo-Darwinian religion and Queensland is suggested by the number of branches which popped up in the 1890s in the coastal towns – though perhaps that overemphasises the small, mainly male, groups which met in hired rooms to answer for themselves the protean question 'What is theosophy'. Dr Edelfelt's group in the Rockhampton School of Arts studying karma and reincarnation in 1894 survived his departure and subsequent death in 1895; it was not reported 'lively' again until 1913. The group at Bundaberg which benefited from the encouragement of Besant in 1894 and funds donated by T.H. Martyn, continued with fortnightly papers on such subjects as 'Theosophic Brotherhood' from Brother Pascoe. In Townsville in the early 1890s there were regular meetings in the Old Town Hall. The surveyor Charlton led another group at Maryborough. In 1896 the hope of Cairns was fulfilled, and it proved the healthiest of all the coastal branches.[25]

Theosophical hope in Queensland was not confined to the coastal towns. In addition to the fitful life of Toowoomba branch, there were possibilities inland in the mining towns – a pronounced feature of Victorian theosophy a little later – which appeared to be fulfilled with the formation of a branch at Charters Towers in 1901. Wowsers and miners had long battled it out in Charters Towers, to the discomfiture of believers in rational progress and the elevated character of mankind. The Charters Towers and Townsville branches of the Theosophical Society appear to have had an intermittent and interchangeable history, and together they illustrate another funnel for theosophic hopes of the 1890s.[26]

In Brisbane, after so many beginnings, the branch re-formed in April 1895, and grew in strength. Improvement was partly due to the success of public meetings, which attracted variable attendances in the late 1890s, averaging about fifty; it was due also to the increasing strength of theosophical women of whom Edelfelt's widow Isabelle was the most capable; and finally it was due to the sound administration of W.G. John, a recruit of 1893, who became secretary in 1896 and president in 1897.[27]

W.G. John (1852–1916), a London-born accountant who arrived in Brisbane via Ceylon, worked hard as lecturer and writer to promote the cause. It was John who discerned 'the great unsatisfied' in Australian religious life. He believed that Besant proved theosophy must be taken seriously, though he also said it was not a matter of personalities or immediacies, but of slow adjustment of domestic, social and political machinery to accommodate the revolution in human thought now underway. Theosophists, 'a group of students who can lay no claim to be considered the intellectual salt of the earth', should stem the tide of indifference and prepare for the day when spiritual powers would be brought to bear. They stood to truth as the early Gnostics stood to Churchmen, he said, a reference to the religious freedom claimed by gnosticism perhaps.[28]

The records of Brisbane lodge, carefully kept, show a sustained program of activities and a steady supply of paper-givers. In 1896, for example,

Brisbane theosophists delivered papers fortnightly across four main areas: theosophical doctrine and propaganda; theosophic reinterpretation of Christian doctrine such as sin, self-discipline and the atonement; alternative religious activities like spiritualism; and papers relating theosophy to current scientific and social questions on subjects like radiography and vegetarianism. During a bad patch for Brisbane lodge in 1900, W.G. John gave at least ten talks-cum-papers. To list six titles – 'Self Salvation or Self-Sacrifice?', 'Is Reincarnation Reasonable?', 'Does Justice rule the World?', 'Command of Mind over Matter', 'Art and Theosophy' and 'Socialism from our Standpoint' – is to bring out the interesting point implicit in the general listing above, that theosophists were not much interested in press sensations about Thibetan masters or in the manoeuvres of Madame Blavatsky. Rather, and on this Brisbane lodge records are the best surviving guide, they sought a stronger personal and social ethic. Amid papers which revelled in rounds and races and firemists, along with the stodge too, there ran a steady stream of more or less standard religious anxiety, and the quest for knowledge on which to build a broader platform to include the insights of Indian religion and women. The records suggest that theosophists' complaints about press misconception had some basis in these earnest early days, though of course there could be no permanent escape from the earliest outrageous claims and actions; and without access to the actual texts it is impossible to say how much of the addresses was simply fanciful.

Mostly the new Queensland branches barely survived the turn of the century. It is also true that in the first phase of organised theosophy, theosophical lecturers worked Queensland hardest of all Australian locations in the late 1890s. Thanks to the sea-route from India via Surabaya, Olcott landed there again on a second and last trip to Australia in 1897. He joined forces with the young New Zealand lecturer Lilian Edger, MA, soon to be adopted by the Australasian sections as federal lecturer.[29] However, it was easier after that to revive interest, as happened when branches re-formed at Charters Towers and Toowoomba in 1914. What happened in Queensland in the late 1890s foreshadowed the fact, never really conceded, that a movement like theosophy could only hope to survive in the cities. Nevertheless, even by the late 1890s branches were not secured in all the major cities.

By 1897 a start had been made in Perth by emigrants from Victoria, Mr and Mrs James Patterson (already met in Ibis lodge, Prahran), carpenter Montague Miller (if he be the same figure traced through the Australasian Secular Association and the spiritualist journal *This World and the Next*), and Mr E. Gregory, an early member of Sydney lodge, who, along with another senior public servant and literary man, Wilhelm Siebenhaar, brought intellectual strength to theosophy in Perth, all encouraged by the popular and conscientious Miss Edger.[30] In 1899 Miss Edger stayed with 'Mr Cook', the government astronomer – apparently the same Professor Ernest Cooke encountered at the beginnings of theosophy in South Australia – and delivered a series of lectures in November 1899, one of them at the Mechanics' Institute, said to have attracted 300 listeners on average. Later, after he became general secretary, W.G. John included Perth in a pastoral itinerary and reported a good response: press coverage was, he said, the best theosophy had had in Australia for years.[31]

By that time Mrs Patterson had started a second branch at Fremantle and there were about thirty theosophists in Western Australia. No attempt seems to have been made in Kalgoorlie. In due course adherence improved, and by 1913 adherence to the two lodges in the west was better than in either Adelaide or Hobart; nearly a hundred enrolled, a proportion of whom were said to reside beyond Perth itself. The problem of a nomadic population faced by all religious organisations in Australia was experienced by Western Australian theosophists. But theosophy found a niche in the old gentry town which was still Perth at the turn of the century.

In fickle Sydney none of the suburban branches survived the new century. Each was the initiative of the spiritually dissatisfied. Mrs Steel's effort at an Egyptian lodge meeting in Oxford Hall, Oxford Street, collapsed for want of interest in her version of 'occult philosophy'. Theosophists certainly did have something to say about drink (and diet) but Dayspring went the way of the Lemurians. An interesting initiative at Mt Rockley, an old gold town south of Bathurst, also proved very shortlived. Meantime the Sydney branch gathered in the survivors and became the largest theosophical fellowship in Australia by 1900, with 76 members.[32]

In Melbourne, thought to be the largest branch throughout the 1890s until figures for 1900 disproved it, there was as yet only one suburban meeting, the Ibis branch formed in honour of Annie Besant in 1894. The Wisdom lodge met first at 200 Walsh Street, South Yarra, home of its founding secretary

Alfred Deakin. Deakin, whose diploma is dated 21 February 1895, resigned the following year, after correspondence with Colonel Olcott about Madame Blavatsky's 'baffling personality', and joined with Strong's Australian Church; but he helped launch a branch said by the other well-known founding member, H.H. Champion, to be in a good way in 1895. Not only did the Ibis branch run all the usual classes, including the more innovatory children's Sunday class, but it also planned a children's holiday home at Mt Macedon, prison and hospital visiting, and even a labour bureau. Ibis claimed a membership of between thirty and fifty up to 1914, and later became the Prahran lodge, meeting at Garden Street, South Yarra, a similarly marginal location to many of the failed Sydney branches of the 1890s, now dwarfed by a large shopping centre.[33]

In Adelaide, which secretary Staples immediately identified as peculiarly indifferent to theosophy, theosophists were pleased to recall that they did not run charities nor were they a school of magic. Having discarded 'the terrible old orthodox God of the Hebrews', they awaited higher things. They were not, said Knox, 'mere idealists'. 'Every noble effort for the reform or for the elevation of humanity begins on the ideal plane and progresses there before it appears here as an actuality.'[34] Such elitism scarcely attracted people to theosophy, as is evident from the *Register* of the Adelaide Theosophical Society for the 1890s, the only such record known to be extant. Between 1891 and 1901 members increased from seven to twenty though more than that joined during the period.

That more sophisticated souls attempted to till the social field in the manner of Brother Besant shows up in the reports of papers at the two largest branches in Sydney and Melbourne in the mid-1890s sent to *Theosophy in Australasia*. Even there, social concern leavened rather than transcended religious talk. Thus Melbourne branch in 1895 heard Mr Debney on the still-vexed question of vaccination, H.H. Champion, presumably a visitor from Ibis branch, on 'Practical Theosophy', and geologist James Stirling on 'Geology and *The Secret Doctrine*'. A similar though perhaps stronger leavening is evident at Sydney branch, with addresses in 1896 on theosophy and kindergartens (Miss Hooper), the work of the Vegetarian Society (from W.D. Campbell), and on cremation from its long-standing advocate Dr J. Creed. Meanwhile in Hobart, secretary Benjamin suggested to a meeting on 9 September 1895 that the branch might 'assist in any well-directed scheme of social improvement'; but over the next few months energy went mainly into preparing by-laws advised previously by Staples as a means of putting branch affairs in order.[35]

Though official publications were slow and erratic in accommodating the fact, by early 1896 the Australasian section was in reality a purely Australian section. The creation of New Zealand section in 1896 involved the loss of about a hundred members. Even so Australian theosophy entered a reasonably good account of itself in its second report to Adyar that year. Though immature, it could point to progress: acting general secretary Martyn noted two new branches and an encouraging outlook. And amid the meanderings and verbosity which must characterise any small and earnest organisation came some overflow into the issues of the day from the spiritual dissatisfactions which brought theosophists together in the first place. The record of theosophy, once started, is remarkably full for so small and obscure an organisation, not because the members believed history was on their side – they perhaps did – but because theosophy attracted men with professional training, accustomed to keep neat records, and 'word-people' – would-be teachers, preachers and writers. Furthermore, in an era when educational opportunities were limited by class and gender, a few of the self-educated in all walks of life were attracted to theosophy. Whether or not the first years of theosophic life assuaged spiritual hungers and appeased psychological needs, they showed a certain busyness.

Table 1, Appendix, showing the section's progress to 1914 puts matters in perspective. Between 1896 and 1901, after six years as a section, organised theosophy in Australia could claim about 400 supporters, if renegades are included. Of the seventeen branches formed in those years, fourteen survived. After 1907, membership grew again.

Theosophists had extended the hand of fellowship. Now the question arose as to whether they could maintain it: Was the section secure? Was the movement cohesive? Could there be a theosophic community? During a gradual rise of the theosophical movement in the early years of the twentieth century, some answers to these basic questions emerged.

Seen in the broadest context, the section was secure. Australian theosophists were represented on the council of the society which, under the revised constitution of 1896, consisted of the president, the vice-president and sectional secretaries. Those who remained under Adyar's wing did not mind that the Theosophical Society was not a democratic society. On the issue of autonomy, the rules read, 'each Branch and Section shall have the power to make its own Rules, provided they do not conflict with the general rules of the Society'. The general rules made it clear that all authority derived from the president, who had the power to cancel diplomas (of individuals), charters (of branches), and rules (of sections). The Australian section was far more exercised by the proportion of votes to members and branches at its own annual convention than by the shadow of presidential prerogative. In accordance with decisions made by lodge delegates (or their proxies) at Convention, the official yearly meeting of the section instituted in 1895, it paid the requisite quarter of annual dues and entrance fees (seven guineas in 1895) to Adyar, and supplied reports for inclusion in the general report of the society yearly (except 1897). Undoubtedly members enjoyed the security of belonging to a cosmopolitan 'forward' movement.[36]

In a narrower context, from the general secretary's seat, the situation was less reassuring. After his appointment to the post in 1898, Dr A. Marques berated Convention delegates because the theosophical movement in Australia was stagnant. Though it was one of the earliest sections, fourth with the Scandinavian after the American, Indian and European, and with a respectable record of branch formation, many members had fallen by the wayside, and really the coverage was poor. Marques criticised the intellectual level of branch life as revealed in *Theosophy in Australasia* (a title retained until 1921).[37]

Part of the trouble sprang from the general-secretaryship itself. It had been a headache ever since the unexpected death of Staples, in England in 1897 to attend the TS council. A series of stopgaps failed to command the organisation. Dr Marques failed too. He was a much shorter-lived incumbent of the post than official records suggest. Marques, an old friend of Olcott's who remained loyal through the American split, now a businessman in Hawaii, had agreed to help out in Australia, but he found Australian ways conservative and the climate debilitating. He arrived late and left early, spending not much more than a year in Sydney.[38]

Then T.H. Martyn persuaded ex-Brisbane president W.G. John to take on the job, from 1902 until his death in 1916. No more was heard about stagnation. Numbers rose, some new branches formed in Victoria, and

Charles Leadbeater's membership certificate

lengthy pastoral tours by John encouraged weaker groups: Hobart lodge for example heartily appreciated his efforts 'to assist us in our search for Truth', and its minutes of April 1903 record that his public lectures were 'well-attended by intellectual and appreciative audiences'. Secretary John announced that dead wood had been purged from the books, and 'the public mind still turns distinctly in our direction'. To cope with expanding clerical work, Convention appointed his wife Isabelle (previously Edelfelt) assistant general secretary in 1905. Isabelle John (1862–1939), English-born and a nurse by training, was a woman of 'robust commonsense with a gift for practical exposition', who had considerable colonial experience and a strong commitment to theosophy. She served the section well for the next twenty years, and is one of the few theosophists to be entered in the *Australian Dictionary of Biography* as such.[39]

It is interesting to note that the small organisation afforded two paid officers. *Theosophy in Australasia* ceased to publish detailed financial information in 1906, and the estimates for 1905 do not include consideration of the new post of assistant general secretary, but nearly half of the balance sheet for 1896 went on 'allowances for the secretary and assistant, $83 of $180, and in 1905, the general secretary's allowance was $150. This may be compared with clerical stipends, high at $400 p.a., and more likely averaging around $230 in the better-off Christian denominations. Since the official

Charles Leadbeater in his study

duties of the chief officer of the Theosophical Society were by no means so exacting as that of a clergyman, the allowance seems a fair thing, as might be anticipated in such a society.[40]

W.G. John earned his allowance. In 1905 he reported that the 418 members in twelve branches constituted a compact little section. Of these members, Queenslanders were still most numerous, though with 126 in three branches as compared with 125 in Sydney and 123 in Victoria, State differences were insignificant. Adelaide branch had grown to about seventy members and Perth increased to fifty. A year later in 1906 John reported the section secured. He believed that the public now recognised theosophists as a firmly established body.[41] Neither of the Johns was native-born, but they were permanent residents, unlike the two previous appointees, and they effected a kind of 'nativisation' of theosophy. Another interpretation might be that they were sufficiently competent to sustain the momentum implicit in Annie Besant's act of sectional organisation.

Sound administration based on Sydney was reinforced by increasingly frequent visitation by theosophical leaders. In 1897 Brisbane branch hoped for another tour by Annie Besant; but, perforce, the branches made do with

Colonel Olcott (by then rather grumpy about the Australian character – too wild and sporty), with Lilian Edger, and later with the general secretaries. Then in 1905 the fastest-rising star in the whole theosophical galaxy came, Charles Webster Leadbeater, his fare paid by T.H. Martyn.[42]

Leadbeater, who became important at a later stage of the story of Australian theosophy, was already well known as the author of numerous treatises published since the mid-nineties conveying the results of his clairvoyant researches on the astral plane, and through joint publications with Annie Besant. His reputation as a theosophical lecturer in London and America was riding high, and the reason for it is obvious from his *Outline of Theosophy* (1902, and still in print). In simple style, this little series of lectures systematically strips conventional religious perception of Calvinist suppositions, declaring an end to sin, suffering, guilt and death in the light of *theosophia*, of which exact information is said to be now available to the earnest student, via clairvoyant experiment, and in the light of spiritual evolution and its evidence. It states that reincarnation is a comforting doctrine.

In Australia in 1905, Leadbeater lectured mainly to closed audiences, members only. This reminded laggards to pay their dues and boosted morale, as did his distinctive teaching of 'the Masters and the Path'. There were some converts, J.H. Haycraft, an Adelaide accountant and inventor, and William Harding of Sydney, also an accountant who recognised in Leadbeater's exposition 'the precise basic principles of the Law', and some worldly friends were made too, like the future Major-General K. Mackay. It appears from correspondence between Leadbeater and the Professor of English at the University of Sydney, John Le Gay Brereton, on psychism and Swedenborg, that Mrs Brereton enjoyed his lectures (with characteristic aplomb, Leadbeater recommended to her his most recent work *The Other Side of Death* (1903) containing 'a clear statement of the evidences of man's survival of that process'). The section was satisfied with the visitor and wished him back again as soon as possible.[43]

Leadbeater did return, in 1914. Before that, in 1908, Annie Besant came again. Membership doubled after her second tour.[44]

One problem which no visitor could affect was sustaining enthusiasm among new recruits. Having abandoned the churches in hope of broader illumination, they still needed more than lectures and papers. Madame Blavatsky knew that when she established the anomalous Esoteric Section in 1888 for 'advanced students'.[45] Without the Esoteric Section (ES) it would be difficult to understand what kept theosophy going. The sense of belonging to a secret society, of entering the inner core, kept theosophists engaged, and special classes in the ES satisfied the need to make progress, a need otherwise catered for only in an impersonal way.

The Esoteric Section operated quite differently from the territorial section. It was a section in the older elitist sense, as originally conceived in New York. Though that concept disappeared from the practice of the Theosophical Society by the 1890s, it continued in the ES, of which Annie Besant was now – after 'the judging of Judge' – the Outer Head and T.H. Martyn her Australian representative. Members applied to join, were scrutinised, and, if acceptable, began the training which took them through processes of initiation up the spiritual path. They were sworn to secrecy and loyalty to the Head. The ES stood in the same relation to the Theosophical Society as the Society of Jesus to the Roman Catholic Church in that Jesuits owed direct obedience to the Pope and ES members to its head. It survived within the society because both leaders and led wanted it to – a loyal phalanx of advancing spirits.

Probably only a minority of the first Australian theosophists belonged to the ES. Who, how many, to what effect, all is undocumented and inaccessible historically. The historical point is that the invisible ES played a role in the rise as well as the fall of the theosophical movement in Australia, though documented only at the fall (and then only partially). It could be either a cohesive or a divisive force. In the first phase of organised theosophy it was probably a cohesive force. Later the dual allegiance of its members, plus reliance on 'the great captains', played havoc.

In another subtle shift of the period the word 'lodge' replaced the older word 'branch' as official designation of a theosophical group. Just as the newer usage of the word 'section' overlaid an occult inheritance and practice, so the change from 'branch' to 'lodge' acknowledged an appealingly ambiguous dimension in theosophic self-presentation. Leadbeater captured the aura when he titled one of his papers in 1905 'The Secret Life of the Lodges'. The new word encompassed hidden purpose, special association, a brotherhood not Brotherhood, with suggestions of friendly societies and freemasonry – all stronger associations eighty years ago.[46]

The new usage conjured up the world of a self-helping working class, in particular the lost ritual convivialities of the friendly society lodges which flourished in the mid-Victorian period. Very likely this reverberation was the work of Annie Besant. She well knew the strength of the old popular culture which – as E.P. Thompson has noticed – in the north of England contained theosophic lodges. At this time, in the early years of the twentieth century, Annie Besant also began promoting a 'co-masonic' movement. The introduction, or revival, of occult ritual and symbol within a masonic order was another attempt to catch the older flavour and culture of 'brotherhood'. Several Australian theosophists testified that the aridity of ordinary masonic life led them to theosophy. Hence the word 'lodge' was a versatile word, suggesting cell, self-help institute, secret society all in one. It sounded more exciting than 'branch', and nothing like 'church'.[47]

Advancement of the latent powers of man may have been the society's third object, but under Leadbeater's influence it became theosophists' first aspiration. Lady Emily Lutyens, an Edwardian convert who became an important theosophical lecturer, recalled theosophy as the body of teaching contained in the occult tradition of all the great religions of the world which identified a Great Being heading each solar system as the source of its life and the evolution of life on earth. By strenuous effort man could join the already perfected men liberated from karma, who formed an occult hierarchy, the Elder Brethren. The hierarchy, described by Leadbeater as a Great White Brotherhood, the inner government of the world, was headed by a trinity representing the Head (the Lord of the world), the Heart (the Lord Buddha) and a practical Arm into the world (Mahachohan), whose influence was transmitted to the world through Manu and the Bodhisattva. Three of the perfected men were especially important to the Theosophical Society, Blavatsky's Masters Morya and Koothoomi, plus the Count, a ceremonial figure who lived in Hungary, not Tibet. All theosophists, Lady Emily wrote, believed in the Hierarchy and the Masters, and longed to become pupils of the Masters, to walk the path of discipleship as *chelas*. Discipleship after probation involved five stages of initiation, which gradually elevated the *chela* to circles of higher consciousness and liberation from karma. From this perspective came such extraordinary statements as 'the future of Australian thought is in our hands', and frequent reference to the spiritual hierarchy governing human destiny, of which Australian theosophists were the remote representatives.[48]

It may have been promoted cohesion, but the occult dimension gave theosophy its unacceptable face, and denied theosophists the respectability which in other respects many may have attained. No wonder that the rest of the world refused to associate itself with the theosophical brothers if they really lived a secret life in the lodges, and believed themselves to be representatives of an occult hierarchy. It sounded either silly or sinister. No matter how forcefully leaders like Mrs Besant argued the possibility of 'perfected men', occult geopolitics put reasonable people off.

In 1909 in Sydney a group of 'arch-optimists' gathered to launch a new headquarters at 132 Phillip Street, the first of many substantial buildings which focused theosophical life in the city. Despite the esoteric aspects of the lodges, and like the freethought movement to which it was, in a minor way, heir, theosophy in the larger cities by the twentieth century made itself manifest in congregations if not communities. Theosophical practices looked increasingly church-like. In some places it was difficult to hold Sunday morning meetings because 'the cars do not run' (tramcars, that is), but in Brisbane regular Sunday morning devotions flourished, and everywhere the main Sunday evening lectures became ceremonial. For instance, pianos were acquired, and introits and other musical offerings became customary. (There were other embellishments too: in 1909, the property of Hobart lodge included twenty-two chairs, one cushion, £10 worth of books, and a potted palm.)

The only universally observed ritual was Madam Blavatsky's birthday, White Lotus Day, on 8 May, 'in remembrance of her who brought us to the chart of the climbing path which leads to the summit of knowledge', when extracts were to be read from the *Bhagavad Gita* and *The Light of Asia*, in accordance with her wishes. (The white lotus symbolised beauty ascendant from muddied waters.) Nevertheless, the weekly digest of lodge life looked increasingly like that of an ordinary suburban church. In addition to lectures and beginners' classes, the larger lodges ran Secret Doctrine classes (like Bible studies), meditations comparable with prayer meetings, and ladies' meetings of the charitable rather than missionary variety, sewing circles for the poor. Theosophists who looked askance at Christian Sunday schools quickly created an alternative for children. To the anxious question 'Is theosophy for children?' came a positive reply, encouraged by the educator Froebell, 'every child is the thought of God' – an advanced soul too perhaps.[49]

First conducted in New York in 1892 on principles advanced by spiritualists, lotus circles were introduced in Australia by Mrs Cooper-Oakley in Melbourne and Sydney in 1893. By the early twentieth century they were widespread, equipped with locally produced hand books. Thanks to teachers like Miss Haycraft, BSc, Adelaide lodge claims the largest lotus circle, offering a thorough plan of work, examinations, and studies with the microscope. Sydney lodge reported good attendances of up to thirty children at the lotus circle by 1909.[50]

Theosophists also took up youth work, following a trend dating from the turn of the century in Britain and America, where a combination of Social Darwinism and popular chivalry produced, in Vermont in 1893, the Knights of King Arthur, precursor of both the Boy Scouts and the theosophical Order of the Round Table. The Order of the Round Table, founded in London in 1908, aimed to encourage altruism among the young. The motto of the order, which took in youth to about nineteen, was 'Live Right, Speak True, Right Wrong, Follow the Light'. Young people were to be organised in tables in a graded manner, through the ranks of page, companion, squire and knight, with a senior knight presiding. The first Australian table was formed in Melbourne in 1909 and Perth lodge had two by 1913, run by journalist Muriel Chase, which concentrated on child and animal welfare. 'Its chief aim,' Chase wrote, 'is to build character so that the companions and knights may become a centre of usefulness and strength to those among whom they live.' Emphasis was placed upon 'the service of the King', and when in 1918 Leadbeater became senior knight and protector of the tables following the death in action in Palestine of founding chief knight Captain Herbert Whyte, he emphasised service of the spiritual king, the coming World Teacher, and the order became an affiliate of the Order of the Star in the East.[51]

Another American idea about youth work also enjoyed some favour, but briefly. The Golden Chain movement envisaged that each child become a link in a world-wide chain of love. Some success was thought to have attended moves to promote the idea in the schools journal of the Victorian Department of Public Instruction. But it seems to have remained the cause of a few devoted ladies, and to exemplify the problem of theosophical youth work, that there were usually more workers than youth. Nevertheless theosophical youth work was ahead of its time. According to a recent student of theosophy and education, lotus circles, round tables and golden chains were, like the spiritualist lyceums before them, attempts to provide 'a grounding in morality without recourse to direct doctrinal instruction'.[52]

Reference to child and youth training leads to the vexed question of *rites de passage*, the marking of birth, marriage and death. Civil registration procedures dated from the 1850s in Australia. Theosophists might ignore christenings, but not ceremonies attending marriage and death at which churchmen officiated.

Need of a ritual to mark death was felt earliest because of the 'passing over' of the first generation of theosophists in the early twentieth century, many of whom had been well into middle age at conversion: Sydney lodge president George Peell, Queensland politician Edward Pechey, Mrs Pickett, and Mrs Sarah Way of Adelaide. Whereas Christian teaching emphasised death and taught bodily resurrection, theosophists minimised the significance of death. Not only Christian teaching but also its practical consequence, burial of the corpse, were seen as vestiges of barbarism; theosophists had always advocated cremation.[53]

The call for reform of burial practices came from sanitary reformers in England in the 1840s. The first effective advocates of cremation in Britain and America formed Cremation Societies in the 1870s. (It may be remembered that the Theosophical Society first attracted public attention when it cremated the Baron de Palm in New York in 1876.) By the mid-1880s the Cremation Society of England had established that burning the dead was not illegal, and the first crematoria were built; but it was not until 1902 that it was legalised by statute. Australian cremationists were first heard in Victoria in the 1870s. In New South Wales from 1886 Dr J.M. Creed promoted cremation bills without success, and it was not until 1923 that the New South Wales Parliament amended the various acts pertaining to public health and burial, enabling the first cremation company at Rookwood by 1925. The situation seemed to be equally unsatisfactory to cremationists in Western Australia and Queensland, but the nonconformist States of South Australia and Victoria acted more speedily with legislation in 1891 and 1905 respectively. There it was possible, though not popular, to die without benefit of clergy.[54]

Theosophists had advocated cremation in Australia since there was a theosophical press in which to do so. They had welcomed the first known cremation in Australia, on Sandringham Beach, Melbourne, in April 1895, generally thought 'a scandalous and horrible occurrence'. Adelaide theosophist, F.S. Hawkins, recalled that the Adelaide Cremation Society in the 1890s consisted of 'a few advanced thinkers, both ladies and gentlemen', a group which certainly included theosophists. In New South Wales they started the NSW Cremation Society in 1908. With Dr Creed as president and Rose Scott on the executive, it quickly gained a wider membership of 300 members, and seemed to make progress. Theosophists' beliefs set them apart from conventional practice, as did an Indian orientation, which added depth to the utilitarian arguments advanced by cremationists. They provided an active constituency and steady support for what was a fundamental belief change, only gradually accommodated by the wider society.[55]

Theosophists were in further difficulty with marriage, relying on sympathetic clergy, or forced to civil ceremonies. Theosophical weddings were performed in Brisbane lodge in 1907. In Melbourne Dr Strong obliged, in Sydney the unitarian Walters. The irritation and anxiety occasionally expressed by theosophists was not resolved until the 1920s. Although the situation must have been unsatisfactory to deeply religious but otherwise quite conventional, even conservative, people, alternative solutions were not easy to generate, or even promote, though their preferences are commonplace today.[56]

It might be expected that as non-Christians the early theosophists would also be set apart in other matters of daily life, dress and diet for example. Both can act as basic boundary lines of alternative culture and community. Unfortunately almost no direct Australian evidence survives on either, though discussions of the associated topics of health reform and animal welfare appeared in the 1880s, and all became more prominent issues in the 1920s. Groups as diverse as the Christian Scientists, Seventh Day Adventists and New Lifers faithful to the 1880s 'Religion of Socialism' also proclaimed 'counter-cultural' practices in Australia before the Great War.[57]

Most likely theosophists were distinctive in diet but not in dress. Maybe some women did favour reformed dress and Annie Besant's Indian style; perhaps a few men in the tropics leaned to looser cladding as was the practice at Adyar and urged by C.W. Leadbeater; but in the absence of even one locally produced pamphlet or lecture, the possibility must be left open. Absence of direct evidence on diet is not so disabling. In principle, theosophists were, and mostly are, convinced vegetarians. Literature abounds. Some of it contains atypically forceful language about impurity and sin. To the classic health and humanitarian arguments for vegetarianism, theosophists added an occult rider, that 'flesh foods undoubtedly [make] the physical body a worse instrument'. Flesh-eating was anti-evolutionary.[58]

The arguments for vegetarianism have not changed much in a hundred years, though the ills to be remedied have – intemperance and incontinence played an important part earlier – and the contexts have shifted from the slaughterhouses of Chicago to the battery-farms of ex-urbia. Recognisable themes of goodness and purity and oneness, and a comparable confidence in the goodness of man in nature, sustained theosophical polemic. As Leadbeater concluded his pamphlet *Vegetarianism and the Occult* (1913),

> [t]here is a golden Age to come, not only for man but for the lower kingdoms, a time when humanity will realise its duty to its younger brothers ... A time will come when all the forces of Nature shall be intelligently working together towards the final end ... universal recognition of ... Brotherhood.

On this subject, Leadbeater spoke in the authentic tone of the second, late Victorian, resurgence of vegetarianism (the first occurred in Britain in the early nineteenth century). As Julia Twigg has proposed, vegetarianism flourishes in periods and among groups looking for holistic answers.[59]

Whether or not theosophists supported the early vegetarian restaurants in Sydney and Melbourne, or the Seventh Day Adventist Sanitarium Food Co., is not known. Perhaps their diet meant they managed with fewer domestic servants. Predictably they opposed compulsory vaccination, a related issue because vaccination introduced alien substances into the body. Certainly they sympathised with the animal welfare movement, or its Victorian precursor, the anti-vivisection movement.[60]

Since a meagre modern literature often argues that such commitments are basically egalitarian, it is interesting to speculate on the class considerations underlying them. Recent historical interpretation based on nineteenth-century Britain tends to stress elements of social control, and over the period, displacement of a humanistic middle class by scientific professionalism. It may also be that theosophists were as much impressed by Hindu as Western reasoning on vegetarianism. In orthodox Hinduism, it has been one of the ethical criteria defining status, hierarchical rather than egalitarian in function. On the other hand even in Hinduism espousal of vegetarianism is fraught with ambiguity, as it is far from universal and its origins lie with more egalitarian movements such as Jainism and Buddhism; radical and adventist sects in the West have also often been vegetarian. Moreover present interpretation tends to underestimate the force of feminism, elements of which have been ardent animal-rights advocates for a century or more; and to neglect changing conceptualisations largely beyond class. Echoes of all these contradictory forces can be heard in the theosophical preference for vegetarianism. In such an uncertain area it is well to stay with the obvious fact that their view of diet did set theosophists apart from a majority of their fellow Australians. How far, and at what cost, if any, can only be guessed.[61]

Thus in the area today called lifestyle, issues of community did emerge. But theosophists were not well placed to meet them, structurally or numerically. Nor did they really wish to do so. Convention provided a forum, but it was seldom used. Apart from the general secretary, theosophists acknowledged no local leaders, and antipathy to a professional clergy remained strong. When a shadow of clericalism did fall, in 1912 in the proposal to endow a two-year training scholarship at Adyar, it was shelved amid agitation. To those of the great unsatisfied who feared degeneration into a mere sect, and thought they detected an inward-looking tendency, W.G. John replied reassuringly that theosophy was too young; it had no fixed literature, and no dominating personalities. Realistically, theosophy saw itself more as a 'forward movement' than a separate community.[62]

The society always insisted that it was a movement in aid of religion rather than a religious movement. Even in its institutionalised activities, propaganda still took first place, hence the persistence of speakers' training classes, voice and elocution lessons, and even, in 1908, Esperanto. Esperanto is the artificial language invented by L.L. Zamenhof in 1887 based on the commonest words in the major European languages and intended for international use. If the first Esperanto Club in Australia was formed in 1908 by artist-historian George Collingridge, the theosophists were not far behind, because in the same year Victor Roinel moved in Convention for a theosophical association of esperanto circles in Australasia. A Guild of Esperanto Theosophists was at work in a minor way by 1910 in Sydney under Mrs Drummond and G.H. Chappel, and in Melbourne Mr Drummond. The guild hoped to ease the work of propaganda both in Australia and in other countries, where 'lingual conditions have hither to constituted a hindrance to the spread of Theosophy'. The inchoate character of theosophy was a constant reminder of the importance of propaganda, as were Australian conditions.[63]

Three such Australian conditions are obvious from annual statistics. All reinforced the sense of theosophy as a movement. First, a proportion of members could never be 'churched'. 'Unattached' members – usually about sixty – were a diminishing proportion, but in the beginning there were as many as 20 percent and, being sixty-five out of 1185 in 1913, remained a large number if a smaller proportion. The unattached living in remote places were a constant challenge to organisers, who established lending libraries, book depots, and correspondence courses. They were also a steady reminder of work still to be done in far-flung parts if theosophy was to take hold. In 1910 a Faith and Works League was established to send theosophical news out to country presses.[64]

Second, acquisition of divine wisdom was as much the result of individual as collective effort, and all too often the latent powers of man, once released, conflicted with brotherliness in lodges. The hint of conflict surrounding Maybank back in 1892 continued to attend lodge formation in the big cities. Besant lodge, formed 1908 to be the intellectual nucleus of Melbourne, faded away. Another way of putting it would be that figures like Mr and Mrs Hunt preferred to lead, and the sources of authority in theosophy were too remote to gainsay them.[65]

Third, as has been said before, *theosophia* often held only fleeting appeal. Unless converts were incorporated into lodge life, or they joined the Esoteric Section, they would often drift away, to be lost forever in the flow of peoples so characteristic of regions of recent settlement. Others did not survive transient enthusiasms, such as Eastern Hill, Melbourne, a cultural group meeting in Collins Street, founded by Dr E. Alleyne Cook and J.B. McConkey in 1906, whose permanent members returned to Melbourne lodge in 1910. Many small suburban lodges failed to maintain the minimal membership of seven with which they began, although hopeful general secretaries kept them alive nominally. In some periods the number of lodges which closed down equalled the number which continued to function.[66]

Frequently the lure of the city lodge proved too great. Only in Tasmania was the situation any different: there were more members in Launceston than Hobart in 1908, just before Besant's return to Australia. But by

1913 there were fifty paid-up theosophists in Hobart, only twenty-four in Launceston. In Western Australia, the impression that Fremantle would be most responsive to theosophy was soon corrected. The Pattersons' Fremantle branch founded in 1900 had only twenty-one members by 1913, compared with seventy-two in Perth. In reality only the central lodges of the capitals could maintain membership.[67]

Indeed, only Sydney maintained a large lodge. Nearly 200 people belonged to Sydney lodge in 1908, compared with just over 100 in Brisbane, and under ninety in Melbourne. Sydney lodge was on its way to being the largest lodge, not just in the southern hemisphere – no great achievement – but the largest theosophical lodge in the world. The third point from the figures is that only in Sydney was there a community potential. Ultimately Sydney lodge grew large enough to experience the churchward tendency deplored by first generation theosophists.[68]

To answer the questions posed earlier, then, the Australian section did feel itself secure after its first decade; there were forces of cohesion and encouragement in theosophical teaching and practice; and there was a potential for community, though it was minimised both by theory and reality. Theosophists experienced a number of problems which kept them at cross-purposes with a Christianised society. It may be remarked that although the theosophical movement belongs within the fold of religious history, the usual typology of religious groups – 'church' and 'sect' – does not seem to be applicable to a group which stood beyond Christianity.

Theosophy seldom became respectable, partly because of the mixture of esoteric and exoteric teachings which offended orthodoxy and drew inspiration from far beyond it, India especially, partly because theosophical leaders frequently offended the canons of respectable society. The fragility of theosophical claims to respectability was to be demonstrated many times in the second and third decades of the twentieth century. A nice example of how uncertain theosophists themselves felt is that, as late as 1905, it was still a matter of debate whether contributors to *Theosophy in Australasia* should attach their names, or even initials. The editor was instructed at Convention to leave the choice to them.[69]

Such caution could be justified. Theosophy remained vulnerable to scandal and charges of immorality. Occultism and advanced thought were always uneasy bedfellows, but bedfellows all the same, and unfortunately in every sense. Within a month of grateful remarks about the learned visitor of 1905 appearing in *Theosophy in Australasia* C.W. Leadbeater was obliged to resign from the Theosophical Society, because of charges of immorality pressed against him by theosophical parents in America. Having entrusted their sons to Leadbeater as tutor, they were horrified to discover that his tutorship included 'demoralising personal practices', and successfully demanded an inquiry, duly held in London in 1906. Leadbeater adopted a 'refuse-to-confirm-or-deny' attitude, and resigned. (Nethercot's researches in the 1960s finally revealed that his moral tutorship included rather dubious masturbatory exercises.) Two boys had accompanied him on his Australian tour without attracting attention – even though one of his many requirements was that the little party should not be split up at overnight stops – but when he decided to return to Australia in 1914 a delicate problem of publicity exercised the minds of his still-reverential hosts. However, the scandal had blown over by then. In 1907 Annie Besant attained the presidency of the Theosophical Society, and it was not long before Leadbeater was reinstated and returned to India to live at Adyar.[70] In 1908 Annie Besant was back in Australia.

When Mrs Besant returned to Australia in the winter of 1908, she had changed, and so had the world. The difference between Mrs Besant and many of her followers was that she knew it and extended her message accordingly. As expected, she brought new vigour to Australian theosophy. This time she came not as a missioner but 'bishop', president of the Theosophical Society, Annie Besant PTS. She had earned the position by fifteen years lecturing in the cause, and innovative educational work in India where she founded the Central Hindu College at Benares to educate Indian boys within their own culture. Succession had not been achieved without the application of constitutional and occult skills in the face of men who thought themselves better qualified. But it was never again in doubt; she served four terms as president, until her death in India in 1933. Nor were any of the alternative candidates convincing to Australian theosophists who voted in the presidential election of 1907. Though mourning the death of the president-founder Colonel Olcott, they welcomed her a year later as 'one who was almost still deeper founded in our affections'.[71]

Those who believed that theosophy was primarily a spiritual movement soon learned what the new president meant by the often-used phrase 'forward movement'. Her first presidential address, London, June 1907, called for unity and tolerance (the usual theosophical virtues), and more propaganda. Considering the work of organisation to be virtually complete around the world, Besant urged theosophists out of the lodges into beneficent activity of all kinds: clubs, societies, and religious bodies. Internal study groups should increase understanding of the three objects of the society. So, she concluded, 'may the Masters guide and prosper the work which they have given into my hands, and blessed'.[72] And so Australian theosophists urged, in words probably written by Mrs John, that

> the time has come to make a decided and general move in the direction of utilising the existing machinery of, not only kindred societies, but some of the hundred and one forward movements of the day ... So long as we can succeed in associating Theosophical Thought with every ostensible forward movement for the betterment of the mass of humanity, without arousing the impression that the Society has an axe to grind, we shall do well.[73]

Mrs John went to Perth to meet the president. Mrs Besant was as vigourous as ever. 'I am exceedingly strong,' she said, demonstrating again the benefits of vegetarianism.[74] This time the lecture tour took in Brisbane and also, en route from New Zealand, the previously deprived Tasmanian cities. Sectional organisation worked, down to surviving balance sheets which showed a profit of £1,000, £600 of which went to the president's 'moiety'. As usual, Sydney was most responsive, and then Perth with the third largest takings.[75]

The bound volume of press clippings preserved in the society's library at North Sydney has her as the event of the week everywhere. The *Bulletin* remarked with surprise that there seemed to be some life in the hazy old cult after all. It also noticed a change of audience: a young and eager crowd, remarkably frilly: 'They're not the occult and hungry-looking throng of weird women and fierce males who generally haunt lectures ... but a crowd with a taste in battery and a profound knowledge of frills.'[76]

Second time round, the Christian clergy paid close and critical attention. Her lectures were more doctrinal, and these days she emphasised theosophy as the servant of true religion, including the Christian religion:

> That which we seek after is Truth, and we do not believe that truth is confined to any one religion, or to any special sect. Over the world searchers after

truth are found in all the great religions which console man during life and encourage him in the hour of death. And, therefore, in speaking to you, in any thing that I may say, I have no desire in any fashion to weaken the hold of Christianity on any who profess that faith. On the contrary, I have known many cases where men and women, puzzled with the problems of existence, unable to solve the difficulties of human life within the limits of the Churches, were leaving the Churches and abandoning Christianity, but came back to it when they found the rational explanations that Theosophy offered of the doctrines which had repelled them. We do not empty the Churches. On the contrary, we bring back to them many of the intelligent and intellectual who have slipped away from them because of the narrow and crude presentment of many a Christian doctrine. We ask people to be more spiritual, to be more liberal, to be more generous towards those with whom they do not agree. We endeavour to spread peace among rival creeds, and to serve every religion in its own country and among its own people.[77]

The first of her *Australian Lectures* addressed 'Theosophy and Christianity'. Theosophy, she said, could restore to Christianity great lost mysteries, and doctrines which had slipped out of sight. Christianity had lost touch with its Gnostic roots. Once knowledge was equally shared. Now, in the hands of the priesthood, it had lost its power. Theosophy also made rational the unacceptable teachings of Heaven and Hell by reinstating reincarnation, and expounding the lost code of karma: 'out of horror of an everlasting hell the revolt has grown, and that horror is only a result of losing hold of the great doctrine of reincarnation'. Further,

> If you believe in reincarnation you say that the suffering that follows evil, and its inevitable result, is remediable, educative and purifying, so that the man is the better, nobler, and purer for it. Heaven becomes rational when it is temporary, and when in that heaven you can become better than when you left the earth ... When you come to think of it, these two absurd doctrines of an everlasting heaven and an everlasting hell are both utterly opposed to the belief in reincarnation.[78]

Exactly, replied the clergy. Mrs Besant's overtures were not welcome, and the tour was punctuated by hostile reaction from pulpit and press which attacked both Besant and her teaching. It hardly mattered whether the response came from liberal (as in Adelaide) or fundamentalist (as in Brisbane) clergy. They denied that theosophy could be a movement in aid of religion, certainly not the Christian religion. Mrs Besant's regrettable progressions had not led her in the direction of Christianity, for all her recent work in *Esoteric Christianity* (1901). Only a few spoke up in her favour, among them predictably the Reverend George Walters.

Theosophy was vacuous, audacious, irreverent, pretentious, and had a link with secret societies in Italy, said 'Viator' in the Catholic *Austral Light*. In addresses delivered to the Anglican clergy of Sydney diocese, the Reverend W.H.H. Yarrington of St Luke's, Concord, took a longer, more learned view, but he saw only an empty bauble, at best refined pantheism. Yarrington's competent discussion of the history and principal teachings of theosophy left no room for doubt that it was a fabrication, and an enemy to Christianity, whatever Annie Besant might now say. It showed what happened when willful people departed from orthodox faith, since it promoted the illusion that 'every man is his own Saviour'. James Neil in Dunedin, seeing spiritualism and theosophy as 'twain brothers of anti-Christ', inadvertently identified the appeal of theosophy when he attacked it for reducing central Christian teaching to mere historical events, bringing Jesus to the level of man and treating the Bible like the Vedas.[79]

In truth, the old freethought fire remained alight. The lectures in effect deplored the intellectual failings of the churches, now depleted of intellectuals and working people, left to women:

> We see, as we turn over Church papers and Nonconformist papers, that they are always complaining of the lessening influence of their particular form of Christianity. Above all, they complain that while very many women come to their places of worship, men are apt to be conspicuous by their absence. We notice, also, that they complain that the manual labour classes are very little found in touch with the churches and chapels ...[80]

When the TS restricted entry to a Sunday talk to members and ticket holders, it fell foul of Sabbath observance legislation as interpreted after 1887, which sought to restrict Sunday entertainments and preserve New South Wales from the desecrations of a 'continental' Sunday, and Sydney got a whiff of the old Annie. Speaking at Concordia hall on 'Theosophy and Christianity', she said the legislation was a reflection on the intelligence of the city and hoped that people would rise up and wipe such a blot from the laws of the land.[81]

Nor had Annie's bias towards Hinduism diminished. It showed when she said confidently that India would never be converted to Christianity, hardly a placatory point when so much church missionary effort went on Indian missions. The very idea that Indian religions were progressive deeply offended Protestant communities, who firmly believed that their own material progress sprang from religious freedoms denied in ancient autocratic codes such as Catholicism, and that the key to progress in backward parts of the world was conversion to Christianity, preferably Protestant Christianity. As a character in Rose Macaulay's *The Towers of Trebizond* remarked, what Turkish women needed was the Church of England. So a good deal of energy went in attacking Indian practices like child-marriage and widow-burning which Mrs Besant should have condemned.[82]

Besant, who had renounced politics after her arrival 'Home' in India in 1893, always defended India. She remarked acidly that missionaries might as well be sent from India to Australia to save spinsters. Imperial tendencies, and other tendencies in the Theosophical Society to be mentioned shortly, meant that more significant Australian shibboleths were not allowed to pass unremarked either. Recent Australian legislation on the colour question was a danger as well as a disgrace to the empire, hypocritical too. Many Australians' skins were darker than Indians', and 'if I am any judge, the residents [of North Queensland] are likely to become a coloured people'. The *Bulletin* reported this affront as: 'She asked with some excitement if it were true that a highly educated nigger might be debarred from landing in the 'Roo country'.[83]

Of course all the old objections to theosophy resurfaced, especially in Perth, at its first exposure to the greatest woman orator on earth. Who was Madame Blavatsky; what about the Hodgson report; and the Masters, after the Judge affair? New difficulties arose after Mabel Besant-Scott entered the Roman Catholic Church. *Truth* made something of it, but both ways: 'it would be well if this SECTARIAN-RIDDEN STATE had more of this Besantine breadth'.[84]

The curious possibility is that Besant was least controversial when talking to the workers. 'Theosophy and the Workers', first delivered by invitation at the Trades Hall, Adelaide, on 10 June, 1908, was an old subject which aroused new ire, not from the workers – in Sydney they gave her an illuminated address and album in appreciation of her efforts on behalf of the workers in all parts of the world – but from the medical profession, who dragged up the birth control question. Actually the lecture was a winning account of the law and necessity of brotherhood, the benefits to those at present disadvantaged of reincarnation, and the morality of karma.[85]

'In many of the political proposals you are dealing rather,' she said, 'with flowers without roots', an idea developed in several ways, the most striking in her account of the proper foundations of the socialist state. As in the trade unions, so in government: a representative hierarchy springing from democracy at the local level would produce ideal government, a family government, experienced. It would represent all, not particular interests; and it would recognise as significant social divisions the dependencies of youth and age, thus embodying brotherhood beyond merely class. In her emphasis on happiness for all when merit governed, she harked back to Edward Bellamy and the influential authoritarian socialists of America.

Furthermore, in a world recognising the reality of reincarnation, all men would be liberated, equal in perfection at last. There would be an entirely different attitude to crime and punishment. Karma gave stern but merciful hope to 'the great mass of human beings who long to be better'. It provided the third foundation of the coming state.

The radical press were hostile as ever to what they saw as her pessimism, fatalism and diversionary message. The editor of *People* closed the letter columns for that reason. But Wilton Hack, by 1908 returned to TS membership, defended her on the birth control issue, pointing out that the 'unhappy and pernicious' Law of Population had been withdrawn years ago; and some socialists said they found her teachings encouraging, like Frederick Allman's testimony that he was a better socialist worker for faith in reincarnation. H.F. Powell, writing from Brisbane Trades Hall, found theosophy the co-requisite mental science to accompany the social science of socialism:

> Theosophy leavens the lump of humanity for the establishment of what Morrison Davidson calls 'the New Order'; Socialism will complete a great

stage of industrial evolution; mental science will convert mental sordid poverty into intellectual lofty luxuriance and Theosophy paves the way.[86]

To the charge that Besant had changed her view, a theosophist replied that she was still a socialist:

> She now taught the recognition of duty, rather than right, the duty of the wiser and the stronger to the weaker, and the duty of the younger and the less wise of the race to respect and reverence the wiser ones of the race. Socialism could not succeed unless it took into consideration the facts of nature, and received the light of theosophy.[87]

Besant herself merely said that she had discovered a selfishness at the heart of socialism and was happy in theosophy 'because I regard life as endless. Because I think our future is completely within our power ... Ignorance is the great enemy of mankind.'[88] Confirming that she wished to raise humanity to the highest level of intelligence and that she approved the rule of wisdom, the expression of obligation, duty and altruism, she added that 'striving for class is an utterly wrong principle'. It was true that she was no longer a socialist; her views had changed long ago.

The invitation to apply reincarnation to social progress was not well received. Frances Levvy of the Woman's SPCA defended 'one universal kinship' with the animal world, but the idea that people should look after their bodies for the next inhabitants attracted derision. Nor were her remarks about smoking, and drinking, and the consequences of poor housing or of the 'coloured water' cures of the average medical man, publicly endorsed.[89]

Mrs Besant could still attract and challenge a wider audience. Some deemed her Sydney lectures an intellectual tonic. The liberal intelligentsia again heard her out, this time from the floor, not as in 1894 from the platform, now occupied by theosophical chairmen. Alfred Deakin, Prime Minister of Australia, was in the audience in Melbourne. *Truth* still said it was claptrap. But some considered theosophy part of modern intellectual equipment: 'the ideas of the theosophists are so widespread that most people have a few of them. Hardly a book is written today without touching upon some point that has been brought forward [by The Theosophical Society]'.[90] The *Sydney Morning Herald* still hoped for a good moral influence, while Sydney sporting weekly the *Arrow* gently satirised:

Both Romanists and Methodists,
'Tis clearly understood,
May now become Theosophists,
Provided they are good!

They need not have too many brains,
Their heads may be of wood;
But, as the Prophetess explains,
They really must be good!

The gloomy Scotchbyterean
Of cold, ascetic mood,
May join in with the Anglican,
Provided both are good!

And gentlemen of African
Or Asiatic blood
Will all be welcomed to the clan
If only they are good!

They may belong to any faith
Invented since the Flood;
Or, so the missionary saith,
Provided they are good!

It is a most convenient creed
When rightly understood,
And even might suit me, indeed
If only I were good![91]

It was a mixed reception, to say the least. Considerations of class, culture and colonialism were all relevant. Mrs Besant's own lofty diagnosis of antipodean circumstance reflected elite assurance in the age of imperialism. But it was a nice twist to blame the Church of England and the clergy, as in an interview attributed in Hobart lodge records to the *Mercury* 14 July 1908:

In England, where the people are mostly cultured, they are taking an increased interest in Theosophy, especially among Anglican Church adherents. The people in Australia seem to be very attentive to my lectures but it is evident that a great deal of it is new to them. I do not think the subject is touched upon in their literature, and it appears that your clergy have not taken it up.

The truth was that Mrs Besant, and theosophy, lived off such tensions; and in Australia and other dependent societies, had the benefit of another, the tension between emigrant and native-born. In new societies, there will always be argument between the two as to the merits of 'homeland' prescriptions, and elements eager to endorse such prescriptions. In Australia, where the demographic balance had but recently tipped in favour of the native-born, these were the years of 'the lion and the kangaroo', of a wider cultural ambivalence.

What no one noticed at the time was how Besant related her message to newer questions. The new questions pertained to the fate of liberalism. Liberals everywhere faced pressures from within and without, from organised labour and from international rivalries which exposed imperial weakness. Whereas hope still attended the 'new' liberalism in Britain, its brief bright day had nearly ended in advanced Australia. Anxieties about the uncertain future of liberalism were, perhaps, felt the more in Australia, where it had never been strong, where Labour was an established party, and where also imperial ties were strong. When Annie Besant addressed Edwardians, she confidently advanced theosophical remedies for liberal weaknesses. Having carried theosophy past the ferment of the eighties, and encouraged it through the guilty nineties, she now offered antidotes to decadence.

Thus, in Brisbane, giving the 'Message of Theosophy to the World', she skilfully incorporated those ambiguities of social development which gave theosophy its entree into Queensland in the first place. American politics had showed the problems of unbridled licence; and there was, she said, a big risk in Australia of allowing irresponsible people an important role in government, which needed educated and experienced men and women. In Sydney she spoke 'forcibly' to educated women urging that they vote responsibly ('and not before it was needed,' added the *Bulletin*). The young

Commonwealth needed to foster art, and idealism, and moral training in the schools, lest it be swamped by materialism and mere class legislation.[92]

Hence, too, theosophical geopolitics in the lecture entitled 'The Guardians of Humanity' included reminders of rumblings in India, the sufferings of Ireland, and the continuing struggle against autocracy in Russia. (The Roman Catholic press at least approved of remarks about the great spiritual powers of repressed peoples; whether or not the Highland Society agreed that the American Revolution was an avoidable mistake is not recorded.) The argument that imperialism should accommodate legitimate nationalist aspirations accorded well with Australian expectations. Of the swing of empires over vast spans of human history, she took the optimistic view:

> Asia had conquered Europe, Europe now begins to conquer Asia; first in the quiet guise of commerce, and then, later, by invading armies. And now in our own days once more in the far East, Japan has thrown her sword into the scale of empire, and it is beginning to weigh down again in Asia, and the end has not yet come. Is there nothing to learn from that strange swinging backwards and forwards, eastward and westward ... no profit out of all these great invasions and tremendous outpourings of human blood? When we look at the results we see that every invasion has enriched the invaded people, every conquest has left the conquered with something that before they did not enjoy ... East and West are different; and therefore it is necessary that they should come into contact, conquer each other ... and with each swing of the pendulum give something of East to West, or something of West to East, until both great types are blended in the perfect man and the evolution of humanity, perfect in all its possibilities, shall be with us.[93]

It was a broader view than Kipling's.

Even doctrinally, Besant stood nearer to the mainstream of intellectual life in the early twentieth century than is at first apparent. Much was made of her pessimistic use of karma and reincarnation, but that should be seen in the context of the irrational and elitist tendencies in advanced social thought, and compared with the grim perspectives of Social Darwinism then applied to urban populations. The theory of urban degeneracy had been fashionable for some time, and the liberal intelligentsia toyed with eugenics as a mode of social engineering to counter working-class predominance.

When Besant said that theosophy cast criminality in a different light, she meant a different light from the degeneracy school. She meant to contrast 'the light of Asia' with illiberal views of crime and punishment which dressed old punitive approaches in new Darwinist clothes, finding in reincarnation for example, fresh grounds for opposition to capital punishment, a cause which made almost no progress after the end of public hangings (in Australia in the 1850s). Unlike the degenerationists and the sociologists, Annie remained an individualist, propounding exotic but still individual and democratic solutions to supposed evolutionary blockages. To her mind, reincarnation belied the pessimists, and karma did away with social controls derived either from religious or secular sources. Against the radically authoritarian interventionists, Annie advocated a new version of self-help. Attuned to finer forces, all men might evolve to the level of genius and avoid degeneracy:

> You know how Lombroso [the Italian criminologist] declared that all cases of genius were cases of degeneration, how they said that genius and lunacy were so closely allied that genius was a disease ... The man of genius shows you what the human race shall be. He is the prophecy of the future. He is not the product of degeneracy. He shows us what men shall become at a stage of higher evolution ... It is only fair to admit that at the present time the genius, the artist of the highest kind, the great religious leader, the seer, the prophet, the revealer, has often a brain too delicate to bear the rough vibrations of the outer world ... Can they be avoided? Yes. That is the answer of the Eastern scientist ... You can train yourself to receive the finer forces, and yet keep the body healthy ... Along that line, then, human evolution will go.[94]

Besant's criticisms of religion and politics grated on many Australian ears, and the press tried hard to puncture her rhetoric. But she belonged in a recognisable undercurrent of pre-1914 idealism and she spoke still to the Great Unsatisfied, those dissatisfied with politics as well as those dissatisfied with the churches.

For theosophists, the president had provided a program for social work. Sydney branch set itself to make more extensive contacts with a program under seven heads. They were: (1) the promotion of religious and moral education in the schools; (2) the union of Christendom in Australia; (3) visitation of hospitals, asylums and gaols; (4) the stamping out of gambling and intemperance; (5) the abolition of capital punishment and establishment of prison reforms; (6) cremation; (7) the establishment of a Chair of Comparative Religion at Sydney University. The Cremation Society and Esperanto Guild have been mentioned already. Here were the makings of a real 'forward movement'.[95]

One new feature noticed by many reporters at the lectures was the response of women. More women than men responded to Besant's message though, as with Adelaide journalist James Leonard Davidge, she attracted new male talent too. A new women's organisation, the Theosophical Order of Service, was formed, and even before the president left the country, Adelaide lodge had its order and others were forming.

To its chagrin, theosophy reaped a 'harvest of opposition' from the Besant lectures, at least in the Melbourne press. But 1908 was still a memorable year; and, said John in *Theosophy in Australia*, it was silly to say 'our day was done'. New lodges formed in greater numbers than since the 1890s. Membership rose to nearly 1000 by 1911, 1400 in 1914, the same steady upward trend as for the Theosophical Society in general, 24,000-strong worldwide by 1914. An organisation which doubles its membership every few years may feel some satisfaction, especially one which measured its progress not merely numerically, by the branch formation which Annie Besant said she had come to encourage, but also, and as she also said, by the extent of its propaganda work.[96]

Rising membership was both matched and encouraged by a dramatic new development on the religious front. It will be recalled that the sixth round would provide new religious insight. Madame Blavatsky had nominated 1975 – a convenient century after the founding of the Theosophical Society – as the beginning of the sixth round. The sixth round would be heralded by another great religious teacher, another Buddha, Jesus, Mohammed. Mrs Besant began developing the inheritance in her famous annual Queen's Hall lectures in London. Concluding a lecture on 'The Coming Christ' in 1909, she said positively that there were signs of the coming of Christ in the current revival of mystic teaching and in the deadlocks of civilisation:

> Unless all that I have been telling you during the past five weeks is a mere dream; unless the very facts that I have pointed you to are utterly without significance, you ought almost to have thought yourselves into the point

to which I fain would lead you now – that we are on the threshold of a new manifestation, and that the mighty Teacher again will appear as man among men. Now, to say that to any people may only make them think: 'But why for us?' So might the Jew have questioned when last He came on earth. That a thing so great, so transcendent, and so rare, should come to earth at any particular time, to be measured by only a few years of mortal time – that that should now be seems too strange, too beautiful to be true. And yet He came before; why not again? If at the birth of the fifth sub-race, why not at the birth of the sixth? Some must be on earth when any such manifestation takes place ... and there is no valid reason that any one of you can give why this age should not be such a time, and the people of this age the recipients of the new flood of spiritual life. Strange, because it happens seldom, but sure, because it happened at similar crises in the story of the world; and the strangeness of it does not mark it as untrue when you see the signs of the coming all around you, if your eyes should be open to recognise what they mean. For an expectation is spreading everywhere of the coming of some mighty Teacher ...[97]

Suddenly a World Teacher was imminent. It was not after all a very big step from the Masters to the Messiah.

In 1910 Leadbeater found him. The irrepressible Leadbeater, now reinstated and housed in a rotunda at Adyar, had been conducting clairvoyant experiments with the aid of a dreamy motherless child, a Brahmin boy born in the hills north of Madras in 1895 called Krishnamurti, who lived on the compound with his father and brother. Leadbeater identified Krishnamurti as the likely vehicle for the World Teacher.[98]

With Annie's endorsement, the idea was taken up with enthusiasm by theosophical teachers at the Central Hindu College, Benares, who created a preparatory Order of the Star in the East (OSE). Mrs Besant's determination to adopt the boy increased as opposition from the boy's father and hostile Christian missionaries in Madras mounted. From London, whence Krishnamurti and a party of theosophical attendants repaired in 1914, the Order of the Star really took off, with ribbons, badges, dues, a journal and a round of activities which were by now almost second nature to leading theosophists. Of the new order, Krishnamurti was for the time being Outer Head; and, though not educable to university entrance standard, as hoped by his sponsors, he edited the *Star* journal, nominally at least, aided by such capable and devoted women as the Lady Emily Lutyens.[99]

Reporting on the new Indian enterprise at the Adelaide Convention in 1911, general secretary, John, claimed to have conceived a very similar idea himself, though he had only gone as far as a Guild of Endless Life. Apparently Melbourne theosophists had been talking about a Coming for a couple of years too. For example, W.R. Rall wrote to Christopher Crisp, the country editor, alluding to 'new and startling developments': 'There is a great psychological wave going over the whole world just now and I think it is a very good thing and the precursor to new & startling developments in the realm of the mind and also of spirit.' A circular calling for intending members to forward particulars to Sydney, with 2/3d. to pay for postage and a five-pointed silver star (brooch or pin), preserved by Melbourne theosophist Elsie Deane, probably dates from 1912. It lists six points. The points, which remained unchanged for the life of the organisation, read as follows:

THE ORDER OF THE STAR IN THE EAST

This Order has been founded to draw together those who, whether inside or outside the Theosophical Society, believe in the near coming of a great spiritual Teacher for the helping of the world. It is thought that its members may, on the physical plane, do something to prepare public opinion for His coming, and to create an atmosphere of welcome and of reverence; and, on the higher planes, may unite in forming an instrument of service ready for His use. The Declaration of Principles, acceptance of which is all that is necessary for admission to the Order, is as follows:

1. We believe that a great Teacher will soon appear in the world, and we wish so to live now that we may be worthy to know Him when He comes.
2. We shall try, therefore, to keep Him in our minds always, and to do in His name, and therefore to the best of our ability, all the work which comes to us in our daily occupations.
3. As far as our ordinary duties allow, we shall endeavour to devote a portion of our time each day to some definite work which may help to prepare for His coming.
4. We shall seek to make Devotion, Steadfastness and Gentleness prominent characteristics of our daily life.

5. We shall try to begin and end each day with a short period devoted to the asking of His blessing upon all that we try to do for Him and in His name.
6. We regard it as our special duty to try to recognise and reverence greatness in whomsoever shown, and to strive to co-operate, as far as we can, with those whom we feel to be spiritually our superiors.[100]

The lodges responded keenly to Mrs Besant's covering note, and to John's hope that the time had come to destroy materialism. At Tweed River, in northern New South Wales, virtually all members joined the OSE. T.H. Martyn became president of the Australian wing of the order, and by 1912 there were 620 members in Australia, even some of the general public, an estimated 11 percent of the New South Wales enrolment. Propaganda began with W.T. Ashford's 'If Christ came to our City', a title reminiscent of W.T. Stead's phenomenally successful polemic, *If Christ came to Chicago*, inspired by the Columbian Expo in Chicago in 1893. Monies were set aside and pamphlets produced for the Christian clergy (unresponsive as ever, and likely to be even more hostile, but Mrs John joked in verse, 'You have woken me too soon / I must slumber again').[101]

Here then was work for the Great Unsatisfied. The evidence is that theosophists seized it hungrily. It only needed the further Leadbeater prognosis of Australia and New Zealand as the home of a new sub-race for the mood to become quite millennial. Perhaps a home could be constructed for the coming World Teacher when in Australia, an Australian 'Krotona', on the lines of a new community in Hollywood? Cudgeen Headland, where the Tweed River lodge conducted summer schools, was suggested, and Narrabeen on Sydney's North Shore, site of a summer camp of one of the half-dozen theosophical study groups operating in Sydney at this time in addition to the established lodges. These eager preparations came to nothing, but they give a perspective on the Star Amphitheatre built on Balmoral Beach in 1923, more of local inspiration than usually allowed.[102]

Meanwhile there was a fundamental problem for white Australians to face. Evidently the World Teacher would not be white of skin. On Empire Day 1908 one lodge remembered the responsibilities of an imperial people:

> ... after the usual music the President opened the proceedings with an excellent little address appropriate to the occasion, in which he reminded us that seven-eighths of the people composing this great empire of which

we are so justly proud, are coloured – a fact we are apt to forget – and that the great body of compatriots must be treated with justice, sympathy and brotherliness if our nation is to remain on sure and lasting foundations.[103]

Empire Day was but a recent innovation, and a suitable time for reflection. Most theosophists earnestly opposed race prejudice. They had also learned of historical arguments which said that religious advance usually came from the margins not the metropolis, as with the dark-skinned Palestinian Jesus. But the White Australia Policy jeopardised the Coming, and posed problems not faced anywhere else in the theosophical world. Some mental wriggling began.

It should not be presumed, said Hunt in Melbourne, that the Great Teacher would occupy a dark-skinned body at all times. Even with the University Extension Lectures advised by Miss Wanliss there would be a problem in Australia. On the very real question of whether the teacher would be allowed into Australia, it was hoped that spiritual status would impress, and that erstwhile labour organiser and theosophical politician Matt Reid of Queensland would do the rest.[104]

Not all theosophical energies were absorbed by the Order of the Star in the East. There were other enterprises afoot before 1914, like the theosophical arts and crafts movement advocated by Mrs Besant, and yet another youth movement, Sons and Daughters of the Empire (Mrs Besant hoped the King himself would head this movement – perhaps the Governor of New South Wales might be persuaded to be local patron?). Sons and Daughters superseded an earlier patriotic proposal from England, a Samurai Order to emulate the selfless virtues of the Japanese warrior class and promote clean and strenuous habits (badly needed in the 'slipshod, disorderly and careless ways which so greatly obtain especially under the Southern Cross'), and was expected to spread the ideal of service, thereby abolishing industrial strife and making war impossible. At a time of increased industrial conflict in England, theosophists advocated service and advanced liberalism – prosperity-sharing as at Lever Bros works at Port Sunlight, near Liverpool – in places like the glossy *Bibby's Annual*, produced by another Liverpool employer, Joseph Bibby. The new Gnosis lodge in Sydney (see Chapter 5) best captured these trends in Australian theosophy, with its

Narrabeen retreat, Guild of Art Workers, Sons and Daughters of the Empire, Pythagorean Music group and so on.[105]

In June 1914, two months before the declaration of war, *Theosophy in Australasia* noted with satisfaction that Australian theosophy was now closely tied to the wider movement: 'Australia may claim as a fixed habit a far closer touch with the Society's headquarters in India than we could have thought possible in former years.' The Australian section had proved itself not only loyal but responsive. It had grown steadily since 1896 with twenty-three lodges and nearly 1400 members, many activities, and, of late, a great hope. The optimists appeared to be vindicated as they basked in the brilliant light cast upon an unsatisfactory world by Annie Besant PTS.

5

To the court of the Faerie Queene

In several studies of the Renaissance Frances Yates has explored aspects of the first theosophic movement: *Giordano Bruno and the Hermetic Tradition* (1964), *Astraea, The Imperial Theme in the Sixteenth Century* (1975) and *The Rosicrucian Enlightenment* (1972). A main theme is the seizure of lost knowledge – hermetic and cabbalistic learning originating in Constantinople and Spain – by sixteenth-century men of science, Renaissance magi like John Dee, to promote a Tudor Reformation and a 'British Empire' in the face of increasing Catholic reaction on the continent. Her last and boldest work, *The Occult Philosophy in the Elizabethan Age* (1979), argues that Edmund Spenser's epic poem 'The Faerie Queene' is a great magical Renaissance poem, not only a poetic metaphor for Elizabethan England but also a response to contemporary states of mind polarised by religion; the chivalric poem is read as a vision of a new age of universal harmony structured by a Christian Cabbala. Less controversially, Spenser's epic 'expresses a "prophetic moment", after the Armada victory, when the Queen appeared almost as a symbol of a new religion transcending both Catholic and Protestant in some far-reaching revelation, and transmitting a universal messianic message' (p. 104). The Faerie Queene, Elizabeth I, thus personified hope of religious reform, the latent powers of Albion and the promise of a British Empire.

Similar ideas sustained the theosophic movement of the late nineteenth century. The threefold aims of the Theosophical Society envisaged a new religious synthesis transcending distinctions of class, caste, creed and gender, and the reconstitution of moral and spiritual authority. The new *theosophia* also produced another 'faerie queene' in Annie Besant, whose spectacular passage to theosophy in 1889 had made her the best-known propagandist for the cause in the 1890s, and from 1907 second president of the Theosophical Society. Under her leadership the small society, primarily an occult and mystical group, gained an influence disproportionate to its size.[1] In the early years of her presidency, before World War I, the new theosophists sensed another 'prophetic moment'.

The means by which the theosophic tradition survived between the sixteenth and the nineteenth century are obscure. But the powerful and poetic symbol of the magical queen whose court was the brilliant hope of her day casts some light on sources of renewal in the nineteenth century. In Britain, where faith in the old magical tradition lasted well into the nineteenth century in popular religion, the nationalist theme, the image of oppressed Albion, became popular in radical circles in the late eighteenth century, in part in response to socioeconomic dislocations. There were various revivals, as of Swedenborg's New Church (secretly admired for universalism), and millenarian surges, with visions of the Second Coming, this time in 'England's green and pleasant land'. Meanwhile, the surge of liberalism across the nineteenth century strengthened popular anti-clericalism, and favoured religious alternatives like spiritualism. Increasingly, and for more elevated people, *theosophia* offered a gloss on forward-looking ideals. Despite defeats a theosophic sense remained viable and renewed itself on the margins of culture, because of restrictions of class and caste, and obscurely at first, constraints of gender.[2]

Theosophical history, like most religious history, pays little attention to women, apart from Blavatsky and Besant; and problems of evidence have reinforced a more general lack of interest in women's religious experience in the past. The passage of women through the age of revolutions is inevitably obscure, the more so because of the variety and intensity of general religious awakening in the Victorian era. Very little, therefore, is known of women's religious behaviour and beliefs, criticisms of which emerged in Europe in the 1880s. But some things stand out. The early millenarians were often led by women, the most famous being Joanna Southcott, a domestic servant who became 'the woman clothed with the sun'. Amid resurgent religious enthusiasm – millenarian, Methodist, evangelical and revivalist – women 'ranters' of the lower classes, and, later, more respectable women preachers of non-denominational revival, found scope for self-expression in popular religion.[3]

Within the churches woman's sphere expanded dramatically in mission and charitable work over the period, mention of which revives folk memories of a flood tide of religious commitment by women in the second half of the nineteenth century. Some historians, noticing that women were much better churchgoers than men in Victorian America, have gone so far as to speak of the 'feminisation' of religion. It should be emphasised that not only did Christianity endorse women's most basic and cherished roles, and comfort them in the performance thereof, but also the churches provided cultural and psychological sustenance not offered elsewhere in a male-oriented secular culture.[4]

Indeed, women had reason to stay with the churches. Too many issues affecting women specifically remained unresolved in a world without churches and churchmen. Feminists vigorously attacked the denigrating stereotypes of women in the Bible; but Christian teaching provided a rationale for Woman's elevated status, and the moral sanction which, it was believed, lifted wives out of the chattel status so often deplored in non-Christian societies.[5] It was apposite to criticise Calvinism as a guide to child-rearing; but at a time when women's nurturing role was being re-emphasised and the family's position as moral core of class society reasserted, mothers often felt moral training was left in limbo. And while there is abundant evidence of female hostility to the patriarchal blight cast by some clergy on their hard-working wives, long-suffering daughters, and impressionable young girls in their congregations (Besant's autobiography covers most of it),[6] still the clergy were often women's closest male friends and strongest allies.[7] That is to say, secularisation, 'a growing tendency in mankind to do without religion', in Owen Chadwick's definition, implied the de-regulation of men.[8] And that, in the dark ages of women's history before contraception, was not a compelling prospect. In those waning days of the old patriarchal order, something stronger than hope of increasing rationality was needed to carry conviction.

Plainly the great theme of secularisation bears but lightly, and then obliquely, upon women's experiences in the late nineteenth century. Far from exhibiting a tendency to do without religion, they seemed to be more reliant upon it than ever. The important question was whether or not revealed religion could keep pace with womankind. Women, especially educated women, looked to religion for affirmation of improving status; but in doing so ran up against a still powerful patriarchal dispensation, its heartland in fact, as the neglected American feminist Matilda Joslyn Gage argued most forcibly. The status quo accorded ill with women's highest aspirations, a contradiction testified to by Florence Nightingale's unpublished theological writings. At that point – roughly in the mid-Victorian years when American women also rebelled against constraints on their work as Christian anti-slavery campaigners – the ancient theosophic sense revived in spiritualist and reformist circles, as resource against oppressions of gender in religion.[9]

The most hopeful moment for religious feminists came later, at the World's Parliament of Religions called in conjunction with the great Columbian Exposition in Chicago in 1893, 'the most comprehensive and brilliant display of man's material progress'. It was felt that this 'great Festival of Peace' would be incomplete unless man's intellectual and moral progress was also adequately displayed, and the aspiration of religious union for the whole human family expressed. It was a sign of the times that women joined wholeheartedly in the pursuit of 'the elements of a perfect religion', ultimately said to be found in Christianity, a universal rather than 'topographical' religion. (Incidentally, antipodean Christianity was represented in Chicago by the Anglican Bishop of Sydney, the Rt Rev. Saumaurez Smith, Dr Llewelyn Bevan, doyen of Melbourne Congregationalism, and the Rev. James Rickard of Brighton.)[10] The record of the World's Parliament of Religions begins, 'Religion is the greatest fact of History'. For the five female paper-givers (some fifty men also performed), the story of man's religious progress must include the equally important historical fact of women's spiritual subjection, and the speedy recognition of sacred feminist principle that 'men and women must rise or sink together', as stated by the Rev. Annis Eastman, analysing 'The Influence of Religion on Women' in terms remarkably similar to today's well-known dichotomy of the Madonna and the Magdalen. They all agreed that the Gospel knew nothing of 'male' and 'female'.

With one voice, these advanced women demanded a return to first principles, a clean sweep of historical constraints, calling in most theosophic manner for truly universal brotherhood. Dr Eliza Sunderland of Michigan, in a scholarly advocacy of the value of 'Serious Study of All Religions' as basis for essential change, actually referred to theosophy: 'the germs of a philosophy of religion may be found in the theosophic mysticism and the antischolastic philosophy of the renaissance' (p. 625). Mrs Lydia Fuller Dickinson spoke to the World Parliament on 'The Divine Basis of the Cooperation between Men and Women', concluding that the enfranchisement of women would restore the basic oneness of male and female and usher in a new era of

>New churches, new economies, new laws
>Admitting freedom; new societies
>Excluding falsehood (p. 508).

For Mrs Laura Ormiston Chant of London, 'The Real Religion of Today' was aesthetic, mystic, comprehensive, the hope of remade humanity, *Prometheus Unbound* at last. In the last paper of the Parliament, the Rev. Marion Murdock plucked a Pauline text [Romans 16:1] on deaconess Phebe to expound 'New Testament Woman'. In the new, Christian, dispensation, women were 'called and chosen':

> [N]ot until the inauguration of a radically new movement in religion were the official barriers in some degree removed. Not until the emphasis was put on that divine love of God which would save all creatures, upon that mother heart of the Deity which would enfold all its children; not until the emphasis was put upon the spirit rather than the letter of Bible literature, upon the free rather than the restricted revelations of God, upon the Holy Spirit in the human soul, without regard to sex or time or place; not until all this was proclaimed and emphasised did the Phebes ask or receive official recognition in the ministry. And it was better so. Under the old dispensation, they would have been strangely out of place; under the new, it is most fitting that they should be called and chosen (p. 799).

The full-blown optimism of the Christian feminists at Chicago was not the only option. Some women took reform from within to mean separate structures, of nuns, deaconesses and missioners, within the Protestant churches. A few passed right out of the existing churches, in search of a new dispensation. Some even set up their own churches, a tendency most pronounced in North America. Analysing the appeal of such a radical alternative to American women, Mary Farrell Bednarowski has shown that women were drawn outside the mainstream into Shakerism, spiritualism, Christian Science and theosophy by a combination of intellectual and social disaffection: hostility to orthodox Christian doctrine of a male deity, a male clergy, and female depravity; dissatisfaction with rigid attitudes to marriage and sex-roles; also by the chance of leadership roles. None of these alternatives envisaged the end of religion. Quite the opposite, as the distinctive presence of women theosophists like Annie Besant and Mrs Cooper-Oakley at Chicago also suggested, religion was 'the most important fact in history' for all of them.[11]

Given the intellectual currents in liberal Christianity and women's various approaches to reform and renewal by the 1890s, it is hardly surprising that theosophy was a beneficiary at the turn of the century. Theosophy offered not merely reform but reconstruction, and special promise for women. Theosophy's best-known leaders were women and the Theosophical Society eschewed sexism both in theory and practice. It appealed to women of the middle class – in Britain the upper middle class, in Australia the middling classes in general – particularly educated women who sought resolution of spiritual conflict and reassurance of intellectual independence in the religious sphere.[12] In a world stirred by secular feminism, some women looked to theosophy to carry them forward. By 1907, when Annie Besant became president of the Theosophical Society, the 'prophetic moment' was almost overdue.

The late Victorian struggle for a 'new consciousness' ran into the sands in the 1890s, and there followed that state of open uncertainty about religion and politics which, according to Samuel Hynes, caused *The Edwardian Turn of Mind* (1967). What happened to the many women who had participated as preachers and teachers of 'the New Life'? An example close to home shows how one woman found a theosophic solution. Clara Codd, who became general secretary of the Theosophical Society in Australia in the 1930s, recounts that she joined the Marxist Social Democratic Federation in England in the 1880s but found it a disillusioning experience. Male members told her there would be no place for artists in the future; the secretary absconded with funds; another member ran off with a wealthy woman. For her 'the rule of the Best' was not to be achieved that way; the socialists must be spiritualised. Later Codd joined the suffragettes and was imprisoned. Later still she attracted the attention of the Liverpool philanthropist Joseph Bibby, who sent her to India for training as a theosophical lecturer.[13]

A sign that the moment had not passed was the success of a new London weekly, aptly titled the *New Age*, launched in 1907 by theosophical writer A.R. Orage. The *New Age* spoke to a new intelligentsia, increasingly perplexed and dissatisfied with political realities, but still idealistic, expectant. Looking back in 1916, the socialist intellectual Edward Carpenter nominated as parts of a torrent of change 'Socialist and Anarchist propaganda, the Feminist and Suffragist upheaval, the huge Trade-union growth, the Theosophic movement and the new currents in the Theatrical, Musical and Artistic world, the torrent even of change in the religious world – all constituted so many streams and headwaters converging, as it were on a great river'. A comparable expectation attended the rise of the Progressive movement in American politics before 1914.[14]

Thus currents of reform on either side of the Atlantic carried theosophy into the Besant era. In 'Imperialism and Theosophy', a lecture delivered at the end of the South African War (1899–1902), Annie Besant said: 'We need an Empire of peace, of justice, within which a new civilisation may ... grow up, a civilisation which should be at peace not war, co-operation not competition, education not cramming, comfort not pauperism.' Her thoughts on the varieties of religious experience – esoteric Christianity, revived Hinduism, even Islam, and the new psychology from which enlarged consciousness might come – poured off theosophical presses in London, Benares and Madras. The prophetic moment arrived with promise of 'the new cycle'. In lectures delivered annually at the heart of the empire, in Queen's Hall, London, the president refreshed the image of theosophy, now offered as the basis of a higher socialism, the solution to cultural deadlock, the hope of *The Changing World* (1909).

Nothing in that addressed women specifically, though the state of the suffrage struggle was one of the more dramatic deadlocks of the day. It is striking how infrequently Besant even addressed women's issues. She often spoke at women's meetings, but her immense published *oeuvre* contains only two lectures on the position of women after her conversion in 1889. One was on the education of Indian girls (1904), following success with boys at the Central Hindu College, Benares; the other a special London lecture delivered in June 1914 in aid of old friends at a frightening moment in the British suffrage campaign, where she capably defended a just cause while deploring a scandalous situation.[15]

The absence of material addressed specifically to women suggests that it was not needed. So do recruitment figures. As will be seen subsequently, in Australia there were more places for women at the court of the faerie queene in theory than in reality, but an increasing number of women became theosophists in the early twentieth century, and an increasing proportion of theosophists were women. The feminisation of theosophy in the 1920s, so obvious after the Great War, began at the turn of the century.

No doubt the rising number and proportion of women in theosophy followed from its outright rejection of the teachings and practices which told against women in the Christian churches. But the Theosophical Society waited a considerable time to reap the benefits of liberal principle. Whatever brought women to theosophy in increasing numbers in the Edwardian years, it was not just liberal principle in religious life. Something more – a good deal more – was involved.

A clue may be found in Besant's lecture on the proper education of Indian girls. It is dangerous to generalise from a single lecture, and especially one delivered to men in a colonial situation, but Besant's argument hardly affirmed liberal principle, wise and bold as it was in other respects considering its time and place. Rather, she looked to a strengthening of traditional roles. The education of Indian girls should be such as to make 'happy households', consonant with 'national' aims, and in accord with Hindu teaching. She advocated a syllabus which would provide moral and religious teaching in the classics, a vernacular literary education, domestic science, and artistic and physical training. It should restore a balance of the sexes, and the dignified liberty enjoyed by Hindu women in antiquity before it was smothered by Islamic practice and swamped by the faster pace of westernisation among men. It was stressed that the sad fate of the enormous number of unmarried women in economic competition with men in the West should be avoided:

> The national movement for girls' education ... cannot see in her the rival and competitor of man in all forms of outside and public employment, as woman, under different economic conditions, is coming to be, more and more, in the West. The West must work out in its own way the artificial problem which has been created there as to the relation of the sexes. The East has not to face that problem, and the lines of Western female education are not suitable for the education of Eastern girls.[16]

Besant addressed a single and exotic issue, women and progress in India. The lecture, however, belongs in a wider context, which may be called 'theosophic feminism'. Although Besant contributed very little to the construction of a theosophic feminism in England at the turn of the century, yet her lecture hints at its strongest themes, themes which go a long way towards explaining the appeal of theosophy to women. Indeed without those themes, without the now-forgotten cultural context which produced them, the appeal of theosophy to educated women would remain a mystery.

The construction of a theosophic feminism began with Madame Blavatsky. Although she is barely recognisable in modern feminist dress, she would probably pass, being a rude Russian rebel who charmed the advanced and often aristocratic circles she frequented in the West by flouting the 'lady' image. And as some women today believe, her writings carried a message of 'liberation', albeit a very different version from today's ideals.[17]

In the first place, she popularised religious history itself as a source of alternative images of womanhood. Blavatsky did not say so in as many words, but the very title of her first treatise, *Isis Unveiled*, drew attention to pre-Christian goddess religions of Egypt, and the Levant. Isis was a comprehensive and institutionalised goddess, and women served as her priests. She had an apparently limitless appeal for women:

> It is quite clear that the religion of Isis provided for the first time in classical antiquity a deity with which women could identify. Her titles (she was called Isis 'of the myriad names') show her as Sister of Osiris, Daughter of Cronos, Widow, Queen, Mother (of Hocus and nature in general) and the Beautiful: in each of the areas of womanly experience, Isis participates by being a woman in that role. She is also the patron goddess of childbirth, of fertility, of sailors, life and magic. Her story shows her as having been a prostitute in Tyre; the legend of her marriage to her brother Osiris shows her as mourning over his death and dismemberment, and seeking to recover the pieces of his body, but she is unable to find the phallus. Isis was remarkably comprehensive, and was identified with all kinds of local goddesses ... her capacity to meet the aspirations and needs of women was therefore limitless.[18]

The religion of Isis extended as far as Germany, carried there in the Graeco-Roman era, and survived in the Nile valley until in the sixth century AD it was suppressed during the reign of Justinian.

Although the goddess religion may not have caused the greater freedom of Egyptian women, yet it strongly supported it; and its influence persisted into the Christian era within the Gnostic sects, now the subject of lively debate as a lost source of Christian feminism. Today's scholarly debates seem rather to confine than extend such sources of encouragement for women dissatisfied with the constraints of conventional Christianity, but in Blavatsky's day they had scarcely been studied, and it is not surprising that some women responded to the ancient, indeed suppressed, female wisdom.[19] One hardly expects to see before the veil of Isis the redoubtable figure of the Baroness Burdett-Coutts, philanthropist and foundress of colonial bishoprics in Australia. But there she is, in the preface to the second volume of *Isis Unveiled*, as earnest of advanced womankind and evidence of true religion, uncontaminated by 'pernicious ecclesiastical systems ... ruinous to man's faith in his immortality ... and subversive of all moral restraint'. The Baroness did later abandon restraint by marrying a man thirty years younger than herself; but hers was an admirable name to drop in 1877.[20]

In *The Secret Doctrine*, Blavatsky offered a signpost rather than a map for theosophic feminism. She remarked teasingly that '*The Secret Doctrine* contains all you want to know – but you won't find it'; and its lovingly compiled index does not mention either sex or woman. It was not until the 1920s, when sexuality became a relevant subject to students of the higher consciousness and theosophists attended to the debate about venereal disease, that a compilation entitled 'The Secret Doctrine and the Problem and Evolution of Sex' appeared. It shows that when Blavatsky considered the problem of reproduction she did so on a grand scale, in the fabled evolution of root-races; and that she took a disdainful view of the practicalities, prophesying the end of sexuality.

In the Blavatsky scenario, sexual division did not even occur until the mid-Lemurian cycle. Previously the rootraces developed from a pure sexless state of mind:

> Reproduction of the earlier Races as follows: First Race – Self-Born. Second Race – Sweat-Born. Third Race – Egg-Born; at first Sexless then Androgynous, and finally separate sexes. All these stages are re-enacted in the stages of the present human embryo.[21]

Then occurred the 'Fall into Generation', or, 'the Sin of Mindlessness' (from which the great beings or masters were exempt). In the fourth race, the Atlantean, a terrible misuse of 'the creative power' occurred, and from ensuing miscegenation, monsters and the anthropoid apes originated (there are recurrent references to monsters), as well as gender division. The iniquity was carried over into the present, fifth, root-race by karmic law; and the battle for sex equality began. Now only the sternest self-control availed. Absolute purity was necessary to recover lost spiritual powers like the third eye, now reduced to the pineal gland. In the sixth root-race, immaculate reproduction would begin again; and in the seventh, 'the great Adepts and initiated ascetics will multiply i.e. once again produce Mind-born immaculate sons'.

Clearly Blavatsky's view of the evolution of sexuality was similar to that in the Book of Genesis, with the important difference that the fall was not caused by woman. And she envisaged the elimination altogether of sex and gender. The sons of the seventh round would be mind-born and only notionally male.

Personally Blavatsky seems to have found sexuality abhorrent by middle age, and suppressed the fact that she had once borne a son, Yuri, by a wandering Central European musician. Nor did she mention other more or less legitimate liaisons in America. For those who have entertained the idea of a lesbian attachment between Blavatsky and Besant, on the basis of Besant's spectacular conversion and subsequent devotion, there is little likelihood and no evidence. The suggestion obscures more than it reveals about the mysterious Madame or implies about Besant's lonely life. Such attachments were common within the nineteenth-century female culture and usually without erotic significance.[22] In this case, dominance and devotion carried no further implication. Apart from Blavatsky's age and health, she taught the suppression of sexuality as fiercely as any more conventional religious teacher, and if anything encouraged Besant's innate puritanism. There was, of course, plenty of repressed male sexuality in theosophy in Leadbeater's heyday, and religious radicals have often been notorious for the free expression of sexuality. But women-led movements have usually gone in the opposite direction, as did theosophy. Sexual suppression rather than expression was a motif intelligible to late Victorians, late Victorian women the more so.

Blavatsky's new theosophy provided a radical religious premise from which to argue the advancement, even the supremacy, of women. The best extant examples of theosophy as feminist resource come from the writings of two influential Edwardian English women, from the prolific but now largely forgotten Frances Swiney and from Charlotte Despard, best remembered as president of the Women's Freedom League, the democratic breakaway from the Pankhursts' Women's Social and Political Union. Swiney developed links between theosophy, feminism and biological theory, and Despard between theosophy, feminism and socialism. Both illustrate the interplay of radical and religious thought, and both saw in theosophy an instrument for the advancement of women.

Rosa Frances Emily Swiney (1847–19??) was an earlier and more elaborate theorist than Despard, with at least seven books to her credit. It is clear from Swiney's titles and her train of thought in *The Awakening of Women* that she was a theosophic feminist. In so far as her work has ever been noticed by historians, it has been as the work of the man-hating Miss Swiney. *The Bar of Isis; or the Law of the Mother* (1907) is said to have contained pathological ideas about the dangers of poisoned sperm, and the right of woman to protect herself against unfit males, spacing sexual encounters to leave pregnancy and lactation times clear. That other women upheld Swiney in the press has done nothing to restore her evident respectability: mother of six, wife of a major-general, president of the Cheltenham branch of the National Union of Women's Suffrage Societies. But it does attest an attentive female culture, which certainly read her in the *Westminster Gazette*, and bought her books, a culture which included Australian feminists. Irene Greenwood of Perth recalls that her mother, Mary Driver, studied Swiney; and Vida Goldstein publicised her books in *Woman's Voice*. *The Awakening of Women; or, Woman's Part in Evolution* (1899) appeared in its third edition (1908) complete with pages of encomia, including one from Goldstein, who recognised from the splendid book 'an enthusiastic co-worker'.[23]

The Awakening of Women is divided into four parts: Woman's Physical Organisation; Woman's Psychological Characteristics; Woman as the Wife; Woman as the Mother. From it, and the more ambitious *The Cosmic Procession; or, the Feminine Principle in Evolution. Essays of Illumination* (1906), Swiney's line from theosophy to feminism emerges. It is a line of thought close to the biology of her day, and much of the sociology. It also runs close to the thinking of the better-known contemporary American feminist Charlotte Perkins Gilman, in so far as Swiney comes near to parthenogenesis, while in books like *Herland* (1915), Gilman merely imagines it: 'it has been proved that only a transitory change in the ions of the blood may allow of complete parthenogenesis of the higher mammalia'.[24] Deploying one of Blavatsky's 'monster' references, Swiney endorsed predictions of the demise of dogmatic religion once women were in total control of fertility 'for the world will have discovered that individuals have it in their own powers to procreate Buddha-like child[ren] – or demons. When the knowledge comes, all dogmatic religions will die out'.[25] As well, Swiney's deployment of *theosophia* foreshadows some of today's debates about the rejection of women in early Christian culture, as in the feminist reinterpretation of gnosticism from recently rediscovered texts: 'the whole system [in Gnostic writings] ... must be immaculate and feminine.'[26] For Swiney, scientific evidence and theosophic teaching together pointed to the pre-eminence of Woman, as not only the producer but as the evolver of the species.

Swiney was not a thinker of the first importance like Gilman. But she was vigorous, an impassioned synthesiser. In discussing reproduction at all, she was unusual, and the remark that the reproductive organs centre on the creation of a living soul had its startling aspect in pre-Freudian times. In fact her ideas were a curious, and doubtless satisfying, amalgam of conventional and advanced thought. When Swiney proclaimed that the bar of Isis rendered inviolable the fruit of the womb, she meant to emphasise that men played an insignificant role in the great work of reproduction, and they should and could limit sexual activities to that. Intercourse should be for reproduction purposes alone, a common view; when it did occur, it was only when the mother's desire was 'sympathetic', an uncommon view; and men must learn to respect the vital evolutionary role of the female principle, an advanced view:

> Now the first step ... will be taken when man, taught of woman, fully comprehends the vital importance of conserving the feminine creative energy within himself for self-development. Its expenditure ... is for birth alone, and then only when the mother's desire is sympathetic. The spirit and power of Elohim, the Divine Mother, will at last turn the hearts of the fathers to the children.[27]

The special significance of *The Cosmic Procession* was the case made out for motherhood, as a feminist concept. Previously motherhood had not been a starting point of feminist demand, which rested on liberal premises of individual rights and opportunities. In the hands of Frances Swiney, motherhood became a weapon. The emergence of the ideology of motherhood from customary behaviour has puzzled and infuriated feminists, and is seen as oppressive patriarchal ideology manipulated by the state. And so it has been. But it also seems likely that biological science at the turn of the century presented feminists with an opportunity; and from a mixture of religious and scientific ideas, feminists themselves created the ideology of motherhood. In Swiney's words:

> The Race of Mind will not be evolved among men until the sublime mystery is understood; until the creative power of woman is recognised at its full worth in the scale of Nature's elemental forces. The mother alone can give physical health to her children; she alone can make all the virtues instinctive.[28]

At its time of writing, *The Cosmic Procession* was abreast of biological knowledge in attaching a special importance to woman in the evolutionary process, or at least legitimate in interpreting the little that was known of it. It was not a respectable subject. Only biometricians and professional plant-breeders addressed themselves to the mechanisms of evolution, even though the chief difficulty of natural selection as the sole mechanism was well-known. The difficulty was that, over time, variation would be eliminated in perfected populations, and there would be nothing left for natural selection to work on. But biology was not yet an experimental science and it was not until 1900 that the laws of variation proposed in 1865 by Gregor Mendel were rediscovered, and not until 1906 that there was even a word to describe the study of the laws of inheritance, that is, 'genetics'. Even then, 'the great lacuna' in Darwin's theory was only slowly filled in, as with the later discovery of chromosomes, and the role of nucleic acids.[29]

Frances Swiney seized on 'the great lacuna', the new importance of heredity, 'the ancestral germ plasm', and the importance of forces affecting the single protoplasmic cell; in short, what happened in the womb. (How interesting that in 1919 a male theosophist in remote Queensland should be worried on this very issue – he wrote to Marie Stopes, the birth controller, to ask if semen was 'sexed'.)[30] There are, Swiney wrote, 'three factors that form the characteristics of all living creatures in more or less degree. First, heredity; second, environment; and third, maternal impressions, which last will be found to be the most important of all as immediately and directly influenced by environment'.[31] In the absence of scientific understanding of the role of chromosomes, her seizure of prime of place for motherhood in evolution is understandable.

Furthermore, in the gloomy climate of opinion which fed off 'the great lacuna', the widespread Social Darwinist fear of the survival by 'artificial' means of the unfit, and race degeneracy, she elevated woman's biological role as fulfilling the imperatives of the evolutionary process. 'The survival of the fittest thus pivots on the selection faculty of the female', being the locus (so she thought) of inherited variation and the selector of external variation. In motherhood, the female transmitted newly acquired traits and eliminated retrogressive ones. Motherhood, she argued, was the 'natural vehicle of determinate progression'.

In Swiney's view, the great impediment to evolutionary progress was the failure to recognise this law, which was appreciated by all the archaic religions. Occult teaching about the nature of the Divine and 'the grandest, most indispensable work of science' could be combined to demonstrate an 'Eternal Creation Principle by which all exists'. The business in hand was to reconstitute knowledge so that it was useful to women: or, as she put it, Eternal Truth, to show 'the phoenix rising from the pyre of our faulty and obsolete conceptions of the reality'. The suppressed religions of the Levant had always envisaged the divine force as feminine; the archaic goddess religion was monistic. The churches perverted the sublimest truths, even including the mission of Christ, who certainly was virgin-born, and diverted natural laws. Citing sociologist Lester Ward, she contrasted his judgement of male superiority as 'pretentious, meretricious, quixotic', with gynarchic communities where women were naturally democratic, socialistic and communistic because of family life. Man, the son, the 'World Fabricator', could not point to a single field where he laboured independently with success. 'Civilisation along exclusively male lines does not tend to make man more human: on the contrary, it fosters his animal passions and vices ...'[32] Women, armed with the latest biological and mental sciences, must reassert themselves through Divine Motherhood. *Cosmic Procession* ends with an object lesson in the evolution of the race, a tour of national galleries and the British Museum where the increasing femininity of the male type is observed, and the ideal androgyny of the ancients. The last words are resounding and apocalyptic:

As through the woman the Divine Man was born, so through the man shall the Divine Woman be born, both owing their origin to the sacrifice of the self ... The one is by the surrender of the body, the other by the surrender of the will. The one is through the redemption of body and soul; the other is through the unity of soul and body.

When this supreme truth is fully recognised ... then ... the Woman-question will be solved ... At present she is the Sphinx of Humanity – the inexplicable Riddle of the World.

Yet She comes – the transcendental One, joint offspring of earth and heaven, of the human and the divine. Before Her the shadows flee, and the twilight of the gods breaks into the perfect day. For in her is manifested the Oneness of the Cosmos; through her is revealed the supremacy of the Divine Feminine – the Living Spirit of God; with Her are ended the birth-pang of the ages, and the former things have passed away.

Obviously Swiney struck far into territory only hinted at by Madame Blavatsky. Despard, whose terrain included Besant's old socialist stamping grounds, used theosophy to rally women from established positions.

Charlotte Despard (1844–1939), a wealthy widow and sister of the famous soldier Sir John French, was one of the most remarkable women of her day, greatly loved and quite unmanageable: socialist, feminist, democrat, Sinn Feiner, theosophist, ultimately a communist. In 1909 she heard Annie Besant in London urge the world to prepare for 'the coming of a new world in which truth and righteousness and justice shall be the moving forces', sentiments with which the radical mystical Despard agreed wholeheartedly. She found in theosophy principles which satisfied her for the rest of her life, probably a means of unifying the conflicting pressures of the many causes she espoused. (Her biographer, Andro Linklater, speaks of 'a thin missionary frost' settling over her mind thereafter, but also confirms her everlasting optimism and activism).[33] Soon her feminist work showed theosophic influence. In 1911 came a pamphlet, *Women and the New Era*, about the direction of a new unrest: 'the woman-force, the labour-force, the child-force. These,' she said, 'are building up energy, breaking down prejudice, so that presently the Truth, for which the world is waiting, may stand revealed.'[34] Like Annie Besant she recognised the crisis of liberalism, though she foresaw a socialist future, where Annie had in mind something altogether more hierarchical. In 1913 she published *Theosophy and the Woman's Movement*.

The reason why the woman's movement was the only truly vital movement in the world today, Despard began, was that it mobilised qualities scarcely recognisable in the modern male: ardour, service, self-sacrifice. The women's movement sprang from a spiritual awakening. It was 'a great international ever-widening-out drama of woman's newly evolved consciousness'.[35]

The force behind the woman's movement, she claimed, was theosophic. Theosophy led out of the man-worshipping religions of the nineteenth century towards liberty, independence and new resources: 'the revolt; the discovery; the momentary rending of the veil ... a new outpouring of the divine ancient wisdom.' Both movements rebelled against the harsh and unnatural relationships of the twentieth century, and a world built on 'grasping principle'. Both demanded a return to first principles, 'Brotherhood without distinctions'. Both were in the direct line of evolution. Indeed – and this was the gist of the book – the women's movement was but a theosophic vanguard. Astonishingly, Despard went on to reveal herself as a follower of the Order of the Star in the East, the order founded by leading theosophists in 1911 to prepare for the coming of a World Teacher; the whole trend was but preparation for 'the one far-off divine event to which the whole creation moves'.

Seen thus, the woman's movement was very far from selfish or sectional, being in the van of spiritual evolution. Standing on the divine wisdom which taught that 'in spiritual qualities there is no sex,' women, mothers and workers, were elevated by the struggle against a male-dominated society. Women had been deprived of liberty longest, since the Middle Ages, and peculiarly hurt by the clash of material and spiritual values in the nineteenth century; they now faced baffling conditions at home after a century of industrialisation, and had special need as wives and mothers of a new order. 'They seek such recognition,' went the Foreword, 'as shall establish their right to true effective motherhood of nations and races.' In Despard's view, the requisite readjustment of human relationships was first of all moral: equality between the sexes, 'unity in diversity'. The second involved the state: higher ideals against male expediency, and an end to the fact that sex and class 'have sat in the seats of the mighty', thwarting labour representation and generating such contemporary evils as the armaments race, monopolies, infant mortality, physical deterioration of workers, and the high cost of provisions. 'Readjustment', 'Preparation', 'First Principles', 'The Vision' are the titles of the last chapters of *Theosophy and the Woman's Movement*. The vision is not entirely optimistic, but it envisages and carries through Armageddon, with women in spiritual and social evolution: 'There can be no doubt that woman, with her intuition, her love-instinct and her life-force, will play a large part in the reconstruction of society, which will inevitably follow the era of destruction that seems to lie in front of us.'[36]

Today Despard's talk of vanguards and the female life-force sounds archaic, if not absurd, as does Cosmic Motherhood in Swiney. Nevertheless, theosophic feminists recognised the vital moment in history and, with the aid of ancient precedent and modern theory, they hoped to seize it. They meant to snatch the evolutionary lead. Like Alfred Russel Wallace, the maverick naturalist who discovered the principle of natural selection simultaneously with Charles Darwin, and later astounded the scientific community by espousing spiritualism and socialism,[37] they argued that the advancement of women was the key to the continued evolution of humanity, the alternative to decay and destruction. Only Woman had the spiritual resource to carry it through. From Divine Motherhood and the 'creative feminine' they envisaged a new ethic along theosophical lines. Their basic position has been restated many times since, though the original ground can never be recovered because the Great War demolished the optimistic social theory which fired the theosophic feminists – who were also, it is clear in retrospect, trapped by that evolutionary theory, and by an incomplete biology.

Meanwhile the women's movement and theosophy advanced simultaneously, and in England shared some common ground. Both movements sensed 'the prophetic moment'. On the one side, the women's movement was as much a crusade as a political campaign, reliant on underused intellectual abilities and pent-up psychic energy of the kind that attracted women to radical religion. On the other, a quasi-religious movement founded by one woman and led by another was bound to flourish in the suffragette years, when militancy both raised and divided women's consciousness. Of course, theosophic feminism was as marginal politically as it was intellectually precarious. But its boldest exemplars and advocates had a responsive audience when they argued that theosophy gave Woman a more exalted role than ever before.

The argument reached the edge of empire. However its dynamic was obscured in Australia by the earlier success of the woman suffrage movement; the vote was achieved everywhere by 1908. Radical women like Louisa Lawson were attracted to the theosophical orbit in the 1890s, when the woman's movement also began, but it was not until later, in the early years of the twentieth century and Annie Besant's presidency, that the appeal of theosophy to some women became obvious. The feminisation of Australian theosophy dates from Besant's 1908 lecture tour, when the *Bulletin*, eagle-eyed and misogynist as ever, had noticed that more, and more respectable, women turned out to hear her.[38]

The president undoubtedly struck a chord in women. In a society where the position of women was widely regarded as advanced (except in Victoria where opposition delayed enfranchisement until 1908), and an optimistic evolutionism swayed men and women alike, it was possible to see her as a role model. Male reporters preferred to think of her as 'a woman of the truest type', leaving the paradox of a good woman who purveyed outlandish ideas up in the air; but most women journalists took her seriously, and many more women revered the name of Annie Besant. Her fight for birth control in the 1870s and its terrible personal aftermath (she lost her two children), her success in organising the Bryant & May match-girls in 1888, and her battle with the London School Board to provide school meals for poor children, had made Annie Besant a heroine. H.F. Powell, writing from Brisbane Trades Hall in 1908, saw her as a queen among women, 'a sample of what we women shall be as soon as the conditions are ripe':

> Strong yet beautiful, forceful yet gentle, intellectual yet teeming with sweet womanliness, united by affinity with all the forces of Nature, pulsating with infinite sympathies, a woman, a citizen, a soul with destiny inseparable from the great heart of the universe.[39]

If the feminisation of Australian theosophy dates from Besant's tour in 1908, so too does the expansion of space for women within it. Besant proposed to mobilise women into several new auxiliary or 'forward' movements. Since these initiatives coincided with efforts by newly enfranchised women to establish themselves politically, theosophic feminism found its outlet, notably in Western Australia. By 1914 theosophy provided one of the platforms from which Australian women sought to work publicly. The story of the rise of theosophy in Australia may be correlated with shifts in the status of women.

Theosophical men, who did most of the talking in the early days, were well aware of the appeal of theosophy to women. For a movement which aimed to modernise religion, the presence of women, and the prominence of some women – a preponderance was yet to come – was a good thing, reassurance that the movement was, as it claimed to be, on the forefront of modern thought. It could be argued that movements like theosophy, which endorsed feminist principle, benefited particularly in frontier cultures where opportunities for equal relations between the sexes were limited outside the best circles, and masculinist codes oppressed thoughtful men (though it was hard to break with conventional wisdom, expressed par excellence by the *Bulletin* when it said, of Besant no less, that 'the intellectual belief of a good woman is of comparatively slight importance').

Thus W.T. Willans, editor of *Upadhi*, the first theosophical journal in Australia, celebrated equality of the sexes in theosophy, writing in 1893 that 'union of male and female – and the ultimate union of masculine and feminine – is that towards which all nature tends'. More soberly, Adelaide accountant Knox said equality was something in theosophy's favour. A decade on, the general secretary of the Australian section, W.G. John, noting that 'ours has often been spoken of as a woman's movement', thought it mainly due to the prominence of Blavatsky and Besant, adding that there were responsible places for women in all the branches. 'Variety in Branch Activity,' it was urged, should include regular ladies' meetings, because the TS 'is essentially a woman's movement'. Robert Wishart of Brisbane agreed, because by 1905 the women's group in Brisbane was so big.[40]

Secretary John rather overstated it when he said that there were responsible jobs for women in all the branches. For a movement which espoused sexual equality, the record of the Theosophical Society in Australia was not remarkable. Women could and did hold executive positions, but not commensurate with men. From 1891 to 1925, after the great split which signalled the decline of Australian theosophy, women constituted at most a third of known office-bearers, that is, 32 percent of presidents and secretaries (see Appendix, Table 2). They were, inevitably, more often secretaries than presidents. In the former, more arduous role, women theosophists achieved near parity with males, but far fewer became lodge presidents.

There were fewest women in executive positions in New South Wales, the site of sectional headquarters, a picture modified only after the terrible split when Adyar intervened in 1924 to put Armidale-born expatriate loyalist Mrs Josephine Ransom in charge of the section. Women did best in South and Western Australia: wherever resources were slim there were women in office. Moreover, equality of opportunity diminished over time. In the very first decade women presidents were less uncommon than became the case later. Between 1891 and 1901 there were five women presidents, notably Mrs D. Parker of Ibis lodge, Toorak, and Mrs Henrietta Patterson of Fremantle. Women sometimes launched lodges of their own, like Mrs Steel's Egyptian lodge in East Sydney (which did not last, however). But then between 1901 and 1916 there was only one female president in all Australian theosophy, Miss Noble in Launceston.

Leadership opportunities for women in theosophy increased during and immediately after the Great War. In Queensland Miss Marcella Clarke emerged from the book depot, and then Mrs Mason Beatty, as presidents, and in Western Australia presidents included Miss Charlotte Priest, Mrs Cooke, Mrs Young and, in 1924, Mrs Stanway Tapp. In the scatter of suburban lodges which sprang up in the second decade of the twentieth century and lasted into the twenties, women also took the lead, as at Glenelg (SA), Chatswood (NSW) and Latrobe (Tas.). All these points were neatly encapsulated in the person of Miss Nina Spasshatt, a doctor's daughter who was president of Armidale lodge from 1916 after Lieutenant Colonel G.F. Braund was killed at Gallipoli.[41]

The number of women at conventions before the war gives another measure of the importance of women in the society's counsels. The Convention itself scarcely functioned on a national basis until the early twentieth century, but then grew quickly from thirteen delegates in 1900 to a maximum of fifty-one in 1912. The number of women delegates grew even faster, from one in 1900 to seventeen in 1912. After 1913, as sixteen of forty-one delegates, women constituted more than a third, and in 1914, at the onset of war, nearly half the assembly. At Convention the women were also more likely to come from the periphery than the centre of theosophical life, Brisbane and Adelaide delegations especially being dominated by women. (Usually Perth was too far away to be represented except by proxy.) Miss Worth and Miss Mildren of Brisbane were elected to the executive council in the years up to 1906, but after that the council, consisting of staff, presidents *ex officio*, and a variable number of elected members, appears to have been composed entirely of male theosophists. W.G. John said in 1909 with satisfaction that the executive council was 'a capital body of capable businessmen'. Perhaps the portrait of the president which hung in every lodge with a building to hang it in sufficed to reassure women with worldly aspirations. Or perhaps the wide-eyed gaze of Madame Blavatsky from so many frontispieces in theosophical publications transfixed women readers in positions of deference.[42]

An increased female presence in theosophy is best shown by recruitment figures, available from 1899. In that year women joined the TS in about equal numbers with men, a considerable advance on the earliest days when Mrs Margaret Woolley of Sydney was the only female fellow. A decade later more women than men took out diplomas (seventy-six of 140; see Table 2, Appendix). That was in the wake of Besant's second tour. The trend continued, and the appeal of theosophy to women as compared to men strengthened during and after the Great War. (Nevertheless, the disproportion of women to men in theosophy was nowhere near as pronounced as in the comparable and contemporaneous Christian Science movement, which on 1933 census figures greatly surpassed theosophy in its appeal to women in early-twentieth-century Australia: in 1933, 5562 of Christian Science's 8878 adherents were women. One of them was that foremost feminist Vida Goldstein and another Ina Higgins, sister of Arbitration Court judge H.B. Higgins.) [43]

It has been estimated from Victorian census evidence in 1911 that theosophical women were the best-educated women of all religious groupings in Australia at that time, and better educated than theosophical men. The ratio of graduates to non-graduates among theosophical men stood at 1:8, second only to professed atheists, but the women's ration was 1:7.[44] Even so, a lot of the work available to women in the Theosophical Society was little different from that done in the wider society. For instance, lodge-building demanded work from willing hands, especially if done along the comprehensive lines recommended by Mrs Cooper-Oakley during her proselytising tour of 1893; or, as theosophists preferred to put it, gave opportunities for active service. Women often contributed to the lodge syllabus by running weekly study classes at both beginner and advanced levels. When theosophical Sunday schools (lotus circles) were established, they were usually run by women. The larger lodges set up lending libraries and book depots, also usually run by women; and women kept the lodges open for enquiries throughout the year, as well as keeping them clean and decorated. (Sydney, the largest lodge, did employ a caretaker ultimately.) Moreover, in maintaining the philanthropic face of theosophy, women did all the work; it was the women who met on Thursday afternoons to sew for the poor of Sydney and listen to readings from *The Secret Doctrine*. It was only right, in view of these customary house-keeping duties, that women should be noticed in 1903 as 'having attended for work in various ways at the principal branches' throughout the year.[45]

But women did not attend the court of the faerie queene to be drudges. The real attraction was Divine Wisdom and intellectual participation, even if 'women's work' often diverted intellectual energies. Women were more engaged than the records suggest, and theosophy attracted capable women from the beginning, evidenced by the very first fellows, Mrs Woolley, perhaps Mrs John Smith; recruits of the late 1880s, Isabelle Edelfelt and Mrs Pickett; and then in the 1890s Mrs Wolstenholme and sympathisers like Mrs Charles Bright. As President Olcott reported, *theosophia* appealed to ladies as well as gentlemen. In the small branches of early theosophy from which the original Australasian section was formed, women were much in evidence, like Mrs Willans, with her husband an active Lemurian. In the many attempts to consolidate the Brisbane branch, the names of Mrs Mary Given, Mrs Mallison and Mrs Robert Taylor recurred. When lodges were formed in Western Australia at the turn of the century, Mrs Patterson took a leading role, and later Mrs Adair. Where the early branches operated as study groups, as in Melbourne, women seemed to participate in equal numbers; participation by women in lodge debate was noted hopefully. When theosophy went on the offensive, as in Sydney, women sometimes lectured.

The door was open, and some women seized the chance to address the public in papers, lectures, and contributions to the section's journal. The evidence is scattered and disappointingly thin for the early years, but bolder women of the 1890s did speak up, after Mrs Wolstenholme's 'Theosophy and everyday life': in Sydney Miss Hooper, BA ('The true educator a theosophist') and in Melbourne Miss Birnie – maybe the daughter of litterateur James Birnie – on reincarnation, and Mrs Crozier ('The new woman'); also Miss

E.T. Mackenzie, BA, later wife of geologist James Stirling ('Women' and 'Agnosticism and theosophy'). When Sister Susman read a paper to the Monday public meeting of Hobart TS in September 1897, it was noted that this was the first occasion on which a paper had been delivered by a lady member and hope was expressed that others would follow. Subsequently women paper-givers seem to have preferred safe topics, as for instance Mrs Petley on 'Jesus of Nazareth' and Mrs Lithgow's 'Notes, thoughts and comments on love', both delivered to Launceston lodge in 1901. Yet, that energetic lotus circle teacher of Adelaide, Miss Haycraft, BSc, FTS, addressed 'Theosophy and modern science' in 1907, as she was well equipped to do.[46]

Being allowed to give lectures certainly was a gain for women, the theosophical equivalent of a clerical role. In that theosophy stood well ahead of all but the Unitarian Church in Australia; and some local women did emulate Annie Besant, Mrs Cooper-Oakley and the Countess Wachtmeister. By 1893 Margaret Lilian Florence Edger, MA (1862–19??) from Auckland was beginning to make her name on the platform. Said to have been one of the first women graduates in the British Empire, Edger established a girls' secondary school in Auckland where she joined the TS in 1891. In the early 1890s she gave up the school and became a full-time theosophical lecturer; at Olcott's urging she joined him lecturing in Queensland in 1897, and was then appointed federal lecturer at £.80 p.a. Just before World War I, two other New Zealand women, Kate Browning, MA and Helen Horne, travelled the Australian circuit.[47] Later came Mrs Leonard of Chatswood, and from Brisbane Marcella Clarke; also Miss Nevill (1908–1911, mentioned as lecturing in Perth), and Mrs Josephine Ransom in 1912. A sample of lodge lecturers in July 1908, during Besant's tour, and therefore perhaps an atypical month, shows women giving about half the lectures – though only one-third in Brisbane, where Mrs Robson spoke on 'Theosophy the Basis of all Religions'.[48]

Ambitious girls went to India, like Edger in 1905. Either they went to Adyar for unspecified training, as did two Perth women, Miss Florence Fuller and Miss A.T. Dixon, or like their Christian sisters engaged in the theosophical version of missionary work, which usually meant teaching in theosophical schools where, of course, the opposite of Christian missionising was meant to occur. The first and least fortunate recruit was Miss Pickett of Melbourne, who, it may be remembered, drowned in a well shortly after taking up her

Lilian Edger, MA, federal lecturer, c. 1897
(*Theosophy in New Zealand*, April–June 1946)

post in Ceylon. To the Musaeus Buddhist schools in Ceylon supported by Wilton Hack went Miss A.J. Davies of Brisbane to join her sister. Perhaps these were the Misses Davies of Armidale reported in 1901 as nobly giving their lives to the faith. In 1905 Miss Leonora Gmeiner of Adelaide, who spent time in the Perth Theosophical Society at the turn of the century, left 'to serve India's daughters' as head of a Delhi girls' primary school for twenty years. Lilian Edger, who developed a disagreeable independence of Adyar orthodoxy in India, was principal of the Central Hindu Girls' School at Benares, 1913–1919, the college where Kate Browning also taught briefly, and Annie Besant's ideas on the proper education of Indian girls were put into effect. It is interesting to think of these women alongside the many Christian women who devoted themselves to mission work in India, for example David Rivett's sister Eleanor, principal of the Women's Christian College at Madras.[49]

The early women theosophists in Australia appear to have published little. Only two women published signed articles in the *Austral Theosophist* (1894–1895) – Edger and Emma Richmond. Edger was in fact chief female beneficiary of theosophy's faith in the written word and its propensity to publish everything, as in her early lecture delivered in Auckland Town Hall in March 1893 (said to be the first published lecture by a local woman), *Religion and Theosophy*. Her contribution to the *Austral Theosophist* was significantly on the great need for brotherhood – 'we are all rays of the One Universal Spirit ' – and it recommended Olive Schreiner's allegory of 'The Ruined Chapel' from *Dreams* (1891).[50] For some reason New Zealand (1903) women benefited most from theosophical publishing, Edger's *Elements of Theosophy* and Catherine Wallace Christie's *Theosophy for Beginners and for the Use of Lotus Circles* (5th edn, 1928) being two examples. An Australian beneficiary was Josephine Maria Ransom.

Mrs Josephine Ransom, possibly one of the Misses Davies just mentioned, the general secretary of the Australian section after 1924, and later quasi-official historian of the Theosophical Society, found an outlet for literary-cum-historical writing via theosophy. In 1904 she went to Benares to join Besant, and encouraged by her, wrote tales with a feminist flavour like *Indian Tales of Love and Beauty* (Adyar, 1912), and *Irish Tales of Love and Beauty* (London, n.d.). Besant, contributing a preface to *Irish Tales*, wrote that no land had produced stronger women than India, 'and to tell of the women of the past is to inspire the women of the present, and to shape the women of the future'. Ransom wrote more romantically,

> I love the great women of all nations. Those of Ireland and India have a special appeal ... The women of both these countries are austere at heart, proud because self-respecting, loved of their men because they know how to serve them yet rule them – and that in cabin or palace (*Irish Tales*, vii).)

Of literary aspirations among theosophical women there were few traces, though *Theosophy in Australasia* did publish poetry. Theosophists of the early generation were not literary people – in the 1930s the older generation still deplored literary material in lectures so the absence is not so surprising. It is a bonus to have found in the catalogue of the Adyar Library at Madras two books by women writers: R. Wilshire *From Cronulla (Poems on Occult Subjects)* published in Sydney in 1911 and inscribed 'To Annie Besant from the author with love and gratitude', and (undated) *Life's Wallaby. Short Stories about Australia, Occult and Descriptive*, published at Norwood, South Australia (the author is entered as ' "Sydney Partridge" [Kate M.P. Stone]').[51]

Since early theosophy took an austere if not unsympathetic attitude to other cultural forms, like art and music, evidence of women's contributions is sparse in those areas. However, theosophical cultural ambitions which became important in the 1920s, not least through the efforts of women, date back to the Edwardian years and to Besant's attempts to ally theosophy with 'forward' movements in culture:

> Theosophy gives back to the artist a world that for a long time he has lost ... new subjects ... new secrets ... in the allied art of sound music, the future lies along the line of Theosophic thought and ideals [as with] that great master of mystic music Wagner ... [and] there is an artistic ideal in life other than the ideal of modern civilisation ... I look to The Theosophical Society ... with its ideal of art in life to change that in the civilisation of Europe which is growing merely rich and ostentatious, instead of beautiful and refined.[52]

Besant urged theosophists to take an interest in the arts (see ch. 8) and there were women artists in theosophy in Australia before 1914, like the previously mentioned Florence Fuller of Perth, whose work so impressed Besant that she persuaded Fuller to shift to Adyar; also Madame Mouchette and Mademoiselle Lion in Adelaide. (An impressive portrait of Annie Besant painted by Berthe Mouchette in 1908 hangs in the rooms of the Adelaide Theosophical Society.) The pleasures of the piano and the song cycle crept over the Theosophical Society in the Edwardian period and music seems to have been the raison d'etre of Eastern Hill lodge Melbourne (1906–1910), where Mr Armes Beaumont and Miss Sinnotte sang. Sydney's new Gnosis lodge, presided over by Miss E.B. Sheridan Moore, the local litterateur's daughter, heard papers on Wagner and Colour-Music; as mentioned earlier, Gnosis lodge ran a Pythagorean Music Society and a Ruskinian art circle.[53]

Published sources reveal very little about women's hopes of theosophy. No significant collection of personal papers detailing intellectual and spiritual development over the early period appears to have survived, nor even materials of a more public kind such as lecture sets or class notes. Despite new emphasis on the arts, no literary records comparable with Rosamund Lehmann's personal testament to faith in the afterlife published as *The Swan in the Evening* in 1967 seem to have emerged. It is therefore very difficult to penetrate the specific and individual responses of women theosophists, though there are echoes of Edwardian impasse in Lehmann's testament. She struggled to accommodate grief at the unexpected death of her daughter Sally, rejecting conventional dogma and practice on the one hand and comfortless materialism on the other. Doubtless more women than now would have endorsed her trek beyond belief to the assurance of the soul's survival of death – 'we are souls travelling through eternity' – and recognised the literature of psychic research which she has studied. Certainly there were many late Victorians similarly trapped between the will and the incapacity to believe, unable to 'sit safe in the bosom of Mother Church' and resentful that the churches asked both too much and too little of them, though the women among them are but rarely glimpsed.

One such glimpse is available, by implication, in correspondence between Susannah Blackmore of Hobart and the controversial New Zealand lecturer and palmistry enthusiast Mark Hawthorne in May 1910. Only Hawthorne's reply survives, but it says something of the problem posed by Blackmore. He assured her that theosophy was progressive, uplifting, and altruistic, a support for the truly religious: 'There are many things – the old ideas of Heaven and Hell, which you mention for instance, which need a larger conception.'[54] Native-born, Anglican, a Labor activist shortly to marry Tasmania's first Labor premier John Earle, Susie Blackmore joined the TS in September 1908. Her sister and her husband also became theosophists.

Likewise the gnostic or mystic element evident in Lehmann's testimony attracted some women, such as Devon-born Phyllis Campbell, the daughter of a Calcutta High Court judge, who came to Sydney with her sister Evelyn Caspersz in 1920 to marry engineer Elliston Campbell, a man active in the affairs of Blavatsky lodge in the twenties. Campbell, who was uninterested in the 'scientific' occultism of Leadbeater, and became a Roman Catholic in the 1930s (returning to theosophy in the last years of her life), presents a quite different thread of theosophic aspiration to those 'mad old women in white dresses and coloured scarves' recalled by Helen Heney as frequenting theosophical congregations in the twenties; and is a reminder of the eclecticism of theosophy. Her progression suggests that the appeal of theosophy to women was no more, and was perhaps less, reducible to the level of marvels than its appeal for men. The dimensions of Phyllis Campbell's commitment may be clearer if more of her mystical poetry, carefully preserved by her husband at Faulconbridge in the Blue Mountains, is published.[55]

Perhaps the difficulty of assessing the scope of women's commitment to theosophy is not simply the absence of records. A clue is offered by the remark attributed to G.K. Chesterton that the appeal of theosophy rested in 'the ordeal of the free man' – and woman. The remark is cited in the story of Ethel Rhoda McNeile, a well-educated north Englishwoman with an evangelical Anglican background whose experience of religious conflict was temporarily assuaged by Annie Besant and enthusiastic espousal of theosophy, which she lived to regret and publicly oppose as intellectual tyranny. Her story, with its return to Christian vocation, as recounted in *From Theosophy to Christian Faith* (London and New York, 1919) is not strictly speaking relevant to Australian theosophy, but it does suggest two further points, namely that theosophy appeared to offer an authoritative reconciliation of conflict, but that for many it was not a permanent solution. McNeile's experience at once increases and confirms the elusive character of commitment.

The extent to which theosophy comforted women in daily life is similarly elusive. There is one pamphlet on *Theosophy and Home Life* preserved in the theosophy pamphlet collection in the State Library of Victoria which rather laments this point, and offers a theosophical version of 'the angel in the house'. In a brief reflection 'Why I am a theosophist' printed in *The Australian Theosophist* in July 1933, Winifred Armstrong, a woman with three children living 'in the backblocks' when she first learned of theosophy from her dentist, stated that 'years of trial, poverty and disappointment would have been almost unbearable' without knowledge of karma and reincarnation, 'the only possible solution to the many apparent injustices and inequalities of life'; and she testified to hope for the future of civilisation, 'under the guidance of the Great Ones'. Gwen Noble of Sydney, who helped type this manuscript, recalls her mother, of Anglican background and artistic temperament, the wife of a stock-and-station agent in the Riverina, purchasing theosophical literature, and regularly reading *The Light of Asia*, which she kept by the bedside. She had a picture of Krishnamurti on the wall near her dressing-table. Although she conformed to a conventional view of woman's role, she preferred poetry to housework; and, being uninterested in the endless round of local tea-parties and entertaining, was something of an outcast in the social life of a country town. This sort of evidence may suggest to the modern reader that theosophical women valued the option of personal autonomy as much as its reality.

One of the most revealing statements on this broader ideological subject made in Australia came from a man. W.G. John, writing in *Theosophy in Australasia* in February 1906 on 'National Ideals and Destiny', allocated to woman a central place in the purification of English idealism (which he compared unfavourably with Indian traditions). In a greedy and careless world of plutocrats and weakening chivalry, the question – 'whether our national ideals are still high enough to preserve us in the forefront ... or whether we are so deteriorated by neglect of our backward classes as to have debased beyond hope our national ideals' – made the contribution of women very important, since it was among women that 'the richest power of sacrifice' lay. On the one hand John stressed that interference with sex-roles endangered evolutionary mechanisms, especially reincarnation; and on the other, that not every woman would need to be confined to a 'household career'. Evolution and Eastern knowledge would ensure selection of really able women such as Annie Besant for the rejuvenation of national ideals.

> Womanhood in all countries must ever hold a great place in the formation of a nation's ideals. Of course, a student of Theosophy soon gets to see that in questions of real life the Ego has no sex. Reincarnation very early shows to us that sex is merely a division for marking off certain qualities which are specially to be wrought into the individual soul. To so arrange the social, commercial, or domestic life of a nation as to unsex the personality is, therefore, to defeat the distinct purpose of an incarnation; to obstruct the development of faculty in the great life of the soul ... But there is no wish to limit woman's sphere. Every woman need not become a mother or confine herself to the household career laid down for her in Xenophon's *Republic* ...

John argued that the great advantage of Eastern knowledge was that it improved knowledge of character and helped identify great women, thus saving the waste of putting advanced women to commonplace work.

It must be admitted that knowledge is hard come by otherwise. Theosophical women in Australia kept a relatively low profile, and even for the emboldened and articulate few basic biographical information is at best patchy. Diana Burfield's case studies of theosophy and feminism in Britain in the 1880s provide a reference point for such biographical evidence as remains. Her findings that many theosophical women came from mixed religious backgrounds strongly flavoured by evangelicalism, and most passed through periods of agnosticism before arriving at theosophy via spiritualism, rings true of the women fellows in Australia. Equally relevant is the finding that these included intellectually gifted women who successfully pursued careers despite various educational and familial disruptions, even though their formal education was frequently incomplete (no bad thing, says Burfield, considering the brutalising and narrow schooling available to boys then). And, like their British counterparts, they do not seem to have been by any means deeply committed to traditional female roles: the proportion of unmarried and childless women overall appears to have been quite high (though this may be attributable in part to the impact of the Great War).[56]

Compared with the aristocratic background of many theosophical women in Britain, Australian theosophical women seem to have come overwhelmingly from the middle class, their fathers and husbands being engineers, chemists, teachers, public servants, accountants, solicitors and clerks. The Theosophical Society did attract a minority from the Australian elite of pastoral and mercantile capital, and from the fringes of governing circles, but these do not seem to have thrown up many active theosophical wives and daughters – Perth journalist Muriel Chase, from one of the old families, is an obvious exception. Nor is there much evidence of generous bequests from such sources until much later, after World War II – though if financial records were accessible they would undoubtedly reveal women's munificence, the decline of which is much regretted by officers of the society today. For example in 1925 Mrs Mary Margaret Wienholt FTS of Brisbane transferred the historic 'Hanworth' ('The Hospice'), a home for elderly gentlewomen which she founded in 1913, to the TS, which manages it today in accordance with the bequest. The likes of Mrs Edith Douglas-Hamilton were scarcely to be expected in the early days of Australian theosophy. (Mrs Douglas-Hamilton, heir to the Wills tobacco fortune in Bristol, left large sums to theosophy, though the amounts were small in comparison with her estate of £1.7 million.)[57]

What the fragmentary evidence does suggest is that Australian theosophy contained, in about equal proportions, women of independent means, wives and daughters of prosperous citizens, and professional women: teachers including kindergarten teachers, journalists and artists, even, in Hobart, a sub-matron at the gaol. Some were active in philanthropy, a few in politics, like Susie Blackmore, later Earle, and Amelia Lambrick

Bessie Rischbieth, JP, theosophic feminist, Perth.
(Battye Library Pictorial Collection, 2452P)

of Melbourne, one of the defenders of sex-reformer Chidley in 1916, otherwise known to theosophists as a worker for the cause at Ballarat. It is noticeable too that whereas many women both in Britain and Australia came to theosophy in mid-life, some of the daughters of the first Australian theosophists maintained a prior family commitment, notably in Adelaide, in the cases of Miss Haycraft, Miss Connie Radcliffe and maybe Bessie Earle (later Rischbieth), reared in the household of prominent Adelaide theosophist W.B. Rounsevell.[58]

A final sociological point can be made. It is often said the theosophists were itinerants, and it is true especially in the 1920s that many colourful birds of passage swelled the ranks. However, before World War I, and among women, there seems to have been a balance between first-generation native-born and immigrants. In that (as well as in class position), they were unrepresentative of the Australian population, but at the same time evidence of a customary cultural dynamic during the long period of dependence, that is, interaction between immigrant and native-born.

Evidence of the character and capacities of theosophical women does improve across the Edwardian years. The increasing number of women who joined the society after Besant's tour created a higher profile for women in theosophy; and Besant moved quickly to capitalise on under-used female skills when she launched several affiliated 'forward' movements. The two most important initiatives were Co-Freemasonry and the Theosophical Order of Service.

Co-Freemasonry (or co-masonry, as the theosophists usually called it) began in France in the 1880s. In 1882 a free-floating masonic lodge of 'L'Ordre Maconnerie Mixte International, Le Droit Humain' initiated a woman, and she in turn initiated other women. The cause was taken up by French feminists, and in 1893 an organisation called co-masonic open to both sexes was formed, La Grand Loge Symbolique Ecossaise de France, Le Droit Humain (Human Duty). Some theosophical women in England joined the new co-masonic order, Miss Francesca Arundale being the first to do so. Besant joined in 1902 and rose to become a vice-president and Grand Commander of the order's British jurisdiction. Partly, it appealed to her increasing love of ritual.[59]

Madame Blavatsky in *Isis Unveiled* had denounced modern freemasonry as degenerate:

> We say nought against Masonry as it should be, but denounce it as, thanks to the intriguing clergy both Catholic and Protestant, it now begins to be. Professedly the most absolute of democracies, it is practically the appanage of aristocracy, wealth and personal ambition. Professedly the teacher of true ethics; it is debased into a propaganda of anthropomorphic theology ... the time has come to remodel Masonry.[60]

Masonry remodelled to admit women 'on exactly equal basis with men' and to restore ancient ritual was, however, deemed consonant with modern theosophy; and Besant seized the chance to promote both causes. She claimed that the French move was legitimised by ancient Scottish rites, and that it would prepare the world for the new dispensation, the coming race, and the new ideals needed for the new order; 'Wisdom as authority shall wed with Liberty'. Soon there were hundreds of co-masonic lodges around the world, attracting people who agreed with Besant that a masonic movement open to both sexes 'could be made a powerful force for good in the world'.

Subsequently male theosophists would stress the benefits of co-masonry for women. It represented, said C. Jinarajadasa (a frequent theosophical visitor to Australia who had been recruited as a boy in Ceylon by Leadbeater and later became president of the Theosophical Society), 'a break in the ramparts erected by the male against the realisation of many noble dreams of humanity': in young countries women were needed in public life, and co-masonry prepared the way. The first co-masonic lodges in Australia were established in Melbourne in 1911 and Sydney in 1912.[61]

Written record of Australian co-masonry is not available, and its significance must be deduced from the cautious and respectful testimony of women close to active women co-masons, like Irene Greenwood, OA, the Perth feminist whose mother Mary Driver was a co-mason; and from occasional references, in for example letters written by Calcutta-born journalist Evelyn Caspersz, resident at the theosophical commune 'The Manor' in Sydney in the interwar years, to Bessie Rischbieth.[62] Rischbieth and other women like Isabella Johnston were active co-masons, and rose to the highest degree. Several prominent feminists also joined, notably Ruby Rich, and actress Enid Lorimer. A Sydney woman who was a co-mason in the interwar years recalls that women enjoyed belonging to a non-exclusive order and reacted to its rituals the more profoundly, while also brightening meetings in their white robes. She thought it a valuable corrective to sexism in male masonry and stressed ceremonial uplift:

> It evoked certain parts of oneself, shall we say, and its processes were largely masonic I believe, though I've never been in a closed order ... you did the same marching, the same bowing, the same uttering as presumably goes on. I'm sure a lot of us just loved the ceremonies we were given.[63]

In this recollection the movement is said to have been based on Egyptian understandings of the great Architect of the Universe, which accords with a surviving list of Sydney lodges in the late 1930s (which list also shows that co-masonry in Sydney was run by theosophical women at that time: of six lodges there were five on the North Shore, administered by Miss V.K Maddox from the Manor). The list conveys the flavour of co-masonry, naming Miss Muncaster as contact for Lodge Osiris Ra, Chatswood, Mrs Stella George for Pythagoras lodge, Clifton Gardens, and Mr George Gillot of Turramurra at Rameses lodge.[64]

The extent to which women of ceremonial temperament followed Besant's example cannot be determined, nor the effect of participation on them. Most of the members never spoke about their experiences, according to Greenwood, though Anne Ridgway of Perth has recently done so in a down-to-earth manner:

> It was exactly like the man's Freemasons with special clues and there were two lodges in Perth, one of which was St. Cuthbert's. I belonged to the second one, I've forgotten its name. Men could go too if they were Freemasons and their wives were members.[65]

Probably most women who became co-masons were already theosophists, and relished ritual otherwise allowed no expression along the theosophical path.

In 1908 Annie Besant launched an order of a different character, the Theosophical Order of Service (TOS). This order was a westernised version of the Hindu tradition of *sannyasi* in which mature adults renounce personal ambition to labour for the spiritual elevation of humanity. Its aims were as follows:

1. minimise the sum of misery in the world;
2. forget self in working for others;
3. eliminate selfishness and substitute love as world rule;
4. live to the highest that is in us.

Today's formulation of the aims of the Theosophical Order of Service reads just as closely to dominant idealisms:

> The ideal of Service is based on the condition that the world problems of human relationships and organisations cannot be solved without recognition that the Brotherhood of nature is a fact of humanity and cannot be contravened anywhere without imperilling the whole social structure.[66]

In 1908 the Order of Service aimed at practical humanitarianism.

For similar reasons to those underpinning the appeal of co-masonry to theosophical women, the order became, in effect, a woman's order. At least that is what the early Australian evidence suggests. Orders of service were set up immediately in Australia. The first, in Adelaide in 1908, reported addresses given at the TOS on penal reform and the abolition of capital punishment (in fact a society for its abolition). Adelaide members were told that the local gaol was in urgent need of support; and many activities suggested themselves. In Sydney in 1909 the order had twenty-five members. Its work was reported to range from a League of Mercy for Hospital Visiting (a tricky exercise for theosophists with their austere attitudes to suffering and death), a Religious and Moral Education League, and the previously mentioned Cremation Society. The Sydney branch of the order was well organised, probably by Mrs John, and its work was thought to have done the society's image good.[67]

The Brisbane exercise began in 1910, Mrs Moss its president. It was as vigorous as it was charitable. Having boasted the largest ladies' meetings in 1905, the monthly Theosophical Order of Service meeting now delivered clothing to the Benevolent Asylum (badly needed owing to cruelly parsimonious state administration), and to poor children in the Valley. It supported creches and the Kindergarten Association, and established a bursary in 1912 for a kindergarten teacher trainee.[68]

The Theosophical Order of Service had its greatest impact in Perth. Everywhere it edged into the mainstream of women's organisations, like the National Council of Women, but in Perth it was itself a promoter of women's organisation. There, Mrs Adair, secretary of Perth lodge, along with theosophical journalist Muriel Chase, and Edith Dircksey Cowan, the first Australian woman member of parliament, launched the influential Women's Service Guild. Adair regretted that the guild was not a theosophical organisation – but theosophical women were prominent in it: its first executive included Bessie Rischbieth (vice-president), Amelia Macdonald (treasurer) and Mrs Stanway Tapp. The Women's Service Guild became an important innovating and co-ordinating welfare organisation in the West. With the specific aims of education on social questions, unity, loyal citizenship, and equality of citizenship, it was the best expression of congruence between theosophic feminism and the advancement of women in Australia. It was in effect a secular Order of Service.[69]

So it emerges that theosophic feminism found expression in Australia in the years before World War I, though under very different circumstances from those attending its most outspoken moment in England. When historians first realised that theosophy and women's organisation went hand in hand in Perth they were amazed. A detailed inquiry into the forgotten congruence is now in progress. Meanwhile Irene Greenwood's statement that 'most of my Mother's friends and associates were theosophists' is interim evidence of a complicated point in Australian history.[70]

Greenwood's statement emphasises the fact that in Perth theosophy provided a viable arena for progressive – and recently enfranchised – women. It is neither possible nor necessary to define that arena precisely here, nor theosophical networks within it. Clare Thompson, who has chronicled the history of Perth lodge, listing the names of prominent lodge members in the early twentieth century, had no difficulty in naming a dozen or so women activists among them for this book. The scope of their activities in the opening decades of this century is impressive. Fanning out from the Women's Service Guild, it encompassed the needs of women and girls, young children and infants, Aborigines, and the environment, along with the more predictable causes of religious women, like temperance and animal welfare. Theosophist and co-mason Amelia Macdonald, JP (1865–1946), an energetic Scotswoman who arrived in Western Australia in 1896 and joined the Theosophical Society shortly afterwards, worked for most of these causes: she was first treasurer of the WSG, member of the Kindergarten Union, active in the Children's Court and a member of the WCTU and the RSPCA. Mary Driver, who lived mainly in the country, ran a guild correspondence network for isolated country women and, at the urging of Macdonald, sent out theosophical literature along with the guild's papers.[71]

Driver, who had read the works of Emerson in her youth, was a strict Anglican at the time. Later, after great personal hardship, she embraced theosophy (and in old age entered a Rosicrucian community in Perth, the resting place of an ardent and active life). Of the women mentioned by Thompson, most seem to have found in theosophy a necessary and sufficient religious position, though some retained prior denominational affiliations too. It seems that the theosophical women of Perth fit the picture already drawn of theosophical women elsewhere, being educated (often self-educated, like Macdonald, who left school at the age of eleven), active, and from the middling to upper ranks of Western Australian society, with a large minority of single women.

The outstanding figure amongst them was Bessie Mabel Rischbieth (1876–1967), a South Australian by birth who married a wealthy merchant in the 1890s and moved to the West. By the 1920s Bessie Rischbieth represented the New Woman as far as Australian theosophists were concerned, and her name retains its lustre in Western Australia to the present (though not more widely). The sight of Bessie Rischbieth stepping off the plane after one or another national and international conference on equal citizenship remained a familiar one in Perth until the 1950s. She devoted herself to the cause of women from the time she joined the Women's Service Guild in 1909 until she relinquished the presidency of the Australian Federation of Women Voters which she founded in 1921 and led for twenty years. Of all the women in Australian theosophy she walked mostly firmly in the footsteps of Annie Besant, a liberal version of Charlotte Despard: like Despard, she was widowed early, and rich, with entrée into the best circles.[72]

Today a certain reticence surrounds the memory of Bessie Rischbieth, a reflection no doubt of a formidable personal style and social distance – 'the lady at the moated grange', or rather the superior suburbs of Peppermint Grove and later Cottesloe – and testimony to an energetic public life. If it is the case that she destroyed many of her personal papers, her biographer faces an unenviable task of reconstruction from the preserved public papers and scrappy autobiographical material. It was clear, however, that she was the most significant theosophic feminist in Australia, one who believed 'women possess qualities that could rescue the world from chaos', qualities such as patience, flexibility and calm judgement; qualities which, it is asserted, she possessed in full measure herself.[73]

Irene Greenwood has said that no one knew Bessie Rischbieth, that she was 'a unique soul'. Unfortunately she said little, indeed virtually nothing to posterity, about her beliefs, except perhaps in books and papers she willed to the Perth lodge of the Theosophical Society which it has not been possible to locate. Greenwood considers that the reason Rischbieth said little about her beliefs was not for fear of satire – theosophy in Perth was 'more than respectable, it was well-regarded' – but because she was naturally reserved; and also because she thought of the Theosophical Society as 'very much a secret society'.

Bessie Rischbieth once stayed in Gandhi's ashram; late in life she showed sympathy for Baha'i; throughout she worked through a theosophical network. But she did not choose to lift the veil of Isis. It is not even certain when she became a theosophist. Perhaps she was reared in it, in the Rounsevell household in Adelaide, where she was educated in an advanced feminist manner; perhaps it dates from Besant's first visit to Perth in 1908;

maybe she joined when in London before 1914, where she is said to have attended theosophical meetings as well as suffrage rallies and heard great feminist speakers of the day such as Charlotte Perkins Gilman, whose lecture 'Men, Women and People' prompted a letter to a fellow kindergartner in Perth redolent of theosophic feminism:

> She [Gilman] brings the points out along the 'biological' lines. Going back with the past evolution showing how it is only when you come to the human race that the emphasis is laid on 'sex'! To the detriment of our whole civilisation. And that is just where we are today and why we have the present outcry. It is absolutely necessary for future progress that women should be humans first, sharing a common humanity before they are 'females'. That is that the whole economic condition of women must change. The sexes must be co-equal.
>
> I am afraid I am expressing myself very badly.[74]

It is also surprising how infrequently Rischbieth features in the surviving records of Perth lodge, though she often conducted her business there, and is recalled with pride by older members.

What is certain is that she retained theosophical commitments to the end of her life. From a considerable estate, she made several bequests to theosophy and associated movements, and willed two temple lamps to the Manor in Sydney. As well as being an active co-mason, she supported the Liberal Catholic Church founded by theosophists during the Great War; she was cremated after ceremonies at the Perth church. The church received bequests too.[75]

Rischbieth's record as a lobbyist, and her career as a theosophic feminist, suggest that the appeal of theosophy was not an appeal to defeated women. This may have been the case with Flora MacDonald Denison, the Canadian suffrage leader who was converted to theosophy in 1914, having been forced out of the leadership of the suffrage movement before the vote was won by conservative forces, especially by 'the stifling force of Canadian Protestantism'.[76] Certainly in both Canada and Australia theosophical idealism enabled women to keep afloat culturally and intellectually, despite discouragement and isolation. Greenwood, for example, concludes that

> ... in the basic tenets of theosophy, which postulated a belief in reincarnation and a future life, there can be no doubt whatever that they thought the

frustrations they were experiencing in this life could be realised in some future life, when they would have earned the right to come back again and be given a second chance.[77]

Nevertheless, in Australia the paradoxical position of women in the early twentieth century – politically advanced, socially backward – gave theosophic feminism a chance. It provided a rallying point for unaligned idealism. In Rischbieth's case, that idealism remained undimmed.

In her nineties she waded into the verges of the Swan River to protest at reclamation for an expressway through the city of Perth and for a car park. Having stripped her lifestyle to its minimum requirements she continued to pursue an ethical position sufficient to combat the violence of the twentieth century. How interesting, then, that when first-wave feminism in Australia petered out in the 1940s, it did so amid conflict between Bessie Rischbieth and Jessie Street on ideological grounds. Rischbieth remained above, beyond, indeed outside, politics and deplored the class-based activism of Street. A prolonged parting of the ways occurred. Theosophic feminism was altogether too high-minded for the modern world, though it had had its moment.[78]

The constructive coincidence of feminism and theosophy in Western Australia in the early twentieth century is integral to the rise of theosophy in Australia. It shows that theosophy progressed in tandem with the women's movement; and it clarifies the appeal of theosophy to women. The women who joined the Theosophical Society were women who had abandoned the churches but not religion. They were thoughtful, active women of the middle class who sought a comprehensive world view to assure, not threaten, progress already made. Annie Besant, evidence of Woman in evolution, herald of religious harmony, moral progress and liberal imperialism, offered reassurance, building into theosophy significant strengtheners of woman's status. In turn, more and more women entered the court of the faerie queene.

6

Men, Mars and the millennium

The Great War of 1914–1918 had a quickening effect upon Australian theosophy. The forces which brought it to an historical climax in the 1920s had already been set in motion, but war and its aftermath increased their momentum, as did Mrs Besant's unexpected entry into Indian politics. The losses and disruption of war made new openings for theosophy; and, after 1916, promise of post-war reconstruction mingled with an intensified messianic urge, dating from the announcement in 1911 of the coming World Teacher.

The war affected tone as well as pace. The tone became increasingly masculine and millennial. Major Jack Bean, who became general secretary of the section in 1919 almost immediately after his return from the war in Europe, spoke incessantly of harnessing the Anzac spirit for the building of a 'New Order'. Meanwhile efforts by Leadbeater and others to seize the hour – to link Mars with a theosophical millennium – had fostered a theosophical version of post-war reconstruction emphasising education and religion. By 1919 Australian theosophists had established a model school and some among them, an ideal church.

Refurbished idealism carried the theosophists into the twenties. By 1921 membership of the Theosophical Society in Australia stood at 2309, almost double that of 1914. Evidently something had been harvested from otherwise inchoate and sectarian middle-class passions during and after the Great War.

Like most religious groups, theosophists hoped the Great War would advance their cause. The Christian churches in Australia foresaw a great opportunity, and issued eloquent calls for repentance and return to Christian morality. Theosophists, initially dismayed by the threat to brotherhood posed by world war, and partly restrained from chauvinistic excess by the vigorous contributions of German-born members to sectional life, were also patriotic, but characteristically forward-looking. While holding conventional pro-war views (suitably expressed in occult terms identifying German aggression with Black Forces), they nevertheless applied occult evolutionism to the situation and offered optimistic views on death 'to those who mourn'.[1]

Happily for Australian theosophists, they were provided with fresh teaching. In May 1914 Annie Besant's right-hand man in all matters clairvoyant, Charles Webster Leadbeater (1854–1934) returned to Australia. He landed at Townsville from India via Burma and Java for a second Australasian tour, beginning in Brisbane where he delivered public lectures on such topics as 'Life after Death' and 'The Advantages of Theosophy'. Australian theosophists who had appreciated his earlier tour in 1905 rejoiced that they were now so close to 'our self-sacrificing leaders'.[2]

Leadbeater was halfway through his tour when on 4 August 1914 Britain declared war on the German Empire. The disruptions of war and the comforts of theosophical homes on Sydney's lower North Shore encouraged him to stay in Australia. He stayed until 1929, settling in Sydney, to become a major inspiration of Australian theosophists and a drawcard for theosophists from all over the world. The former immediately recognised their good fortune, noting, for example, that he brought to the 21st convention in Melbourne during Easter 1915 'a distinct impulse to [its] intellectual and spiritual activities', and attracted public interest to theosophical teachings 'regarding the condition of the soul after death; particularly in relation to death in wartime'. The young dissident J.M. Prentice, however, deplored Leadbeater's advent, noting the latter's hostility to women in his audiences.[3]

An imposing figure and prolific writer, Leadbeater was by then sixty years old, and a considerable guru. In 1937 the *Theosophical Year Book* memorialised him as a 'Great Seer whose books have robbed death of its terrors; Master-Scientist of Occultism, who unveiled to the world the hidden side of life; Lover of Humanity and Spiritual Teacher of tens of thousands; Co-worker with Dr Annie Besant for over forty years in the Theosophical Society'. He had not always been so impressive. Recent research by Gregory Tillett has adjusted the colourful version of his back ground circulated during his lifetime to evidence of lower-middle-class provincial origins, and establishes that he was ordained a curate of the Church of England in the diocese of Winchester in 1878 as a 'literate', that is a candidate without academic qualifications, establishing also that he was not the same age as Annie Besant as claimed but seven years younger. This obscure curate, powerfully affected by the revival of spiritualism in the 1870s and an early recruit to theosophy in 1883, impulsively abandoned his curacy at Bramshott, Hampshire, to go with Madame Blavatsky to India in 1884, where he proved useful in Ceylon and at Adyar. The erstwhile Anglican espoused Buddhism and, according to the Year Book, 'unfolded and perfected his psychic abilities'. As well, he produced a *Smaller Buddhist Catechism* (1889), the first of many books, a number of which are still maintained in print by theosophical publishing houses.[4]

Returning to London in 1889, Leadbeater was thereafter tutor to aspiring theosophical families and, as a theosophical lecturer, achieved some didactic success by the mid-nineties. His thoughts on 'the astral plane' attracted the attention of far-off Alfred Deakin and in 1897 an article in *Lucifer* by Leadbeater on dreams was read at Hobart lodge for example. During the 1890s his position was strengthened by a chaste liaison with Annie Besant, which was notable at first for such co-productions as *Thought-Forms* (1901) and *Occult Chemistry* (1908), and subsequently as an inviolate partnership. 'I, his nearest colleague, united to him by ties unbreakable, knowing him as none other, living in the outer world, knows him, I stand by him in storm and sunshine,' she testified in 1923.[5] She had always stood by him. As mentioned earlier, in the last days of Olcott's regime he had been temporarily forced out of the society, but Annie Besant PTS quickly restored his credentials.[6]

The man, however, was irrepressible. It was Leadbeater, newly returned to Adyar, who perceived in Krishnamurti the makings of a World Teacher, the announcement of which caused so much trouble before the war: first in India in theosophical schools thus lost to the cause by over-enthusiastic promotion of the preparatory Order of the Star in the East; then in Europe, where virtually the whole German section split off in protest at the new doctrine to form the Anthroposophical Society led by Rudolf Steiner in 1913; and then in the courts. Besant fought the boy's father all the way to the Privy Council, where in May 1914, on a technicality, she succeeded in retaining custody of Krishnamurti and his younger brother Nityananda.[7]

It might have been hoped that Leadbeater's most creative days were over, that he would settle down in remote Australia to a congenial figurehead role. But with his favourite causes now protected by the Privy Councillors, he soon perceived possibilities in his new home. In a series of four lectures delivered in Sydney in August 1915 he proclaimed 'Australia and New Zealand as the home of a new sub-race'. He had detected, especially in Queensland, a new antipodean racial type characterised by intuition and powers of synthesis evidently a new sixth sub-race of the fifth Aryan round, foreshadowing the next more advanced sixth round as envisaged by Madame Blavatsky. Leadbeater urged his audience to align themselves with evolutionary law, assuring them that present confusions were merely transitional. He held that, despite distance and a small population, the Antipodes provided a favourable site for inauguration of a new era of brotherhood and cooperation, being neither decadent like Britain nor overblown by capitalist pride like America, and not yet delivered into unworkably democratic systems of government by 'too-young souls'. There was crudity, and reverse class legislation, but the wholesome environment held promise.

In Leadbeater's view, antipodean evolutionary advantage was partly fortuitous – a facetious reference to the White Australia Policy – but substantial, too, because of the glorious sacrifice of war dead. The Australian war dead had earned special evolutionary rights for the incipient sub-race. It would be important to purify child-rearing practices, by abstinence from alcohol, meat and tobacco, and to educate the next generation correctly, along Montessorian lines. The reward would be the coincidence of a new sub-race and the World Teacher in fifteen or twenty years' time.[8]

Leadbeater gave these lectures at various lodges around Australia, and it was reported at the 1916 Convention that all 2000 copies of the printed version had been sold. On the suggestion of Mr (from 1917 Senator) Matt Reid, provision was made to donate a further 10,000 copies to schools.[9]

By the time of the first conscription debate, Leadbeater had enunciated 'An Occult View of the War'. Stripped of various occult pieties, it advocated conscription and struggle to the end. It also contained a peculiarly virulent anti-German message. That German theosophists had been recently unpleasant, indeed utterly unscrupulous, was a mere coincidence. The larger reality was that the war re-enacted a prior cataclysm in Atlantis, when 'the Lords of the Dark Face' challenged 'the Ruler of the Golden Gate' for the right of separate evolution. Punished by the submergence of Atlantis, they had returned to try again. Despite the best efforts of the powers directing evolution, the fifth root race could not now advance as a whole, and Germany must be beaten. The arrogance, the moral decline, of Germany was not easily explained, but was evident in comparative crime statistics. Democracy, admittedly 'an unlovely stage', was better than aristocracy: 'this War is essentially one of principles.'[10]

Ultimately for Leadbeater, however, the main issue was preparation for the Coming. Though appalling, the war should be regarded as part of world preparation. He hazarded that there might be no other way of getting sufficient unselfish and awakened egos to establish the sixth sub-race. 'Many of those who die will be worthy of birth in the new Sub-Race, but so also will be many of the women who have bravely sent forth their nearest and dearest to answer their country's call.'[11] A similar view is elaborated in *The Coming of the World-Teacher*, and *Death, War and Evolution*, a selection from the writings of leading theosophists made by Leadbeater's secretary Dr Mary Rocke in 1917.

As Leadbeater desired its widest possible circulation, arrangements were made to print 5000 copies of 'An Occult View of the War ', for sale at 3d. each. Convention delegates in 1916 earnestly recommended distribution to 'Statesmen of the Empire, France, Russia and Italy'. Later theosophists were proud to have produced so many volunteers.[12]

How the message appealed 'To Those Who Mourn', Leadbeater's other main wartime statement, is now difficult to comprehend. The bereft were told that sacrifice was inevitable, probably beneficial. Perhaps the complexity of the sevenfold nature of man propounded in theosophical texts, and confusion about the three extra-terrestrial components, distracted the earnest student's grief. Ancient wisdom revived seems cold comfort. But theosophists who had always deplored 'the Victorian way of death' seem to have found in war radical confirmation of their view that death was a relatively unimportant event, to be interpreted constructively, merely an incident in spiritual evolution. T.H. Martyn, perhaps the most important of Australian theosophists at the time, was among the many to address 'The Fear of Death'. J.L. Davidge, exploring 'The Eschatology of War' in 1916, wrote that it proved the reality of angels, as with the Angel of Mons; he felt that war eased the transition called death by creating more helpers on the other side.

> In ordinary peace times a legion of trained helpers wait the hosts of souls who pass over by normal death or by sudden disaster, but in the poignant stress of war the bands of invisible helpers are strengthened from many sources [as] the narratives from soldiers at the front testify ...[13]

It was asserted that much had been done to remove the fear of death and the hereafter, so haunting to previous generations.

It was also asserted that theosophy comforted men at the front. Melbourne theosophist S.T. Studd, retiring president of the section, felt certain in Easter 1918 that 'by the campfires in the trenches, and in the dug-outs at the front, the enlightening truths of Theosophy have found a ready welcome and acceptance in the minds and hearts of the thousands of noble men who are freely giving their lives for King and Country'.[14]

A report that theosophists at the front faced death fearlessly is plausible. But it appears that neither theosophists nor theosophy made much headway with the soldiers. Two sets of papers of theosophist-soldiers survive at the Australian War Memorial, donated by Major John Willoughby Butler Bean, MA, MD (1881–1969), younger brother of the war correspondent C.E.W. Bean, and Sergeant (later Lieutenant) John Murdoch Prentice (1886–1964), a clerk from Moonee Ponds who enlisted in May 1915. They do not provide much evidence for Studd's assertion that 'noble men' welcomed the truths of theosophy, a possibility more firmly attested by the number of high-ranking military sympathisers after the war, such as Major-General Kenneth Mackay, an old friend of Leadbeater's, Major-General Sir C.B.B. White, a founder of the AIF much admired by C.E.W. Bean, and Lt-General Henry Gordon Bennett, whose family contained several leading theosophists of the 1920s.[15] Nor are they very illuminating on the value of theosophy at war, though that is not surprising since neither donor was primarily a soldier, and both spent considerable time out of the war in England, Bean in military hospitals and Prentice in administration at Horseferry Road, London. Dr Bean did write en route to Gallipoli in April 1915 that theosophy helped 'a bit': 'it is only occasionally the utter tragedy of [the war] smites me ... Theosophy helps me a bit – it makes me feel that after all it is just a moment or a few short hours of pain perhaps & then you go on leading a wider life elsewhere'.[16]

By 1916, still in Cairo in army records, Prentice felt theosophy had failed him; but he was conducting theosophical classes at the same time, and soon recovered himself in England.[17]

In May 1918 *Theosophy in Australasia* stated that the theosophical roll of honour stood at sixty-seven. An early casualty was Armidale lodge president Lt-Col. George Frederick Braund, MLA (1886–1915), accidentally killed at Gallipoli while commanding officer of the 2nd Battalion (1st Infantry). A teetotaller who always wore his Star in the East badge, Braund impressed other theosophist-soldiers in Egypt, but his mess arrangements were unpopular. Prentice felt himself regarded as 'an amiable mad man'. Even Bean ultimately fell out with army authorities, amid vigorous debate with his unit's padre on the true meaning of the Second Coming.[18]

The two collections cast contrasting light upon theosophy at war – as indeed the donors intended they should, since they held passionately opposed views on concurrent developments in the Theosophical Society. But it is possible to detect common ground too, as in their changing responses to war. Prentice, initially charmed by the camaraderie of army life and enchanted by 'psychic Egypt', wrote home after Gallipoli that 'war is so cruel that only the Gods can stand it'. 'The World will not better for it, but I am afraid worse. I am getting very pessimistic over the whole thing, and the more I see of the soldiers the less do I consider that War under any circumstances can be for upliftment.'[19]

Similarly Bean, bound for Gallipoli, wrote to his parents in Hobart that war was wicked, and, recuperating in Alexandria after the Gallipoli landings, deplored the un-Christian growth of hatred and bitterness in the world. But by February 1916 Prentice, seeing the war as the work of 'deep forces', believed that 'everyone who is really required for the purpose of evolution will be drawn in'; and Bean's mind was restored to optimism. While still convalescing in England in October 1915 Dr Bean met 'the young Hindu theosophists' and immediately joined the Order of the Star in the East, affirming his faith in the physical coming of Christ.

> When one thinks of how utterly the Spirit is conquering the Flesh in our splendid men as they rush from their trenches to certain death not in a white heat of rage but quite calmly & quickly – when one thinks of the thousands of men & women all the world over whose lives the war has made unselfish & useful, instead of selfish and useless, one can see the Spirit of God is at

work – I believe myself in the probability & desirability of an actual physical return [of the Christ].[20]

Neither man retained antiwar attitudes, though Prentice was prone to fatalism and keen to denounce British conduct of the war. But, commissioned at last, he wrote from the front in 1917, 'Of course we must fight on – the blood and tears of the world are required to wash away the over growth and the artificial effects that have grown up through the world'.[21]

The letters reveal shock and horror at immorality in Egypt and England, and a common anxiety about sexual purity. Bean, a bachelor, channelled his anxieties into treatment and study of venereal disease and schemes to protect Australia from VD after the war. Prentice fared worse, being charged by a theosophical mother in Melbourne with corrupting Melbourne boys in Egypt, a charge he most vigorously denied, defending his many friendships and deploring the ignorance of folks at home. Intermittent comment by Prentice, who thought London worse than Cairo, suggests strain almost as severe as war itself. Such evidence says something about theosophy at war too, indicating another way in which the older chivalric code was tested – and survived.[22]

A contrast is apparent in the two men's views of the future of theosophy. Most theosophists agreed that the Guardians of Humanity had foreseen the war and would make use of it. More recognised that the world would never be the same again. But there was no agreed perspective, and Bean and Prentice drew contrasting lessons, effectively foreshadowing post-war divisions within the Theosophical Society. Bean epitomised the orthodox lesson, that the leaders of the Theosophical Society were right, that a new cycle was beginning, that the World Teacher would come. War translated his hope of the Coming into certainty. After seeing the Sphinx, he reflected that 'a mighty spirit is guiding humanity on the upward path towards unity and co-operation between East and West'. At sea near Lemnos he and Dean Talbot of Sydney read *At the Feet of the Master*, purportedly written by Krishnamurti, which he regarded as a modern 'imitatio Christi'. In London he joined all the theosophical organisations, expressing total satisfaction with theosophy as 'the Church Militant on the intellectual and spiritual planes'. Mabel Besant-Scott became his spiritual adviser, and his admiration for Annie Besant knew no bounds – 'I have such complete faith in her wonderful purity, spirituality and Wisdom that I know joining [the Esoteric Section] will be the greatest of Spiritual blessings for me'. We Beans, he said, are 'honest hero worshippers'.[23]

By contrast, Prentice increasingly felt that theosophy had taken the wrong turning, and he wrote freely from London in 1916 to his parents in Melbourne about a deluded, authoritarian and even idiotic leadership preoccupied with incense and 'Indian kids'. An occultist, astrologer, also a good public speaker, Prentice gained confidence in the army and in London, but transferred to the front in 1917 became increasingly withdrawn and negative. It is hard to tell from the deposited correspondence covering 1915–1919 what his general position was in the end, except that by 1918 he was an implacable opponent, not just of Leadbeater but also of Besant – to the distress of his mother in Melbourne. It seems that he was already looking for an alternative channel for his theosophy, or a coup. As early as 1916 he wrote to his mother 'The Master's work is left utterly undone':

> The T.S., which was the one organisation which might have spoken with no uncertain voice in the great conflict is a broken, bankrupt and useless channel, and (save for a handful of individuals scattered abroad over every land) the light of Occult teaching dimmed for another fifty or sixty years. God knows what 1975 will bring to light. H.P.B. and Judge again, let us hope.[24]

To an outsider the most interesting question is not which of the two men was more realistic, but why Bean welcomed and Prentice opposed the millenarian turn. The well-educated Bean displayed what now seems astonishing confidence and credulity, while Prentice's aggressive assessments seem backward-looking. It was largely a matter of class. Bean, the Anglo-Australian, belonged to the same liberal, imperial post-Anglican culture as Besant, and shared her perspectives, as did his family in a sense. Explaining his forthcoming ordination to his sister Jessie in 1896, Bean's father Edwin, a Broad Churchman, wrote, 'What appears to me to be our chief duty here is to form *the very highest idea of God that our race and age permits*'.[25] Prentice, a country boy from Buangor, now of the suburban shopkeeping class, detested those perspectives – the more so for having seen British liberalism and a liberal version of Empire at first hand – and felt threatened by them. He remained an outsider, colonial and xenophobic, his true position in conflict with Anglo-Indian theosophy. That is to say, differences over Mars and the millennium exposed class differences between the men, though such differences would never be acknowledged by supporters of the Brotherhood religion.

Both men spiritualised their war experiences. They would have agreed with S.T. Studd that war had enhanced theosophical teachings, while disagreeing vehemently on which ones, and despite neither having drawn much obvious comfort from them. Later, others would judge that Bean and Prentice had themselves been enhanced by war. Whereas most would-be knights of the Great War suffered the demise of chivalry, these theosophic warriors from Australia endorsed and renewed its elevated code, transcending the lessons which ordinary irreligious men drew from total war.[26]

Theosophy may have been cold comfort 'to those who mourn', and of uncertain value to those who fought, but it contained a message for those who stayed behind, the survivors. At first, like many church people, theosophists were tempted to think that maintenance of theosophical life for the dura ion of the war was itself sufficient achievement. By 1915, when a lodge led by accountant William Harding was established at Chatswood on Sydney's lower North Shore, there were twenty-four lodges in Australia, the largest number ever; and although some smaller lodges collapsed, others were established. The section's most intellectually ambitious lodge, Besant lodge in Melbourne, collapsed, but HPB lodge in Newtown, Sydney, seemed to replace it, with forty-two members in the middle of the war and successful evening discussions on topics like 'Reconstruction of the Empire'. By 1918 the number of lodges stood at twenty-two, only one less than in 1914. Lodge life, including children's work in lotus circles and round tables, was sustained. The former were now equipped with hymn book and literature: the January 1915 number of a lavishly produced issue of the *Lotus Bud's Journal* is preserved in the Mitchell Library, complete with references to *What Katy Did*, also Miss Christie's *Theosophy for Beginners*.

But, willy-nilly, war brought more people to the TS than ever before. Not all wartime recruits stayed, but an increasing membership spoke for itself. By 1918, the Order of the Star Conference attracted 200 people, and with a membership of 1664 the Order was almost the size of the TS itself. As well, the theosophical presence in Australian cities became more impressive. New buildings were occupied in Adelaide (at 212 King William Street); Brisbane (with its own premises at Concordia Hall, Charlotte Street); Melbourne (where the lodge moved from Flinders Street to Collins Street); and, the most grand, in Sydney, where an eight-storeyed sectional headquarters in Hunter Street was dedicated by Leadbeater on 22 April 1916. Queen's Hall Melbourne and King's Hall Sydney were said to be among the most modern in their respective cities. The King's Hall was a special wonder, 'the most beautiful as well as the most acoustically perfect auditorium in Sydney', with seating for 700. Like Brisbane, Sydney lodge had its own orchestra, largely of professional musicians. S.T. Studd remarked that 'the fact that money always flows into the Society's coffers, when needed for a specific purpose, is a potent sign of the vitality of our movement'. The Hunter Street building was valued at £70 000 in 1925, and the exceptionally well-sited Melbourne lodge cost £16,000 in 1916, £1000 of which was donated by Judge (later Sir) Henry Hodges.[27]

The self-assured Leadbeater made a great difference. In return, theosophists treated him with the reverence due to a Grand Old Man. From 1917 Convention was held in Sydney instead of rotating around the capital cities as in the past, not because of the superior facilities at Hunter Street, but to spare the ailing Leadbeater the strain of travelling. Convention voted him a gif t of £1000 in 1920. Naturally, theosophy in Sydney benefited most from his presence. Sydney lodge reported average lecture attendance of 300 during 1916–1917, and the lodge more than doubled its membership between 1914 and 1920. From 384 members in 1914 it grew to 591 in 1919, and a reputed 800 by late 1920. Nor did this exhaust the theosophical potential of Sydney, where Chatswood lodge was an earnest of suburban growth; lodges were also formed at Manly (led by Victor Chidgery) and Strathfield, both middleclass suburbs like Chatswood. Chatswood lodge survived in the local School of Arts for many years, moving up the line to Roseville in the late twenties.

It was almost as if there had been a conscious reversal of policy. In the past it had been thought desirable to associate theosophy with other progressive causes. Now theosophists were increasingly inclined to urge the world to come to them. As T.H. Martyn said in Easter 1917,

> My Brothers, do not let us slumber through these momentous days! But rather let us be very awake to the opportunity given to us to hand on all

the grand principles that our Society stands for just at this critical moment, when ... old shibboleths are in the melting pot.[28]

In 1918, Convention established a publicity department, run at first by Gustav Köllerstrom and Ian Davidson, and then by enthusiast Karel van Gelder, who also wanted a sectional publishing house. The publicity department circulated 32,000 pamphlets in its first year, directed at returned soldiers. The American pamphlet, 'Why we go over the top', was recommended on the grounds that the war had fostered theosophic ideals: and pamphlets giving 'scientific' proof of life after death were distributed widely, as in a handbill distribution in Annandale in 1920, and during Mrs John's platform work in the Domain on Sundays.

Theosophists had interpreted the losses and disrupt on of the early stages of the war optimistically. They endorsed the war with increasing fervour. (Mrs Bright of Melbourne, the woman who accused Prentice of corrupting her son in Egypt, said by way of reproach, 'I gave him up to the Masters to go to the War without a tear'.) They did not feature in anti-war protest, against conscription for example, or against the secret treaties which radical liberals believed had caused the war. Nor are there many references to humanitarian war work in annual reports, excepting the frequently mentioned Red Cross. Two stand out: Besant lodge, Melbourne, formed a branch of the Purple Cross (later called a Victoria Service) to provide medical comforts for 30,00 troop horses, and sent a substantial sum to the founder, Miss Lind-af-Hageby in London in 1916; and Brisbane women supported several relief funds (in 1917 they supported a branch of the Babies' Kit Society founded by Dr Mary Booth in Sydney in 1914).[29]

Later they responded with optimism to talk of post-war reconstruction, which began in England in 1917. Leadbeater said from the beginning that sudden death in a noble cause created a bank of souls ready to reincarnate for higher evolutionary purposes. Since the dead would return, albeit at some later and variously calculated stage, as advanced souls in an evolving world, a basic duty of loyal theosophists was to prepare the way. Early in 1917, quick to detect secular trends, he lectured in the reconstructionist mode on the 'Unseen Influences' of war. Although an atrocious anachronism, an awful slaughter, war was also progressive, impelling new political unities, as between British political parties, and between Britain and Ireland within the empire. It also promoted social reform between classes. Typically, Leadbeater referred to the elevation of manhood, minus alcohol and meat, and the magnificence of sacrifice, especially by women. But he also noted – what has become an historical truism – the relationship between war and social change in the twentieth century: ' though the war itself is an awful waste of money, yet it has also had this effect: it has taught us that money can be raised in prodigious amounts, and if it can be done for destruction, why can it not be done for construction?'[30]

In 1918 it was claimed that theosophists were ardent philanthropists:

> Philanthropic efforts of all kinds in Australia today, the free Kindergarten Schools, societies for the promotion of public health, the Red Cross and other war activities, are all enthusiastically supported by members, and thus come ... into the wider circle of the Theosophical Movement ...[31]

By 1919 they were ardent reconstructionists – or at least the new general secretary of the section was.

Major Bean, who became general secretary in April 1919, had been mulling over schemes for 'reconstruction' since 1916 when, in the first flush of theosophical excitement, he wrote home, 'Isn't the world bubbly and "yeasty" with God's new life wave just now inaugurating the New Age?' His schemes, however, developed out of grimmer experiences in military hospitals among the victims of venereal disease. Bean became increasingly troubled by what he saw as the army's mechanical and punitive approach to the problem. He tried to promote purity and continence among the troops. His first attempt was a League of Sociable Service, launched in the Star meeting rooms in London in January 1917, which aimed to create wholesome leave networks and a pattern of class cooperation for after the war. Later in 1917 at Bulford Hospital near Salisbury Plain, he launched an Australian League of Honour (motto, 'On Active Service'; oath, 'I promise with God's help to safeguard Australia's Honour and race purity by Temperance in alcohol and Continence'). He wanted General Birdwood to head the league and invited his brother Charles to be its secretary. Such a league he thought would appeal more than a rival religious proposal for the protection of women, 'The White Knights of Dartmoor' emanating from Beatrice Chase and John Oxenham, because it would be headed by a man, secular, and 'Australian'. Bean saw it as a step towards reconstruction, for 'building after the War that Australia which is still an Ideal'.[32]

By 1918 Bean was anxious to get home quickly to join the anti-VD campaign. On the boat he advanced the notion of a League of Active Service for the great task of social reconstruction: 'We are to be the immediate reconstructors of our country,' he wrote for the benefit of the Diggers. 'How necessary it is that we should keep the spirit of chivalry and knight errantry lit by the war ...' He reminded them of the great and idealistic work that lay before them, listing 'the reconstruction in Politics, and in Social Affairs, the great questions of Venereal Disease, Alcohol, Public Health, Education, Child Welfare, Unmarried Maternity, Housing, Land Settlement, Irrigation, Industrial Expansion etc. ...'[33] A league would be needed to promote debate, maintain morale, and fulfil the sacrifice of the fallen 'who ... may be reborn in Australia as our children to carry on once more their service for King and Country'.

Nothing came of these schemes during the war. But having found what he regarded as his natural office in life as a 'missionary along my own special lines', he renewed his efforts from a far more hospitable platform. Settled in Surry Hills, Sydney, as general secretary of the Australian Theosophical Society, his first plan was a Digger's Parliament in King's Hall. A letter seeking help from his now famous brother Charles (C.E.W. Bean) shows that by 1919 he thought in terms of maintaining the AIF spirit as a basis of reconciliation and co-operation. Otherwise the diggers themselves would suffer, from drink, idleness and incomprehension, and society would drift unchecked towards bloody revolution:

> I can see that more and more the country is dividing into two utterly hostile parties – more than two perhaps. They are both in earnest at bedrock, but both need educating to avoid prejudice, hatred, misconception. At present we are sailing blindly on towards horrible bloody Revolution & social Chaos just as surely as we sailed on towards the World War, & only Co-operation and above all Education can stop it.[34]

Bean wrote eloquently in his first *Theosophy in Australasia* editorial of a 'living peace', a phrase of Carlyle's, and the priority of social over spiritual reconstruction, preaching the lessons of the war as learned by a man of his class:

> In our hands, Australians, have they left the trust ... It is for us in the years immediately ahead to clear away the debris of an outworn system, and lay sure the foundations of a new life and outlook in religion, politics (national and international), industrialism, economics, social intercourse.[35]

There must be no return to the old indifference. What was needed immediately, he said, was 'no polluting public houses to surround our Diggers when they reincarnate', free treatment of venereal disease, eugenic examinations, an anti-slum crusade, city planning, preventive medicine, domestic hygiene, child welfare, diet reform in the tropics, physical education, changed attitudes to the criminal, and educational reform.

Theosophy in Australasia 1919–1920 overflowed with reconstructionist zeal, and 'the Australian Spirit'. Bean looked to the best of the AIF to run the country and prevent red revolution (in which the bourgeoisie could expect to suffer most because of its 'shameful past'). He urged industrial harmony and the co-operative spirit. Where was the 'creative faculty in industry'? What was the solution to conflict between capital and labour? The One Big Union should be capital and labour conjoint. 'Political reconstruction' also had a place – as in electoral reform and proportional representation advocated by Miss M.E. McCabe.

There were specific projects to be advanced too, like national kitchens. The advantages of national kitchens included wholesale food purchasing; expert cooking; conservation of leisure, energy, health and income; promotion of industrial harmony by improved digestion; the opportunity for food reform by teaching national domestic science in the kitchens: 'pure foods, food values, well-balanced meals, and good cooking (especially of vegetables in their skins, conserving their natural mineral salts, so priceless as blood cleansers).' National kitchens were presented as one of the most practical and far reaching of the higher social reforms, part of the HIGHER SOCIALISM:

> HIGHER SOCIALISM [means] the deliberate sacrifice of the leisured, moneyed, cultured, classes in the service of those who have none of these things. Misery, Squalor, Despair, can generate that hate which is the driving steam-pressure of Revolutions. But HATE cannot reconstruct nor regenerate National Life. Love alone can do that ...[36]

Bean's most ambitious reconstructionist effort was 'The Entente', a Sydney club 'to promote a sociable entente between people in Australia interested in national welfare', open to both sexes, all classes, and every possible opinion, drawn from such groups as the WEA and the Anglican Church, with John Simpson, a returned soldier of Weymouth, Matilda Street, Bondi, formerly the English delegate in Australia of the Men's League of Women Suffragists, as secretary. An impressive executive was nominated in January 1920, with Dr Richard Arthur, MLA, as president and thirteen vice-presidents (including the Bishop of Bathurst, the Dean of Sydney, Capt. C.E.W. Bean, Sir Joseph Carruthers, Professor R.F. Irvine, G.V. Portus, Dr Constance D'Arcy, Mrs Consett Stephen and Mrs Palmer), and an overlapping committee of fifteen (adding, among others, A.W. Green, Mrs Mary Gilmore and Miss I. Gullett to theosophical stalwarts John Mackay, Dr Bean, Mrs John and Miss Mackenzie). Bean suggested a monthly program of impromptu speeches at the Better 'Ole Cafe by T.H. Martyn, G.V. Portus, Dean Talbot, Mrs Greville, Ivy Gullett, Mrs Mackinnon and others, beginning with 'If I were Dictator'. Whether or not this club, or the larger plans for co-operation also envisaged, really attracted the support said to have been given by the WEA, NCW, RSSILA and the ATNA, its planning reveals theosophic aspiration for the new age. Bean looked forward: 'the ferment of our time, however terrible, is but the birth pains of the new system.'

The new political system would be characterised by a complete specialisation and co-ordination. In preparing for the Advent of the Great Friend – the Grand Uniter, the Prince of Socialists, the Prince of Peace, the Christ Himself – it was necessary to 'rehearse the great "Soviet system"' so that the world would eventually adopt it. Bean believed the Soviet system was in essence the way forward (also the way back) for the great Aryan race. It reconstituted effective hierarchies and the best national spirit.[37]

Bean's 'Entente Ideal' envisaged the returned servicemen giving a lead in public-spiritedness and proposed outlets for altruism, now threatened as 'the glow of true heroic idealism has died down'. 'Our returned sisters' could be travelling organisers of the patriotic spirit and, via the National Council of Women, in industrial and commercial welfare work (adequately paid). Bean believed that the best hope for Australia lay with its female population: 'Personally, I look above all to our women. Our women must be "National", a great active resistless organised driving force to uplift our land.'[38] It was pointless, for example, to preach evolutionary reincarnation if returning egos were to be housed in diseased bodies, bodies ravaged by the newly controversial venereal diseases. Gustav Köllerstrom represented the TS at the first VD conference in Australia, the WEA Conference on the Teaching of Sex Hygiene held at the University of Sydney in late 1916.[39] Thereafter, theosophical publications devoted increasing space to such issues as sexuality, motherhood, child welfare, child and adult psychology. In July 1917 *Theosophy in Australasia* publicised an Infant and Child Welfare Conference, and in March 1919 carried a prospectus for the newly formed Royal Society for the Welfare of Mothers and Babies, from its president, S.R. Innes-Noad, in the same year also publishing 'The necessity for future legislation for the protection of women and children' by A.W. Green, president of the State Children's Relief Board. Naturally the Entente Club's program included visits to child welfare centres, and lectures on the future for women. Altogether, it was hoped that the Entente would be a breeding ground for 'bright regeneration reconstruction ideas'.

Concurrently, an economics study circle was formed. Bean wanted to update theosophical expertise in economics and psychology, and encouraged people such as Mary Gilmore to attend Professor Irvine's lectures at the University of Sydney. Unfortunately not much progress was made with economics, probably because those most interested, like the accountant William Harding, adhered to the 'underground economics' of their youth, especially the single land tax. Both he and T.H. Martyn contributed to the economics study circle, Martyn commending a form of guaranteed minimum income drawn from a flat-rate 20 percent tax on all incomes.[40]

Hope of post-war reconstruction has received almost no attention from Australian historians. Agitation by and for returned soldiers has always been seen as more significant. The former derived from radical liberalism at the heart of the empire and spoke of duties rather than rights in idealistic language enfeebled by war. Generally, middle-class idealism which linked 'Mars and the Millennium' lacked focus in Australia. But that same idealism was situated in the mainstream of Australian society, and the men who promoted it were not divorced from emergent ideology – as is apparent from the Beans. The distance between Jack and his brother Charles was not very great. The family, Anglo-Australian with Indian experience, was sympathetic to what they called 'Jack's schemes' (at least his brother kept the records of them) and tolerant of his theosophy: they reflected liberal opinion, which had always tolerated the theosophists, and the more so after the upheaval of war.

Probably Leadbeater's platform work – 'think imperially', he once said – improved establishment opinion. There was, however, a more compelling reason for renewed attention. In 1913 Annie Besant, aged 66, returned to politics after a twenty-year abstention, with a rousing pamphlet, *Wake Up, India!* Why she did so is a complex question: she said she acted on instructions from the Masters, that it was her duty 'to claim India's place within the Empire'. Perhaps she thought it timely to change gear. Whatever the motivation, the effect was to transform Indian politics.[41]

First she organised among theosophists, and in January 1914 began propaganda for Indian self-government by acquiring a weekly paper, *The Commonweal*, then in July 1914 a Madras daily, renamed *New India*. Her aim was unity of the various warring factions in the Indian National Congress and with the Muslim League. The war added force to her comprehensive arguments. Unlike Ireland, in India the question of home rule was not shelved for the duration of the war. Rather it was posed the more effectively as the Indian army made its enormous contribution to the defence of the empire. A fragile unity emerged among the nationalists, with Besant forcing the pace. Explaining that she preferred home rule to self-rule, she campaigned against autocracy with her old fiery competence, proposing the Home Rule League in 1915, the year Gandhi returned from South Africa. By September 1916 the All-India Home Rule League was a reality. The government of India, increasingly perturbed, interned Mrs Besant at the southern hill station of Ootacamund; but this only added to its difficulties, and she was freed in September 1917. In December of the same year she was elected president of the Indian National Congress. Although the terms of debate turned against her in 1918, hers was a remarkable achievement.

Besant's contribution to Indian nationalism was profound and cannot be weighed adequately here. But during the Great War she stood at its centre, at a time of crisis when India was still the jewel in the imperial crown. No wonder that beyond India opinion divided on whether she was traitorous or heroic, short- or long-sighted – theosophical opinion too. Some theosophists deplored her 'Sinn Fein' activities. Leadbeater, ever the staunch Tory, feared privately that she would wreck the society. And Jack Bean's London enthusiasm for the Home Rule League did not last, though he loyally stuck with his leader: 'We have a great deal to be ashamed about.' Prentice, who detested the British and their black empire equally, hoped the Indian government would not make a martyr of her, and regarded her political work as disastrous.[42]

However, Australian theosophists supported her. For most of them Annie Besant was still 'the greatest living woman', and Besant's program for India accorded well with the facts of Australian history. In 1915 Convention expressed sympathy for the aspirations of Indian brothers to self-government under the Crown, and endorsed Besant's Model Parliament in Madras. To ensure that Australians continued to understand that her program was 'absolutely constitutional and law-abiding', Besant despatched a copy of a statement drawn up mid-1917 'that Australians might know that autocracy rioted in India under the Union Jack'.[43]

Plainly, the president was exhilarated by the enormities of war and the promise of Indian nationalism. She recalled Blavatsky's prophecy that in the early years of the twentieth century the accounts of the nation would be made up. Assuming a British victory, she believed India's part in that victory assured liberation from autocracy. 'Never again can [Britain] ... treat the Indian Nation as a subject race.' She stood on principle and for free speech, within the society as without, a traditional and impregnable position held the more assuredly in that she had been re-elected to a second seven-year term as president in mid-1914 by an overwhelming majority.[44]

In Ransom's resume, these were the years of 'Theosophy Applied'. Not only were theosophists everywhere busy defending the new initiative in India;[45] morale also rose at the thought that the society was 'the standard-bearer of the coming civilisation'. Besant addressed this prospect too. It was in part simply her style – the elitism of Edwardian social theory found one expression in Mrs Besant, who, like Lenin, was ready and willing to take command under the right conditions. It was also a deployment of the increasingly insistent rhetoric of reconstruction, for the Masters and the Messiah.

In January 1918 President Besant listed six tasks for the society: to penetrate the atmosphere with theosophical ideas, recast education, reform penology, raise labour from drudgery to creative joy, lift the disinherited classes, and eliminate the double standard of morality between men and women. Meantime, a rather less conventional agenda had already been established along lines suggested by Leadbeater in 1916. Ransom cites correspondence between Leadbeater and Besant which established operational priorities. According to Leadbeater, the Occult Hierarchy recommended that the society now show how things should be done, in three ways. The three ways were in education, religion and ritual: a model school, an ideal church, and co-masonry.[46]

This was an inspired stroke. All the accumulating forces came together – Leadbeater in Sydney, the carnage in Europe and talk of a New Age, Annie in India, and of course the coming World Teacher – in a kind of theosophical home front. The survivors must prepare the way. The Australian section embarked immediately upon its tasks. First, the school.

By the second decade of the twentieth century theosophists were ready to embark on comprehensive educational experiment. Some had long cherished visions of an ideal school, since interest in education reached back almost to the beginnings of modern theosophy.

It will be remembered that from the earliest days theosophical leaders had promoted educational reform in India, and that the education of theosophical children had become an issue in the 1890s. Melbourne theosophists had discussed Froebel in the mid-nineties and in Sydney Dr Carroll moved on to 'child study'. Support for the kindergarten movement, which began in earnest in the late 1880s in Sydney, increased in the twentieth century, and turn-of-the-century developments in educational psychology were noticed: Besant in 1907 was one of the first English-speaking advocates of the dazzling methods currently employed by Italian reformer Dr Maria Montessori. Although the Theosophical Society had not previously contemplated setting up its own schools outside India, unlike its rival in California where a Raja Yoga school flourished at Point Loma, the idea of model schools was welcomed – partly perhaps because so many theosophists were teachers, maybe nearly 10 percent by 1918, but mainly because theosophists generally were sympathetic to the tenets of 'the new education', and had now a particular interest in 'alternative' education.[47]

Having rejected original sin, they deplored the physical and mental coercion of innocent children, and many testified to the baneful effects of punishments at home and at school which they had endured in childhood. In the theosophical belief system, the child occupied an exalted position, being the spirit reincarnate, the soul wearing new clothes as Leadbeater put it (adding that the clothes should be clean). If theosophists were to attain progressive spiritual evolution, education had a special role to play, and teachers a special responsibility: Leadbeater said they should remember that they were dealing with souls of roughly equal age. Furthermore theosophists were now to lead the way into the new age. They must be ready to serve the World Teacher.[48]

Leadbeater was himself a teacher. But the chief exponent of theosophical educational theory was a younger man, George Sydney Arundale (1878–1945), who became the third president of the Theosophical Society after Besant, and was the most important, historically, of Besant's many recruits for her Indian schools from Britain, America and Australia. An orphan reared by his aunt, Miss Francesca Arundale, one of the earliest followers of Madame Blavatsky in England, Arundale was educated at St John's College Cambridge and converted by Annie Besant in 1902. He dedicated himself to her service, and went to India in 1903 to teach history at the Central Hindu College, Benares, where he rose to become principal in the years 1909 to 1913. Unfortunately he became obsessed with Krishnamurti, which undermined confidence in the college, and the theosophists were obliged to withdraw. Besant immediately established a Theosophical Educational Trust, which by 1915 ran fifteen schools in India. Meanwhile Arundale returned to England with Krishnamurti. Increasingly disenchanted by the rather ineducable Krishnamurti, and in fact rejected by him, Arundale promoted the trust's work vigorously and found a good reception for a new prescription, a small book called *Education as Service* (1912). Purportedly written by Krishnamurti, but heavily influenced by Arundale, this book described an ideal school where children grew harmoniously through adolescence in a loving atmosphere, nurtured by teachers with high vocational ideals.[49]

Educational experiment was in the air. Not only were the pre-war years marked by vital contributions to educational theory (as names like Montessori and Dewey indicate, also less well-remembered ones such as Edmond Holmes), but developments in public education, especially secondary education in England since 1902, were not to theosophical liking. It was not long before discontent with secular schooling was given theosophical direction by an English Educational Trust and, by 1916, a Theosophical Fraternity in Education. The former promoted several experimental schools, including the Letchworth Garden School. The latter was primarily aimed at teachers. The thinking behind these initiatives is clear from the aims of the Education Fraternity, forerunner of the influential New Education Fellowship of the thirties. The fraternity stood for child individuality, self-discipline and self-government, co-education, vital religious teaching, the elimination of competitive practices, and citizenship training. It aimed to improve the status of teachers, and enlarge their professional freedom; and to awaken public interest in the new education, promoting lifelong education for all. A pamphlet introducing the Theosophical Fraternity in Education filed in the Education Pamphlets of the State Library of Victoria lists the founding personnel: Arundale as president, Charlotte Despard and the Lady Emily Lutyens among the vice presidents and Beatrice de Norman (later Ensor) secretary. When the influential Mrs Ensor came with the New Education Fellowship to Australia in 1937, a significant event in educational history, she spoke on Radio 2GB and urged fellow theosophists to support her as they had done in the early days in London.[50]

Arundale outlined his views on many occasions. A pertinent example appeared in *The Theosophist* in November 1917. In this article Arundale related the theosophical life cycle and education. Years one to seven represent the years of self-discovery for the child, still an 'elemental', recapitulating race experience. The years between seven and fourteen should be years of general education, when the child acquires 'family virtues', and then, until twenty-one, self-expression and the beginning of specialisation should be foremost. From the age of twenty-one to thirty-five, it is laid out, a man will be devoted to citizenship and the family, and in the next stage, from thirty-five to forty-nine, citizenship will be paramount. But at fifty, the stage called *sannyasi* by the Hindu, the years of personal renunciation begin, and one's duty is to humanity at large. Finally, consciousness expanded, the individual passes into the wider world.

The particular work of theosophy in the natal stage (as distinct from the prenatal and post-mortem stages) and of theosophical teachers, Arundale wrote, was to identify the individual's special service to the world, to enable successive initiations of consciousness and successful passage through life's stages. He said that the Montessorian method should be applied to all levels of education. The teacher is an ego-trainer. And the theosophist will have a special respect for the child ego, guarding carefully against its corruption in reincarnation, encouraging the will to achieve and to maintain an upward path. Ultimately theosophical schools would produce enthusiastic citizens, 'a powerful force in National Life'. Occasional examinations would be allowed as a concession to worldly necessity. Citation from Herbert Spencer on the evolution of self-discipline, and self-government, completes the discourse.

The proposed theosophical role at all educational levels was bold and challenging; in theosophical terms, comprehensive and coherent on 'unfoldment'. The basic argument was to be elaborated many times thereafter in theosophical and progressive education publications.

In Australia educational experiment was also in the air. Before the war theosophists had been most interested in the education of very young children in lotus circles and kindergartens. By the second decade of the twentieth century lotus circles were well established, but educationally oblique, as recalled by Marjorie Bull, 'a very gentle experience':

> Our lotus circle room [at Hunter Street, Sydney] was painted so that it shaded from deeper purple up to pale pink to azure blue ... it was very expressive of what we were taught about auras and atmospheres.
>
> I know you had to collect a very nice little saying every Sunday and bring it to the Circle, and I expect a lot of teaching went on ... I remember the sort of thing I would bring would be a very ordinary little statement 'God is Love' ... But I always remember a whole meeting being galvanised ... when a boy I knew ... stood up and said 'never trust a stranger', and the whole philosophy of the thing was wrong.

There was no catechism:

> Oh no ... We had *At the Feet of the Master*, which was of course basic theory which all theosophical children were given. But nothing like a catechism. Our upbringing was extra-ordinarily free from any sense of guilt. It was a philosophy of one's evolution within the human system and the divine system ... if you were theosophical you were very special.[51]

Theosophists were always more interested in the 'special' than the 'normal' child. Indeed they rejected the notion of the normal child, and deplored wastage in the public system which neglected 'super-' and 'sub-normal' children. Their attitude, an amalgam of idealism, ideology and philanthropy, came together in ardent support for the kindergarten movement, a respectable women's philanthropy which by 1910 had established thirty-two kindergartens in Australian cities; as Bessie Rischbieth wrote encouragingly to a kindergartener friend in Perth, it contained 'the spirit of the new age', because although there was plenty of talk about ending competition, 'children from infancy are taught to compete ... in all our schools, & are not shown their inter-relationship & their social place'.[52] Mrs Mabel Mackay, who joined the Council of the NSW Kindergarten Union in 1913 as president of the Golden Fleece free kindergarten in Chippendale and served until 1921, is a good example of the interest taken by theosophical women in kindergartens, as are numerous references to advances made at Blackfriars kindergarten, Sydney, before and after the war. Orders of service everywhere supported kindergartens, and the Brisbane OS provided a bursary to train teachers. Most strikingly, in 1916 theosophists presided over both the Queensland and New South Wales kindergarten organisations: Mrs Moss in Brisbane and John Mackay in Sydney. Mackay, a retired grazier and prominent theosophist, presiding for the whole period his wife Mabel was on the NSW council, maintained an association until 1926.

They also took an interest in the (newly defined) 'delinquent' child. Mrs Lily Hynes of Melbourne lodge, active in its lotus circle and attendant children's work, became a special magistrate in the Victorian Children's Court for instance. It was thought the kindergarten movement should be strengthened. 'Gaps' should be filled as in Auckland with Mothers' Thought Guilds. Efforts should be made to improve the environment. Marcella Clarke of Brisbane reported success with civic parks in North America. And news of Maria Montessori's work with slum children in Rome was welcomed. Whether Lillian de Lissa of Adelaide, who established the first Montessori school in Australia, was a theosophist is unknown, but co-worker Lucy Spence Morice was a member of Adelaide lodge and the vigour of the Adelaide lotus circle suggests she was close to its teachers.[53]

Just before the war, interest widened and quickened. It is recounted that members of the Order of the Star distributed 7000 copies of *Education as Service*. In 1913 Gnosis lodge in Sydney announced what was by 1915 presented as 'a bold departure ... from all conventional methods in education' on the northern coast of New South Wales (probably at Normanhurst, a northern Sydney suburb, however). And there were already some avowedly theosophic educators. When it came to finding a principal for the new school in Sydney, it emerged that the Misses Lily Arnold and Jessie Macdonald had been offering a theosophical education to sixty pupils at Apsley House Girls' School, Stanmore (now the Concordia Club) since 1913.[54] In 1915 another private theosophical school was launched in Devenport, northern Tasmania, by leading lights in Olcott lodge. *Theosophy in Australasia* of May 1918 refers to an 'open air school started nearly three years ago' there, most likely Lilian Outhwaite's 'Lindula', forerunner of her relatively long-lived theosophical school, St Margaret's (1918–1928).[55] The point about an 'open air' school refers to the fact that the country girls enrolled there learnt the novel art of eurhythmy and were among the first in Australia to excel at it (soon all theosophical schools taught eurhythmy).[56]

The most convincing evidence of increased enthusiasm for 'alternative' education before 1914 comes from a more familiar and socially secure source: Winifred West's Frensham founded at Mittagong in the southern highlands of New South Wales in 1913. Frensham was not a theosophical school and West denied theosophical influence. But the school espoused comparable ideals, notably 'true religion'; and West's teaching experience in England at Harrogate, a theosophical stronghold, her impressive cultural range and lifelong idealism, bespeak a common culture, if not shared aspiration. Her success at least shows what was in the air.[57]

R.C. Petersen has made a careful study of the history of experimental schools in Australia since the beginning of the twentieth century, in which he reviews a score or so of cases. He shows that most were highly derivative, but concludes moderately that the limited Australian experience of 'progressive' education nevertheless does illuminate the wider movement from which the experiments derived. He also suggests that the Australian response to experimental schooling has always been extremely cautious. But the theosophists, whose efforts account for no fewer than four out of six of the experimental schools identified in the first phase of experimentation, moved very quickly once the section had agreed to launch a school. In addition to British models, and the Zeitgeist which Winifred West said inspired her to found Frensham, the Australian section had before it the prospect of the sixth sub-race. They now believed, as Marjorie Bull was taught, that there was something special about theosophical children in Australia.

The ways in which the special needs of theosophical children could be met were addressed in terms of the 'new education' and a model school, as at a conference of TS workers in education in Sydney on 25 April 1916 (and earlier in New Zealand). Parents of children showing signs of sixth sub-race characteristics were located. On the motion of L.W. Burt, seconded by J.B. McConkey, Convention in 1916 approved in principle the founding of a theosophical school along the lines laid down by *Education as Service*. At the 1917 Convention, T.H. Martyn announced the formation of a school affiliated with the Theosophical Educational Trust through the section executive. It would stand for a truly religious education and the unfoldment of children individually, living under enlightened conditions. Delegates said they wanted a school where 'religious instruction should be imparted, cramming eliminated, and each individual child studied with a view to unfolding its particular genius'. Martyn thought the prognosis very fair, since the school would attract both local and Far Eastern children whose parents wanted the benefit of association with Leadbeater. Four hundred and twenty pounds was raised instantly.[58] At a concurrent conference of TS class leaders and propagandists, Stanley Sprott Fisher, a leading Perth theosophist and senior public servant, successfully moved that 'this conference is of the opinion that the question of the Newer Education is a matter of vital importance. It therefore recommends that Lodges throughout Australia ... study the question with a view to assisting the Theosophical School movement, and to secure reform in the existing State and Secondary School Systems'. In 1918 an Australian Educational Fraternity was launched by a committee of theosophist-teachers. By then, a Theosophical Educational Trust of Australia had things well under way. Convention delegates were able to inspect their own school, Morven Garden School.[59]

They were impressed. With typical acumen the trust had acquired a splendid site, five and a half acres of land on Morven Lane, just off the Pacific Highway at Gore Hill on Sydney's lower North Shore, about half an hour's drive from the city. It contained a functioning gentleman's residence, and commanded views of the harbour and towards the Blue Mountains. At £3,500 it was cheap. In the presence of local dignitaries, Leadbeater laid the foundation stone for a teaching block over copies of *Education as Service* (the school's motto) and the signatures of Annie Besant and Krishnamurti.[60] Soon after, on 9 April 1918, Morven Garden School opened with twenty pupils. By early 1920 it was operating as an all-age co-educational day and boarding school with an enrolment of 112 – fifty-eight girls (forty of these boarders) and fifty-four boys (thirty-four boarders) – probably the only co-educational boarding school in Australia at the time apart from Friends' School, Hobart. Sixteen acres of bushland were added to the grounds, donated by Sydney member Captain Russell Lloyd Jones, now a New York bookseller. Aided by the Reverend Kay, senior master of the boys' school which opened in 1919, the Misses Arnold and Macdonald presided over a flourishing and cosmopolitan school, which implemented many progressive educational principles.[61]

In 1921, aged fourteen, Sydney writer Helen Heney enrolled as a boarder at Morven Garden School, on the advice of her aunt Dr Lucy Gullett, because it was coeducational. She vividly recalls theosophical life at the school in the early twenties – vegetarian meals, Greek dancing, concerts at the Conservatorium, Knights of the Round Table ('a very clever wheeze in that everyone had a duty so that half the work of the school was done in the name of spiritual development') and visits by prominent theosophists, Annie Besant and Krishnamurti, 'a beautiful boy, unspoiled, unflawed, gentle'. There were far fewer boys than she had expected, and more domestic labour, such as window cleaning, but 'we had a very nice time'.[62]

Heney remembers that the students themselves insisted on an adequate education, especially 'a small turbulent minority of girls'. Though some girls were withdrawn, she and her friends Hope Clay on and Dorothea Hughes (Thea Stanley Hughes, later a eurhythmics teachers and Australian sponsor of the Women's League of Health), stayed the course. Although she was mistakenly allowed to drop maths, Heney duly matriculated, and recalls able women teachers, Miss Macdonald, Olga Moss from Brisbane, and Roseen Guiterman, said to have been from a prominent Zionist family. By 1928 Helen Heney had graduated BA (Hons) from the University of Sydney and rejected theosophy, but perhaps retained sympathy with the culture which produced what she now calls 'jazz religion', a thought prompted not only by her career as teacher, social worker, author and animal welfare worker, but her statement in *Who's Who of Australian Women* (1982):

> 'As I believe that human reincarnation is the only belief consistent with our hope of a merciful as well as a just and wise deity, I am trying to use the time remaining to me to cultivate and express compassion to as much of creation as may be without fanaticism'.

The ups and downs of Helen Heney's education notwithstanding, the school and staff of ten was judged satisfactory after state inspection in 1922. Seemingly its closure in 1923 after six years of teaching followed from a wider crisis in the society rather than from its educational principles. However, these were very advanced for Australia, and the trust had already fallen into financial difficulty, as it tried unsuccessfully to sell the school early in 1922; so the crisis of the section was the coup de grace for its school. To look ahead briefly, it was closed at the end of 1923, sold in 1925–1926, and the outstanding debts of the Educational Trust amounting to £6000 finally paid off by 1928. Its site is now occupied by the Sunshine Home for intellectually handicapped people, established in 1924 by Dr Lorna K. Hodgkinson (1887–1951).[63]

It is interesting to speculate on Dr Hodgkinson's links with theosophy. Affinities are evident in that she was trained as an infant teacher in Perth, taking courses in kindergarten and Montessori methods, and, after teaching in Perth and Sydney, was employed by the State Children's Relief Board, training delinquent and backward children at Carlingford. In 1920 she went to America as a student at Harvard University's newly established Graduate School of Education, where she was the first woman to receive a doctorate of education in 1922, with a thesis on 'Diagnosis and Treatment of Atypical Children in Public School Systems'. Returning in late 1922 she was appointed Supervisor of Education for Mental Defectives in New South Wales until the post was terminated in May 1924; shortly afterwards she established the Sunshine Home at Gore Hill. It would seem that Dr Hodgkinson was at least a congenial lessee of Morven Garden School. Theosophists would have sympathised with her work, whether or not she sympathised with them.[64]

The story of theosophical educational experiment did not end in 1923, though official involvement did. In 1924 Arnold and Macdonald founded the Garden School at Stanton Road, Balmoral, as a private venture in a large stone house with wide grounds (only the stone fence survives today). They continued as theosophic educators in Sydney until 1946, although the Garden School did not survive the depression. St Margaret's in Devonport lasted until the late twenties when its proprietors died. As for the most radical of the four theosophical schools, the tiny, boys-only King Arthur Home School at Neutral Bay, it ran for about a year in 1922–23 under a newly arrived Leadbeater disciple, the young Dutch coffee heir J.J. van der Leeuw, who was previously and briefly in charge of Morven Garden School – a peculiar young Dutchman, said Heney, 'who tried to run the school on Boy Scout lines'. (Vasanta Garden School established by New Zealand theosophists in Auckland in 1919 survived until 1959.)[65]

Theosophical schools were really exotics, with shallow roots. They did not become a permanent feature of alternative education in Australia. Nevertheless they occupy a substantial place in the rather flimsy history of alternative education (as perhaps do Steiner schools after World War II). Morven Garden School especially represented considerable novelty and commitment in 1919, with over £8000 already expended. Its corporate individualism may not seem very progressive today, but it was abreast of its times, and exploited bourgeois aspiration and anxiety effectively. In 1919 the school library received a copy of C.E.W. Bean's *In Your Hands, Australians!*, and he and Major-General White donated their portraits to the school's proposed gallery of 'Australia's Master Builders'. How many disciples for the coming World Teacher were produced is another, more painful, perhaps suppressed, issue; but Helen Heney and friends are evidence that some interesting young people passed through its briefly opened doors.[66]

The threefold program of Leadbeater–Besant in 1916 included religion and ritual as well as education. Shortly after the war two large buildings standing side by side in Regent Street, Redfern, near Sydney's Central Station, proclaimed the other two priorities. One, a co-masonic temple, was not particularly controversial, embodying commitments made before the war, now intensified because Leadbeater himself joined the order in 1915. The other, previously a Methodist mission church, renamed St Alban's Pro-Cathedral, stood for something altogether new and problematic, the idea of a 'theosophical' church, called first the Old Catholic Church and then in 1918 the Liberal Catholic Church. Now organised internationally and quite

St Alban's Liberal Catholic church and co-masonic temple
in Regent Street, Sydney, 1926 (ML)

independent of theosophy, it has small congregations in most capital cities. The 'ideal church' progressed almost as quickly as the model school. By late 1918 several private oratories and two churches had been established, with a local clergy to serve the predominantly theosophical worshippers.

The Liberal Catholic Church was not an attempt at an 'Australian' church like Charles Strong's venture thirty years earlier. Its roots lay in England where, in A.H. Nethercot's helpful reconstruction, it had 'a strange and not very respectable history' through the old Catholic movement dating back to opposition among Catholics to the doctrine of papal infallibility enunciated in 1870. These and certain disaffected Anglicans took heart from the survival of an Old Catholic Church in Holland. There, Dutch Jansenist bishops of the OCC retained a legitimate, that is, true and apostolic, succession, and were willing to ordain and consecrate renegades. The chain of events leading to an Old Catholic Church in England – and ultimately to the Liberal Catholic Church – began when Arnold Mathew (1852–1919) was consecrated as a bishop in Holland in 1908. He subsequently ordained others, marginal and doubtful candidates of comparable but lesser stature to the extraordinary Rolfe, the self-styled Baron Corvo, Scourge of the Papacy, or 'the great beast', Edwardian occultist Aleister Crowley. There seems to have been a flow of hopefuls thrown up by counter-revolutionary currents and hieratic dissatisfaction in the 1890s. In 1913 Mathew ordained James Ingall Wedgwood (1883–1951), a member of the great pottery family, previously an Anglican and a convert to theosophy in 1904. Mathew also ordained and elevated a defrocked Anglican clergyman, Willoughby; but realising his mistake, dismissed Willoughby six months later in May 1915. For good measure Mathew closed the Old Catholic Church in England in December 1915, returning himself to the Roman fold.[67]

Wedgwood, general secretary of the English Theosophical Society 1911–13, and co-ordinator of comasonry 1913–15, was at Adyar in autumn 1914 and in Australia throughout 1915 promoting various ritual movements. Not to be deprived of his new-found clerical status, Wedgwood rushed back to England and in February 1916 the remaining bishops, including the tainted Willoughby, consecrated him Presiding Bishop of the Old Catholic Church. Dressed in garments becoming the status of a presiding bishop, which also protected the wearer from military attentions – these were the days of conscription in Britain – Wedgwood returned to Australia, and a warm welcome in Perth, in mid-1916.[68]

Annie Besant was soon surprised to learn more of the wandering bishop. When he arrived in Sydney, Wedgwood consecrated Leadbeater as a bishop too, in novel rituals performed at the Köllerstrom home, 'Crendon', Neutral Bay, on 22 July 1916. Leadbeater, presenting her with the *fait accompli*, wrote that 'the movement would fill a niche in the scheme', and that the church would be a channel for the coming World Teacher, blessed by the Lord Maitreya. Besant loyally supported the ecclesiastical adventure, outlining its credentials in *The Theosophist*, on the grounds that it was 'likely to become the future church of Christendom when He comes'. A spate of mainly keen articles followed in the Australian journal.[69]

Nethercot correctly observes that promotion of the Old Catholic Church (as it was first known) launched 'a disastrous avalanche of trouble in Australia'. But many theosophists responded with wholehearted enthusiasm. Wedgwood, an impressive and upstanding young man with a private income, made successful proselytising tours of Australia and New Zealand in the later war years. Would-be members of the ideal church gathered in theosophical backrooms to witness with some wonderment celebration of the Mass in the vernacular. The spectacle of Wedgwood in purple cassock and mozetta caused quite a stir, since very few of the new worshippers had previously seen such items close up. Men immediately came forward for ordination from most of the large lodges. Soon Sydney was a mecca for male persons with clerical aspirations.

The first services were held in Melbourne in June 1916, even before Leadbeater's elevation. John Beatty McConkey (1864–1951), lawyer and long-time leader of Melbourne theosophists, president of Eastern Hill lodge 1907–1909 and of Melbourne lodge 1914–1915, was ordained in Sydney on 21 July 1916. David Morton Tweedie (1857–1941), was rebaptised and confirmed at his mansion, 'Straven', at Glen Osmond, Adelaide, by Wedgwood en route for Sydney, and later ordained at the TS building, Adelaide, on 5 July 1916, the first of the attendant priesthood (later he went to Brisbane as priest-in-charge of the Liberal Catholic church there, 1921–1932). A few months later Gustav Köllerstrom, mainstay in Sydney since the early days, also entered the ranks of the new priesthood at another ceremony at 'Crendon'. In Perth, Stanley Sprott Fisher (1881–1950), who had joined the TS in 1899 and served for a decade as secretary of Perth lodge, achieved his heart's desire of ordination later, in 1918, by Julian Adrian Mazel, a Dutch associate of Leadbeater's and bishop of one year's standing himself. Mazel baptised and confirmed forty-three people on that visit to Perth.[70]

The early twenties saw many more such ordinations in Sydney, usually performed by Leadbeater, with candidates from near and far, as near as Leadbeater's personal secretary, the young Harold Morton, and as far as Amsterdam and Shanghai, when van der Leeuw and ex-Baptist missionary Spurgeon Medhurst were elevated. The world of theosophy, once firmly anticlerical, was increasingly complicated by the translation of some of its stalwarts into clerical garb, and the addition of cosmopolitan talents. T.H. Martyn, upset by the trend, proposed a series of resolutions to the 1918 Convention which, if successful, would have dissociated the OCC churchmen from the Theosophical Society: these proclaimed the neutrality of the society, opposed the use of TS facilities by churchmen, and prohibited the use of clerical titles on theosophical platforms. Martyn said that if titles were allowed the lodge syllabus would soon look like a churchman's outing. But, after heated discussion, the motions were suitably toned down to a restatement of the traditional position of TS neutrality:

> That the Australian Section of the T.S. in Convention assembled, in view of misconceptions which have arisen, disclaims any official association with any and all divisions of the Christian Church, or with any other religious organisations, and reasserts its firm adherence to the first object of the Society, i.e. to form a nucleus of the universal brotherhood of humanity without distinction of race, creed, sex, caste or colour, and its sympathetic interest in the spiritual work of all religions alike.[71]

The many attendant 'clergy' affirmed that their new church was indeed a separate organisation. This was all meant to produce a consensus that the ideal church was a help to theosophy – 'made an opening' – and that its voluntary clergy would remove one source of popular mistrust and difficulty for true religion, namely the paid clergy. Martyn himself offered the olive branch: 'Many people mistrusted "religion" in Australia because they distrusted the professional priesthood.'

They were not more likely to be wooed by the gorgeously arrayed representatives of the new church. Reports trickled back from London of unsavoury demeanour, and the hostility of men like Prentice intensified: 'That damned fool Wedgwood wanders round in purple clothes and a cross nearly two feet high hung in front of him.' The new church attracted renewed attention from hostile Christian churchmen, a fresh wave of anti-theosophical pamphleteering which attacked the new church's credentials and intentions. It was, argued English pamphleteer Stanley Morrison, a blasphemous theosophical front, neither old nor catholic. The gap between the church's public presentation and its inner teaching increased its vulnerability to such attacks, for, as Gregory Tillett has explained, it was claimed that the new church existed to forward the work of her Master Christ and was inspired by faith in the living Christ, but the Master Christ was not necessarily the same person as the Christian Jesus and the Living Christ was really the Lord Maitreya, head of the occult hierarchy, now preparing to revisit the world.[72]

Controversy seldom harms a timely cause. The church flourished, especially in Sydney where, despite dusty surrounds, services replete with

'Oriental luxury and elaborate ceremonial' were celebrated in accordance with Christian ritual laboriously revised by the bishops to enhance magical and mystical forces and diminish demeaning practices. Just as the freethought movement of the late nineteenth century perished because of its own aridity, and freethinkers drifted in all sorts of more emotionally sustaining directions in the 1890s, so the abstruse and impersonal theosophical program was wide open to a ritualistic raid. Not only were many theosophists really in search of the perfected church, but also the sectarian rigidities of Australian religious life intensified the impasse to which unbelief had brought so many. As presented by the articulate and cultured Wedgwood – he was an organist, and organ builder of some repute – the new church could seem a positive step to the religious, still yearning for ritual and a cultivated theology rather than the various fundamentalisms of their youth. As expressed today, the aims of the ideal church promoted by Leadbeater and Besant in 1916 are:

> [to combine] the traditional sacramental form of worship – with its stately ritual, its deep mysticism and its abiding witness to the reality of sacramental grace – with the widest measure of intellectual liberty and respect for the individual conscience.
>
> It uses a revised Liturgy in the vernacular, wherein the essential features of the various sacramental forms are preserved with scrupulous care, but from which outdated forms of worship expressing fear of God and His wrath, and attitudes of servile self-abasement and appeals for mercy, have been eliminated as derogatory both to the ideas of a Loving Father and to man whom He created in His own image.[73]

In September 1918 the Old Catholic Church Wedgwood–Leadbeater style became the Liberal Catholic Church, of necessity as well as preference in that the Old Catholic Church in Europe disowned the English off shoot. But, as is obvious already, the church forged ahead. Accounts of its progress in Australia are available from three adherents, all women, the veteran Adelaide theosophist and legator Constance Radcliffe, Elsie Deane of Besant lodge, Melbourne, and the young Marjorie Bull of Sydney.

Constance Radcliffe (1882–1978), daughter of an Adelaide homeopathic chemist, recalled exactly the steps by which the Liberal Catholic Church at Regent Street, Redfern, Sydney was acquired. She was a convenor of the first Sydney meeting of sympathisers held in Star rooms in Elizabeth Street in early 1917. Services were held in the Oddfellows temple, Clarke Street, in 1918. Then, aided by Martyn, they discovered the vacated Wesleyan church beyond Central Railway, a bargain, worth over £10,000. £1100 was promised on the spot, and £500 paid over by John Mackay in August 1918. On the Sunday morning of 17 November 1918, three bishops, seven priests and fourteen acolytes performed a consecratory service, with eight choirmen.[74]

Elsie Deane was the daughter of a railway engineer, London-born Henry Deane (1847–1924), a theosophist best known as surveyor of the transcontinental railway line, and of Matilda Deane (1870?–?), of literary inclination. Among her papers – which also reveal great frustration during attempts to attain economic independence, in journalism, secretarial work and then, more assuredly, in historical research – are retained evidences of the Old Catholic Church's beginnings in Melbourne. Elsie Deane responded to McConkey's requests for support in ways that reveal agreement with Besant's rationale, and typical theosophical perspectives. Although an Anglican herself, Deane thought the revived or Old Catholic Church might contain the nucleus of a great movement in the future; she would join if the ideal church was closely allied to TS aims, and offered more intelligent ceremony and ritual than the Church of England. She regretted that she could not, alas, contribute financially to this or to any other movement in which she was deeply interested, as she was not well enough paid as a secretary to save money. She subsequently contributed. She came to see, as she explained to the local Anglican minister, that the OCC was 'just what I need'.[75]

Deane, whose spiritual difficulties sprang in part from a mixed religious parentage – mother Catholic, father Quaker – and in part from personal dissatisfaction with the narrow evangelical Anglicanism she adopted, recorded her satisfaction with the new church in early 1918. She attended service in a disused Pentecostal chapel in Punt Road, and now gave 1/- per week. She was apparently pressed to that, according to an undated circular received from McConkey's aide, H.S. Hesselman of Hawthorn. From it the full import of the 'ideal church' is seen: 'It is hardly necessary to point out the grave responsibility with which we have been entrusted or the priceless opportunity of actively assisting in establishing a Church, which will receive the World Teacher when He comes.' Elsie Deane was not one to shirk responsibility. As well, the time had come for the new dispensation:

'Great things must happen now if the full value of all the sacrifice is to be received.'[76] So, in women like Elsie Deane, the new church found its congregation.

No doubt the appeal lay in the way the new churchmen stripped Christianity both of Calvinist and of Catholic terrors and retained the aesthetic and therapeutic pleasures of religious practice – in the elaborate ritual and sacramental expressiveness of the church, its main feature and perhaps function. But its motor was clerical. And their liberality was not apparent. The new officers were not to be servants of a congregation but trained priests, albeit voluntary and unpaid. It is ironic, but quite understandable, given its origins, that recollections of 'the ideal church' come from women, observers excluded from the priesthood, as were lower-class men.

Marjorie Bull recalls her father Oscar Degen, later caretaker of Adyar House, as a devout church man, revelling in ritual and the new priestly order, but, having no formal education, never more than a 'blue man', the lowest of the sub-orders of church servors: 'my father was a blue man, and he always carried the banners, that's all he ever did'. At least he was part of the sacristy, where no women were allowed. Women composed the music for the service, and designed and embroidered the gorgeous clerical garments, but 'it was a very male-dominated thing ... really very high church, and not an ounce of sin anywhere'.[77]

And yet, for the young Marjorie Bull, a sensitive child set apart from her fellows at Paddington elementary school by her English accent and her theosophical upbringing, these new services were entrancing, as they were for the other schoolgirl, Helen Heney. The excitements of religion came to her from the men at St Alban's, especially Wedgwood whom she revered:

> What I got from it all was my almost bewitched listening in the Liberal Catholic Church, to what those beautiful people would be saying ... I know that I listened in a particular way because I can remember my face being taken into the hands of many people and held under the chin. They used to say 'This little girl listens so much to what we have to say'.

She too felt the powerful sense of a new dispensation, its urgency. When asked about attending Sunday services in the now blighted Regent Street, she vividly portrayed the pre-automobile era, the trek with fellow worshippers from the tram stop at Central Station through streets deserted of all but the nearby Christadelphian worshippers, and the feeling of doing something tremendous for humanity, 'building up this tremendous thought form from the Mass and Eucharist and really sending out a great blessing all over the area ... giving something to the Sydney area where the service was taking place'. To the same services the poet Christopher Brennan sometimes repaired.

Theosophical churchmanship remained a controversial issue. It would not go away. But that is a story of the twenties, heyday of St Alban's, when it boasted a choir and a magazine and its services were broadcast weekly on Radio 2GB; and, at last, churchmen performed theosophical weddings, as between Lilian Outhwaite and Dr Walpole of St Margaret's, Devonport, and when Dr Bean married Isabelle John, his brother Charles as witness, in 1922.[78]

The Liberal Catholic Church was the turbulent creation of turbulent times. It was established during the Great War by men who tapped the longing for comfort and reassurance, and for new ideals in religion and education. The appearance of the court of the faerie queene changed dramatically a t that time. Before the war sober men and thoughtful women were the main attenders. Now they were transformed or overshadowed by egregious clerical courtiers. As usual Mars meant a new lease of life for male rather than human values, though that was not obvious at the time to most theosophists, fully stretched by the busy round from lodge to temple to church to school. The best thing to do when anticipating the millennium is to keep busy.

7

The height of expectancy

The 1920s in Australia have often been characterised as a mean and disappointing decade: politically reactionary, culturally repressive, and manic economically. In the famous slogan of the times, what mattered was 'Men, Money, and Markets'. Otherwise, it has been observed, Australia's innocent image was protected with unprecedented zeal. Gough Whitlam, launching Donald Horne's biography of Billy Hughes in 1979, encapsulated it when he said that World War I changed independent Australian into a British province.[1]

At the same time, the new suburbs and the big stores promised plenty on a quite unBritish scale. A contrasting view takes in the Americanisation of Australian society since the twenties, seen as the vital take-off point for contemporary consumerism. Furthermore, the 1920s saw the establishment of an independently minded Australian heavy industry, making of Australian manufacturing an altogether new force.

Not surprisingly, Australia experienced some of the same tensions as both British and American society. The legendary turbulence of the twenties in America, simultaneously experiencing both cultural rebellion and, as in Prohibition, reaction, foreshadowed comparable transitions in Australia. The British fear of internal conflict (culminating in the General Strike of May 1926) and of imperial decline had obvious reverberations in Australia. Over all hung the spectre of the Bolshevik revolution in Russia. It is no wonder that every effort was made to calm the common people after the war.

If there were few unambiguous indications of a new postwar order, the old order could not be restored either, and conventional opinion had many reasons for anxiety. In the religious sphere, evidence of malaise, especially a resurgence of spiritualism, alarmed Christian orthodoxy, which witnessed a puzzling range of sects and cults of increasing appeal according to interwar censuses. The range of minority religious movements was known to encompass not only spiritualist revival and renewed fundamentalist zeal, but also adventist sects and perfectionist or millenarian cults. To cite three famous examples, these were the days of Aimee Semple Macpherson, Californian evangelist extraordinaire, Christabel Pankhurst, student of biblical prophecy, and the Armenian guru, Gurdjieff, with his Institute of Harmonious Development outside Paris where Katherine Mansfield died.[2]

There was a good deal of adventism in the twenties, after the Great War. Historically, movements proclaiming the imminent return of Christ to this world have flourished in periods of cultural unease and transition; and at no time in modern history was a literal reading of the biblical book of Revelations more plausible. Its visionary representation of the apocalypse, Armageddon, the millennium and the Last Judgement related readily to recent experience. Mostly twenties adventisms were orthodox and as in the past came to nothing. But the theosophical version was different, eclectic, exuberant, the ultimate in reconstruction. 'We hold,' said one Australian theosophist in *Theosophy in Australasia* in May 1919,

> that this mighty New Thought movement sweeping over the world ... Christian Science, the Eustace Miles and other food reform movements, physical culture, the women's movement, spiritualism, Bahaism, and many other great spiritual movements, as well as the regeneration, reinterpretation and reconstruction of the old-established world religions, – all these are the John the Baptists of our day, preparing the paths of the Great Lord ... till He shall come and 'guide our feet in the way of peace'.

Annie Besant, speaking at the Golden Jubilee of the Theosophical Society at Adyar on 27 December 1925, nudged historical necessity in troubled times:

> We stand then today at this critical point, a new type appearing in the human kingdom. You notice that it has lately been said that the World Teacher will soon be amongst us. It is known to some of us that He has slightly hastened what we may call the date of His coming because of the troubled and almost hopeless condition of the modern world, rent by quarrels of every description – quarrels of Nations, quarrels of classes, quarrels of the

various vocations even, that are the functions of national life and so, it is the great need of the world which calls Him from His own secret retreat in the Himalayas to the rescue of a world which threatens to perish for the lack of Him. At this great crisis then in the world's history – to say nothing of those earlier millennia – when the Theosophical Society has existed for fifty years, having proclaimed in all countries the great basic truths that are held in common by all religions ... it would be strange if ... the World Teacher did not come back to His world as a man among men, to guide it along the path of its further evolution.[3]

The very next day, a man among men, the 30-year-old Krishnamurti assumed the mantle, mentioning his mission for the first time. In two much-quoted sentences he promised:

I come for those who want sympathy, who want happiness, who are longing to be released, who are longing to find happiness in all things. I come to reform and not tear down, I come not to destroy but to build.[4]

With this, those theosophists who supported the Order of the Star in the East reached the pinnacle of religious experience. Their leaders' prediction of evolutionary advance had come to pass. Concurrently in Australia as elsewhere the Theosophical Society reached its peak numerically. A dramatic change in the character of theosophy was effected. Amid a blaze of controversy, it transformed itself into something like a millenarian cult, leaving by the wayside a host of doubting Thomases. Ultimately, the twenties proved to be the 'great days' of theosophy in Australia; but they began in tribulation. Tribulation lasted until 1925. What happened during the height of expectancy between 1921 and 1925 is best introduced from the centre, in Sydney, locus of conflict and a lovely site for the Coming. Fortunately for the fullness of historical understanding Mrs Besant reappeared on what can only be described as a disturbed scene in 1922.

Sydney in the twenties was already Australia's most vital and cosmopolitan city, with the kinds of trading links along which theosophical ideas might readily travel, from North and South Asia and via the Pacific. It was in Sydney that the theosophical presence was the most convincing. There more than anywhere else in Australia theosophy continued to emit an aura of vitality, verging on respectability, the sense of which can still be

The magnificent Manor in Iluka Road, Clifton Gardens, Sydney, a theosophical community since the early 1920s. (*TinA*)

felt in the hope of aged theosophists in remote parts who would like just once more to come to Sydney. In the twenties about one in three Australian theosophists lived in Sydney.[5]

The theosophical presence was affirmed by an imposing and valuable building at 69 Hunter Street, just off the city's administrative spine and within its cultural core. The building was fronted by a bookshop and flanked by St Michael's flats and the King's Hall – both modern, and the latter used for public meetings, plays and concerts. It housed sectional headquarters, and Sydney lodge with its busy program of lectures, classes and meetings.

Since 1901 Sydney lodge had been the largest in the section. On 27 January 1921 the retiring president, T.H. Martyn, reported a total membership of 695, a net annual gain of 104. The year 1920 was one of unprecedented growth, and the lodge was now an efficient 'all-embracing' organisation for the service of the Masters. However, 1921 proved to be an even better year in the service of the Masters, under the presidency of lecturer and Liberal Catholic L.W. Burt: Sydney lodge claimed 800 members, and boasted a lively program including lectures on the advanced topic of psychology. There were also several suburban lodges, at Strathfield, Chatswood, Ashfield (Western Suburbs lodge) and Enmore, plus 'Study Centres' at Marrickville, Manly, Redfern and Forest Lodge.[6]

In the suburbs, especially on the lower North Shore, lay scattered a comfortable theosophical community – the envy of poorer theosophical families in the inner city – focused increasingly around Mosman and the Manor. Previously known as 'Bakewell's Folly', this 55-roomed Edwardian mansion in Iluka Road, Clifton Gardens was acquired in 1922 as a home for Leadbeater; and with some thirty-five other residents including several families by 1923, the Manor was soon to be presented as 'an interesting experiment in community life' with an 'expert manageress'. The representative men of the theosophical community in Sydney were T.H. Martyn and John Mackay.[7]

Led by such worthy men it is understandable that Sydney lodge was reputedly not only the largest but also the richest theosophical lodge in the world. Adding to the sense of presence and community were the model school for theosophical children at St Leonards and the ideal church at Redfern. With Leadbeater in seemingly permanent residence, the lure of the community increased, promising spiritual and, by then, clerical advancement.[8]

Theosophical listings for Sydney suggest a considerable European leavening. After World War I there was a pronounced Dutch colonial flavour. For example, the male delegates to annual convention now included K. van Gelder, founder of a Javanese Section of the TS, Adrian Vreede, a doctor of Dutch law who transferred his membership from Java in 1919, and the learned young Dutchman van der Leeuw. A military stiffening also showed in delegations by 1922. Along with Dr Bean came Raymond Perdriau, MLA, a corporal in the AIF (3rd Division artillery) and, from Tasmania, the redoubtable Prentice. Noticeable also are the names of professional men like accountant William Harding representing the suburban lodge effort, and an ever-increasing contingent of administrative staff, George Chappel and Loris Ingamells, servants of an optimistic cause.[9]

Although Sydney convention delegations usually included a fair number of women, few emerge from the sources independent of their husbands apart from Mrs John (to become Mrs Bean in 1922) and the musical Mrs Greig. It is easier to say something of the men, though they mostly remain as names too. The evidence suggests a cross-section of the middling class. Of fifty-one New South Welshmen attending conventions in 1920 and 1922, the occupations of less than a third are discernible: stockbroker, grazier (retired), printer, lawyer, jeweller, estate agent, ex-clergyman, teacher, tax accountant, rural politician, three doctors, two lecturers, perhaps a builder. Some evidence also suggests that many were immigrant, and so they were perhaps self-made men. It may also be proposed that they were 'edgy', on the margins of Sydney's not inconsiderable commercial and professional classes: there are few names of known independent status in Sydney society.

Sydney theosophy may have been of uncertain social status in the twenties, but events like the psychology lectures suggest that it flourished by keeping abreast of advanced thought. In 1921 Dr Donald Fraser – probably the same Dr Fraser who was expelled from the Presbyterian Church of NSW in 1896 and started branches of the Australian Church in Newcastle – was lecturing from G.F. Tansley's *The New Psychology and its Relation to Life* (London, 1920), a successful popularisation of Freudian concepts which went through ten impressions in five years. Theosophists had always been interested in psychology, as the society's third object – study of man's latent powers – indicates. Though sympathetic to the new teaching, they soon discovered that Freud and Blavatsky were worlds apart, and increasingly deplored preoccupation with the abnormal in a new discipline.[10]

Unfortunately, lectures in 'abnormal' psychology provided poor protection against certain realities which increasingly disturbed members of Sydney lodge. Behind the facade the lodge was deeply divided over Bishops Wedgwood and Leadbeater, and their sinless church. From 1919 onwards, evidence of homosexuality in the Liberal Catholic clergy filtered through from London. By 1921 the whole section was disturbed by similar rumours in Sydney.[11]

Watchful enemies in America saw the makings of an interesting crisis in the 'AB Society'. Because he decided to act against the church men, T.H. Martyn virtually lost faith in Annie Besant, who in April 1921 deposed him as ES leader in favour of Leadbeater. In August, at the invitation of Dr Fraser, a sizeable minority of Sydney lodge members and its executive formed a TS Loyalty League to reassert theosophical objectives, proclaim the society's religious neutrality and oppose the use of lodge premises by clergy. In September Sydney lodge itself stated publicly: 'There is no Theosophical Society Church.' In November the league launched a bi-monthly magazine, *Dawn*, for public purchase, as a rallying point for freedom of opinion – and, more daringly, to mock 'There is no Religion Higher than Credulity'. Soon

Dawn was to claim evidence of moral corruption in high places, and it was all over the daily press of Sydney.[12]

It might be thought that the dissidents found the situation titillating, but the temper of the times must be remembered. While restraints were relaxing in theory, social anxieties had heightened. Both sex and religion were avoided as topics in polite conversation. Neither the criminal code nor social standards sanctioned sexual deviance. It is also pertinent to recall that the lurid face of anti-catholicism, with its endless imaginings of depravity in religious orders, intensified in the 1920s. In truth, priests and perversion were equally appalling to respectable theosophists and orthodox Christians.[13]

Perhaps if the problem had been confined to homosexual practices among priests it would have been manageable – they might have survived discreetly in a society proud of its tolerance, protected too by occult distinctions regarding the physical and astral body. After all, *Ross's Monthly* later said, religious teachers were often sexually abnormal, and what was the point of moral mudslinging?[14] Moreover the Liberal Catholic Church was highly ritualistic, and might have served as harmless sublimator.

The association of ritualism and male homosexuality is longstanding and, it has recently been argued, pronounced in late Victorian religious history. As the distance between male and female spheres widened and social practices were increasingly regulated, so deviant sexuality became more conspicuous. Respite was to be had in some large hierarchical organisations, notoriously the army and the church. Within the Church of England there remained some haven for latent male homosexuals (though 'muscular Christianity' among the Broad clergy was increasingly constricting too). Some of those unable to conform sought new structures to accommodate the ritualism which until then had been an effective sublimator. As much may be inferred also from curious private and magical cults of the 1890s, leading Edwardian lights of the OCC, and the rush to purple a decade later by Wedgwood and the aged ex-curate Leadbeater. They certainly worked hard at constructing formulae for their new church.[15]

However, critics of the church were not simply bothered by male homosexuality by priests – and /or perversion – delicate as that issue was. Increasingly involved was the resurgent and unpalatable domestic problem of Bishop Leadbeater, tutor of boys. That was a more complex issue, scarcely manageable today under the heading of paedophilia because it involves minors (and parents).[16] Apparently the situation was akin to the problem of religious cults today, charged with alienating children from their families.

There was a further twist. A major problem for dissident theosophists was that theosophical parents accepted Leadbeater, a guru or *Arhat*, as spiritual tutor to their sons, who resided with him, all house-guests of wealthy theosophists; in Sydney first with the Martyns, and then with their neighbours, the Köllerstroms. In general, all parties were in collusion for the sake of religious advancement.

Moreover, the distress was very much *ex post facto*. It is recounted by the hostile J.M. Prentice, and was testified by Mrs Martyn to the NSW CID, that she rejected Leadbeater as a resident at St Michaels (4 Raymond Road, Neutral Bay) because he interfered with her marriage, and also with the boys. No such scandal ever emerged from the Köllerstrom household. Nor, despite her nervous collapse, did T.H. Martyn take his wife's difficulties seriously until Leadbeater and company encumbered theosophy with a priesthood.[17]

The fact that Leadbeater never retracted his advice on the desirability of masturbation could and sometimes did tell in his favour. That he was said to detest (married) women as impure seems to have offended nobody in theosophical circles except Mrs Martyn and her maid. And there was a chorus of adult testimony, from ex-pupils, clergy and single women as to the bishop's pure moral stature.[18]

Nevertheless, many feared the worst. Privately, some came to regard the church as bogus, merely a front for the procuration of boys. Leadbeater lay low, working on *The Science of the Sacraments* (1920, 2nd edn., 1929). Dr Bean, writing to his family at Christmas 1921, predicted that 'the old feud between the Liberal Catholic Church and the Anti-Church Party in the TS' would probably lead to a split this time, and to his own demise as general secretary. The increasingly real prospect of the presidential presence at the next Convention kept the lid on an unsavoury stew. Surely Annie Besant could handle it.[19]

In Australia, Annie Besant was always a figure larger than life. The *Daily Telegraph* reported electrical restlessness as the train from Perth drew in at Sydney Central on 9 May 1922. Marjorie Bull, a retired Sydney social worker,

Annie Besant arrives at Central Station, Sydney, May 1922.
With Leadbeater and Jinarajadasa.(Campbell Collection)

then an eight-year-old Lotus Bud, remembers moods of 'absolute awe and wonder'. Aged seventy-five, Besant was still a powerful personality. The encounter was for Mrs Clare Thompson of Perth one of life's rare moments: 'she took me into another dimension.' Dr Bean's adulation of the 'Christlike' Annie was still so intense that she had rebuked him, he confessed to his brother Charles.[20]

As with people, so with situations. That Dr Besant – she received an honorary doctorate of letters from the Hindu University in 1922 – came at all meant action. Though the president's purposes were not disclosed, her presence extended the scope of the simmering Sydney dispute. In her wake came publicity, politics, even sexual politics, all new and disagreeable dimensions. She had enormous authority, both formally and personally, and was still quite capable of exercising it.

What she did stunned the dissidents. She told them to call the police. There was a Gilbertian public meeting where the chair (Senator Reid) gagged debate and hustled through a motion condemning disloyalty. Loyalty Leaguers were expelled from the secret Esoteric Society, run by the president, and she established a separate new lodge for the faithful. With that, after three unpleasant weeks in Sydney, Dr Besant returned to India, a disagreeable duty done, she said, only a storm in a puddle.[21]

Nevertheless, the situation was quite transformed. T.H. Martyn angrily said she had been bluffing about the police. Others said her approach was unproductive. Perhaps so, but she was on sure ground. Under the circumstances, how could a case be mounted against Leadbeater? Marion Piddington, prominent Sydney feminist and birth-controller with an abhorrence of masturbation, recounted to British birth-controller Marie Stopes that there was evidence: 'We had evidence of worse things. But we preferred to base our decision *on his own confession* that of teaching young boys to masturbate before the age of puberty, and that he *handled them himself*.'[22]

But this was old stuff. Where was the charge, and where was new (and corroborated) evidence? James Brown, a Sydney theosophist since 1900, saw the difficulty: 'a self-created 'Bishop' is blamed but no-one sees the acts committed and those who suspect (and not without strong reason) have to be careful of the law of libel and other things.'[23] Besant seemed to carry the day when she said that those who had evidence of a felony should produce it, and that they should carefully distinguish between questions of conduct with which the law does and does not deal.

Even so, it is a moot point whether she would have acted so boldly had she known that there was already a police file on Leadbeater. It was opened in 1917 at the instigation of Besant's American rival, Katherine Tingley, head of the alternative Universal Brotherhood and Theosophical Society at Point Loma, California, maybe alerted by controversy in Sydney *Truth*. Via J.H. Fussell, she recommended police investigation because 'the presence of such a man as Leadbeater is a menace to the youth of your city', warning also that with so clever a psychic, investigation would take time.[24]

It did. The police, duly instructed to inquire, reported that although some neighbours regarded him as 'a sodomist', they had been unable to obtain any relevant information. A further report, from CID in late 1917, was more positive: the Martyns' 'magnificent home', the Mackays' wealth, and interviews with some of the boys led to the conclusion that Leadbeater was not instructing his pupils in pernicious practices. Indeed, the lads 'appear to be pictures of health, and show no symptom or indication of having practised masturbation'.[25]

The Minister of Justice, however, kept up inquiries, and there was a further CID report on 10 September 1918, even more favourable, resting on police interviews with Messrs Martyn and Köllerstrom and a local GP. So on 17 September 1918 a letter went to Madame Tingley stating that after careful investigation no evidence of immoral teaching and practice had been uncovered. There was further cursory attention 'Re a man named Leadbeater' in November 1920. Then, the Under-Secretary of Justice called for the papers again on 8 May 1922, just before Mrs Besant arrived in Sydney.

The upshot, as advocated by the *Daily Telegraph* and applauded by Sydney lodge, was another police inquiry. The investigating officer reported that Leadbeater exercised remarkable influence over the theosophical community. In his claim to be a Master he commanded not only respect but patriarchal veneration, and power over the neophyte boys. Although he probably was a 'sex pervert', it would be difficult to establish a charge since all the parents except the Martyns were alarmed and unwilling to testify; the closed theosophical world made it hard to interview even ex-theosophists. In early August the Crown Solicitor advised that neither police inquiries of the complainants nor transcripts of police interviews made voluntarily (and later carefully corrected) by a selection of Leadbeater's boys had produced sufficient evidence to lay any charges. Revealing as these uneasy documents are, they testify to little more than masturbation and the odd priestly grab. Sydney lodge, however, submitted a more incriminating document about the boy 'A', which apparently supports testimony by Mrs Martyn that Leadbeater took some of the boys into his bed, and emphasises masturbation.[26]

Leadbeater was not subject to police interview himself, due to poor health; nor did he join the party of volunteer interviewees. Action was not thought feasible since the available evidence was uncorroborated and /or undated. Hence it was hard for Leadbeater's opponents to enlist the support of the law and the state.

Perhaps there was protective lack of interest at the highest levels. The then Minister of Justice in New South Wales, the unlovely T.J. Ley – later known as 'the Minister for Murder', having been convicted of the 'Chalkpit murder ' in London in 1947 – belonged in the same Progressive corner of polities as many theosophists, Raymond Perdriau, MLA, for instance, and his unscrupulous methods included condoning child molestation and murder in the Puddifoot affair in 1923. But there is no evidence of ministerial direction. Most likely, Ley simply had no interest in exacerbating difficulties for the theosophical world: in those 'troubled times', theosophy reinterpreted and upheld endangered moral and political attitudes, and though it was then both heretical and scandalous, it did have some establishment links, as with the military previously mentioned; mostly theosophists were respectable middle-class citizens; and in Annie Besant they had an impeccable leader. 'All the best elements gave me a warm welcome,' she said of Sydney in 1922. Furthermore, Ley had no personal interest in intensifying controversy; he lived by the double standard himself with a well-hidden mistress; and the underlying issue of male sexuality, of increasing concern in the 1920s, as evidenced by feminist interest in the Leadbeater affair, would have been anathema to him.[27]

Whether or not class interests had much to do with Leadbeater's survival, the scandal exposed deviant sexuality to unusual scrutiny, and this was in part due to the increased presence of women in public life. For quite different reasons Besant, Tingley and Piddington all endorsed police action. Besant intended to suppress conflict and clear the way for decisive action in the interests of the society; Tingley, her rival, deeply deplored perversion and psychism; and Piddington saw in the case both masturbatory horrors and anti-female practices (James Brown likewise deplored 'this terrible teaching which encourages young men not to marry and makes them hate women'). Whereas feminists, and theosophical feminists too, had actively defended the sex reformer William Chidley only a few years earlier, because his teachings implied improved sexual status for women, in the Leadbeater affair they were not impressed (quite the opposite) by apparently advanced teachings on masturbation and, as suggested by Marion Piddington's indignant letters to Marie Stopes, actively opposed them. Her husband, A.B. Piddington, read the Madras evidence tendered when Krishnamurti's father opposed Besant's control over his son in 1913, and went so far as to resign as president of Sydney University Public Questions Society when it refused to cancel an address by Besant on India, on the grounds that her evasive and authoritarian behaviour rendered her unfit as a teacher of public morals. But the issues, and the forces, remained elusive from a feminist perspective.

Of an unsatisfactory outcome, Marion Piddington wrote: 'members of the Theosophical Society have turned Leadbeater out and he now runs his Church and Lodge himself with his followers who must be all hypocritical.' [28]

In the very public aftermath of the Sydney crisis, three things emerged. The dissidents lost. It was they who were turned out of the Theosophical Society. The Sydney lodge had continued to agitate for 'a judicial and impartial investigation' into Leadbeater's behaviour with boys since 1914, as sketched by general secretary Bean in *Theosophy in Australia* in April 1923. Drastic action followed. Sydney lodge was expelled from the section, its leaders from the society. In June 1923, following deliberations by section council, Adyar withdrew the lodge's charter and cancelled the diplomas of twelve FTS (listed by Prentice as Mr and Mrs Martyn, Mr and Mrs Eberle, Mrs and Mrs G.C. Barnes, Mr and Mrs J.E. Grieg, Messrs Wiedersehn, Harrison, J.M. Prentice and Loris Ingamells).[29]

In a related fateful development, organised opposition died away. The dissidents, with access to the police report and support from American critics, established to their satisfaction that their fears were justified. Not that they went quite so far in their agitations as the Washington critic Stokes, who referred to the 'LCC sex-pervert gang'. But they failed in an appeal against what weaker brethren feared was a harsh and unjust measure (and H.G. Oliphant of Adelaide deemed unbrotherly action). Nevertheless, they did have some support from disaffected Tasmanian and Queensland theosophists. On 28 October 1923 about 600 Sydney lodge members constituted themselves the Independent Theosophical Society, with T.H. Martyn president and Dr Fraser vice-president. Then, unexpectedly, Martyn died in October 1924 on a business trip to Ipoh in the then Malay States. It was a great loss, an insuperable loss.[30]

G.C. Barnes assumed the presidency, supported by Prentice and Mrs Martyn. The busy lodge round continued. In January 1925 the ITS launched *The Path*, a bi-monthly magazine, successor to *Dawn*, which addressed itself to people repelled by societies and prepared to focus theosophical dissatisfaction internationally. It projected anew the image of a theosophical movement, in the great cause of Humanity and the service of the Masters:

> The Theosophical Movement is that great effort set forth ages ago by the Occult Rulers of Humanity, whereby successive movements have been

brought into the world, under the guise of religions etc. for the amelioration of the distresses under which Humanity has suffered. In every effort to improve conditions, to free the spiritual consciousness in man, to combat professional priestcraft and dogmatism, to join issue on the life side as opposed to the form side – there the theosophical movement can directly be perceived.[31]

But *The Path* survived less than two years, through five issues. Amid talk of federation (not universal union) the weakened sponsor ITS itself faded from view.

Perhaps members were moving closer to sympathisers in America, like singer Dorothy Heimrich who left Sydney shortly after the end of World War I and found repose in the anonymous United Lodge of Theosophists in London in the 1920s. J.M. Prentice reappeared as a force revitalising the Tingleyite Universal Brotherhood wing and the so-called fraternisation movement of the late 1930s which hoped for reunion between Adyar and Point Loma. (In 1938 he took over from the aged Willans as president of the UBTS.) Others like Dr Fraser disappear altogether from the record. A last mention of the Independent Theosophical Society came in 1955, following a court determination that the proceeds of sale in 1938 of the building at 69 Hunter Street retained by the ITS be distributed among those who belonged to Sydney lodge back in 1923. All too quickly then the proposed revitalisation withered away. In the process the dissidents lost everything.[32]

The Adyar-based organisation survived, retaining the official name of the Theosophical Society in the face of threatened litigation in Equity in 1923, with the loyal Australian section more or less intact. It was acknowledged that the stigma of sexual depravity remained 'in the minds of the reading public'. And there were casual ties. The assiduous Bean was eased out, along with Mrs Bean, who had served the society since the 1890s; and expatriate loyalist Josephine Ransom was 'invited' to take over as general secretary in early 1924. There were also losses, of members and assets. Loss of members, down below 2000 again in 1923, was said to be salutary, attributed to outflow from psychology classes, previously the rage. Assets lost included Morven Garden School which the section decided to close in 1923, being also obliged to shoulder a £6000 debt managed before by the Educational Trust, a section committee containing many Sydney lodge members. Perhaps the worst loss was King's Hall, subject to litigation also and finally relinquished to the ITS, with £3000, in 1927.[33]

Undaunted, members of the new loyalist Blavatsky lodge formed a company to build new headquarters and, with customary resource, found £110,000, it was reported in the issue of *Building* for 12 November 1924, for a nine-storey building at 29 Bligh Street (just around the corner from the objectionable ITS). The section, the lodge, and Adyar Hall were all operational by mid-1925 in Bligh Street; indeed Adyar House soon became a Sydney landmark. That resources remained abundant is also suggested by the appearance of an extraordinarily glossy magazine the *Pacific* (1923–1925), into which venture it is said John Mackay poured thousands of pounds.

Recovery owed a lot to the Coming. Just as it was an aspect of the split, so it helped restore stability among the survivors. According to Dr Bean, the events of 1921 and 1922 had been an attempt 'to spoil the Coming', orchestrated from afar, and fierce reactions were justified:

> When you are on 'active service', when you are just about to go into a fight (and surely for the very many who believe in it, the 'Coming' of the Christ is going to be just that), you cannot afford civil war in your ranks, nor can you win through on 'civil' methods.[34]

Later, he emphasised the benefits of the split, because it sorted out the more advanced souls needed for the Coming.

> The past year, tho' the stormiest in the history of our Movement in Australia, has been salutary for us all.
>
> It has sorted out those with true vision and genuine solidarity to their brethren, those loyal to great Leadership, from others, some of them sincere and earnest, but not yet ready to discriminate between the real and the unreal, nor to advance to the severer tests that must await all of us at the 'Coming' of the Lord.

Bean's days were numbered by then, but his rhetoric is instructive, because it expresses the cult of great leadership.

Theosophists were always strong on leadership, but after the split faith intensified. The status of the leadership was in fact enhanced. Bean urged the dispossessed members of Sydney lodge to recall the merits of the leadership, to restore historical perspective by reading Besant's *Autobiography*, evidence of truth and purity and sense. To the faithful, he stressed the potent powers of the leadership: 'We, the great majority, believe that Mrs Besant and Bishop Leadbeater are His two chief Heralds and the greatest spiritual Teachers of the world until He comes ... Mrs Besant, above all, we believe is the official representative of the Masters for the Outer World.'[35]

Privately Bean hoped he was not overdoing it. Even so, his own faith in 'great leadership' and the Coming had intensified by 1923. Upset at the spectre of the Adyar guillotine hanging over the heads of the dissidents, and hoarse from pleading the cause of the starving children of Russia and Eastern Europe in the Domain, he took time out in January 1923 to write 'dear old Chas and Eff' a thoroughly convinced letter. In this astonishing document, Dr Bean recounted to his brother and sister-in-law various travellers' tales from Thibet and inner China supporting the theosophical view of 'the true Westminster', the sacred city of Shamballa in inner Asia where Great Spiritual Beings governed the world and Annie Besant sometimes attended conferences ('though not in her physical body'); and timely archaeological findings in South America, the Caribbean, the Middle East and New Guinea. The letter waxed eloquent on the coming smash-up of all orthodox beliefs, and the imminent triumph of esoteric knowledge:

> Those who are too mentally ossified to rid themselves of time hallowed traditions will have a very bad time – 'The Desolation' when the spiritual foundations of their world seem shattered. Those who can rise up out of it all into the grander scope of Xt's New Message will experience 'The Rapture'. Other good earnest people will cling in spite of all evidence, to the dead forms of the passing Age but will be quite happy having an inner spiritual knowledge of the Living Mystic Xt [Christianity] which no outer cataclysms can touch.[36]

What did Bean mean by 'great leadership'? Since 'the leader' was an increasingly important political concept in the interwar years, theosophical reverence for great leadership bears analysis. Plainly for Bean, Besant, and to a lesser extent Leadbeater, personified great leadership. Both were great teachers. They were heralds of the new order, and Besant was representative of the remote hierarchy which could, or did, govern the world. Great leadership by implication came from spiritual sources, from big minds and great souls, from above and on high.

Annie Besant's leadership has not stood the test of time. Lasting success attended neither her spiritual nor her secular prescriptions, and her reputation declined rapidly. During her life-time she experienced constant and increasing criticism from within, and biographers have failed to find the spiritual strengths of a great religious leader; indeed they have increasingly emphasised weakness, dependence and even credulity in her association with Leadbeater. Something remains of her political reputation, but it is partial, and ultimately incoherent. Yet her stature was plain enough at the time. In 1924 the cream of progressive opinion gathered in London to honour Besant's fifty years of public work, an event reported respectfully by Dr Marion Phillips to *Labour Woman* ('A Great Gift to Humanity', 1 August 1924). The question arises as to the source and extent of her authority by the 1920s.

Two historical dimensions have been lost. One, the dimension of 'the lost woman leader', however tantalising, is probably gone forever. The other, the Indian dimension, may be reconstructed. It may not rehabilitate Besant's reputation, but it restores her stature in the secular sphere and renders intelligible her otherwise incredible commitment to the Coming. The basis of Besant's authority had changed over time. By the 1920s it derived from the Indian dimension in imperial history, just as twenty years earlier it rested on the challenge of secularism to the established order. The shift is itself sufficient to rescue Besant from the charge of captive credulity to Leadbeater and the clerisy. Without her leadership theosophists would have had about the same social standing as flat-earthers. By the 1920s Besant's India envisaged an imperial salvation, and not just for the latter-day wise men who looked for 'a star in the East'.

It is amazing how completely and how quickly – since the 1960s – the historically rich Indian perspective has disappeared from Australian awareness. Today Indian realities impinge with ever-increasing faintness from Perth to Sydney. India represents a tourist option, a psychic stopover. It hardly features in progressive opinion, representing a failed alternative, unappealing to all but minority cultural and religious interests. Prompting facile comparative observations about the distribution of wealth, India projects a conservative image.

Sixty years ago the undivided subcontinent carried quite different connotations. While it was correct to note mutual ignorance between Indians and Australia ns in the 1920s as reported in Besant's Madras daily, *New India*, no one underestimated the strategic and political significance of India itself. By the early twenties India was the flashpoint of empire, more so even than Ireland with all its troubles. In a world agitated by the Bolshevik revolution and an empire where frontier tension between Russia and the Raj was endemic, a lot depended on the path taken by India now that Indian nationalism must be reckoned with as a· popular force. In the wake of the terrible Amritsar massacre (1919), and the rising tide of Gandhian non-co-operation, the situation was serious. Besant said, when reflecting on the inadequate British response to Amritsar, that it was bad for the empire that Indians who had fought for the liberty of others were unable to obtain it for themselves.

When Annie Besant revisited Australia in 1922 she stood on the plateau of her political career, the untiring voice of constitutional reform, self-government and dominion status for India within the British Empire. Indeed, her Australian journey had to be postponed because of uncertainty in India. An advance party from Adyar, arriving in Sydney in time for the Easter Convention, sounded discouraged: spokesman Jinarajadasa compared the unpopular constitutionalists with the impact of Gandhi, and stressed the dangers of direct action, citing the Russian case of reversion to barbarism. But then Gandhi was arrested, and in the political respite Besant set off, more optimistic. On arrival she told a packed Perth Literary Institute that Gandhi's extraordinary status amid an intensely religious people was undercut, Indians were freedom-bound, and the time was ripe for a constitutional convention. Over the next two years, culminating in the first Labour Government in Britain, her position seemed to strengthen.[37]

Warm appreciation attended her efforts in Australia. Although to a later generation Gandhi's tactics were enormously impressive, public opinion had not yet grasped the import of civil disobedience. Rather, it applauded Besant's statesmanship. The Adelaide *Register* for example, approving her widened mission even though she plainly said she had no particular mission at this time, saw her as 'a most capable and ardent champion of the legitimate aspirations of the Hindu peoples'. The Sydney *Daily Telegraph* conceded as much, seeing her as an old-time statesman, with the face of a strong man. It was unusual, said Herbert Heaton from the chair in Adelaide Town Hall, to hear Indian problems discussed by 'a white woman who had lived in India and studied them on the spot'. The *Sydney Morning Herald* said she spoke with freedom and authority on India. These responses rested on the shared premise of 'legitimate aspiration', a century of constitutional aspiration and achievement in the colonies of white settlement; and were nourished by the common hope of imperial modernisation: 'India and England together mean the world's peace, both in Europe and Asia. Britain and India ... 'will be the redemption of our world and the progress to a new era of peace, brotherhood, happiness and helpfulness.'[38]

That Dr Besant aimed to save India from revolution, as the headlines put it, held none of today's negative implications. The press, though more critical than ever of theosophy, remained attentive and respectful of her politics. It was possible to encompass her claim that Britons and Indians originated from the same race in the orient. She spoke to a civic reception in Sydney of the empire as 'a great experiment in welding free peoples together into one great Commonwealth'.[39]

Shades of Mrs Besant's Fabian past! But also common coin of the English-speaking peoples until the 1950s, and, in 1922, vital and visionary, ahead of the institutional declaration inaugurating the British Commonwealth of Nations in 1926. The first volume of Sir Keith Hancock's masterly *Survey of British Commonwealth Affairs. Problems of Nationality 1918–1936* (1937) includes a discussion on 'India and Race Equality' which helps escape anachronistic judgement. Hancock delicately exposes the position of postwar India as 'an historically conditioned mood' which reached the limits of nineteenth-century liberalism: the conflict in the theory of imperial citizenship between the rights of man and the mobility of labour. The British Empire was not cosmopolitan like its predecessors, the Roman, Russian and even French empires, but 'multicellular'; freedom of movement by diverse populations within the Empire was a source of constant and increasing difficulty.[40] To liberal imperialists Besant's program seemed to be the way forward. It was not totally self-deceiving of her to conclude that the result of her Australian tour would be to convince the Australian public that theosophical study 'brings very practical suggestions for the solution of the vital problems now facing the Nations'. The full and particular relevance of this will be shown subsequently, but it is exemplified by J.K. Powell's remark in *Spark's Fortnightly* that she set a practical example, and saving India from Russian reforms would mean an upward movement in practical universal brotherhood.[41]

Annie Besant's authority derived from that hope. It is worth digressing briefly to take in the secular details in her Australian schedule. To do so is to further expose her underlying strengths. Throughout she tried to dispel ignorance about India, and to prepare the way for a further – in fact overlapping – tour of Australia by Indian Privy Councillor Srinivasa Sastri. Both touched on Australian obstacles to a liberal imperial citizenship, that is, on the White Australia Policy.

Besant's theme everywhere was 'India for the Indians, within the Empire'. She was tireless. During three weeks in Sydney amid theosophical hullabaloos, she attended at least thirty-four meetings – not a bad record for an old lady of seventy-five, as Nethercot remarks – a significant proportion of them public meetings. In addition to vice-regal attentions and a civic reception, she gave three public lectures, a written address on 'Indian aspiration' to journalists at Farmers (the first woman speaker, according to *New India*); and, to cheering undergraduates at the Public Questions Society's meeting at Sydney University where Professor Alexander Mackie replaced the indignant Piddington in the chair, she spoke on 'The Future of India'. She produced two newspaper articles on 'India's Past and Present'. She also spoke to the League of Nations Union and a women's meeting. Through the southern capitals the story was the same. In Melbourne she lectured at the Town Hall, and at the University, on 'India and her Position in the Empire' (where Justice Higgins of the Arbitration Court did the honours and pioneer sociologist Professor Meredith Atkinson proposed the vote of thanks).[42]

In 1914 an enterprising journalist in London had asked Annie Besant if she had a message for Australia. She did. As published in August 1914 in *Theosophy in Australasia*, the message was threefold: Australia must look to its professional artistic and middle classes if it were to have a hopeful future, remembering that 'a nation does not consist of its manual labouring classes'; second, democracy must be imposed by safe leadership, and show a willingness to submit to discipline, a sense of reverence for great ideals, a love of country and a spirit of self-sacrifice, that is, practise self-control; and third, overcome racial prejudice. By 1922 the relevance of these themes theosophists thought amply demonstrated. For Annie herself, racism had assumed the greatest importance, as an Indian and imperial question; and of all her efforts at uplift and the advancement of India during those weeks the way she dealt with racism is the most striking. At the Communist Hall, speaking 'down' as it were on 'Education and Nationbuilding', and again in Adelaide, she complained that 'Australia appears to be a labour nation and nothing more'. The race question in Australia she said was an economic question, and there were two ways forward: admitting Indians into trade unions, and modernising the education system. Australian children left school too early, tempted by high wages and independence; but to achieve a thoughtful and progressive nation, higher education should be undertaken. In this way, 'all can meet socially on a common basis of knowledge'. Australian education needed a filter of progressive thought too, along Montessorian lines.[43]

Besant, received in government houses and mayoral suites, as easily addressed rulers as the ruled. The regrettably scrappy Australian collection in the Adyar Archive contains a Memorandum about a visit to the Prime Minister of Australia, arranged by the indefatigable Senator Reid. Over morning tea in Melbourne on 3 June 1922, amid electioneering, Hughes listened to 'India and the Policy of a White Australia', a transcript of which also survives at Adyar.

Here, using the governmental plural 'we', meaning the coming government of India, Besant spoke the language of diplomacy, continuing to sympathise with the White Australia Policy as an industrial problem, even dismissing it – 'The Empire is large enough to include many race cultures' – especially when independent India industrialised. However, existing inequalities must be remedied; the position of indentured Indian labour in South Africa for instance was inappropriate to a citizen of empire. All that was currently required of White Australia was citizenship of resident Indians, not otherwise too badly treated.[44]

The practical difficulty for Prime Minister Hughes proved to be the old one. The Japanese might claim the same rights. His response to the view that a strong India would defend Australia in an emergency is not recorded, nor whether he found promising the idea of rich India relieving debt-ridden Australia.

Here then was statesmanship. She had prepared the way for the imperial mission of the Rt Hon. Sri Srinivasa Sastri. It shows how fully Indianised Besant was that when the trains carrying her home and Sastri forward on the first day of his ambassadorial tour of the dominions met, mid-Nullarbor, and a brief exchange was effected 'in right Irish fashion', she felt refreshed: 'Seeing an Indian face ... hearing an Indian voice and Indian news was like a shower of rain on a thirsty land.'[45]

It is necessary to say something here about Sastri and his mission, as it illuminates 'the Indian dimension' of theosophy in Australia. The commitment was to an Indian messiah, an unlikely proposition in White Australia where the likeliest populist admission was that Indians were 'not quite niggers'. The race question looms large (unusually so in religious history), and Sastri addressed it according to contemporary conventions. Back in India, Besant expected this high type of the motherland to dispel ignorance, and have a great effect, not least because 'Australians are not accustomed to hearing flawless English'.[46]

Sastri's mission was straightforward. He was policing the so-called 'reciprocity' agreements made at successive imperial conferences in London between 1917 and 1921. Reciprocity meant that the government of India accepted immigration controls in the dominions, in the expectation of similar rights when independent, and in return for citizenship rights for Indians currently resident in those countries.

By the 1920s the number of 'Indians' in Australia, never substantial, had dwindled, partly because of the colour bar on immigration since 1902. At the 1921 census, the Australian population included a little over 4,000 persons from the regions of the Raj (classified as Afghans, Baluchis, Cingalese and Hindu), of whom the great majority, 3,576 or over three-quarters, were 'Hindu', 619 of these being Australian-born. The number of 'British Indians', who were the subject of Sastri's mission, that is of resident Hindus and Cingalese born beyond Australia, amounted to a mere 3,160. Neither theosophists nor anyone else except perhaps residents of farthest camel country paid attention to these people, and they suffered numerous disabilities in addition to exclusion from the Commonwealth franchise. A small delegation waited on Sastri in Perth – as had earlier on Annie Besant – and in Adelaide to state their ancillary grievances, such as exclusion from government positions, age pensions, miner's rights, and the cane-fields of Queensland.[47]

About these other issues, and petty discrimination, Sastri could do little, observing that 'the ordinary people have a very poor conception of Indians'. However, the Commonwealth agreed to franchise and other reforms for British Indians in 1925, and Sastri's mission was fulfilled without much difficulty or controversy.[48] Despite Japan, it was argued, in the words of the Melbourne *Herald*, reprinted in *New India*, that 'the concessions can be granted without in any way prejudicing our racial purity, our industrial position, or our relationships with other Dominions.'[49] But Indians were not to go to New Guinea. And they still suffered at State level, their lowly position unchanged.

Harder heads shook disapprovingly. In Australia, the *Bulletin* was not assuaged; and E.J. Holloway of Melbourne Trades Hall asked why the Indian intellectual class did not devote itself to reform at home. There was a flurry following rumours that Australian troops might be used to dispel disorder in India. Back in India, Besant could not afford to be so bland about dog-in-the-manger attitudes, claiming that ultimately Australia would be compelled to admit Indian colonisation to develop and protect the north. Since Gandhi had awakened India, there were many there who failed to appreciate Sastri's strategy, and rejected entirely the insulting White Australia Policy.[50]

Strategy it certainly was, and, as Hancock judged, historically conditioned. For Besant and Sastri – 'two great imperialists' said *New India* – Australia, with achieved nationhood, had only a limited role in India's advancement. Nor were they deceived by the limited enthusiasm for racial harmony in remote Australia. But they believed dominion status for India was imminent, and together they highlighted the wider imperial predicament.

In the early twenties this predicament brought all things Indian to the fore in Australia, and reinforced a conservative Australian nationalism. Australians were only too pleased to stand with moderate Indian opinion, for fear of worse (Sastri harped on this, predicting that Gandhi would be worse than Lenin because of the obscurantism of his total program).[51] That is, Australian nationalism in the 1920s fitted easily into aspirations for a British Commonwealth of Nations which included India. But it did so on its own racial terms, terms which moderate Indian opinion had accepted for pragmatic purposes, even while finding it abhorrent, as did the Japanese. Resident Indians were not equals in this short-lived strategy, merely symbolic.

It may be presumed that theosophists stood at a distance from the racist fears of their countrymen. The first object of the Theosophical Society remained the promotion of brotherhood regardless of racial distinction. In practice, the realities of the White Australia Policy were hard to handle, and not all agreed that the question should be viewed in the broadest perspective, as evidenced by Prentice's hostility to Besant lodge in Melbourne where the Hunts preached racial tolerance and Bernard O'Dowd sometimes spoke against institutionalised racialism. (O'Dowd appears in the section's journal in 1912 denouncing the White Australia Policy as unbrotherly, undemocratic and unscientific.) They frequently feared for their Indian visitors, and in 1918 the Jinarajadasas apparently had difficulty in obtaining entry. As well, Madame Blavatsky's theory of history was at best ambiguous on the race question, and could encourage patronising attitudes. But the teaching acknowledged the spiritual importance of other races, and by the twenties, Besantine theosophy had thrown in its lot completely with India. Theosophists had every reason to be among the few who spoke positively on the 'colour question', even leaving aside the point made by E.G. Docker that in the early twentieth century it became increasingly unfashionable to speak slightingly of Blacks. By the twenties, theosophical opinion favoured not only imperial race reform but also Aboriginal advancement.[52]

Cynics may suggest that theosophical class interests overrode concern about colour, that a middle-class group like the theosophists were merely quick to appreciate the servant question. Those fortunate enough to visit Adyar experienced at first hand the benefits of a large black service community, albeit slow and still undernourished. Whereas wealthy theosophists were among those who bought into Sydney's first serviced flats, the Astor apartments in Macquarie Street, for the double convenience of labour-saving devices and proximity to Sydney lodge, in later, more depressed days the service argument against institutionalised racism surfaced, to give an ironic class twist to the reiterated theosophical protest that the White Australian Policy was a labour question.[53]

Class interests certainly do illuminate both the sources of modern racial policy, and protests against it (usually ineffectual). What was – and still is – unusual in Australia is a specific commitment to racial tolerance and diversity. All along appreciation of non-European cultures was fundamental to a theosophical orientation, even though the original fierce hostility to European Christianity expressed by Blavatsky abated in a communion consisting, in the West, of Christians and ex-Christians, and despite Blavatsky's view that many representatives of non-white cultures appeared decadent or atavistic. The Aboriginal people of Australia were doubtless seen as atavistic, but might still be custodians of the spiritual insights from which an authoritative religion could be constructed; and the diminished leaders of once great civilisations should also be respected. A rough class equivalence served to bolster liberal sympathy, as when Dr Bean wrote in 1919 on the colour question that high-caste Indians as much as Australians had an instinct for race preservation and that the time had come for spiritual as well as constitutional reciprocity:

> Above all, in exact proportion as our racial instinct shrinks from experiment of blood intermixture may our Divine instinct expand towards spiritual fusion and brotherhood, so that by eager courtesy, frank trust and warm comradeship we may prove that race prejudice and race preservation not only should be, but actually are, in our lives as far apart as the poles.[54]

It is interesting that theosophists, who were not by and large the marrying kind, did not shrink from 'blood intermixture', as there were numerous marriages between English and Indians in the twenties, the most stunning and then impressive of which was that of George Arundale and Shrimati Rukmini Devi, a high-caste Hindu daughter of an Indian judge, then aged sixteen, in 1920.[55] Theosophic idealists like Dr Bean continued to scan journals for anthropological and ethnographic evidence for the refreshment of rejected and apocryphal perspectives which would, as Mrs Besant put it, break present deadlocks. In short, theosophical tolerance of racial diversity rested on theosophical 'theology': on idealism, not materialism.

Again, Besant best captured the good intentions and marshalled the materials for a synthesis of political and religious aspiration which exalted India and Indians. The materials included of course religious materials. Here the task of assessment is daunting, not least because Besant's own scholarship was substantial: her writing on Indian religions included translations and commentaries as well as essays and lectures and polemical works. (The library at Adyar built up impressive historical resources.)[56] It is safe to say that Besant was most deeply engaged by Hinduism (rather than the Buddhism espoused by other early theosophists), responsive to the mixture of romance and authority in the basic texts, and fully appreciative of the adaptability and strength of an ancient civilisation now in decay. While she did not espouse Hinduism as did her compatriot Margaret Noble, the revolutionary disciple of Swami Vivekananda, she was at home in it and saw there a structured moral economy to remedy the defects of Western religious and moral authority, as well as strength sufficient to liberate India.[57] Today there is nothing unusual in the perception that colonisers have much to learn from the colonised. If these attitudes are not always adequately scrutinised now, they were a powerful novelty in Besant's day, when the processes now called decolonisation had not begun.

Besant once commented that it was easy for Gandhi amid a basically religious people to seem semi-divine. Yet at the same time she herself was promoting Krishnamurti as the coming Christ. It is one thing to advocate the rights of Indians and the virtues of Indian religion to Europeans and another to offer an Indian messiah. Some have wondered how so experienced a figure fell for millenarianism. Others have seen it as a secular stratagem to disguise spiritual bankruptcy. Most have seen her as a figurehead, a victim either of Leadbeater's manipulation, or her own loyalties, or of both.

It is true that Leadbeater manipulated. The candidate, the lavish preparations, the cult, all were his untiring work. But Besant was not a victim, and more than a figurehead. She was committed to the idea all along, and firmly believed in the Coming herself, a belief stated as early as 1909 when she rehearsed arguments on the historical necessity for a new Christ. 'The Coming Christ' (1909) presented a rollcall down the ages correlating sub-races and religious teachers, and the assurance that 'such a Teacher, the Supreme teacher of the worlds, makes himself manifest as a man at the beginning of every sub-race'.[58] She and Leadbeater together promoted the World Teacher, and neither expressed any doubt about it until it was too late – indeed Besant never expressed doubt in Krishnamurti. Basically she created the secular synthesis upon which public readiness for the Coming depended. She proposed the turning point, the new dispensation, the appropriate revelation, and that she was equipped to recognise it. At least she did not proclaim herself the World Teacher, nor assume divine status, as have many such minority religious leaders. The project also relied on her eloquent advocacy, which never faltered.

Krishnamurti aboard ship.
(NLA Loc D1)

Her confident synthesis could hardly be replicated today. It included something from the evangelical inheritance; something from positivism and the secularists' idealist view of history; and a great deal from India, where great teachers are common. When Leadbeater reported that he had found the appropriate vehicle for the World Teacher in the young Krishnamurti, the pieces fell into place. A radical past had taught her what is standard religious sociology today, that new religious forces usually arise at the margins not the centre of culture, from among the dispossessed.

The pieces stayed in place partly because the theosophical dream of what was soon to be called the world religion required a world teacher; and partly because, by whatever means, Leadbeater chose well. The young Krishnamurti shaped up as vehicle for the World Teacher, and the lavish attempt to turn him into an English gentleman enhanced rather than undermined his exotic aura, a bonus to twenties photographers and their many versions of 'the Beauty of Holiness'. Slight, modest, 'unflawed ' in Helen Heney's recollection, Annie Besant's adopted Indian son enjoyed in early manhood both personal beauty and, it emerged, integrity. If the creed of Annie Besant was thought to be a queer creed and her message absurd, yet she had lived with it and fought for it, and the fullness of 'the Indian dimension' is what made her 'the Great Leader'. Alongside her record, the efforts of a few rebellious anti-clerical theosophists in remote parts paled. If they thought her bad for theosophy, many more thought 'radical Annie' assured the Coming.

From 1921 serious efforts were made, especially by Besant, to galvanise the Order of the Star in the East and its nominal head, Krishnamurti, by then a well-travelled young man of twenty-six with a taste for fast cars and tennis. Krishnamurti first came to Australia in 1922, one of the party from India attending the traumatic TS convention in Sydney. It was after the many embarrassments of that visit – not merely of the Leadbeater affair and press attention, but also at blatant racist reactions to him in the streets – that he turned to self-preparation. His childhood friend and biographer Mary Lutyens has described his travails in *Krishnamurti. The Years of Awakening*. From sources published there, it is clear that he suffered considerably, particularly in late 1925 with the death of his brother and companion Nityananda, his only link with the Indian world from which the two theosophists wrenched him in childhood. Lutyens' sympathetic account of his painful 'process', as it was called, beginning in the theosophical retreat in a high southern Californian valley town of Ojai after the Sydney fiasco, and continuing during trips to Europe, suggests panic and horror, inspiring in the reader respect and, perhaps, pity and terror at the prospects for so dislocated a being, who by then saw no escape: 'My difficulty is, I feel so small and incapable to do the mighty work; I still lack confidence in myself and I don't think I shall ever be conceited.'[59] Particularly striking is his gradual appreciation of public derision, after years of private coddling by rich Europeans. Crude Australians laughed in his face.

Reportedly Leadbeater found the 'process' puzzling, a terrible drama, an incomprehensible preparation, but accepted Besant's view that 'the whole proceeding is under authority'. Ultimately, Krishnamurti came through, confident of new powers; and, having assumed Star work under duress in

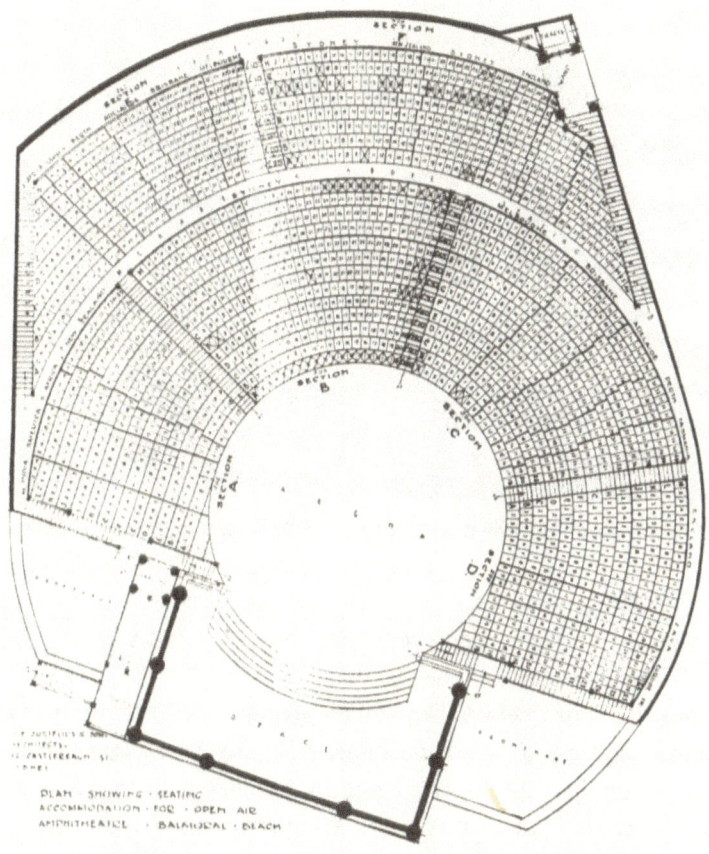

The seating plan for the Star Amphitheatre at Balmoral Beach, Sydney.
Members were invited to purchase 'Founders Seats' by marking a position
on the plan, 1923. (*TinA*)

1921, gradually gathered confidence as speaker and writer, producing poems in the manner of an Eastern mystic.

By 1925 a lot hung on the Coming. Inevitably, the nearer Krishnamurti came to his role, the more convincing his appearance and utterances, the more complicated it all became. Loyalists, faithful to great leadership, drunk on dreams of a decisive step forward, being aware through Star publications of 'the process' and culturally prepared over time, hastened ahead. Would-be disciples must prepare the path, and prepare themselves. Adelaide lodge, reporting a busy round of lectures among its 126 members

The Star Amphitheatre at Balmoral Beach, Sydney. (Campbell Collection)

in 1923, including educational charitable and reform activities, reflected that 'along our corridors, ere many years are past, may walk feet more blessed than we know ... These are but practising days.'[60]

Preparations proceeded apace in Sydney. In 1923, in her annual presidential address to the Theosophical Society, Dr Besant referred to a huge and beautiful amphitheatre being constructed in Sydney for the World Teacher, 'when He Comes'. In 1924 Dr Besant congratulated the organiser, Dr Mary Rocke, for the splendid success of a daring dream of beauty. She added that Sydney was to be a great theosophical centre in the future and the two great works planned when she was in Sydney in 1922 (that is Adyar House and the Star Amphitheatre) were nearly complete.[61]

The other side, now the Independents, watched with wonder. *Dawn* could not reject the Coming out of hand; it was possible, although Madame Blavatsky had nominated 1975 as year of the Torchbearer. It contented itself with the hope that the amphitheatre would prove an expensive washout, given Sydney weather; and a crack about the view over the boys' bathing shed on Balmoral Beach from the back of the amphitheatre.[62] The amphitheatre, which lasted on Balmoral Beach until it was demolished in 1951, provided one enduring urban myth, that an adventist group built the amphitheatre to watch Christ's return, walking on the water, through

Sydney Heads. Like all good myths, it rested firmly on fact. Between 1923 and 1924, on three blocks of splendid harbour foreshore facing east into the Pacific, sympathisers built, at a probable cost of £20,000, a platform for the World Teacher.[63] It was used for Star lectures and even once or twice by Krishnamurti, returned to Sydney in early 1925. Perhaps there was some dramatic landing scheme. Even *Dawn* admitted the site was replete with beauty. Dr Mary Rocke, Leadbeater's personal physician and prime mover in the venture, celebrated the Star amphitheatre as a dream of beauty:

> The amphitheatre in one sense is naught but a shrine for Nature's ever-changing perfection, and no art gallery, no museum, or university could probably equal it in power to raise aspirations and inspire the lives of the multitudes who daily throng the beach, or in bestowing upon all who enter a peace and a blessing of which many are quite conscious.[64]

Well, perhaps a few. The multitude remained unmoved, the press derisory (except of the actual construction by local architects and builders). But the Star Amphitheatre on Balmoral Beach in Sydney was meant to command the spiritual, as well as the geological, heights.

At the same time, self-preparation intensified. Members of the OSE duly regarded the six points intended to strengthen faith: living worthily, keeping His name in mind, devoting some daily time to definite work for His Coming, practising Devotion, Steadfastness and Gentleness, praying twice daily, and revering greatness, in cooperation with spiritual superiors. The Manor, with Leadbeater ensconced, became like a great factory, as recalled by Lutyens, of occult promotions for young and old, from near and far, much to the distaste of Krishnamurti, who was increasingly hostile to ceremonial and occult practices.[65] Spiritual superiors especially stirred themselves for the new dispensation, and the officers of the Order of the Star in the East made final frenzied calls for money.

There were at that time over 40,000 members of the order in forty countries, about two-thirds theosophists, and some 2000 people from all over the world rallied annually at a Star camp site in Ommen, Holland, in the early twenties – one of whom was the well-loved British Labour leader, pacifist and internationalist George Lansbury, an enthusiastic member since 1918. The order received land in Australia suitable for camps but no Star camps in the European style seem to have been held. At the Star camp at

Ommen in 1925 leading theosophists, led by George Arundale, declared themselves Higher Initiates and Apostles of the Coming Lord.

Ten were nominated, with two to come presumably: Besant, Leadbeater, Jinarajadasa, Wedgwood, George and Rukmini Arundale, Lady Emily Lutyens, Oscar Köllerstrom, Nityananda and Raja, the Indian vice-president of the TS. Since this did not meet with the approval of either Krishnamurti or Leadbeater (not so easily usurped as one and only Initiator), it is not always mentioned in theosophical histories. However, since so many leading theosophists were involved, it reveals a full-blown millennial cult, established by mid-1925. With thousands of would-be disciples and ten would-be apostles, all that was now required was that the Lord speak through Krishnamurti.[66]

And, at the meeting of the order of Adyar on 28 December 1925, immediately after the Jubilee Convention, about a month after his brother died, the 30-year-old Krishnamurti spoke: 'I come not to destroy but to build'. Some thought he was merely quoting Scripture when he spoke in the first person, but others were electrified. Its significance did not escape Annie Besant. 'The Coming has begun,' she said, adding, 'That there should be opposition is natural; did the Hebrews acknowledge Him, or the Romans welcome Him, when first He came in the body of a subject race?'[67]

8

To theosophise Australia

Over seventy Australian theosophists attended the Jubilee celebrations at Adyar in December 1925 when, it was claimed, the Lord spoke through the chosen vehicle, Krishnamurti, for the first time. Leadbeater's party returned in early 1926 hugging the idea that the Coming had begun. They brought with them the young Peter Finch, abandoned at Adyar by a gallivanting Buddhist grandmother; and, more auspicious, Annie Besant's loyal lieutenant since 1902, George Arundale, with his beautiful young wife Rukmini.

Although Arundale had never been to Australia before, he was almost immediately elected general secretary of the Australian section, on Leadbeater's recommendation, which post he held from 1926 to 1928. The delighted and now orderly section presumed, correctly, that exciting days lay ahead. They had been delivered in Arundale a Cambridge-educated Englishman, with glittering theosophical credentials dating back to childhood acquaintance with HPB herself, twenty years' service in India, including foundation of the Order of the Star in the East. In 1925 during an exciting week of clairvoyance in Holland, Arundale had entered, and subsequently rose to be regionary Indian bishop of, the Liberal Catholic Church. It would be perfectly proper for his new hosts to address the impressive newcomer as 'Bishop Arundale' or Dr Arundale – *honoris causa* from the would-be theosophical world university planned for Madras in 1925 – though he often appeared as the Rt Rev. Arundale, and liked 'Bishop George'.

Mrs Ransom, in command since 1924, departed gracefully for a new tour of duty in South Africa with the assurance of an administration ready for the transformation of Australia into a great theosophic community, which, it speedily emerged, was Arundale's plan of action. Convention responded keenly to his slogan 'theosophise Australia'.

Initially, 'to theosophise Australia' meant doubling membership, increasing cash flow, putting theosophy 'across Australia', and uplifting the nation. The time had passed for technical discussion of karma and reincarnation. Arundale announced in exemplary fashion that he had already joined nine brotherhood movements in Sydney, the League of Nations Union, the Prohibition Society, the Food Reform League, the Humanitarian Society, the RSPCA, the British Union for the Abolition of Vivisection (NSW branch), the Good Film League, the Peace Society and the WEA; and agog with such dynamism, Convention in April 1926 rushed to maximise good fortune. It heard about a new *Advance Australia* publishing company and endorsed a plan to transform *Theosophy in Australia* into a monthly magazine. A.E. Bennett, partner in the new publishing company, also reported a bold technological initiative: the newly developed medium of wireless would be deployed in a proposed theosophical broadcasting station at Adyar House, to be linked with the Manor, the Star Amphitheatre and St Alban's Liberal Catholic Church, to spread theosophy and a first-class program of music and lectures over Australia. The pioneering possibilities of a spiritual community in Sydney, mentioned by Leadbeater, regained an optimistic glow, now that a maker of theosophical men had arrived. The record states primly that all Arundale's plans were endorsed, though what happened to the idea of a theosophical museum is not known; and members restricted their 'terrific enthusiasm' to Australian projects, shelving the idea of making the society a base for a world religion, as mooted at the Jubilee.[1]

In a matter of months, theosophising Australia began in earnest. *Advance! Australia*, a political monthly, did not replace *Theosophy in Australia*, which continued under the symptomatic name change, *The Australian Theosophist*, but the monthly duly appeared, with official backing from the section, in July 1926, forty-eight pages, sixpence, co-edited by Arundale and South Australian journalist James Leonard Davidge. A month later, on 23 August 1926, the Theosophical Broadcasting Station Pty Ltd, headed by Arundale, officially launched Radio 2GB as a 'B' class station, that is, financed by advertising. Atypically for 'B' class stations, it was to be resolutely highbrow. (2GB, in other hands since 1936, is a major commercial broadcaster in Sydney, to the present day retaining a reputation for thoughtfulness.) Two new press agencies, Fidelity New Service and the Country Press Agency, dispensed favourable theosophical information.[2]

The new general secretary galvanised Bligh Street, now more vital and bustling than the old Hunter Street building had ever been, with many new departments of work. Publicity was especially busy, despatching 4,000 magazines per month to influential people nominated by members. Adyar Hall, advertised as the most beautiful hall in Sydney, attracted substantial bookings, and provided cultural space for members with artistic abilities: for art displays, lunch-hour concerts arranged by the Music Lovers' Concert Committee and given by the Theosophical String Quartet formed to service 2GB, and topical midday lectures. It was decreed that Wednesday evening lodge meetings henceforth would revolve around a program of music (the section now had a musical director, Edward Branscombe, who formed the Adyar Ladies' Choir): socials; debates, preferably on the lives of great men; and Star meetings.[3]

The irrepressible Arundale and Australian theosophy awaiting the World Teacher made the preparation of other sections look simple-minded and staid. Suppressing doubts about the expensive amphitheatre, undaunted by the closure of the model school, Australian theosophists rallied, this time to the call of culture. Never before, and never again, would the Theosophical Society in Australia assume such a high profile as in the late twenties, the Arundale phase.

At first Arundale could not be sure what to make of Australians. But, as a pupil of Dr Besant, 'the greatest statesman the world has at present', he began by talking: on radio stations, from pulpits, and through the house journals. Like previous theosophical visitors, he saw a rare type inhabiting this hospitable land, combining the key theosophical virtue of brotherliness with a promising pioneering spirit. A young country appealed to Arundale the theosophic educator. And there were good vibrations. 'I feel in the air of Australia,' he wrote, 'a certain intangible something which presages a wonderful future not yet, except by the idealistic visionary few, contacted by the people as a whole ... Nowhere in the world, I imagine, should the Great Teacher win a warmer welcome.'[4]

Since theosophists never doubted that they were the visionary few, word that they should now give a lead to Australia was welcome. It was not just a matter of permeating national life with brotherliness, as first thought, but of setting true national standards. Arundale's 'The Australia Section: A Vision' had them living in peace, harmony and hygiene in suburban communities with beautiful libraries and the wireless, preparing to serve their fellows, inspired by 'Christ's immediate presence'. Strenuous work lay ahead of the lodges, instructed to build up a noble Australian citizenship: 'every lodge and every centre a community'.[5] Theosophical keys must be applied to every area of life, political, religious, social, educational and industrial. Australia, perceived as a melting pot, at a time of political experiment, was 'open to the influence of great ideals and far-reaching schemes for human betterment'.

The rhetoric improved with use. 'It is the task of members of the Order of the Star in the East and of the Theosophical Society,' continued Arundale, 'to see to it that Australia perseveringly treads the appointed pathway, for members of these movements are the truest pioneers even in this land of pioneers.' A Fellowship of Pioneers to celebrate the lives of world benefactors formed immediately, with Arundale addressing its Anzac Day ceremony in 1926 (the program included the recessional, chamber music, a reading from poet John Masefield and the national anthem). Thereafter, Thursday lunch-hour at Adyar House featured readings from great lives. *Advance! Australia* pamphlets, 3d each, included 'A Pebble of Goodwill' and 'Theosophy and an ideal Australia'. While Arundale familiarised himself with Australian life, and offered more exact strategy, members reminded themselves how small Australia was compared with India, and basked in 'colossal ambition'.[6]

There were indeed powerful new grounds for hope. With a magazine and a radio station, the old obstacles of incomprehension and misrepresentation could be removed. (That hostility derived from the public perception of theosophy as non-Christian, and even anti-Christian, never seemed to be taken quite seriously.) Also theosophical standards in personal, social and political life, if explained clearly, would win respect and influence. By 1927 both *Advance! Australia* and 2GB were running well, with the magazine at a print run of 5,000 monthly, and theosophists responded to calls for support for the station. For the first time, the theosophical claim to public attention extended beyond the lectern. To put it colloquially, theosophists had come out.[7]

What then did a fringe group like that have to offer? As we have seen, they had considerable resources, wide rather than deep, avowedly alternative to the mainstream. How far theosophical values in personal, social and political life represented the promised alternative in the twenties is the most interesting question of all those raised by the history of theosophy in Australia.

The answer is complicated by the fact that theosophy was an esoteric culture. Even at its most open, in the late 1920s, with sources which make assessment possible virtually for the first time, the fact remains that by definition they are still usually incomplete, and at crucial points, unsatisfactory. Esoteric culture always exists in some sort of relationship to the general, or exoteric, culture, sharing a common tradition even while interpreting its basic realities quite differently, so that tense and unstable juxtapositions are the norm. A neat example of the silences, and the relationships, which also illustrates how far theosophical values posited alternative values, emerges in the story of the *pièce de résistance* Radio 2GB.[8]

As noted earlier, the broadcasting idea went to Convention in Easter 1926. However, Karel van Gelder of Blavatsky lodge was experimenting with transmission from the Manor as early as 1923; and in 1925 a group of theosophists had formed a theosophical broadcasting company in Sydney. Like some spiritualists, notably E.T. Fisk, managing director of Amalgamated Wireless from 1916 to 1944, theosophists readily appreciated the possibilities of the new medium. Not surprisingly they were quick off the mark in establishing a station – though not quick enough to claim their first choice of call-sign, 2AB, AB for Annie Besant, this call-sign having already been claimed by Mr A.V. Badger of Neutral Bay. As is now fairly well-known, the theosophical broadcasters therefore had recourse to 2GB, Giordano Bruno, thought to be a previous incarnation of Annie Besant and an old freethought hero, a sixteenth-century martyr to 'true science'.[9]

Credit for 2GB probably belongs to Alfred Edward Bennett (1889–1963), a theosophist since about 1920, who managed the station 1926–1936. One of the large family of Melbourne schoolmaster George Jesse Bennett and younger brother of Lieut.-General Henry Gordon Bennett, A.E. Bennett was an accountant who set up in Sydney in 1922, having previously managed meat-works in Victoria and Western Australia. Arundale, with whom Bennett was to have a dynamic partnership, gave him the credit, but also implied that the station was his own initiative, prompted by the discovery that the infant medium was not a monopoly in Australia as in Britain, and by personal success lecturing on citizenship over Trades Hall stations in Brisbane and Sydney:

> I dreamed a regular program of good things, things which would provide refined enjoyment, develop public taste and appreciation. Good music, not the rubbish we mostly hear, interesting addresses on art, on science, on literature, on the great social problems, on the various movements working for Australian betterment, on Australian ideals – political, religious, social, educational, on international questions, short addresses on Theosophy and its application to the problems of life, topical views ... such could form the ordinary program.[10]

Publicity for theosophy, scope for theosophical lectures, and a demand for theosophical literature would all flow from this limitless opportunity.

Whatever the inspiration, theosophical money and skills were readily to hand, and it was astute to be early on the broadcasting scene. The proposal caused anxiety, not only to the residents of Mosman, fearful of interference with existing reception from the new masts at the Manor, but also because the idea of religious broadcasting in a sectarian community frightened liberal opinion. Later claimants were less successful, and many bars of classical music traversed the airwaves before fears abated. A.E. Bennett assured *Wireless Weekly*, 'we have no axe to grind'. But, of course, they had several. The main one was never alluded to. Nowhere in the public statements are the origins of 2GB linked to the coming World Teacher. However, correspondence of the faraway Perth Lodge, now deposited in the Battye Library, credits the radio scheme to a Star conference in Sydney in April 1926, where £1,700 in £1 shares was raised, about half the amount required to launch 2GB. Senator Reid spoke slightly out of turn when, in April 1927 he stressed support for 2GB 'to broadcast our wonderful message concerning the World Teacher'.[11]

As for the other publicized prospects, less and less was said about benefits to theosophy, and more and more about Australian uplift. Radio 2GB made theosophy respectable:

> The Theosophical Broadcasting Station has put the Theosophical Society on the map in Australia. As a mere gesture, it counts for much. No other body, Church, Social Organization or Educational, has established a Station out of its own resources for the altruistic work of uplifting Australia.[12]

In mid-1927 *The Australian Theosophist* cited its old enemy, the *Daily Telegraph*, on 2GB as the strongest bureau of culture in the State.

The initial share capital was about £3,000 over four years. Theosophists invested around £6,000 in the station. Along with a few unspecified private debentures, the section's interest amounted to £2,500, with individual members holding a further £1,500, and theosophists almost all of the 2,000-odd £1 shares. In 1928 the station earned dividends for the first time, and in 1930-31 paid 6 per cent on a revenue of £12,000.[13] In 1930 the section looked to the station for financial support. By 1930 the strong support of theosophists was not so badly needed, though no doubt they had done their bit by selling 2GB-endorsed radio sets, 'talking-up' the programs, holding listening parties, writing in requests, and patronising advertisers, like Dearborn's Shampoos and the Yellow Cab Company, as urged by Bennett in 1927, when, alas, they had also to be reminded, they were really visionaries with wider purposes: 'We believe the World Teacher is here. Will this Broadcasting Station be of service to Him?'[14]

Arundale projected 2GB as an ideal broadcasting station. It was the sixth Sydney station after 2BL, 2FC, 2UW, 2UE and (some may think it significant) 2KY, the Trades Hall station. Leaving aside the claim to possess the most powerful transmitter in the southern hemisphere (and possibly the British Empire), 2GB's programs did offer an alternative to the fare of rival stations, especially in music. Inevitably, the opening night on 23 August 1926 meant speeches from Arundale, but also W. Arundel Orchard, director of the Conservatorium, the station managers, Bennett, engineer E.G. Beard and Arthur Burton, and, best of all, the blessing of NSW Minister of Education Tom Mutch, who hoped the new station would help rather than hinder the work of his department. This was interspersed with music from Mendelssohn ('Songs without Words' to begin), Mozart, Wagner, Schubert, Boccherini and Haydn, and a string quartet to close. The 2GB Quartette (plus accompanist presumably) compromising Monica Horder, Dan Scully, Ada Brook, Murielle Lang and Lloyd Davies, broadcast nightly thereafter. In 1927 the popular baritone Clement Hosking formed a vocal quartet attached to 2GB for Wednesday concerts. A trio, presenting popular selections from the great operas, formed under Hilda Boyle. Radio 2GB, an independent commercial broadcaster, aimed to be more highbrow than the ABC's precursors 2BL and 2FC.[15]

On the opening night, Arundale promised programs 'as good, as beautiful, and as true as they could make them ... for the uplift of Australia, and the inspiration of listeners'. Within six months, with transmission times steadily extending, 2GB targeted new audiences, not only children, about whose education theosophists had strong views, but also women. Special features included announcer J.K. Powell, editor of *Spark's Fortnightly*, in command of the 6.45 children's slot as 'The Cheerio Man' (originally 'The man from Dreamland'), extending his work to psychology discussions in the first of two women's day-time sessions, and sponsorship of 'welfare bodies' such as the Racial Hygiene Centre in the second. These sessions aimed at educating women in domestic science and advising them on extending their domestic and national influence. Another afternoon talks session with Nell Dungey featured guest speakers like Dr Lorna Hodgkinson. Evening sessions were devoted to music and theosophy, 'straight or diluted', with *Advance! Australia* lectures liberally included, and short talks on, for example, the League of Nations. On Sunday the faithful, the curious and the hapless alike could tune into Holy Eucharist sung splendidly through four microphones at the Redfern LCC church in the morning; and in the evening Blavatsky Lodge lectures were broadcast after church. In 1927 2GB concluded daily transmission not with prayer, but with Great Thoughts from Great Minds, extracted by 'Professor' Ernest Wood, a Northcountryman, briefly Leadbeater's secretary at the Manor.

Really 2GB was a phenomenal success, with Bennett contemplating a string of theosophical stations in Australia by 1928. Whether or not it could ever theosophise Australia, the station was a striking instance of the thesis which claims a modernising capacity for esoteric culture, in that alternative conceptions of reality may give cultural leverage on the status quo. However, the mission to theosophise Australia through broadcasting is an ambiguous example of creativity in the alternative culture. On the one hand, the history of radio in Australia would not have been much different without 2GB – it became one of many commercial broadcasters at the time. On the other hand, it was a product of theosophical culture, and it was innovatory. It set a cracking pace for commercial broadcasting, first by delivering an up-market female-dominated audience to advertisers, and second by leading the drive for American-style entertainment (in 1934 2GB brought Grace Gibson to Australia). It also produced in A.E. Bennett a convincing spokesman for commercial broadcasting in the thirties: Bennett was a prime mover in establishing an Australian transcription industry and served as president of the Federation of Commercial Broadcasters 1934–36. Unfortunately actual program content cannot readily be assessed. However the key probably does lie with musical programming. 2GB offered a real alternative there, and prefigured FM. It was therefore an alternative within the dominant culture. The station was evidence of theosophical enthusiasm and creative support for the dominant culture at a point where in Australia it was weak, rather than a critical alternative to it.[16]

Advance! Australia, supplementing 2GB's position and programming, is a more conclusive source of the direction of theosophical culture – a touchstone for the innovatory claim of esoteric culture, and a particoloured refraction of cultural life in the twenties. Other sources may portray the twenties as drab and disappointing, but contributors to *Advance! Australia* were earnest, exhortatory and optimistic, also confidently eclectic. In the more modest Melbourne version of theosophical high profile, the cardinal sin was 'NARROWNESS'.

There was nothing modest about *Advance! Australia*, subtitled *A Monthly Magazine of Australian Citizenship and Ideals in Religion, Education, Literature, Science, Art, Music, Social Life, Politics Etc.* A blue and gold cover, emblazoned 'The Industrial Crisis and the Way Out', and an Australian poem, launched the magazine upon the reading public in July 1926. Readers were promised practical idealism and sane reform, plus leadership: 'until the real leader comes the work of leadership must be done by the few.' From the profuse editorial comment accompanying this and every other issue it seemed that neither Italian fascism nor bolshevism provided an approved model. Arundale outlined the theosophical platform:

> purified patriotism, the promotion of a noble type of Australian citizenship, vitally Australian, eagerly conscious of Australia's specific place and part in the building of the future, no less eagerly conscious of the wider and equally vital citizenship involved in Australia's membership of the British Commonwealth, and recognising too ... there is a World citizenship, the obligations of which may no longer be ignored. (p. 9)

The magazine would be a harmonising force, conducted as an open forum, on chivalric lines, setting a much-needed example of a clean press. Naturally, it would also publicise the achievements of theosophy in the Outer World.

Contributions to *Advance! Australia* came in roughly equal proportions from local and other sources. Like many Australian papers before and since, it reprinted material from overseas journals, and relied heavily on its staff, many of whom were theosophical itinerants, like Arundale. But it also published significant Australian material, from local theosophists and sympathisers, including a number of female theosophists, with a leavening of 'names' in Australian public life, like Dr Richard Arthur, NSW MLA; Professor Griffith Taylor, the geographer; Walter Burley Griffin, architect-planner; and Adela Pankhurst Walsh. Between them the contributors envisaged reform of almost every level of Australian life. From a theosophical point of view they touched on most of the levers to uplift Australia.

It was not a learned advocacy. Contributions seldom exceeded a thousand words, and format emphasised topical paragraphs for editorial comment on events. In thirty-four issues, the format changed little: copious comment 'Without Fear or Favour', notice of 'Brotherhood' movements, cultural features, and a dozen or so articles, with some graphics. What it was like can be seen from a description of its first and last issues.

In the first issue, a lot of space went on platforms and dedications, so that it contained fewer articles than became normal. Editorialising extended from criticism of artificial industrial regulations and disputes and the need for leadership to save the party system, to religious tolerance, needed by Catholics, animal and child welfare, divorce and the press (which should not be sensational), and finally international affairs. That included support for Egyptian independence moves, attacks on Christian missionaries in India, and criticism of Bolshevik Russia, which might be better off under the Bolsheviks but lacked freedom.

The last issue, published in April 1929, still touched on industrial unrest and child welfare, with pars on diet, beauty, and prohibition, but its criticism was directed at Australian employers, said to be well behind their American counterparts. By 1929 the original regular cultural features had gone, despite a strong beginning with Enid Lorimer (winner of the Chips Rafferty Award for services to Australian drama in 1981), Edward Branscombe on poor performing opportunities, and Arundale on education and art. (Later he proposed a Ministry of Fine Arts.) Likewise brotherhood movements faded into the body of the magazine. The first list was, however, typical in its span: the League of Nations Unions, National Council of Women, NSW Prohibition Alliance, and the British Anti-Vivisection Union.

The first issue had eleven articles, the last fourteen. In the first issue there were articles on immigration, the new race type, church reunion, Richard Wagner, Sir Henry Parkes, builder of the Commonwealth, the renaissance in music, the cinema, and the need for a Teacher. A lot obviously came from the pens of Arundale and J.L. Davidge, the English-born journalist converted by Annie Besant in Adelaide in 1908 and recruited to Sydney in 1926 to become the mainstay of theosophic journalism in the interwar years. By April 1929 *Advance! Australia* was straining for local content, though still attracting significant political comment. Of the latter there was Adela Pankhurst Walsh warning that the communist revolution was nigh; problems of the Pacific, outlined by Persia Campbell of Sydney University (in 1924 Dr Bean had drawn attention to the need for a Sydney branch of the recently formed Pan-Pacific Union); the inevitable failure of utopias; and the prospects of 'sane democracy', by Joseph Hamlet FTS. From Perth Amelia Macdonald sent an account of that recent innovation, women police; and it was asked, 'Can we dispense with marriage?' The chances for a new national anthem were broached.[17]

A theosophical flavour was unmistakable. But it can be seen that the magazine struck a moral rather than religious note, and that it was even more determinedly secular than 2GB at the outset. Leadbeater wrote occasionally, and numerous curious fragments bespoke esoteric interests; but apart from advertisements placed by the United Spiritualist Church, *Advance! Australia* was not an obviously religious production. Advertisements for Victor Cromer's Spiritual Healing Institute in Burdekin House, Macquarie Street, the Hygienic Banking Company in Castlereagh Street, and lavish promotion of Marmite by the Adventists' Sanitarium Health Food Company, carried the lesser implication of links with advanced thought.

The field *Advance! Australia* sought to enter was dominated at the weekly level by the *Bulletin* and *Smith's Weekly*. *Triad* (1915–1928) and the glossy women's journal *Home* (1920–1942) were the main monthlies. Otherwise there were none of the substantial monthlies and quarterlies which had stimulated intellectual life in Sydney and Melbourne in the late nineteenth century. There were no little magazines as in America, with the special and shortlived exception of the Lindsay artistic manifesto *Vision* (1924) and the curious *Muses Magazine* (Brisbane, 1927/1929). And the day of the mass circulation women's magazine the *Women's Weekly* had yet to come. There was room, or an amorphous space, which Arundale hoped to fill.[18]

'I want controversy' said Arundale. But *Advance! Australia* could scarcely be regarded as lively. Its many opinions were weighed down with a welter of well-meaning prose and fine feeling. Superficially it lacked focus, and good causes proliferated on the page. What it attempted was a compendium of progressive thought in the 1920s. In retrospect, that makes it a valuable source.

Just as theosophy had found houseroom in late Victorian cultural ferment, so it made its way again in the troubled twenties. It did so by exploiting paradoxes of advanced thought, and identifying points of impasse. It could do so because theosophy combined in itself many of those paradoxes. Its projected relevance depended upon unresolved contradictions between the spiritual and the material life, culture and society, individualism and collectivism. Those contradictions were obvious the late twenties, and it might be added remain largely unresolved today, being inherent in industrial capitalism and intensified by the onset of consumerism.

By 1926, the Theosophical Society had lived with its own powerful combination of paradoxes for fifty years, during which time Annie Besant had steadily addressed her mind to 'Civilisation and its Deadlocks'. It had survived as a secret society, on mainly occult prescriptions; but these had a secular application and novelty, being in part enriched by Indian culture; and it always claimed to be a movement for brotherhood in the twentieth century, not just a nineteenth-century brotherhood. In Australia historical conjunction of strong leadership, multiple resources, and the Coming revived intellectual confidence. Not for the first time the esoteric culture overlapped with the avant-garde.

Over the next three years the Australian Section of the Theosophical Society urged reform of Australian life. For theosophists the new age, the next round, was at hand. Eager for signs and portents of the coming era within the existing culture, they swam with the current of the twenties, revitalising old concerns and canvassing some new ones. Old concerns included anti-vivisection, cremation and feminism; newer ones were birth control, the environment and the arts. Interest in psychology in the early twenties proved to be an indicator of the ground to be traversed. A disillusioned industrialist reported that his experiment in worker co-operation had failed, and that the middle of the road was untenable: but, splendid affirmation, 'when the industrial World Teacher comes, He will lead us to the Middle of the Road'.[19] That 'reform of Australian life' might eventually lead into murky political waters, to conflict rather than consensus, was not foreseen. Despite impasse and unease, theosophists were among the respectable citizens who believed that right political action and social engineering would lead to the good society.[20]

The theosophical prescription for an advanced Australia mingled many diverse elements. These may be grouped under three general headings: personal, cultural and political. The argument was that reform, or more precisely purification, of personal, cultural and political life would advance Australia.

The first aim should be the pure personal life. It may be remarked at the outset that in some respects, theosophists stood squarely behind Protestant norms, and displayed similar insensitivity to class difference in matters of consumption. Not only did *Advance! Australia* advocate prohibition, a decreasingly convincing proposition in New South Wales as well as America for the uplift of the working classes, but it also published Richard Arthur's case for child endowment to be financed by taxes on 'luxuries', meaning alcohol and tobacco.[21] In stressing the problems of indigestion, constipation and insomnia produced by starchy diets, the magazine reflected bourgeois preoccupations, feeding off the kind of neuroticism which made Christian Science such a success at the time. Possibly technological advances in the mass-production of food in the early twentieth century offended theosophists and this helped revitalise dietary reform as a basis of the pure life. But in other respects theosophists were in advance of creedal and class positions. They drew, that is, on a different tradition. Dietary reform was a mainstay of *Advance! Australia.*

Arundale objected to public funding of cancer research on the presumption that Western dietary preferences cause cancer. Many contributors were free traders, and by extension supporters of the rural interest; but readers were urged to disregard calls to eat more meat for the support of an industry purportedly losing ground to Argentinian rivals. Sometimes promoting vegetarianism had its amusing side, as with the marvels of marmite, or horror at a monster barbeque held for the visiting Duke and Duchess of York. More often contributors earnestly addressed practical problems.

Readers learned of the perils of white bread and white sugar. They received information on vitamins and protein. They were urged to eat pure foods, preferably raw, or if cooked, without unnecessary water and fats. There were recipes for salads and meat substitutes and articles on better breakfasts and the packed lunch. Bertha Crowther and May S. Rogers wrote many of them. Occasionally Australian exigency overrode theosophical horror at animal pain, as with sharks, but it was going too far to worry about vegetable pain, said to be minimal.[22]

Concern for animal welfare revived in Australia in the 1920s. Reasons for revival have yet to be established, but theosophists in *Advance! Australia* and other sources played a part. (They had also been a source of continuity: it has been argued that medical progress in the early twentieth century crushed the late Victorian anti-vivisection movement which became the domain of 'quackery and battiness', meaning theosophists, spiritualists and vegetarians.) When branches of the British Union for the Abolition of Vivisection (BUAV) were established in most capitals in the twenties, theosophists were enthusiastic and in some places prominent supporters. Some ardent souls at the TS Convention in 1924 thought that every lodge should sponsor a BUAV branch; and Miss Richardson reported that the Melbourne Anti-Vivisection Society founded in 1922 mainly by theosophists now had 700 members. Miss Charlotte Priest, president of Perth lodge at various times in the twenties, was also president of the Perth British Union branch; and Mrs Elsie Horder, secretary of Chatswood lodge 1922–25, became secretary of the NSW branch during the late twenties, as did Miss Sheridan Moore. Mrs Herder, a ready contributor to *Advance! Australia*, asked forcefully, is 'New South Wales a Vivisector's Paradise?' Late 1927, spurred by the same cancer research criticised by Arundale, Mrs Winifred Sealby of Saratoga NSW, apparently a relative of aviator Charles Kingsford Smith, formed a society to debate the evils of vivisection. Some theosophists joined this tiny ginger group (which became the Sydney Anti-Vivisection Society in 1936), notably founding committee-woman Mrs Maud Hilliard, a Sydney solicitor's wife who was a member of Blavatsky lodge and at that time joint tenant of the Star Amphitheatre, Balmoral, and also Miss Sheridan Moore. It appears that theosophists were more interested in the anti-vivisection cause than in animal protection societies, though issues raised by cruelty to and exploitation of animals belonged on a continuum of concern extending from diet to death in theosophical 'theology'. As 'Fore Runners of the Golden Dawn' (Mrs Sealby's cry) contributors to *Advance! Australia* such as Miss N.G. Sharpe of Adelaide protested against 'Our reliance on animal death'.[23]

Associated aspects of the purified personal life included hostility to compulsory vaccination, a populist horror since the 1870s; and to newer mechanical intrusions upon the body's integrity, like contraceptives. However, on contraception, old objections to interference with reincarnation gave way to fears of more dangerous obstructions. Purity and chivalry were not enough in the syphilis-worried twenties. I. Anson, another ready contributor, struggled to find a middle way between the birth-controllers and the Catholic Church, concluding that contraception was 'a sorry makeshift', but a lesser evil until humankind learned self-control – or as M.E. Orr put it, looking for 'The Moral Standards of the Future' in the pieties of the past, men learned continence. Leadbeater, characteristically, worried about the favourite Edwardian issue of class differentials in fertility, and the future of the race depending on maternal hygiene, but principally 'prospective parents ... among the cultured classes'. Anson too hoped for improved externalities, listing a simpler life, healthier living, co-operative housekeeping and changed attitudes to marriage. The magazine endorsed the work of the Racial Hygiene Centre, and even mentioned Marion Piddington in approving tones, believing now in information and perhaps even the eugenic principles which were beginning to make headway in Australia by the twenties. There were articles from Marie McLennan, billed as president of the NSW Racial Hygiene Centre (she was also a member of the TS Arts and Crafts Fellowship), and from Lillie E. Goodisson on 'Racial Hygiene'.[24]

The pure personal life required a pure social as well as bodily environment. Arguments for community and the environment appeared in *Advance! Australia* – notably Walter Burley Griffin's 'Building for Nature' and 'The outdoor arts in Australia'. The former is a rich and revealing document, not only a mature statement on the art of architecture but also of theosophic idealism. It argued that the art of architecture had dwindled since the Middle Ages into a mere cult, and while the machine age offered great promise, arrogant despoliation of nature had produced cities 'dirty, monstrous, disorderly, and desolate'. Griffin hoped for the awakening of 'disused powers of the universal mind', an 'organic communal life' and 'a practical religion', seeing in this 'present hectic age' signs of renewal as people looked inward to rediscover 'the possibilities of co-operation between head and mind in social service and creative effort' and the chance of 'broader psychological and emotional contact with life'. It was the architect's problem to observe 'simple equations' of the elements of the problems of life – laid out in a complex table – as illustrated most attractively at Castlecrag, the ideal suburb being constructed under his supervision on Middle Harbour, Sydney.[25]

Griffin spoke of 'this modern intellectual age of renaissance'. *Advance! Australia* reported that Castlecrag belonged to the New Age. After a guided tour by Marion Mahony Griffin in 1927, Anson wrote that it combined beauty and utility in co-operation with nature. Since the Griffins had only recently settled in, and the scrubby promontories showed few signs of developing into today's superior residential suburb, the experiment in 'organic communal life', closely and lovingly supervised by WBG, had not yet progressed far; but, Anson wrote, 'the unusual conditions attract a special type of people', and some theosophists moved in along with the radical Adelaide doctor, Edward Rivett and early anthroposophists, Mr and Mrs Williams.[26]

The Griffins were the theosophists' favourite planners not simply because they were theosophists but because they tried to resolve the problems of individualism and urbanism communally not collectively. As it happened, in 1929, probably out of disdain for what Marion later scornfully called 'the Christ event', they were converted by the Williams to an alternative *theosophia*, anthroposophy: that 'science of the spirit' developed by Austrian-born Dr Rudolf Steiner. In 1913 Steiner had led most of the German section out of the Theosophical Society in protest against millenarianism to form the Anthroposophical Society. Support for anthroposophy seems to have begun in Australia in the early twenties following lecture tours by a German philanthropist known as Alfred Meyerbold. Marion Griffin first read of anthroposophy then and was restored to optimism, though not yet persuaded to join the organisation.[27]

The anthroposophical community developed mainly by Marion Griffin in Castlecrag in the mid-thirties is not relevant here, though it will be touched upon again in Chapter 9 because it shows what *theosophia* as distinct from theosophical organisations meant to people. What is relevant is the Griffin ethic in the twenties and its bearing upon the promotion of an ideal

Australia. First, it exemplifies that quickening of environmental concern among the middle classes which saw increased agitation for urban leisure space, as in the parks and playgrounds movement led by C.E.W. Bean, and the beginnings of bushwalking. W.G. Lillingstone's article in *Advance! Australia* on coral gardens was noticed by Marion Mahony Griffin as evidence that Walter was 'not the only one complaining'. Some contributors called for wild life preservation. Arundale launched a Crusade for a Beautiful Australia and called for a Scenery Preservation Society. If neither seemed to get anywhere, they were signs of the times.[28]

Second, better than most, the Griffins convey the forgotten feel of the New Age, with its hope of a comprehensive spiritual reconstruction, since overshadowed by the Great Depression. Walter's densely packed article is important evidence, as is his commitment to Castlecrag, and its 'natural formula' for renewal: 'After a hundred years during which every alternative has been introduced from every corner of the earth this natural formula is now being tried out at Castlecrag in [sic] Sydney Harbour.' Castlecrag was, as Donald Leslie Johnson has said, Griffin's testament, 'an intimate expression of [his] philosophy of life' and 'the first statement of an architecture inspired by and derived from Australia'.[29] It is not reducible to class interest, nor was it simply 'naturalist'.

Equally revealing but far less manageable evidence is available in 'The Magic of America', an unpublished retrospect constructed by Marion Griffin, probably in the 1940s after returning to her native Chicago in 1937 when Walter died in India. The fourth section of 'Magic of America' called 'The Individual Battle', arranged around some twenty-eight designs, is interspersed with biographical information and other papers, mostly undated, to convey a version of the Griffins' life and times. Amid an array of materials is evidence of their intellectual life in Australia from 1914, and an account of Marion's gradual move towards anthroposophy.

Despite much bitterness at Australian ways, they found many friends: among the single-taxers and anti-conscriptionists in Melbourne (Marion mentions especially the young Adela Pankhurst Walsh whom she laboured to convert from communism, another bureaucratic form of dictatorship), and in Sydney. She wrote of many friends 'now moving towards a common centre from which one could grasp the earth and humanity as totality'. Steiner gave her a new lease of life:

> Before then I had been saying what a pity the Lord, who had created the wonderful beauty of stone and bush and animal, had made the fatal mistake of creating man who devoted all his energies to destroying these beauties. But now I grasped this reversal of things and realised instead of man's standing at the top of the tree of evolution through these kingdoms, they had all ... derived through eons from him. Surely there was some more constructive, creative work he should be undertaking now.[30]

It may be that her writings reflect preoccupations of an old, lonely and rather embittered woman. Nevertheless, the thoughts of WBG on human evolution in the twentieth century towards co-operation and efficiency, and the restoration of harmony of mind and matter, retain interest; and the themes of a paper on altruism, proposing the organisation of citizens into a threefold commonwealth to deal with politics, abilities and co-operation and ensure thereby freedom, rationality and mutuality, will recur in this chapter, especially in the subsidiary view that economics is a matter of values, of distribution not ownership. The point here is that the Griffins by the late twenties were both in their fifties, and at a low ebb professionally speaking, regarded as eccentric – Marion especially, recalled with a 'tomahawk profile and theatrical demeanour' and wearing slacks. Gnosis (and design contracts for municipal incinerators) not only kept them going, committed to the ideal suburb, but ready for the great culminating experience of India in 1936–37, where Walter's designs and Marion's draughting attained fresh splendour. That is, their idealism remained crucial, and through it they demonstrated an important facet of the ideal Australia.[31]

Advanced Australians, it seems, would be advanced individualists, purifying their lifestyles in harmony with nature, with the aid of planners. But that was only the first area of general concern. Cultural advance was necessary too. The second aspect of an advanced Australian should be the promotion of culture, and a rise in cultural standards. The advanced Australian would live a creative and cultured life. To the question 'Are We Barbarians?' English émigré Edward Vidler answered optimistically 'No'. He observed enterprising cultural communities in the main cities of increasing size and improving taste, the second being most noticeable in older women – and thereby gathered several motifs, culture, community and female participation.[32] Like other religious leaders, theosophical leaders had long complained about the Australian enthusiasm for organised sport, with its attendant evils of drink and gambling; but they had not been conspicuous in either denunciation or reform. The question arises whether the idea of a cultured citizenry was merely a revamped criticism of 'materialism'. How far did the second theosophical aspiration to more culture represent an alternative?

Theosophy has few claims to lasting historical importance. Where it does have claims, in the cultural field, commentators have often bypassed them, because they have found religious culture, including theosophy, unpalatable, incredible or inaccessible. Moreover, Australian theosophy in the late twenties did not take the observer close to the sources of innovation in the arts, that is, European innovation. At its most outward-going, though, it did something to disseminate high culture, as in 2GB's musical bias, and in the original features of *Advance! Australia*. Along with the work of prized theosophical figures like the Russian composer Scriabin, it promoted orchestras and mounted art exhibitions. In the twenties, any group which actively promoted the arts in Australia was important.

The claim does not encompass literature, the cultural enterprise which until very recently attracted most attention from cultural historians. A surprising number of obscure contributors to the annals of Australian literature are noticed in these pages, evidence of aspiration if not achievement among the theosophically inclined. But organised theosophy paid very little attention to imaginative literature. The most that theosophical publications did was to publish the occasional poem. These were usually of mystical or encouraging import, old favourites by Shelley, Walt Whitman, Tagore, Olive Shreiner, and suddenly by Krishnamurti. If there were local poetasters, few published as theosophists or for theosophists. *Theosophy in Australasia* published a few – for example, in May 1919 a sonnet by Edwin Bean, called 'Colonial Life'. Probably theosophists had quite enough imaginative literature generated by the society's own publishing houses without secular baubles.

However, many theosophists were largely self-educated, therefore great readers. There is a better explanation for the lacuna. For theosophists, the arts were primarily a vehicle for spiritual illumination. The function of art was not to represent the world as it is, but to penetrate beyond appearances to show spiritual realities. The artist was literally a medium, whether as creator or performer. Artistic effort would be judged by how effectively it reached into the unseen spiritual world. Thus it could be ranked in a hierarchy of perceptiveness, with untidy, impure and individualistic literary expression on the bottom, art and music on the topmost level of impersonality and purity, and sculpture and drama, showy arts, somewhere in between, according to the transfigurations achieved. The theory allowed for literary classics in that time distilled impurity; history did the sorting of 'the best that had been thought and said' – Matthew Arnold's definition, with which theosophists concurred, on their own terms.

Those terms were, nonetheless, perfectly intelligible. As summarised by art historian Sixten Ringbom, they were that art, religion and true science are inseparable, all moving towards the same goal. As interpreted by Wassily Kandinsky, *Concerning the Spiritual in Art* (1912), they proved to be particularly influential for modernism in painting. In 1979 the eminent Australian art historian Bernard Smith, pondering the origins of modernism in Australia, proposed that 'a thorough account of the history of spiritualism, theosophy, and anthroposophy in Australia as abroad is much more relevant to an understanding of modernism than say Einstein's theories'. It is in art that traces of theosophical contribution to culture in the 1920s are most likely to be found.[33]

A brief account of the general case shows why. In the first place, Madame Blavatsky allowed great artists status as initiates:

> The public must be made acquainted with the efforts of many world-adepts, of initiated poets and writers in the classics of every age, to preserve in the records of humanity the knowledge at least of the existence of such a philosophy, if not actually of its tenets.[34]

Annie Besant took the idea of artist as magus a step further. Through theosophy the artist could be precursor as well as preserver. Her view of theosophically inspired artists leading into unconquered realms has been cited earlier but bears restating:

> Theosophy gives back to the artist a world that for a long time he has lost; opens ... up possibilities among non-human races of beings, whole series of new subjects, ... new secrets of colour. For there are colours of the astral world rarer, finer, and more exquisite than in the physical – beings subtler

and more beautiful. As art and philosophy join hands, these beings ... will come down into the prepared sensitive brain of the artist, and to the vision of the sculptor, as new forms of beauty.[35]

In the early years of the twentieth century, theosophists became increasingly hopeful of restored harmony between religion and science through art, especially in Europe, where the general secretary of the German section from its foundation in 1902, the prodigious Dr Rudolf Steiner (1861-1925), was making his way to what has become known as anthroposophy. Besant offered spiritual sponsorship to the increasingly fashionable notion of the avant-garde.[36]

In the second place theosophists contributed practically to the making of modernism. In *Thought-Forms* (1901), Leadbeater and Besant published enticing abstract impressions of the astral plane, in much the same way as they had earlier tried to envisage the elements of the atom. Ringbom claims that the clairvoyants' efforts predated non-figurative art by almost a decade. One writer goes so far as to claim them as the pioneers of modern art. The original illustrations for Thought-Forms have recently been discovered at Adyar, and exhibited by the Bede Gallery Jarrow and comparisons made with the works of Kandinsky and Mondrian.[37]

Third, the groups which launched non-figurative art were well acquainted with and in some cases inspired by theosophical theory, particularly the 'Blue Horseman' group in Munich and maybe similar groups in Paris before World War I. It has been convincingly argued that they owed much to Leadbeater, Besant and Steiner. Kandinsky believed he stood on the edge of a new era, the Epoch of the Great Spiritual. Mondrian, who was a member of the Dutch section of the TS, produced abstract art which may be related to basic theosophical texts.[38]

Thus, theosophy appears to have played a vital role in the emergence of modernism. On reflection, it is obvious that the mature ideology of modernism, its attitude to art and to artists, harks back to a set of expectations as to a cultural turning point. The perceptual breakthroughs confidently proposed by leading theosophists coincided with and stimulated the efforts of the avant-garde. The context is now obscured, but the influence of those innovators has been immense. Herbert Read, who attaches great importance to the development of Kandinsky, concludes that though the great Russian was too austere for easy assimilation, his influence on the development of modern art has been immeasurable:

> Who are the disciples of Kandinsky? They are those artists, and they are now numberless, who believe that there exists a psychic or spiritual reality that can only be apprehended and communicated by means of a visual language, the elements of which are non-figurative plastic symbols.[39]

Perhaps, given Leadbeater's residence in Sydney from 1914, there was a theosophical dimension to modernism in Australia. The question were there theosophical modernists at work before World War II has been asked since Ringbom's article alerted art historians to theosophical influences on the emergence of modernism in Europe. If there were, they would surely have been enlisted in the cultural campaign to theosophise Australia. 'If people do not as you [say] care much about Art they must be educated to it – for as Mrs Besant has said, "it is a matter of life or death for the building of a nation". Australia cannot do without it' was the way Sydney artist and writer Jane Price put it.[40]

Judging from contributions to *Advance! Australia*, there were not too many modernist missionaries advancing Australian art along the lines laid out in pre-war Munich. Leadbeater's reiteration that mental states have colour equivalence and several articles by Violet Teague, such as 'Thoughts on Art' restating faith in the historical unity of art and religion, stand out in a thin field, which included also mention of Indian art. Only the question of artists' status in fascist Italy roused any controversy. Responding to an ambiguous report, Ethel Wood from the Italian consulate in Sydney affirmed that Mussolini was an idealist, a reconstructor in art. Actually, the journal preferred the established simplicities of national purpose to the complexities of cosmopolitan art; and achievements endorsed in London, as in the case of successful expatriate sculptor, Bertram Mackennal, whose Shakespearian group stands opposite the NSW Public Library.[41]

Theosophy in Australasia indicates sympathy over a longer period. Despite the unpromising atmosphere noted by Jane Price (and many others) the new approach to art trickled through. Not very vigorously, organised theosophy fell in with the Edwardian policy of encouraging art and artists. Before World War I, the magazine published occasional dollops of theosophical aesthetic theory, for instance on 'Psychic Painting' in November 1908, describing the feats of drawing mediums, usually untrained, said to produce bizarre but delicate work by astral precipitation or impression. Sundry notes on the true or spiritual basis of art appeared, also on 'The science of colour'. The Korman Guild of Art Workers founded by the short-lived Gnosis lodge in Sydney interested itself in cultural illuminations, and 'Colour Music'. But the section could not boast a native talent like the Irish poet-painter 'AE'.[42]

The boundary between religion and art, sharply drawn by nineteenth-century evangelical Protestantism and corroded by its opponents in the late nineteenth century, seems to have been blurred even further in the second decade of the twentieth century. It is rarely remarked that in the early twentieth century the term 'modernism' was used to describe a liberalising tendency in theology. As shown in Chapter 2, there were few theological modernists in Australia: but some evidence survives to show that those early modernists were concerned to strengthen the association of religion and art rather than diminish it, and unexpectedly from Brisbane. There for several years from mid-1911 Unitarian Reverend Douglas Price MA produced a bi-monthly magazine *The Modernist* affirming that beauty is truth. Price, previously an Anglican clergyman who defended Annie Besant in 1908 against the fundamentalists of Brisbane and who wrote several fictional works between 1912 and 1916, was reported in 1915 lecturing on art as an antidote to materialism. For him, art was 'the inspired Bible of the human spirit', not merely a polite accomplishment but an aspect of holiness. 'I will be a priest of beauty,' he said, adding that 'morality is simply beautiful conduct.' Art conceived by a 'priesthood' has become an increasingly familiar notion in the twentieth century. In a Christian population the association between art and religion still held, and modernisers in both fields sought the higher ground, the ground staked out by theosophy.[43]

In 1917 a Theosophical Arts Companionship was formed at Adyar in response to what its supporters believed to be 'a body of veritable theosophical art'.

> Art [is] coming naturally from a Theosophical conception of the Universe, and therefore much more significant and spiritually vital than the Arts of the past. Already the movement has thrown various workers in Arts together: exquisite pictures, beautiful music, dramas of spiritual beauty ... the beginnings of a great renaissance of the Arts on a higher spiral, which will help build the House Beautiful for the Lord.[44]

In Australia, the yearning among theosophists for a 'higher' art found expression after the Great War, as in a Convention paper by Elsie Deane on art and the coming reconstruction. Efforts were made for alternative bases for theosophical artists and, on a different plane, to reunite pure and applied art. Here theosophists were moved by the British arts and crafts movement, dating back to John Ruskin, and to William Morris, once a co-worker with Annie Besant. In June 1923, Marie McLennan, Theodora St John, Eleanor Ashworth and Hugh Noall formed a Fellowship of the Arts and Crafts at Mosman. In 1929 a fellowship was also formed in Perth, dissociated from theosophy but, it is claimed, inspired by theosophists. The theme appeared in *Advance! Australia*, when Margaret Joske of Melbourne addressed the artists of Australia on the loss of craft functions and the need for good design, in this case on biscuit tins: 'the hoardings and shops are the galleries and museums of the people'. By the 1920s, theosophy allowed room for both pure and applied art, and even the efforts of the untrained, in the name of the spiritual in art.[45]

Most theosophical artists were women. They were great wanderers, for example, Perth theosophist Florence Fuller who closed her studio on St George's Terrace to follow Besant to India in 1908, or the singer Amy Fuller, who collected wildflowers there for a time. Alice Adair, secretary of Perth lodge in 1908–1910, activist and theosophical worker for twenty-five years in Australia and India, devoted some of her considerable talent to lecturing on Indian art (she finished life at the Medina Hotel, Weston-Super-Mare, England). After the war, Ethel Carrick Fox was probably the major figure. Another great traveller who spent time in India, Ethel Carrick was in Sydney in the mid-twenties long enough to take Violet Teague from Melbourne and Queenslander Vida Lahey as pupils.[46]

Had there been an impressive male theosophical painter in Australia at the time, he would certainly have been mentioned. None were.[47] Nor was much attention paid to art except for providing exhibition space. That women were more attracted to the possibility of 'the spiritual in art' is hardly surprising, given the preponderance of women in all forms of religion in Australia. That they should find a home in theosophy is not surprising either given the capacious theosophical ethic. One of the very few skills that gentlewomen could decently acquire was a proficiency in art; and the theosophical world was very gentle. It also provided an international network for free-floating but respectable women of indeterminate means and status.

Modernism, it is often said, came late to Australia. Several features of Australian cultural life in the interwar years served to disguise and obstruct its progress, the most important being a dismissive secularism, anti-intellectualism and sexism. The art world was reluctant to admit the spiritual in art; it failed to appreciate the intellectual bases of modernism; and as Mary Eagle has implied in a look at modernism in Sydney in the twenties, modernism intimidated men probably more than women, but women's work was disregarded except when it could be accommodated as decorative, as with Margaret Preston's work.[48] *Home* interviewed Annie Besant in 1922 sceptically. However some leading male artists expressed interest in either the ideas or the techniques of non-figurative art: the latter congenial to Max Meldrum, the former too challenging for George Lambert.

The new ways irritated Norman Lindsay, a secret spiritualist with his own ideas about a renaissance in art in the Antipodes. If Lindsay rejected new theory 'by which rhythm becomes the basic structure or geometrical pattern of any work ' because all theories lead to 'Egyptianism', he was probably rejecting the underlying theosophical drift in modernism, because Blavatsky originally spoke about secret doctrines emanating from the temples of Luxor in Egypt. Sydney artist Frank Hinder recalls mounting interest in 'transcendental painting' in the thirties:

> The view was current that the classic philosophers' search for the reality behind the world of appearances, the world of forms ... was not essentially different from the mystic's search for unity with the One [and] Mondrian was only one of many artists and thinkers to be interested in theosophy, anthroposophy, Steiner's views, Rosicrucianism, and all forms of Eastern philosophy.

His wife, sculptor Margel Hinder, was interested by all of these, finding inspiration for her own work in various places, including Egypt and India. No doubt the building of the Sydney Harbour Bridge did more for modernism in art than theosophy, but in the confused transition, theosophy played an early and surreptitious part.[49]

Stanley Dobbyns, defending 'modernism' against ill-informed ecclesiastical criticism in *The Australian Theosophist* in 1929, correctly stated that advertising, its chief vehicle, merely reflected its modes without comprehending its spirit. He affirmed that the modernist, ignoring all forms, rituals and conventions, struggled afresh to contact 'life itself'. He too saw the artist as priest. 'The beautiful and true is ageless and heralds the New Age.'[50] If many shared these elevated sentiments, few saw theosophy as the channel for the art of the future.

In Australia, as in many other countries, it was not until after World War II that the diverse possibilities of abstract art were appreciated, as with the return of Godfrey Miller (1893–1964). The mystic Victorian artist Christian Waller (1895–1956) was not rediscovered until the 1970s. Both Miller and Waller were out of the country in the interwar years (Waller briefly, however); and when they did return, both lived as recluses.

Of the two, Miller provides the more straightforward evidence and achievement. Born in New Zealand, he began painting in Fiji during the Great War, an ANZAC invalided out of the army. He then travelled in Asia, migrating to Melbourne in the 1920s where he devoted himself to painting. In 1939, having spent the thirties in London, he settled in Sydney. Of all this he wrote, 'I got nothing from Europe – Cezanne or otherwise. It is the great India'. He also said, 'Indian philosophy gave me the key'. It does seem, however, that he studied Kandinsky closely in London, and for years, anthroposophy. Miller is the non-figurative painter par excellence in Australian art, and his beautiful lattice-like interpretations of the landscape set him apart from the representational nationalist mainstream. That theosophical aesthetic played a crucial part in Miller's thinking is reflected in the Buddhist mantra with which he concluded an undated political reflection:

> I stood in the Presence of the Splendour of the Forms
> But my Intuitions were not yet pure.[51]

So Miller's contribution was a long time in the shaping, and of a later period. He died a member of the Theosophical Society.

At least pursuing correspondence with spiritual reality did not drive Miller into total seclusion, as happened to Christian Waller. Conceivably, single-minded pursuit of such correspondence ultimately had an oppressive rather than a liberating effect on women artists. The seven linocuts of Waller's major work *The Great Breath: a Book of Seven Signs*, published by the artist in Melbourne in 1932, are fiercely symbolic, of astrological and numerological significance. The richly lettered introduction spells out a cosmography closely connected to *The Secret Doctrine*, explaining that each design is a symbolic rendering of the impulse behind each root-race of the present world cycle. The first five are Astral, Hyperborean, Lemurian, Atlantean, and Aryan, and the Sixth, portrayed via 'The Shepherd of Dreams', calls on the Christ principle to lighten the pathway to 'Man Perfected' in the last and seventh race.

In 1939, Waller went to New York to the temple of Father Divine, a black American who in the thirties declared himself God immortal, later attracting a following called the Peace Mission Movement. What Waller found in this expressive but authoritarian sect is impossible to say, since on her return she withdrew from the world; inspiration, the hope of reincarnation perhaps. 'One must be alone and know that the one within can meet all needs' she wrote in 1941.[52]

Like her husband the monumental artist Mervyn Napier Waller (1893–1972), best known for his designs at the Australian War Memorial in Canberra, Christian Waller was an arts and crafts figure. Her influence would appear to have impinged most strongly on him.[53] It certainly did not impinge upon the task of theosophising Australia. Apparently, the resources of the occult tradition were not required.[54] It is more surprising that the resources of Indian art were not brought to bear, but then this was well before the era of mass reproductions and travelling exhibitions, and the traffic was rather the other way. As explained by Florence Fuller,

> When I left West Australia it was to go to India – and I went in search not only of beauty and light and colour, and the picture-esqueness in general, which delight the eye and emotions of all artists – but of something deeper – something less easily expressed ... I think all who begin to touch realities must feel this.[55]

James Cousins's deluxe *Modern Indian Artists* (1923?), preserved in the Art Library of the State Library of Victoria, is a rarity. To the editors of *Advance! Australia* it mattered little that there were limited resources to mount the cultural side of the program. The important thing was coverage, and the best of everything, now.

Channelling the performing arts proved more manageable. In dance, a recent theosophical interest, the best came as Pavlova (currently on tour) and dance-drama, as in eurhythmics and theorhythmics, taught in theosophical schools and at the Star Amphitheatre. In 1923, newly arrived from London as the Art Director of the amphitheatre, Enid Lorimer announced that the striking venue would educate Australians for the new age of brotherhood and reconstruction, 'largely by plays'. She envisaged the new open-air theatre as a venue for dance, drama, film and choral concerts, and the home of a new school of drama 'to revive the spirit of truth and spirituality' and 'to give life to the old dramatic art-forms by restoring them to the divine purpose from which they have in modern days degenerated'. Lorimer proposed to train dancers, and began recruiting players for a troupe free from the tyranny of the star system then dominant in commercial theatre, intending to present Greek drama, mystery plays and an uplifting modern repertory.[56]

The Amphitheatre Players' first production, Henry Van Dyke's 'The Other Wise Man', came a year later in November 1924, and was well received. Subsequently the amphitheatre had a chequered career as theatrical venue and did not fulfil Lorimer's hopes though it functioned as a school of dance into the 1930s, when the Australian dance teacher Joan McKenzie, who later established a school of classical ballet in Honolulu, taught Greek dancing there, to the delectation of Balmoral residents who overlooked beautiful performances against sea and sky by barefoot pupils clad in Greek tunics (reportedly one pupil was the Australian film star Ann Richards). Commercial theatre in Sydney almost collapsed in the thirties, and little theatre, especially lively on the lower North Shore, struggled for survival. But theosophists had played a part in encouraging hope of a more cosmopolitan and craft-oriented theatre. They also nurtured and encouraged the actor Peter Finch through a turbulent childhood, some of which was spent at the Manor and at the Garden School at Stanton Road, Balmoral, up the hill from the amphitheatre, the private theosophical school established by the Misses Arnold and Macdonald when the section closed Morven School in 1923. (Other pupils included Mary Drake, who recalls the two headmistresses as 'extremely large women who dressed completely in white, even to their shoes and stockings', and the co-educational school as being run on 'rather unconventional lines'.)[57]

Finch revered Lorimer as 'a great detached maternal influence'. She was the first drama writer for *Advance! Australia*, replaced by Douglas Vigors in

1927. *Advance! Australia* argued that greater national effort was required for theatre to flourish in the late twenties. Approving Louis Essen's Pioneer Players in Melbourne, it called for a national theatre company and state subsidies to encourage what it – and Doris Fitton of the Independent Theatre North Sydney which trained Peter Finch – called 'better plays'; and also to protect the theatre from blatant commercialism.[58]

A danger referred to in numerous editorials was a flood of pernicious foreign films, particularly American films, feared as a travesty of decency and British civilisation, against which citizens should organise in watchdog committees. Following the example of Dr Bean at the Roseville Community Services Club, another theosophical innovation, the Good Film League, was launched. Readers could support it by sending in reports from local picture theatres of showings offensive to women, children or Australia. *Advance! Australia* also detected a need for a quality film house, and announced showings at Adyar Hall in September 1926. This marked the beginning of a cultural tradition in Sydney, theosophical sponsorship of quality films, from Adyar Hall to the Savoy (1930) to the present-day Walker Street cinema in North Sydney.[59]

Music was just as important to an advanced Australia as art and drama, if not more so. Theosophical interest in music was apparent from the beginning of the century, when the possibility of music as spiritual was first canvassed. With such work as that Scriabin (1872–1915), the Theosophical Arts Companionship could remark in 1917 on the growing body of theosophically inspired music. Phyllis Campbell writing in 1931 on the role of music in world revolution emphasised the cosmic life-releasing work of early twentieth-century composers, at once closer to ordinary life and nearer to abstract realities than in the past, citing film music and the 'scintillating works of Stravinsky' as evidence of the former tendency and Scriabin's 'Prometheus', Holst's Planets suite, Debussy, and even Satie's 'Socrates' as evidence of the latter. Liberation from the diatonic scale via Eastern and alternative scales was also seen as a sign of the new age. In a recent restatement of these issues, Australian composer Peggy Glanville-Hicks has described Oriental and especially Indian influences on her own work. Walter Burley Griffin felt that music was the most successful of modern art-forms, because it kept pace with scientific progress:

> Music is, so far, the one great art that has been developed in modern times, because it has kept pace with science, as that has clarified the phenomena of sound, and with the mechanical progress that has opened new avenues of musical expression.⁶⁰

In principle, theosophists welcomed modernism in music. At the same time Australian theosophy increasingly sponsored performance of classical and religious music, especially in Sydney where Charles Boult organised the Music Lovers' Concerts mentioned previously. Both Sydney and Brisbane lodges formed orchestras in the second decade of the twentieth century, the former led by Mrs J.E. Grieg. It may be recalled that Sylvia McConkey, graduate of Melbourne Conservatorium, composed a musical service for the LCC. In the twenties, the section boasted a musical director in British-born Edward Branscombe. Branscombe, like fellow HQ worker Norman Ingamells, a bassoon instructor at the NSW Conservatorium, did something in Sydney to promote advanced religious music. With local talent, Arundale's passion for classical music, and the programming at 2GB, there was no shortage of fine music in theosophy by the twenties.⁶¹

Advance! Australia added a further dimension to the argument for elevating cultural standards in music, and was quick to perceive that gap in Sydney's musical life after the departure of Belgian-born Conservatorium Director Henri Verbrugghen, a gap filled in part by 2GB, and then, in the early thirties by the ABC. Of its several contributors on music, mystic poet and composer Phyllis Campbell was most interesting. Campbell, who filled a slot on 2GB for a time, played a vigorous role in the musical life of Blavatsky lodge, organising concerts at Adyar Hall and popularising the work of contemporary composers, particularly and controversially, Scriabin. In her own work she was influenced by Egyptian and Indian modes, Hinduism and Sufism, though she regarded Bach as the master, and at the same time took a lively interest in the development of an Australian musical culture. A student and friend of composer Alfred Hill, encouraged by the British theosophical composer Cyril Scott, she had close links with the Conservatorium. She advocated a musical culture both theosophical and Australian, finding some encouragement in the American experience and more in Australian history where Isaac Nathan's arrangements of Aboriginal melodies, Henry Tate with his idea of an Australian scale based on bush bird song, Percy Grainger and Alfred Hill had shown the way. Australia, she said, needed a school for composers who would write music inspired by local, perhaps Aboriginal, sounds and ideas.[62]

In the long run, of theosophists Dorothy Helmrich probably did most to elevate cultural standards, and that in a later period. Helmrich, born in Mosman, studied at the new NSW Conservatorium of Music and won international recognition as a lieder singer. Committed to taking the arts to the people, in 1943 she founded the Council for the Encouragement of the Arts, forerunner of the Arts Council. Helmrich died in Sydney in 1984 aged ninety-five, and at her request excerpts from the *Bhagavad Gita* and *The Light of Asia* were read at the service at Northern Suburbs Crematorium – as they had been read at Adyar on the first anniversary of Madame Blavatsky's death almost a century ago.[63]

Neither the 'new life' nor the 'new age' sufficed to theosophise Australia. That was always basically a political task. The third requirement for an ideal Australia was political. Political involvement came as second nature to Arundale, used to 'a strenuous political life in India'. He arrived in Australia during the first Lang Labor government in New South Wales (1925–1927), and political propaganda from theosophical sources extended through the Bavin administration (1927–1930), to the second Lang government, dismissed by Governor Game in May 1932. The years 1926–1930 were five years of deepening economic recession, worsening industrial conflict, and class cleavage. The storm centre of political life was NSW, but Commonwealth politics proved increasingly unstable too, with the defeat of the conservative Nationalist-Country Party coalition (October 1929) and a short-lived Labor government (1929–1931) at the depth of the depression. Arundale and his lieutenants proposed to give a lead.

Advance! Australia deplored the tone of Australian politics. Australians only accepted wise leadership in crisis. Otherwise, political life presented 'a nauseating spectacle of intrigue and wire-pulling, with its apotheosis in New South Wales'. Worse still, in a prosperous land, industrial conflict threatened progress. To advance, Australia must find ways out of political and industrial conflict.[64]

Arundale wrote that the way out of industrial conflict depended upon improved industrial relations, called by him scientific comradeship in industry, along the lines pioneered by Henry Ford (himself a theosophist, and one whose public expressions of faith in reincarnation endeared him to other theosophists). Employers must lead; workers, by now also consumers, had more to gain in wages and leisure from co-operative partnerships than sterile confrontation and artificial arbitration; the public should boycott non-co-operators. The way out of political strife depended on patriotism. *Advance! Australia* aimed to promote a nobler type of citizenship, as with the series on 'Great Men' and 'Builders of the Commonwealth'. Noble citizens could recognise true leadership.

In orthodox theosophy at this time true leadership referred to the coming World Teacher. In the meantime, until the real leader comes, 'the work of leadership must be done by a few'; *Advance! Australia* aimed to encourage 'practical idealists'. Hence the *Advance! Australia* dinner club – vegetarian – attendance Dr Richard Arthur and the Hon. R. Sproule, both MLAs, Arundel Orchard, Walter and Marion Griffin, Creswell O'Reilly, film censor, T.G. Dawson from Scots College, Dr and Mrs Jenkins, and various TS people. The editors also proposed that Australia needed a permanent Commission of the Wise operating alongside the party system. Who would serve in an Australian Academy of the Wise? People, especially female people, 'who cared only for Australia, who were tired of parties and classes and sects, and wanted Australia instead'.[65]

In approving the political advancement of women, male theosophists endorsed the aspiration of equal citizenship which after twenty years of enfranchisement, had scarcely impinged on the male political machinery. Bessie Rischbieth, a friend of J.L. Davidge and prominent spokeswoman, is cited in *Advance! Australia* on the need for a new social order and a national voice for women. Issues discussed and reported at federal councils of women, and international conferences, justified hopes for an elevated citizenry: 'What an enormous amount of good work can be carried out by a strong-minded and intellectual group of women organised for the benefit of mankind.'[66]

Male office-bearers of a predominantly female organisation, founded and led by women, had every reason to uphold feminism. They were of course conservative feminists, and *Advance! Australia* made more of motherhood than any other issue. It published a good proportion of women contributors; and women contributors themselves focused debate. Elsie Horder, decrying the gap between image and reality in 'Australian Motherhood', noted the problem of a nation's most valuable parents, suicidally overburdened as high wages and shortened hours diminished the pool of domestic labour. Unhappily for constructive debate on the servant question, that angle on the rising cost of living encouraged several well-known single-taxers back in to the fray.[67] What the journal was really concerned about was extending the pool of middle-class leadership, which it did by portraying suitable female role models; Besant, of course, and nationally, along with Rischbieth, Rose Scott and Catherine Helen Spence.

Organised hostility to the party system recurred in the twenties, conspicuously in 1920, 1925 and 1929. During years often regarded as quiescent, between 1926 and 1929, *Advance! Australia* carried a full complement of 'anti-political political thought'. In September 1926, it published a manifesto of an Australian Reform Association (ARA) launched the previous July by persons unspecified, calling for increased nationalism and 'harmonious reform'. It thought existing financial, industrial and social legislation quite unsound and called for intelligent reconstruction with constitutional reform in the direction of unitary government, advocating a flat-rate land tax, freer trade and closer imperial links. It also promised to stand against 'all movements tending to subvert the Constitution and to substitute revolution for ordered progress'.

Other non-party manifestos appeared too, like 'The Peoples' Federation' suggested by W. Watson, independent MHR for Fremantle, one of several enthusiasts for proportional representation (which had in fact operated briefly in NSW in the early twenties). George Cann, independent Labor candidate for Lakemba, warned against the 'red rules' of Lang Labor. The manifestos emanated from the direction of Arundale, who by Easter 1927 had evolved a theosophical policy for Australia. This advocated free immigration (a mutual betterment to the British unemployed and Australian productivity); prohibition, wise government with more women legislators, educational uplift, creative leisure, and religious tolerance.[68]

In November 1927 the president of the non-party ARA, which shared *Advance! Australia* rooms at Adyar House, announced that citizens should support T.R. Bavin in the forthcoming New South Wales elections because he was a man of principle. A month earlier when the Nationalist party contracted with 2GB to broadcast its election campaign, A.E. Bennett insisted that theosophy was 'above party, or at least above present parties'. 2GB stood simply for 'Australia First'.[69]

The underlying premise of political advance in Australia was imperial progress and reform. It was believed that the British Empire had not yet reached its zenith. On the contrary, 'God's experiment in empire building', and the coming World Teacher, envisaged India as the new focus and strength of empire, from which a world-state would evolve. Thus, as part of a nobler citizenship, *Advance! Australia* aimed to strengthen both imperial and international sentiment. That entailed a radical strengthening on the race issue. An advanced Australia must improve its record on race relations.

For those who foresaw that the empire would founder on the 'colour question', the White Australia Policy continued to present formidable difficulties. But the difficulties remained obscured by uncertainty about India's eventual status in the empire. Arundale did what he could to foster sympathy for home rule for India, but his Australia-India League announced on October 1926 and its monthly *Bulletin* seemingly had little effect – probably because the cause of Indian independence itself made little progress in the late twenties. (In fact Indian leaders drew back from discussions with the incoming Labour Government in Britain in 1929 which may have led to the dominion status advocated by Besant.)[70] *Advance! Australia* sustained Besant's line that Australian racial prejudice resulted from ignorance, while accepting the White Australia Policy as an 'economic and moral necessity' for the time being.

By the mid-twenties, the plight of the Aborigine impinged more strongly upon the conscience of the urban intelligentsia. This was reflected in *Advance! Australia*'s references to a dispossessed and decimated black population said to be dying of despair and disgust at white civilisation. The journal endorsed the view that the condition of the Aborigine dishonoured Australia. Aborigines were proven capable of mental development, and theosophists should recognise an ancestral obligation for 'a younger brother in the human family'. It published a review by the geographer Griffith Taylor headed 'The Australian Aborigines and Their Allies' in 1927, and several reports generated in Adelaide on plans for a model native state in the Northern Territory, either in Central Australia or in Arnhem Land. Some contributors touched upon positive aspects of Aboriginal culture, music being one example already cited. Typically, the journal called for federal responsibility. More oblique but equally to the point, it saw 'big questions' building up – warning that through karma cruelty returns.[71]

Some unbrotherly and unfortunate admissions did appear. Dawson's preference for 'family life' as a comprehensive ideal and ex-NSW Premier Holman's hope that the empire would protect white civilisation drew rebukes. Others wrote in uncertain tones of a new China. The Japanese Consul-General in Sydney, I.M. Tokugawa, contributed a defence of Japanese intentions. Elsewhere, William Morris Hughes, perpetual hope of middle opinion in the late twenties in Sydney, struck the firm note: Australians might be surprised to discover that a remote body like the League of Nations could impinge on the White Australia Policy.[72]

Theosophists in the 1920s were ardent advocates of the League of Nations. The Bean connexion worked here, through C.E.W. Bean, an early supporter of the League of Nations Union in Australia. In 1927, Adelaide lodge reported that most of its members belonged to the union, and several were active workers, as was Elliston Campbell at Sydney University where he lectured in engineering. The League of Nations Union topped Arundale's early list of brotherhood movements. Since the British Empire was to be the evolutionary base for the world state, no contradiction existed between imperialism and internationalism. Thus, along with nationalism, and imperialism, *Advance! Australia* co-opted Viscount Cecil of Chelmwood, chairman of the originating British Union, Raymond Watt, devoted secretary of the NSW branch, its vice-president Laura Bogue Luffman, and prominent Sydney worker, Persia Campbell. Arundale, Ernest Wood and van der Leeuw also contributed. In 1929, the NSW branch of the union rented a room in Adyar House.[73]

Although the League of Nations Union was not very successful as a pressure group it gathered an array of forces which help situate theosophy politically. In NSW, the union was strongest among church people and academics, while in Victoria, politicians were more prominent. So in Sydney theosophists sought common ground with the churches, the Red Cross, the Millions Club, esperanto societies and peace groups. In internationalism, theosophists touched the high notes of middle-class political idealism.[74]

Overall, the political plan for an advanced Australian consisted of a hierarchy of nationalism, imperialism, and internationalism, resting within Australia on harmonies of class, race and sex. Despite the alternative prescriptions for personal life, and the 'advanced' aspects of theosophical culture, the ideal Australia turned out to be an intellectualised version of conventional liberal hopes. Theosophical brotherhood did not admit pressure from below: indeed the labour movement attracted little attention, and scant sympathy by implication. Leadership and national unity were sought instead. That it spoke in more elevated and alien tones than was customary in political discourse is obvious from the fact that it always referred to Australia as 'the Motherland', an unrecognisable and alien usage, perhaps even offensive to the Australian ear.

In the cry for nobler citizenship, purer politics and evolution towards ever more rational political forms, it is not hard to detect a carryover from the 'new liberalism' of Edwardian Britain. Although the new liberalism in Britain did not survive the Great War as a political force – Lloyd George saw to that – ideological continuity is evident in the progressive causes which *Advance! Australia* also espoused; and an ideology which tried to contain class conflict and to balance individual and collective interests by means of corporate and communal innovations retained relevance. A difficulty was that in Australia the day of the new liberalism had long since passed with the 'Fusion' of liberals and conservatives effected by Deakin in 1909, whereas in Britain consolidation of the Labour Party was slower and hope of liberal revival lasted into the twenties. Nevertheless, the upheaval in Australian politics which followed the first great Labor split in 1916 challenged the class-based organisation of politics achieved before 1914, and the initial challengers, Hughes and Holman for instance, remained in politics; post-war electorates proved ever more volatile, especially for the conservative forces but also for Labor, as new sectional interests above all the Country Party entered the political arena; and by the twenties the elusive but crucial ingredient of nationalism had been transformed by war. *Advance! Australia* rhetoric, directed at a secularising middle-class, aimed to strengthen the middle-class version of nationalism which valued social harmony, national unity and strong leadership. The presumption was that if Billy Hughes would but stake out the territory, or some other national figure like Sir John Monash could be persuaded to enter politics, theosophists, and many more, would endorse him.[75]

All this took place amid mounting economic depression. Theosophy was not bereft of suggestions. Joseph Hamlet, prominent in the early thirties as a 'populist cure merchant' – he claimed his father represented North Dublin in the House of Commons in the Tory interest, but he was an Australia-first man – wrote extensively for *Advance! Australia*, for example.[76]

It was almost with relief that theosophists seized upon the very latest solution to the mounting problems of the material world, that is, social credit (or, as it was often known after its founder, Douglas Credit). T. Kennedy, Secretary of the Irish section of the Theosophical Society, a social-credit organiser in Dublin, wrote to Arundale in mid-1927 urging FTS to acquaint themselves with the writings of Major Douglas, whose social scheme would 'lead Humanity into an era of Peace and Plenty'. His letter appeared in *The Australian Theosophist*, September 1927, headlined 'Credit Reform. A Social Policy for Theosophists'. W.G. Bow, president of Perth lodge; responded eagerly.

> The world today wants peace and brotherhood. Theosophists must offer a definite plan to that end. Our leaders have given us wonderful conceptions of the purpose of life and the trend of affairs. They have told us what is wanted for the New Age. It is for us to apply those conceptions to the practical detail of life ...[77]

Even the economic system might be arranged in an idealist way.

In Australia as in Britain, social credit made its way through theosophical circles. This was especially true in Australia, where theosophical study circles and discussion groups in Perth and Sydney were among the first to attend to the teachings of Major Douglas. By mid-1928 five articles on social credit had appeared in *Advance! Australia*. Throughout, *The Australian Theosophist* carried social-credit material. Perth theosophist and social-credit activist Douglas Riddett kept it before their attention, and Perth members were the most persistent in urging the section to study social credit, 'the greatest brotherhood idea since the introduction of Christianity'. It was claimed that in Sydney in 1930 a class of eighty had met in the Order of Service rooms to discuss it.

Major Douglas, a retired Canadian engineer, wrote four books between 1918 and 1922, in which he developed the view that the age of plenty had dawned: both production and distribution had been transformed by mechanisation; the problem now lay with a maldistribution of purchasing power. Private control of credit distorted price mechanisms and prevented the operation of the law of supply and demand. Douglas argued that the present system caused poverty amid plenty, and servility, through manipulated scarcity. Credit, being *cultural heritage* rather than private property, should be socialised; artificial pricing replaced by the *just price*, dictated by demand and regulated by experts; wages should be superseded by the payment to all of the *national dividend*. Socialised credit would prevent enslavement to international financiers and power-hungry bureaucrats.[78]

Social credit, which belongs in the underworld of economics, was one of the lost causes of the interwar years. Douglas's theorems have been dismissed as simplistic by economic historians – as 'funny money'. As a form of political expression social credit was in itself probably neutral, but it acquired an unsavoury taste, or worse: it was reactionary in its extreme individualism, proto-fascist because of implication of a financial conspiracy which fostered and still fosters anti-semitic sentiment. Versions of 'community credit' served to strengthen the hand of weak regional politicians, for example, Tasmanian Laborites in the thirties. However, some of the hostility to social credit in Australia arose simply because its electoral impact in the thirties was such as to cause Labor anxiety.[79]

Timing is important in explaining its appeal. Douglas's emphasis on credit and consumption revitalised nineteenth century moral criticism of capitalism, and of liberal economics. It also predated Keynesian underconsumptionist theory. Further, in the early twenties, after the war and the Russian Revolution, believers in 'the Religion of Socialism' were in disarray. The socialisation of credit was a godsend as a new idea.

Promoted by the influential English editor, A.R. Orage, social credit gained ground in a number of disenchanted circles in the 1920s, among ex-guild socialists, radical intellectuals and high churchmen who saw social credit as 'the next step'. That it promised a step away from bureaucratic regulation by the state, whether capitalist or socialist, told in its favour; that it offered both a practical and a moral step appealed to people undergoing the bitter experience of political 'secularisation' as the old 'Religion of Socialism' crumbled. Hope of peaceful evolution to a new economic order was yet to be tested by capitalist crisis in the Great Depression, and unreconstructed by Keynesian liberalism.[80]

Douglas credit appealed to radical religious groups because of its assumptions about human nature, and its ideal of social reorganisation. Both could be incorporated at the margins of Christian social thought. Douglas desired to liberate the individual, and to promote economic functionalism: 'a satisfactory modern co-operative State may be broadly expressed as a functionally aristocratic hierarchy of producers accredited by and serving a democracy of consumers.'[81]

This appealed on the one hand to Catholic and Anglo-Catholic social theorists who harked back to a rosy medievalism of imagined liberties and moral regulation under the one true church, untainted by the grasping Protestant spirit; and on the other to Quaker and theosophist groups, the former approving freedom from regulation by worldly authority. Theosophists, always harder to pin down, shared Anglo-Catholic enthusiasm for the ancient moral order, and some of the Quaker enthusiasm for high individualism. They constituted a natural constituency for social credit. They too held an optimistic view of human nature, faith in the machine age, and the hope of a self-regulating social order. Their class position by the mid-twenties predisposed them to socialised consumption and regulated leisure, while they preferred solutions from 'above'.

In Australia between 1927 and 1934 social credit gained an adherence. Its highest electoral return came in 1934, in 'middling' electorates, a theme to be picked up shortly. It may be of interest to add that it took hold mainly in the cities, unlike comparable societies of Canada and New Zealand. No doubt theosophists remained stalwarts, even when social credit sank to the status of a lost cause.

Nearly three years of theosophising Australia produced no evident result. Still the World Teacher had not come. The long-awaited leader failed to materialise. Theosophists, presumably the chief readers of *Advance! Australia*, lost faith in political journalism. The section had given generously, but the ambitious journal proved a fearful financial drain. The first budget allocation in 1926 is not recorded, but between January 1927 and December 1928 the section expended £2786 on the journal, recouping only £888. A final allocation of £450 was needed in 1929 to close it down – that is it lost at least £2,500. In the meantime, *The Australian Theosophist* suffered brief closure, to be resumed privately under Leadbeater's editorship for nine months, 1928–29, when the section rectified an unfortunate situation.[82]

Convention abandoned the journal without demur in April 1929. J.L. Davidge, who had done most of the work on *Advance! Australia* and was regarded by Arundale as an essential worker, was transferred grudgingly to the office as assistant general secretary. The section was once again clear of politics, a situation infinitely preferred by the more conservative or more spiritual members who treasured TS 'neutrality'. Melburnians, just as energetic, and broadcasters too (of necessity on other people's stations) disapproved of Sydney bombast.

In retrospect proposals for an ideal Australia emanating from a religious minority had little chance. Mistrust of the clergy in politics ran deep in Australia. Confusion about the intent of theosophy was inevitable given the strong smell of money in theosophical enterprises. Despite the firm prefatory note attached to her novel *Ride on Stranger* (1943) that all the characters are entirely fictitious, it could be concluded that the novelist Kylie Tennant had intimate experience of the campaign to theosophise Australian and found it humbug. At one point, the novel's heroine Shannon Hicks is employed as private secretary to Abbott Southwell Vaughan Quilter, a handsome Englishman whose distinguished manner and 'big sweeping ideas' at first thrill her. But she soon rejects his super-salesmanship (goaded by the discovery that he had a wife in England), and departs the scene for radio 2QR. The Middle Way proposed by the Abbott and the Order of Human Brotherhood to which he is attached are both satirised and condemned as exploitative, notably of women.

The fiction, however, does not exhaust the facts. Two are important. One is that the times encouraged political debate, at both ends of the political spectrum. An equally small minority in the labour movement simultaneously hoped for a revolutionary transformation of capitalist Australia; and the spectre of secret armies organised by returned soldiers lurked in the political shadows. Meanwhile the electorally crucial middle ground vacated by Deakinite Liberals in 1909 had been forcibly cleared in the early twenties by coalitionists Hughes and Holman. It was then a confused area, affected by numerous small but significant electoral changes, a weak three-party system, and a considerable number of mavericks. There was room for all, even theosophical claimants as alien and abrasively earnest as Arundale.[83]

Furthermore, the ideology advanced under theosophical auspices anticipated fresh pressure on an already unstable political system. The most striking thing about the campaign to theosophise Australia was the way it appealed to people feeling that pressure early. Eventually they were absorbed as new talent on the conservative side of politics. A.E. Bennett is the key example. Others heard through *Advance! Australia* were Professor Griffith Taylor, chairman of the Adelaide Emergency Committee which was formed to absorb populist threats from below in 1931; Adela Pankhurst Walsh, soon to organise the Australian Women's Guild of Empire financed by Sydney employers as an anti-communist front; and Norman Keysor, one of the Rotarian instigators of the All for Australia League in Sydney.[84] Again the question of leverage by the esoteric culture comes into view.

The second fact is that regardless of Convention decisions, commitment to political action actually intensified in 1929. Theosophical lecturers had promoted 'the ideal Australia ' since at least 1922, and the darkening political sky increased the rhetoric. At the 1928 Convention, discussions in a symposium on the 'ideal Australia' ignored a comment that the tense political situation only showed an advanced working class. It preferred to discuss the drift to civil war and the need for a 'goodwill campaign', fostering 'intense patriotism'. Working-class assertiveness could only be contained by more patriotism – on which panellist Leadbeater waxed strong.[85] The next year delegates heard both Leadbeater and Arundale in full cry on 'theosophy and patriotism', and the great crisis in Australia. Leadbeater, still hopeful of theosophising Australia, remarked amiably on the backward nature of the land he was about to leave after fifteen years of residence. (He was returning to Adyar to be with the ailing Annie Besant.) He deplored strikes: 'We see all these strikes and industrial quarrels. No-one can suppose that this is doing Australia any good. It is obtaining privileges for a certain class ... but for Australia as a whole that sort of thing is very bad.'[86]

In early 1929 'world-citizen' Arundale returned from a world tour to control of the Manor (now bereft of Leadbeater). What Arundale noticed most in the outer world was the failure of the average Australian to put Australia first. He was therefore quite unrepentant about the losses of *Advance! Australia*, and immediately announced his support for a new fortnightly for political propaganda, to be called – of course – *Advance! Australia*. Under the circumstances, the incoming general secretary, the young Harold Morton, could only hope for 'balanced progress', the middle way for theosophy itself and for all those members far from the shouting and tumult of Sydney who preferred mysticism and magic to politics. Actually, Convention did urge lodges to consider political groups, following A.E. Bennett's suggestion of separate study groups for Labor and Nationalist sympathisers – the aim being to cleanse the Augean stables, and diminish class conflict.[87]

In February 1929 in New South Wales a long and bitter lockout began on the northern coalfields. It called up memories of the recent British General Strike of May 1926. In its dying days, *Advance! Australia* published a paper by F.R.E. Maulden, then district tutor of the University of Sydney at Newcastle, later Professor of Economics at the new University of Western Australia and an authority on coalmining. Could the Davidson Royal Commission solve the coal quandary? Not if communism got a hold, implied another late contributor, Adela Pankhurst Walsh. So goodwill, and earlier sympathy for 'Labor's place in the changing social order', ebbed away in 1929.[88] New efforts to define the middle of the industrial road seemed amply justified to the Arundale circle.

If Australia was at war with itself, as pronounced by *The Australian Theosophist* in August 1929, theosophists must rally to ardent and arduous responsibilities. They belonged, it was asserted, not to the leisured classes but to the working classes, and had a message for them. Theosophy belonged to the kitchen no less than the drawing room, and theosophists' civic duty was inescapable. But there was again no collective response. In mid-1929 the Arundale circle turned to voluntary action.

It was reported in September 1929 in *The Australian Theosophist* that a study group had been meeting in Sydney on Saturday mornings to discuss Australian problems in the light of theosophy and patriotism. The group proposed fourteen points for Australian regeneration, exclusive of what were said to be divisive issues, like prohibition. It produced a slogan, 'Patriotism a substitute for tariffs'. It adopted an Australia-first policy. Only Australia-first could settle the vexed question of tariffs or free trade:

> If every Australian will sedulously encourage Australian industries even at a greater cost to himself, if in default of Australian products he will prefer empire commodities, only turning to foreign goods if the worst comes to the worst, the whole question of trade will resolve itself, without having recourse

to those expedients which always hit the consumer hard, and often stir to violence those national jealousies already too easily aroused.

The idea was that International Groups for Patriotic Citizenship would spring up everywhere, under the umbrella of the Theosophical Order of Service, of which Arundale was now Chief Organiser in Australia. Meanwhile, *Advance! Australia* resumed in Sydney, 4 pages, fortnightly, subscription 2/- p.a. Ultimately the campaign to theosophise Australia led to a patriotic league.

Two ways of looking at theosophical capacities to find a middle way had emerged. Previously theosophists had deemed themselves 'path-breakers'. Arundale, drawing on his Indian experience rather than any Australian realities, expected the TS to provide a power base for forward policies. Unfortunately it declined to do so.

An Adelaide chemist Edgar Pritchard expressed a new view. Citing Besant on the need to build the new civilisation within the old, observing also that the two-party system had an inherent tendency to extremism, he interpreted theosophy in politics to mean 'we should hold the balance'.[89]

The difficulty was this was a follower's view, and it was still necessary to find a focus for theosophical goodwill. Then in late 1929 A.E. Bennett resolved all the issues. He was capable, articulate, handsome; he would lead, posing the focal question 'Who's for Australia?' Individuals including individual theosophists would follow by joining the Who's for Australia? League of which he would be general secretary and only named executive. Together, using 2GB, they would test the balance. Given the continuity of political aspiration and anxiety in the Arundale phase, it was perhaps coincidental that the first intimation of a new patriotic league came over 2GB on Armistice Day 1929. It came hard on the election of a Commonwealth Labor government in October 1929, which was also the month of the great crash of the New York Stock Exchange. But in the first month the new league attracted only 300 members. It was really galvanised by the alarming industrial situation on the northern coalfields of New South Wales.

At Rothbury, on 16 December 1929, a young miner named Norman Brown was shot and killed during an armed confrontation between miners and police. This followed the Bavin government's determination to reopen three of the mines with scab labour. The death of Brown, a mere bystander and an Anglican communicant, horrified many Australians. When the first issue of a newspaper *Who's for Australia?* appeared on 15 January 1930, it emphasised the situation on the coalfields, a reign of terror, 'Ill will and Violence or Australia Last!'. Nothing could be expected from the respective vested interests of capital and labour. Mussolini was not the answer (though his achievements were impressive). The trouble was seen to be that if the tyranny and selfishness of both sides persisted, Russian antisocial propaganda would gain a foothold. Citizens must organise for 'true democracy', overriding divisions of class, party and creed in the name of peace, justice and prosperity. 'A leader *will* come'.[90]

From January 1930 the three objects of the Who's for Australia? League were unity, Australia first, the empire second. First came 'common comradeship for common action among all who ardently believe in Australia's great future'; the second object, Australia first, was meant to relate to every area of Australian life: in religion tolerance, in education civic duty, in industry Australia-made goods, in politics interparty co-operation and women in parliament, and a distinctive Australian culture. Third came imperial honour, for Australia and Britain. The league's platform, as outlined in an undated Rules and Regulations, rested on twelve basic 'non-party' principles, with ten further points as extra options. The twelve basic points were as follows: a united national spirit; enlistment of the citizenry by the state; national civic education; federal sovereignty; equalisation of States' rights; a Commonwealth Economic Council consisting of experts in government and industry, with representation of consumers, employers and employees; the end of overseas borrowing and repayment of existing overseas loans; equal status for women; uniform industrial legislation, conciliatory, not compulsory; encouragement of private enterprise; the illegality of strikes and lockouts; and the rigid enforcement of law and order. The optional platform included fewer parliaments, non-party cabinets, constitutional change to break party controls, scientific tariff, compulsory annual wage-fixing conferences and family allowances. In general the League reran the themes of the old *Advance! Australia* with a dash of the new social credit, and the strong new ingredient called by Bennett 'economic patriotism'.[91]

The Who's for Australia? League originated at the heart of Sydney theosophy. Australian theosophists first heard of it from the 'Who's for Australia?' song published in *The Australian Theosophist* on December 15 1929. The first and last of its six stanzas read:

> Who's for Australia, the Golden, the Youthful?
> Who's for the land of Christ's Cross in the South?
> Whose is the heart that soars high in her splendour?
> Who thanks his God he was born on her soil?
>
> Who's for Australia, the Queen of the Future?
> Who's for the Child of a glorious past?
> Hark! She is calling us: 'Who's for Australia?'
> Who's for Australia? Who thunders forth 'I'?

Later they learned that the league was work set for them by the Elder Brethren.

The league quickly reached a wider audience, but it depended on its theosophical base through its fifteen-month life. It operated out of Adyar House, from A.E. Bennett's office. 2GB carried it financially at first, providing space and secretarial staff, bearing the costs of printing, postage and other publicity. More significant, it provided air-time free, with morning and afternoon slots for league speakers. It gave staff support: in February 'Uncle George' was enrolling under-sixteens into a junior section of the league. 2GB musicians performed at the rallies which soon became the league's chief activity. Some 2GB staff like Doris Gowlland promoted the league. Arundale broadcast regularly for the cause, including it in the standard fare at Adyar Hall and the Savoy Theatre. Intense propaganda emanated from the station daily, and 'listening-in' was an approved way of starting a branch.[92]

The league also owed its newspaper to theosophy. In January 1930, it took over what was left of *Advance! Australia* and retitled it *Who's for Australia?*, offering subscriber continuity. *Who's for Australia?* lasted fourteen months, until February 1931, appearing as a four-page fortnightly to June 1930, when it increased to eight pages, changed from magazine to newspaper size and was priced at one penny. What was left of the old journal's staff went with it. No editor was announced for *Who's for Australia?*, but it was in fact edited, not by Bennett as might be expected, but none other than J.L. Davidge, whose duties since April 1929 had included responsibility for the truncated theosophical press agency, and probably that fugitive fortnightly called *Advance! Australia*. In 1930, Davidge's salary came from three sources, £100 from the section, £50 from 2GB for news services, and £50 from the league.[93]

The new ingredient of theosophical politics, economic nationalism, soon attracted a wider support. Support was manifest immediately in the new paper with a call for Australian-made automobiles, and a plug for Harkness and Hilliard, motor agents of Five Dock, Sydney. At its first public meeting convened by Mrs Harkness of Drummoyne on 18 January 1930, workers were assembled to hear Bennett's diagnosis of present troubles and the league's solution. International panic, a worsening balance of trade, and unhealthy extremism in Australia must be met by idealism, self-sacrifice and increased consumption of Australian-made goods. Neither tariff protection nor arbitration sufficed in a situation requiring economic nationalism and a strengthened state. 'What Mussolini has done for Italy we can do for Australia.'[94]

From that point the league grew by 1,000 members a month, reaching 8,000 by July 1930. Thereafter the general secretary – Bennett – spoke wherever district organisers (thirty-seven listed as appointed by February, predominantly married women in suburban Sydney) could gather twenty listeners; at whatever factories meetings could be arranged (usually by management); and in suburban town halls, often outer Sydney suburban, chaired by local government dignitaries. Very few organised groups affiliated with the league – the two main ones being the Australian Legion of Ex-Service Clubs and the renegade Railway Service Association.

With the aid of suburban newspapers, friendly cinema proprietors, housewives and some aldermen, the league made good progress promoting patriotism for employees. In June 1930 the league claimed nine 'business branches' in Sydney, in clothing, electrical and furniture factories. Bennett's technique of reminding workers that they too were consumers – the gospel according to Henry Ford – brought the argument vividly home at the shop-floor level: did Emmco workers at Waterloo use Emmco billycans? In the suburbs of Sydney the league claimed thirty-five branches. Bennett invited audiences there to check their footwear and powder compacts for imported labels. 2GB organised a permanent exhibition of Australian-made domestic appliances, and in June enthusiasts at Drummoyne organised a *Who's for*

Australia? goods exhibition, opened by ex-engineer, J.R. Lee, NSW Minister for Justice.[95]

A.E. Bennett thought the success of the league assured. 'We have the League. NOW FOR THE MAN'. Did Bennett, whose photograph sold to 'hero-worshippers' for 1/-, see himself as the man? Subsequent events suggest he might have been tempted. In August 1930 he signed the front page article of *Who's for Australia?* for the first time, on 'Dictatorship or Democracy'. The enlarged paper, carrying an improving proportion of Sydney advertising, grew increasingly frenzied about 'the leader', and the need for councils of action when party politics were stalemated. Bennett believed that one third of the population, 'the nauseated third', were left leaderless and should be organised: 'We cannot countenance vulgarity, whether from Mr Bavin or Mr Lang, and Australians should inundate such men when they degrade our civic life with letters of protest.'[96] But still no leader actually emerged.

In August 1930 the league slowed down, attracting a further 2,000 members at most. A variety of difficulties and obstacles emerged once the moral strictures had been uttered. Some proved intractable. The league met the challenge of growth by appointing trustees; by elaborating a constitution which organised members upward in a hierarchy said to be party-proof – and which resembled Besant's often-cited model Indian village government system at the lower levels. It adjusted its rules and regulations. And it welcomed similarly motivated groups in other Australian cities, in Melbourne, in Adelaide, and at mid-year, with the aid of TS stalwarts Muriel Chase and Stanley Fisher, in Perth. Demands to exclude all but the native-born, and especially Italians, were resisted. Bennett indignantly rebutted rumours that he was in it for the money, or for Billy Hughes, currently floating an Australian Party in the suburbs; or even for the NSW Chamber of Manufactures which he said was unpatriotic: 'If manufacturers, distributors and consumers do not all work to Australianise Australia, then the inevitable result will be that America will Americanise Australia.'[97]

But in July 1930 the NSW Labor Party had rejected the league's claim to be 'non-party'. Though Paddington branch reacted favourably to Bennett's advocacy, the NSW ALP executive declared the league black for white-anting the labour movement with propaganda in the capitalist interest, also for diverting electoral forces. Lang's triumph shortly after in October 1930, and the deplorable prognosis of British emissary Sir Otto

Niemeyer in August, seem to have taken the wind out of the league's sails.

Who's for Australia? acknowledged the legitimacy of Lang and his large majority, while still berating both the main parties for their extremist wings, and warning especially against communistic elements in the Labor Party. The call for far-reaching solutions and for pure leadership went unanswered, and a hopeful glance in the direction of the British Labour radical – as he was then – Sir Oswald Mosley caught no answering eye. The league's first birthday passed with far less fanfare than might have been expected. Speakers at the Savoy Theatre were Bennett, E.A. Rushbrooke, secretary of the Ex-Service Clubs, who recalled past unities, W. Fletcher of the Railway Service Association, and E. Lindsay Thompson, who lamented the loss of verve in Australian politics since the days of Deakin. Increasingly what troubled the league was others' extremism.[98]

Printed sources suggest the Who's for Australia? League disappeared after one last attempt to rally support for a non-party platform, headlined as 'A Platform for The People' in its paper's last issue of February 1931. Policy in this last pronouncement crystallised as five (conflicting) points: federal sovereignty, economy in public expenditure, elimination of unemployment by national resource stimulus, economic expansion and Empire economic union. Urging an autocracy of the wise, its rhetoric collapsed into individualistic assertion; and worn-out theosophical prescription showed through, even in the paper's lighter sections. Simultaneously, in February 1931, the Premiers' conference met to formulate what became known as the Premiers' Plan, a deflationary agreement meant to meet the financial crisis in Australia. Coincidentally or otherwise, the New Guard also began in Sydney in February 1931 as a rallying point for an increasingly agitated middle class, its numerous recruits effectively portrayed by Phyllis Mitchell as being both 'men of ideals and men intent on preserving their own interests'.[99]

Evidence of links between the Who's for Australia? League and the New Guard has not been advanced, but it is unsurprising that theosophists who remember the league do so with some embarrassment. In both theory and practice, middle-class idealism in politics tended in a fascist direction by the late twenties, with fearful results in Germany; and the theosophists' stress on the middle ground and the need for a leader foreshadowed a more ambivalent and extremist stance by the New Guard in New South Wales. However, it should be remembered that New South Wales opinion divided sharply during the second Lang administration and the entire middle class felt itself to be living at the edge of a volcano. As a young girl at Government House, Bethia Foott recalls that by early 1931 'everyone' was alarmed: 'Everyone we met, from [the unemployed] to our old friend the Turramurra station-master, the public servants, the barristers and the doctors: all were worried for the future.'[100]

As well, Billy Hughes's attempt to launch an Australian Party at this time suggests that middle-class anxiety and idealism could be channelled in various ways. Of course the New Guard did not spring from nowhere in February 1931, but it mobilised what founder Eric Campbell called 'service types', and it did so at a later stage. Its appearance marked new tensions and a shift of focus, from federal to State politics and specifically Labor politics: 'The New Guard owed its existence to a fear and hatred of Lang and Communism.'[101] The New Guard anticipated breakdown, whereas the prior Who's for Australia? League had anticipated breakthrough.

Looking back on the league's efforts, Bennett judged it work well done: 'a smouldering fire burst into flame'. He pointed out that it had preceded the many patriotic leagues which sprang up in 1929–1931. The league, he claimed, had a remarkable effect for unity and patriotism, not just in NSW but throughout the Commonwealth. Theosophy, and 2GB, had been 'building Australia':

> 2GB set out to wake up Australians to a sense of unity and citizenship and a realisation that the prosperity of the individual citizen or the individual business is related to the whole nation, and that they are interdependent. Hence 2GB supported first the Advance! Australia movement, then the Who's for Australia? movement, and now it is endeavouring to weld all existing leagues into one or two united bodies generally clarifying the political situation.[102]

It was however wishful to say that these organisations extended the league's influence; rather the league's forces were redirected into the new All for Australia League (AFAL), formed in Sydney in early 1931, in whose counsels Bennett pressed successfully for co-option (his brother General Gordon Bennett was one of its executive). In turn, the AFAL was absorbed into the emergent United Australia Party. Bennett became one of the five AFAL representatives, along with five Nationalist Party representatives, on the NSW Council of the UAP launched by ex-Labor minister Joseph Lyons in April 1931.[103] The revolt against democracy which the league sought to focus – against the voting system, the tyranny of parties, caucuses and professional politicians – did not lead to a new politics.

Not that the ferociously antiparty AFAL segment in NSW proved as easily digested as its State counterparts elsewhere in Australia. As late as May 1931 Bennett hoped to win control of league policy: 'I am trying to acquire the All for Australia League here' he wrote to Bessie Rischbieth. In the federal election of December 1931 Bennett stood as AFAL candidate for the Sydney seat of Lang (the old stamping ground of the Who's for Australia? League), winning 19 per cent of the vote. It was not quite 'the nauseated third' but, it has been estimated, it came mainly from '1929 Labor voters', that is, the modern 'swinging vote'.[104] His candidature reflected some of the critical conflicts and tensions of dark days. But it was the end of the road as far as politics from a theosophic base was concerned. Theosophic patriotism had its sinister aspects, but it had run its course, a harbinger of alarm in the Protestant middle class.

The campaigns mounted on theosophical resources in Sydney in the late twenties aimed to make theosophy a force in the land. Spurred by Arundale, stimulated by new technology, and sustained by the promise of the coming World Teacher, men like Bennett and Davidge worked hard to marshal support to theosophise Australia, to give a lead. They gave theosophy a high profile, as did the threefold prescription for an ideal Australia. Theosophy became more or less respectable at last. But prophecy of a new age led to defence of the old order. Moreover the campaign rested on a small, weak and probably timid base, and it was fired by a receding faith. Running through it all was the promise of a leader, and they could not summon one up. As became increasingly obvious – Arundale knew it all along – they did not even have one themselves.

Appearances were deceptive. According to reports from lodges in the capitals, lodge life flourished. In 1927, thirty-three lodges answered Convention rollcall. In 1932, with thirty lodges, the section was still apparently well off. Adelaide lodge especially came into its own, stimulated by the new cultural emphasis. It maintained links with groups like the WEA, the NCW, and the Aborigines' Protection League, to list just some affiliations;

it was also drawn closer to the centre of theosophical life. Ex-Adelaidian Davidge used his Adelaide connections to keep *Advance! Australia* afloat. Public lectures there in 1927 included J.C. Genders on the proposed native state, J.H. Vaughan, chairman of the League of Nations Union, Clive Carey from the Conservatorium on 'Folk Song' and Miss E.C. Rischbieth. Perhaps this compensated for loss of the lodge's gentle but dedicated president since 1908, H.G. Oliphant, who resigned in disgust in 1925.[105]

Nevertheless, about half the theosophists in Australia belonged either to Sydney or Melbourne lodges – and even Melbourne lodge felt insecure. Whereas Blavatsky lodge, Sydney, succoured suburban initiatives at Manly, Mosman and Ku-ring-gai, Melbourne gained little by absorbing declining suburban lodges like the historic Ibis lodge at Prahran where Alfred Deakin had served briefly as secretary in 1895. Not only was Blavatsky in Sydney the largest lodge, but in 1929, nine of the thirty-three lodges in the country were to be found in suburban Sydney. Elsewhere resources spread increasingly thin.

Despite a boost in 1926, the trend in annual membership belied the plan to theosophise Australia. Consecutive general secretaries consoled themselves with the thought that more and more Australians had heard of the Theosophical Society. But fewer and fewer joined it. Membership by 1931 was only slightly higher than in 1914. Internationally TS membership increased steadily across the 1920s to peak at 45,000 in 1928. But in Australia the split destroyed momentum much earlier. Though the damage was disguised, decline was unmistakable by 1931. Expressive campaigns failed to restore the healthy glow of the early twenties. Rather they served to sustain the faithful and to divert attention from disappointment and decline.

When the Star amphitheatre was under construction at Balmoral Beach in 1923 the Melbourne *Argus* remarked snidely that there seemed to be no shortage of money for theosophic enterprise. Shannon Hicks, in *Ride on Stranger*, observing that people thought 'anything connected with money cannot be altogether mad', noted the flourishing finances of the Order of Human Brotherhood, and the Abbott's preoccupation with fundraising. Existing TS funds did not suffice to theosophise Australia, however. Arundale's methods of raising money worked initially, but by 1930 the society was in straitened circumstances.

During the Great War it had been said that money always flowed into the society's coffers when it was needed. Since membership dues seldom exceeded £700 p.a. – and a proportion of that was remitted to India – the Hon. Treasurer was often obliged to call for donations to balance the books in those simpler days. Donations came sometimes to finance essential activities: in 1926 Miss Astill of Melbourne donated £429, enough to finance lodge lecture tours. Members also ably supported the larger visions of the post-war years as shareholders and subscribers. It will be recalled that in 1918 the section acquired a school at St Leonards at the modest price of £3,500, raised in trust; theosophists also helped buy the Liberal Catholic church and adjacent co-masonic temple at Redfern, Sydney. In 1925, necessity compelled the section to rehouse at a possible cost of £10,000. By then, the Order of the Star in the East had committed approximately £20,000 to the Star amphitheatre at Balmoral. How much its trustees raised to acquire the Manor as a theosophical commune is not known, though like other property acquisitions in the early twenties it probably came cheap, and the rate exemptions enjoyed by religious organisations kept it so. When Arundale arrived in 1926 supporters of theosophic enterprises were indebted to the extent of £13,000 (£6,000 on Morven Garden School, £7,000 on the amphitheatre) and had made outlays in the region of £200,000 in Sydney alone since 1918.

The society now had substantial assets. The Order of Human Brotherhood, in Kylie Tennant's portrayal, 'owned a city church, small rich and dim, where the bishops and their flock assembled on Sundays; a hall and a network of lecture centres, a share in a printery, the rent of three city buildings and other miscellaneous enterprises'. Business men conducted the Theosophical Society's affairs on business principles, so the profits and losses are not easy to sum. Optimism prevailed about large outlays in the Arundale years. Not only were the big debts cleared, but a new project like 2GB attracted £6,000 of theosophical money – as stated earlier, £2,500 from section funds and £3,500 from individual members.

Of course section funds also meant the members' money, and more of it, to theosophise Australia. Witness again the cost of *Advance! Australia*. In 1926 Convention lifted per capita dues from the lodges from 6/- to 10/- (it seems that lodge dues themselves were set locally and varied from place to place) without an uproar; and they remained at that level until 1932. From early 1927, the usual collections and donations were vastly augmented by a 'tithing' device called the Active Service Fund which Arundale and the executive hoped would bring in 1000 half-crowns weekly. Members were urged to forego ice-creams, personal adornment, tram fares, maids and to work overtime to answer a call greater than war-service, to be Co-Workers with Christ:

> ARE WE FOLLOWERS OR CO-WORKERS WITH CHRIST?
>
> Of greater result to each of us in Australia than all our daily meditations and individual efforts is our response to this Call. SHALL AUSTRALIANS LEAD THE WORLD, OR SHALL THEY DROP INTO THE BACKGROUND AND STOP THERE?
>
> THE CHRIST IS HERE ON EARTH, AND HE WANTS US TO BE, NOT FOLLOWERS, BUT CO-WORKERS WITH HIM. HE GIVES THIS WORK OF THEOSOPHIZING AUSTRALIA INTO OUR HANDS AS TRUSTED FELLOW-WORKERS. SHALL WE PROVE WORTHY?[106]

In 1927, the section received £767 in dues etc., £1,239 in donations – one of £1,000 from William Harding, single-taxer – and £4,377 from the Active Service Fund, somewhat more than the anticipated £6,000. In 1928, the following year when 621 members kept on tithing, only £2,040 was available for disbursement: £1,300 went to *Advance! Australia*, £293 to *The Australian Theosophist*, compared with £355 and £53 respectively from subscriptions; and £445 to administration. By contrast the section collected £659 in dues and fees with few donations. At the same time, Arundale launched a fund to celebrate the eightieth birthdays of Besant and Leadbeater, to which Australian theosophists were expected to contribute £3000 – though as noted earlier Leadbeater was actually seventy-three at the time.

Assuming again that theosophists were the main subscribers to theosophical magazine, in 1928 members contributed over £4,000 to HQ in Sydney; that is, on average, two guineas each, over four times what they were compelled to pay by dues. It is impossible to calculate their true expenditure on theosophy given local variations and local calls, but as late as 1931, it cost £2/10/- (males) and 10/- less for women, to join Blavatsky lodge in Sydney. If the claims of associated activities like the Star in the East, the Liberal Catholic Church, and co-masonry could be entered, it would be apparent that poor theosophists were at a considerable disadvantage within what must have been by the later twenties a very comfortable congregation. No doubt the pennies of young Marjorie Bull and the scrimpings of Elsie Deane told equally with large benefactions in the eyes of the Masters.

Rumblings about the Active Service Fund were heard from Melbourne immediately. They abated a little in 1928 in response to the pleas of A.E. Bennett, who was, it emerges from passing references to the Reverend Bennett, another of the LCC clergy. The fund continued until 1931 with support stronger in Sydney, and with the basic weekly contribution cut to 1/6. There began to be persistent problems with the annual dues, from Perth and Brisbane particularly, resisted until 1932 in the name of balanced budgeting. In 1927 the budget balanced at £6,170. In 1930, with a projected expenditure of £3,000, all seemed set for an old-style deficit. The section's finances collapsed – why is hard to say since no budgets were published after 1928. It was unusual even then to have such a detailed account in print, proof of the increased preoccupation with money in the Arundale phase. Although the money question was brushed aside, by early 1930 Melbourne lodge had had enough:

> Instead of being helped by the present regime the Lodges have been drained both in money and in enthusiasm, and Headquarters is becoming merely a money collecting and spending machine ... This has resulted in a steadily diminishing membership notwithstanding the vast amount of money that has been expended. It has damped the enthusiasm of many of our best workers and created a certain amount of distrust in the minds of many more.[107]

The facts were on their side. The malaise went deeper still. Leadbeater muttered to himself the dreadful truth: 'The Coming has gone wrong.' The leadership lost its leverage in the dying days of the decade, as the reality gradually dawned on the rank and file.

Nothing much had been heard of Krishnamurti after the Jubilee Convention in December 1925. Then in January 1927 after a long spell at Ojai California with her adopted son, Annie Besant confirmed to the press that the World Teacher had indeed arrived. It proved a traumatic experience for members of the Order of the Star in the East. The new Krishnamurti, in circuit from Ojai California, Ommen Holland and India over the next two years, spoke with real authority. But in 1929 he dissolved the Order. Then in 1930 he resigned from the

Theosophical Society. Both events were noticed in the Australian press.[108]

At this point it is best to let Krishnamurti speak for himself. At the Star camp at Ommen, in Holland in August 1929, in his thirty-fourth year, he said:

> I maintain that truth is a pathless land, and you cannot approach it by any path whatsoever, by any religion, by any sect. That is my point of view and I adhere to it absolutely and unconditionally. Truth, being limitless, unconditioned, unapproachable by any path whatsoever, cannot be organised.
>
> I do not want followers. I mean this ... Because I am free, unconditioned, whole, not the part, not the relative, but the whole Truth that is eternal, I desire those, who seek to understand me, to be free, not to follow me, not to make out of me a cage which will become a religion, a sect. Rather they should be free from all fears – from the fear of religion, from the fear of salvation, from the fear of spirituality, from the fear of love, from the fear of death, from the fear of life itself ...
>
> For eighteen years you have been preparing for this event, for the Coming of the World Teacher. For eighteen years you have organised, you have looked for someone who would give a new delight to your hearts ... who would give you a new understanding. And now look what is happening! You want to have new gods instead of the old, new religions instead of the old – all equally valueless, all barriers, all limitations, all crutches. You are accustomed to being told how far you have advanced, what is your spiritual status. How childish. Who but yourself can tell whether you are beautiful or ugly within ... Although you have been preparing for me for eighteen years, when I say all these things are unnecessary, when I say you must put them all away and look within yourselves for the enlightenment, for the glory, for the purification, and for the incorruptibility of the self, not one of you is willing to do it.
>
> So why have an organisation?
>
> After careful consideration I have made this decision to dissolve the Order ... For two years I have been thinking about this, slowly, carefully, patiently, and I have now decided to disband the Order as I happen to be its Head. You can form a new organisation and expect someone else. With that I am not concerned, nor with the creating of new cages, or new decorations for those cages. My only concern is to set men absolutely unconditionally free.[109]

Jinarajadasa, Annie Besant and J.I. Wedgwood, Star Camp, Holland, 1927.
(TAT)

Furthermore Krishnamurti resigned from the various trusts administering Star property, and returned property vested in him by would-be followers. Whatever his status – a vexed question – plainly he had no use for churches, and very little for amphitheatres and radio stations, much less for organisations, office blocks or patriotic movements.

The dénouement was a long time coming and a painful process for all. In January 1927 Star members learned definitely that 'the World Teacher is here'. But Krishnamurti's position was increasingly heretical. After another of the Star camps at Ommen in 1928, when he revealed that he found theosophy mainly unintelligible, the faithful Lady Emily Lutyens tried to sort out the mounting confusion:

> The time has come for us all when a great and serious decision must be made between a dead past and a living future ... He is making us do our own work, mentally and emotionally, and that is the last thing we expected of him. Some people are returning home, naked and alone, their foundations shattered ... some are feeling a sense of bleak desolation at the prospect; others are feeling a feeling of a joy and freedom such as they have never known before. Some will begin at once to gather again the broken pieces and rebuild them on the old plan.[110]

Some, then, responded positively. 'We ourselves must be the reconstructors', realised Marcella Clarke, Australian Star organiser; R.E. Bennett, A.E.'s younger brother, followed Krishnamurti all the same; and John Mackay remained his agent in Australia. In general young members responded better than the old, more willing to think of self-realisation as a theosophical idea. But while the generations debated Krishnamurti's teaching, many more drifted away from the lodge discouraged, depressed, despairing or just plain bored. Even Lady Emily eventually rejected the impersonality of Krishnamurti:

> I began to feel that Krishna's teaching was inadequate. Krishna, who had written and spoken so beautifully of the 'Beloved', who proclaimed that he and the Beloved were one, now seemed to me to be rejecting all beliefs, even in the existence of God, whom he maintained man had created out of fear; whereas for me, a Beloved, someone to worship, was a necessity.[111]

In 1926, after those thrilling messages at Adyar in 1925, it seemed as if Krishnamurti would serve as bodily 'vehicle' of the World Teacher. Then it was thought that, far from being an empty vessel, he was participating in a 'blending' process, being 'overshadowed' by the Lord. Finally it emerged that he spoke as no one but himself: 'Friend, concern not yourself who I am: you will never know...'[112]

In 1928 Leadbeater published a booklet, *The World-Mother as Symbol and Fact*, suggesting that 'a mighty Angel' might be delegated by the Hierarchy to console mankind, or rather, womankind. There was talk in Australia of this 'big conception of Motherhood' and some skirting around the nomination of Mrs Arundale as earthly symbol of the World Mother. It was mainly talk. The big problem was what to do about Krishnamurti. Early in 1929, readers of the theosophy journal learned that the ruling executive of the Theosophical Society had decided to let Krishnamurti go his own way, the so-called 'separate paths' policy. The organisation finally rejected Krishnamurti's program, which could have destroyed it, and in 1928–1929 came close to doing so, when Krishnamurti persuaded Annie Besant to disband the Esoteric Section, and to abolish all religious ceremonies on theosophical land. But the organisation was saved from such iconoclasm: unable to withstand the conflicting pressures, the ageing president – now 82, in her fourth term – soon authorised section and ceremony again. That was the last straw for Krishnamurti and he resigned from the TS.

So the leadership, all but Annie, dissociated themselves from their erstwhile World Teacher, a set of responses wryly analysed by Mary Lutyens in *The Young Krishnamurti*. She remarks that the very people most eloquent in warning that people would reject the World Teacher because he said unpalatable things did the same themselves.

It seems that the Australian section – that diminishing body – swung into line very slowly. They still hoped in early 1929 that Krishnamurti would visit Australia again, presumably to clear things up. Their hopes were unavailing, even after a Convention resolution in 1931 that 'this gathering heartily welcomes the teaching of Krishnamurti as powerfully contributing to the spread of the spirit of Theosophy'.[113] With that, they virtually accepted the 'separate paths' policy, and caught up. They had always been far from the scene of action. It was hard to relinquish years of self-preparation at Star meetings. Having held the line so long, they were scarcely the ones to relish Krishnamurti's remarkably astute diagnosis of their historical condition.

Besides, as Arundale told Krishnamurti, 'I also have something to teach'. He shored up the organisation and the will to believe. What Arundale actually taught is better assessed by theosophical historians from the vantage point of his later presidency (1934–1945). He was marking time in Australia in the late twenties. All he did, he said, was release the avalanche of service accumulated and husbanded by Leadbeater, now settled permanently at Adyar:

> The Australian Section today, its influence upon the life of the Commonwealth, its definite contribution to the unification of Australia, its stand for clean politics ... its ardent call for a fine patriotism – all these are the fruit of Bishop Leadbeater's work.[114]

In large part he was right. The vitality of the Arundale phase derived from his mobilisation of forces already present, and the actual climate of opinion – as revealed by the personnel and content of the campaign to theosophise Australia. It also derived from Arundale's own determination to save the Theosophical Society during the difficult days of Krishnamurti's 'apostasy': he said it was loyalty to Annie which restrained him from public disavowal of K. Having presided over a colourful climactic, Arundale departed in April 1931 on yet another world lecture tour. Though he returned from time to time, and maintained his entry in *Who's Who in Australia*, it was a decisive departure. The 'great days' were over. The stalwarts of the first generation faltered, and their world view collapsed under unprecedented political and economic crisis.

The day of Annie Besant was also effectively done. She had been the other source of vitality. Her great age and immense prestige, and a sad personal decline from the late twenties, spared her the knowledge that it had really been downhill all the way since 1925, when her twin hopes of a world religion and home rule for India both slipped away, just as they seemed to be within her grasp: the great evolutionary leap forward through politics and clairvoyance never came, despite extensive and excited preparation. Meanwhile the world rejected reform liberalism with all its prescriptive intent. She died peacefully at Adyar on 20 September 1933, and was succeeded as president of the Theosophical Society by George Sydney Arundale. It was once said of Besant's peer, British Labour leader James Ramsay MacDonald, who was expelled from the British Labour Party in 1931 when he formed the National Government, that he was like Hamlet – without him the life went out of the play. Whatever the merits of Arundale, the same could be said of theosophy once Besant and Leadbeater lost their grip.

Thus the campaign to theosophise Australia was not merely diversionary, it was doomed. But because everyone was waiting to see what the World Teacher would do in his newly assumed role between 1926 and 1929, it brought out the hopes and fears of the theosophical community and culture as never before – and never again. Theosophy and the Theosophical Society survived. But by the early thirties, the theosophical movement was very subdued, and more evidently divided than ever.

9

The end of an era

The contrast between theosophy in the 1920s and the 1930s could hardly be greater. Whereas the 1920s are rightly recalled by theosophists as 'great days', the 1930s are rarely mentioned. Evidence of theosophical exuberance in the twenties abounds, but very few records were even produced in the thirties and those that survive are shrouded in an entirely understandable gloom. After fifty years of growth and a high profile in the climactic twenties, in the thirties theosophy in Australia almost disappeared from view.

1931 marked the centenary of Madame Blavatsky's birth. But there was not much to celebrate. Suddenly divisions which mattered nothing in brighter days stood out. In the forty years since Blavatsky's death in 1891 there had been half-a-dozen splits in America, the German severance, and home-grown division in Australia in the early 1920s. By 1931 even the two largest groups were in trouble. The Universal Brotherhood and Theosophical Society in southern California suffered the death of its leader the redoubtable Katherine Tingley in 1928 and the Point Loma community was close to bankruptcy. The Indian-based Theosophical Society, reeling from Krishnamurti's glancing blows, had recently recorded its first downturn in membership – in 1929 it claimed 43,600 members throughout the world, but by 1933 this number would shrink to just under 31,000 – and Annie Besant had virtually relinquished command. Moreover the opportunity for reunion between the two offered by the centenary passed with maximum umbrage being taken by both sides. Divided and dispirited, the theosophical movement entered its own version of the Great Depression.[1]

Worse was to come for the Theosophical Society in Australia. It had always been the dominant group, and with Arundale still present, it could afford to disregard lesser ones, the objectionable ITS in Sydney with its outposts in Brisbane and Hobart, and the tiny, indeed invisible, UBTS soon to be augmented by some of the rebels, including Prentice. The TS celebrated the Blavatsky centenary in assured but solemn manner. All the speakers at a symposium in Melbourne stressed her moral stature: her dedication to freedom, wisdom, humanitarianism and cleaner politics. Most of them had been converted in the Besant–Leadbeater era, and few if any apart from Arundale had ever met the amazing Madame, who would probably have been amused. Under the circumstance the symposium's confusing slogan 'Forward to HPB' was all too appropriate. Instead of addressing the big questions – whether the twentieth century had vindicated her teaching and how the society might recover its standing – the assembly behaved like a congregation of pious Protestants taking for granted that she had found the means of reconciling 'science' and 'religion'.[2]

Australian theosophists had been renowned in the theosophical world not only for their wealth and hospitality but for loyalty to 'great leaders'. When the great leaders of the TS 'passed over' in the early thirties they were bereft. Annie Besant died at Adyar on 20 September 1933 and Charles Webster Leadbeater six months later at Perth, en route for Sydney, on 1 March 1934. It is scarcely too much to say that the majority of Australian theosophists consisted of women who revered Annie Besant and men who admired Leadbeater. Without Besant and Leadbeater the TS fell further into disarray.

No journal appeared in the mid-thirties, only a duplicated *Notes and News*. Conventions did not recover until 1935, the sixtieth anniversary of the society. The number of lodges declined steadily, and decline in membership was not arrested until 1937. Statistics show that stability had been restored by 1939 but membership figures were comparable with those of the first decade of the twentieth century. It was obvious that theosophy now appealed to an even smaller proportion of the population, and that it had lost its momentum.

In 1936 the Theosophical Society lost its greatest remaining asset, radio 2GB. The station flourished in the early thirties, despite fresh competition from other religious broadcasters, 2CH (Council of Churches) and 2SM (St Mary). A sample of two hundred housewives rated 2GB the top commercial station in 1932; in the same year, A.E. Bennett, managing director and vice-chairman of the board, reaffirmed the station's theosophical purposes. In 1934 600 listeners joined 2GB's Psychology Club and thirty-four of these became members of the Theosophical Society, forming Radio lodge, the only new lodge of the decade. Profits rose and theosophical propaganda continued. Both benefited the TS, at least in Sydney: 'Sydney is the best informed theosophically of all the cities in the world.' With Arundale still chairman of a board consisting entirely of theosophists, all seemed well.[3]

It is not easy to follow what happened next. It appears that Bennett lost patience with his co-religionists. At some point between 1933 and 1936 he gained control of the society's interest – 'confiscation,' cried accountant William Harding – and flying high on success as a leading commercial broadcaster, he facilitated takeover by Denison Estates, a Denison family company which already held a fifty percent share in radio 2UE. (It also had a six percent interest in Associated Newspapers, publisher of the Sydney *Sun*, Sir Hugh Denison being chairman of both companies at the time.) Ultimately Bennett flew too high and lost out himself, being compelled after complex litigation to abandon his own financial interest and depart the station in 1937. By then he was but a bitter memory to the TS, as he resigned, possibly as early as 1935, after Convention failed to respond to his call for another 'forward movement' and in the face of tension between residents of the Manor and 2GB staff working at the transmitter erected in the grounds in 1926.[4]

As far as theosophists were concerned there had been a lot of chicanery in an unequal contest. With Elliston Campbell, Evelyn Caspersz at the Manor fought much of the battle. She complained privately that few of the male theosophists were up to it. Sometimes the *Sydney Morning Herald* supported the theosophists, sometimes the residents of Clifton Gardens (as when 2GB applied to lease land adjacent to the Manor in Chowder Head reserve for a new transmitter, a move which also raised the ire of environmental groups like the Wild Life Preservation Society and the Parks and Playgrounds Movement, founded by C.E.W. Bean in 1930). Eventually Arundale salvaged something in the courts: the sum of £25,000, shared by the society, the Manor trustees, the Liberal Catholic Church and co-masonry, and an allocation of air time on 2GB. The society was granted four sessions per week for twenty-one years, retaining a more limited allocation to 1980, and 2GB agreed to broadcast the Sunday morning service at St Alban's.[5]

There was some public feeling that the society had been diddled out of its radio station. Thoughtful management of its remaining rights improved the society's image somewhat. The management committee practised 'stewardship of the air' and shared out its entitlement with other 'altruistic organisations' in a familiar manner. It is recorded that all the organisations approached accepted the offer to share in the envisaged round of public welfare broadcasting, these being the free-libraries movement, the National Council of Women, the Australian Institute of Public Affairs, the Constitutional Association, the RSPCA, the Kindergarten Union, the Far West Childrens' Health Scheme, the Parks and Playgrounds Movement, the British American Cooperation Society, the League of Nations Union, the New Economics Society and the Racial Hygiene Centre. Continued access to radio 2GB is probably the main reason why the word theosophy still strikes a vaguely familiar note to Sydneysiders, some of whom can also recall attending meetings at Adyar House, eating vegetarian meals in its basement restaurant and seeing foreign films at the Savoy Theatre.[6]

In this way theosophy retained links with 'forward movements' in Sydney. The 2GB settlement also succoured what Besant and Leadbeater used to call 'the allied movements' like the now autonomous Liberal Catholic Church. There are two Liberal Catholic churches in Sydney today, and the LCC is represented in most capital cities. A large co-masonic temple stands on Regent St, Sydney, next to a service station which was built on the site of the original St Alban's church. And in May 1936 the Manor was paid off by a generous donation from Dr P.W. van den Broek, a Singaporean physician, thereby securing what is by now one of the oldest religious communes in Australia.[7]

With the 2GB settlement the worst was over for the TS. Aided by Arundale who succeeded Annie Besant as third president of the Theosophical Society after a bitter election in 1934, women like Caspersz, Mary Neff and Clara Codd had held it together during the dark days of the mid-1930s when Elliston Campbell was probably the most capable of the men. The society still retained considerable property. Its presence was maintained in all the capital cities, and in 1937 Convention celebrated the opening of a new and impressive Melbourne lodge built on the prime site in Collins St, central Melbourne, acquired in 1916. A mainly ageing membership meant losses but also some material benefit, as from the Rounsevell bequest which enabled

Adelaide lodge to announce itself unencumbered in the late 1930s (as did the historic Toowoomba lodge).[8]

In 1937 the trustees of the Star amphitheatre at Balmoral finally sold the amphitheatre, to the Roman Catholic Church, and with it went the last vestigial theosophical connection and material reminder of the millenarian twenties. The sale symbolised return to what Arundale called 'straight theosophy'.[9]

Meanwhile Krishnamurti went his own way. From his Californian base, he visited Australia twice in the 1930s, 1933–34 and 1939, his agent John Mackay. Some of the younger ones were inspired, A.E. Bennett's younger brother Reginald being one. In 1939 a small Krishnamurti school 'Baringa' was set up in one of the northern beach suburbs by Mrs E.M. Arthur-Smith and other progressive educators who had been followers of the Star in the East, which lasted for several years.[10]

The friends of Krishnamurti were few but firm, and in the 1970s his message attracted fresh attention, partly as a result of Mary Lutyens' moving biography and the wider dissemination of his thought by Penguin books, but also because Krishnamurti has proved a singular survivor. For Krishnamurti, dissociation from what he called the unfortunate theosophists ushered in 'the years of fulfilment'. He has continued as an educationalist and as a moral teacher. There are Krishnamurti foundations in Britain, America and India. In the course of research for this book in May 1982 I visited the Ojai valley in southern California where in 1927 Annie Besant announced 'The World Teacher is here', and happened by chance upon an outdoor Krishnamurti summer school. About a thousand people awaited a Krishnamurti talk. When he appeared, a small, refined, casually dressed figure aged eighty-eight, he sat upon a canvas stool and spoke for an hour or so to the injured of the affluent society, gently reproaching them for relying upon external crutches and urging them to depend only on their own inner resources. In the best Besant tradition he spoke directly, without notes or gestures, and when he had finished he walked away. Krishnamurti disdained the role of World Teacher, but the long preparation has stood him in good stead.[11]

A glimpse of the fate of the Independent Theosophical Society in Sydney is provided by the letters of Marion Mahony Griffin to her husband Walter in India in the mid-1930s: 'King's Hall will be turning Anthro if they don't watch out.' Marion reported that when she and other anthroposophists lectured at King's Hall in 1936 they attracted the largest audiences for some time. It appears that the ITS held on through the thirties but, despite the fact that it was not, as Marion Mahony Griffin put it, 'under bondage to the Adyar group re the Christ event', it failed to attract a following in the next generation.[12]

'I think I have won that thing called a quiet soul,' wrote Marion Griffin in October 1935 (a statement which would doubtless have surprised her intimates, who seem to divide between those who gloried in her flamboyant style and those who deplored her overwhelming personality). Her peace came from anthroposophy, which as mentioned earlier was that alternative *theosophia* expounded by Dr Rudolf Steiner stressing human rather than divine sources of wisdom, and which gained its first adherents in Australia among artistic minorities in the interwar years. Walter and Marion Griffin joined the Anthroposophical Society in 1931. There is as yet no history of anthroposophy in Australia (nor anywhere else for that matter); but Marion Griffin's writings suggest that anthroposophy was the most vital and confident refraction of the theosophical impulse in Australia by the 1930s.

Its focus was Castlecrag. According to Marion Mahony Griffin the model suburb at Castlecrag was 'a truly live spot in Australia', a step towards the ideal Australia. To her all-seeing eye, Castlecrag became not simply a special suburb demonstrating the benefits of integrating the built and the natural environment, but also an expression of spiritual truths. Her memoirs refer to many and wonderful friends in Sydney 'now moving toward a common centre from which one could grasp the earth and humanity as a totality'. In her heyday, anthroposophical discussion was an everyday occurrence at Castlecrag, and there were anthroposophy lectures and weekly study groups. In 1935, with the blessing of the secretary of the Anthroposophical Society and the help of lecturer and singing teacher Miss Lute Drummond, an Anthroposophic Festival was held to increase appreciation of the significance of the changing seasons. And though the residents of the estate were by no means all anthroposophists, Griffin recalled them as responsive to their special environment: 'Each citizen of Castlecrag, stirred by the opportunities for self-expression, could find no rest till his particular interest or faculty could take its place in community life.' There were committees for every conceivable community purpose: festivals, parties and ceremonies like the open-air Christmas parties for children, and numerous cultural activities, beginning with Louise Lightfoot's enthusiasm for dance and a drama club, the Dais. From these activities emerged the recently restored New Haven Scenic Theatre, an open-air amphitheatre set in a picturesque gully where great plays were performed to appreciative audiences from the wider society, some of whom wondered that such things could be done in a suburb. Some, like Griffin's friend from Chicago days Miles Franklin, simply enjoyed the vitality of it all; others like Mitchell librarian Ida Leeson contributed what they could by helping on the estate.[13]

It seems that the Griffins preferred anthroposophy to theosophy because they found it more progressive: more individualistic, pluralistic, and cerebral, and free of anti-Christian bias. 'Anthroposophy is applied Christianity,' Marion once said. However, her late-won assurance came from feeling that she had found 'a practical religion': she gained 'a quiet soul' because the environment of Castlecrag confirmed her belief that the natural and material worlds were both living entities, and reassured her that the destructive modes of nineteenth-century science could be transcended in a progressive manner by free men and women equipped with the 'spiritual science' of anthroposophy. Castlecrag did not flourish in the depression and the small community became more mundane when the Griffin presence was withdrawn after Walter's death in India in 1937 and after Marion returned to Chicago. But residents of Castlecrag still send children to the nearby Steiner school 'Glenaeon' at Middle Harbour and the Griffin heritage is now cherished.[14]

A survey of the several expressions of *theosophia* in Australia in the 1930s shows that the scene was not quite so drab and dispiriting as it had been in 1931. Theosophic aspiration found fresh expression in sections of the urban middle class. And for organised theosophy, there are continuities as well as discontinuity to be observed. Nothing came of the 'fraternisation' movement sponsored by Melbourne members of the UBTS in the late thirties which hoped to find a way to reunite the three groups of theosophists, so that in 1939 the Theosophical Society remained the largest and best-organised expression of *theosophia* in Australia. With its organisation intact and with worldwide publishing enterprises to feed the bookshops which have kept its name before the public, the TS survived to benefit from the next upsurge of dissatisfaction with materialism in the 1960s (and from the sixties boom in urban property which meant that substantial sums were made from the sale of both Sydney and Melbourne lodge sites at that time). Nevertheless the historic groupings of the theosophical movement have not regained the ground finally lost in the 1930s. It would be impossible for them to do so. The thirties were not just a low point in theosophical history, but the end of an era.[15]

That era lasted from the 1880s to the 1930s. During that time theosophy attained a precarious status in Australia, appearing as a non-Christian religion in Commonwealth censuses from 1911 to 1947. If census returns are any guide, many theosophists had always hedged their bets. To 1933 less than half the numbers appearing on TS membership lists showed up at census, and in 1933, when 540 people declared themselves theosophists, less than a third. The elusive theosophists were not required to forswear orthodox religious affiliations – in Annie Besant's day, quite the reverse – and from 1933, when the religious question on the census schedule was marked voluntary, they were not pressed by the state to choose. By that time theosophy was in disrepute, and due to the impact of the White Australia Policy, respect for non-Christian religion was probably at its lowest ebb. Many theosophists simply faded away. Others sought more secure or promising religious positions, as when Phyllis Campbell turned to Roman Catholicism and H.G. Oliphant became a lay brother of a Franciscan foundation in America – fugitives both from a secularising society.

The impact of secularisation first showed up in Australia in the 1930s. The 1933 census showed that the Christian churches had lost their hold on as many as 20 percent of the population. But the long anticipated weakening of organised religion was small comfort to its critics. Liberalism and freethought suffered equally, while the resurgence of spiritualism after the Great War proved short-lived. The figures showed that Unitarianism and the Australian Church were as much in decline as theosophy.

What lay beyond belief? The answer seemed to be indifference, a fatal obstacle to theosophy which also lacked the capacity for self-renewal. Perhaps the material resources were there – the 1933 census showed a high proportion of adherents in the top income bracket. But it also showed an ageing adherence. And whether or not theosophy was for children, there were strikingly few theosophical children. Marjorie Bull was one of the few actually 'born into theosophy', but now she has 'not even a wistful nostalgia' for the faith she left in her twenties. Never evangelical and no longer topical, in later days theosophy became rather introverted. Several people have remarked to me that they walked in off the street to theosophical meetings in the 1940s but found them drab and unrewarding.

A perplexed Jack Bean quizzed his brother Charles in 1933 on why theosophy failed to attract the typical Australian, 'tho' many or most of our folk are decidedly intelligent & freethinking [if] not deeply cultured'. The reality was that secular ideologies were gaining ground. Fortunately for theosophists the mission to rescue religion collapsed of its own audacity before fascism seized upon the social strains of modernity. Nor were their worst fears of the Leviathan realised. The path of individualism to collectivism has proved more or less manageable, as the law increasingly fills the gap left by organised religion. On the other hand, the petit-bourgeois strata of society from which theosophists were mostly drawn, that is the ranks of small employers, the self-employed, marginal professionals and white collar workers, had swung away from liberalism to the new conservatism, and the rebels of the next generation rejected organised religion altogether. Norman Lindsay was a secret spiritualist. His son Jack is an active Marxist. The independent women who were probably the back bone of Australian theosophy went, perhaps more slowly, into conservation and feminism, as Bessie Rischbieth's last years suggest. Theosophy was a prototype of secular ideology; but generational change and cultural shifts in a crucial strata of Australian society during the interwar years made it seem an anachronism.

History tends to back winners. The historical situation is clear enough. Theosophy in Australia is best understood as an alternative religious position dating from the age of imperialism. The ground it stood on was undermined by the crises of the early twentieth century. Finally it was obvious that there could be no magical formula for the recovery of lost certainties; and that contradictions of the imperial order could not be resolved from within. Those same conflicts of class, colour and creed for which theosophy sought a moral remedy destroyed liberal imperialism, which was increasingly unable to guarantee the world's peace and progress. Theosophists hoped that it could, and that the baton would pass to them. In the process they contributed much to national culture and sounded a warning against the triumph of materialism. Whether they were winners or losers is largely beside the point. The counter-culture has a longer history than we think.

Notes

Chapter 1 ~ The first fellows

1. Josephine Ransom *A Short History of the Theosophical Society* TPH, Madras, 1938, p. 81.
2. Citation as in *Harbinger of Light* 1 June 1891, p. 4421.
3. J.A. La Nauze *Alfred Deakin. A Biography* vol. 1, MUP, 1965, p. 39.
4. *Harbinger* December 1879, p. 1693; 'William Henry Terry', *ADB* 6.
5. *Harbinger* 1 March 1880, p. 1747, 1 September 1880, p. 1841, 1 October 1880, p. 1863 and 1 April 1881, p. 1969; Mary K. Neff *How Theosophy came to Australia and New Zealand* Australian Section, TS, Sydney, 1943, ch. 1.
6. Neff *How Theosophy came*, p. 42; Gilbert Elliott 'Esoteric Buddhism' *Melbourne Review* VIII (October 1883), pp. 403–423. Acceptable applicants for membership received, for a small fee, a diploma, and one of three ranks of fellow: Active, Corresponding and Honorary. Since active fellowship involved ceremonial initiation until 1885, and honorary fellowships were conferred by the society, it seems likely that the first Australian theosophists were mostly corresponding fellows; see C. Jinarajadasa *The Golden Book of The Theosophical Society* TPH, Madras, 1925, p. 26, and Ransom, *Short History*, pp. 104–5, 547.
7. Exact numbers of FTS in Australia 1879–1889 who sought TSA are not presently available. Twenty-nine New Zealanders joined the TS 1879–89 (*Theosophy in New Zealand* 7, 10, April–June 1946, pp. 54–55).
8. *TT* I, 1 (Bombay, October 1879), p. 7. For a useful and succinct definition of 'theosophy' in the abstract, and in India (compiler's distinction), see *A Dictionary of Comparative Religion* ed. S.F.G. Braddon, Weidenfeld and Nicolson, London, 1970.
9. Peter Fuller 'Strange arts of ancient Egypt' *New Society* 18 March 1982, pp. 444–45; Raoul Mortley *Womanhood. The feminine in Ancient Hellenism, Gnosticism, Christianity, and Islam* Delacroix Press, Sydney, 1981, p. 19 ff.
10. *Isis Unveiled. A Master-key to the Mysteries of Ancient and Modern Science and Theology* Theosophical University Press, Pasadena, 1972, 2 Vols. (first publ. J.W. Bouton, New York, 1877), introduction, 'Before the Veil'. The grip of rationalist historiography was broken only recently by for example Frances A. Yates *Giordano Bruno and the Hermetic Tradition* Routledge & Kegan Paul, London, 1964. For the late eighteenth-century occult revival, see Christopher McIntosh *Eliphas Levi and the French Occult Revival* Rider, London, 1972; and for the role of freemasonry as transmitter, Marsha K.M. Schuchard, Freemasonry, Secret Societies and the Continuity of the Occult Traditions in English Literature, unpubl. PhD thesis, University of Texas, Austin, 1975 (Dissertation Abstracts International 1975, v. 36). 'Science, Rationality and Religion' *History Workshop* editorial, 9, 1980, offers a useful discussion of the wider historiographical questions touched on in this paragraph.

11 Bruce F. Campbell *Ancient Wisdom Revived. A History of the Theosophical Movement* University of California Press, Berkeley, 1980, p. 35.
12 James Webb *The Flight from Reason* vol. 1 of *The Age of the Irrational* Macdonald, London, 1971, ch. 3.
13 Campbell *Ancient Wisdom Revived*, pp. 35–36.
14 Neff *How Theosophy came* p. 43; H.W. Hunt 'The Early Days of the Theosophical Society in Australia' *TinA* 1 August 1919, pp. 157–58; Dorothy Green 'Towards the Source' *Southerly* 37, 4, 1977 (on Maitland); Samuel T. Studd 'How I came into Theosophy' *TAT* 15 June 1927, pp. 222–24; *Harbinger* 1 September 1881, pp. 2046–48 (review of *The Occult World*), and 1 September–1 November 1883 (three-part review of *Esoteric Buddhism*).
15 Documented in *The Theosophical Movement 1875–1925. A history and a survey* (no author), E.P. Dutton & Co., N.Y., 1925.
16 Numerous sources for Blavatsky's life are listed by Richard A. Hutch 'Helena Blavatsky Unveiled' *JRH* 11, 2, 1980, p. 320, n. 1. Marion Meade *Madame Blavatsky. The Woman Behind the Myth* G.P. Putnam's Sons, New York, 1980 is the most recent and substantial biography (I thank Jean Bedford for this reference). See also Howard Murphett *Hammer on the Mountain. Life of Henry Steel Olcott 1832–1907* TPH, Wheaton, Illinois, 1972.
17 Ransom *Short History* pp. 115–22.
18 A.H. Nethercot *The First Five Lives of Annie Besant* Chicago University Press, 1960, p. 292; and cf. Diana Burfield 'Theosophy and Feminism: Some explorations in nineteenth-century biography' in Pat Holden (ed.) *Women's Religious Experience* Croom Helm, London & Canberra, Barnes & Noble Books, Totowa, New Jersey, 1983, that early London theosophy was 'overwhelmingly upper and middle class ... needs no further demonstration than to note that its London meetings in the 1880s closed at the end of the Season' (p. 28); see also Alannah Hopkin 'Womanly Wilde' *Irish Times* 23 July 1983. I thank Avril Keeley for this reference.
19 W.D.C. Denovan *The Evidences of Spiritualism: Lectures, Addresses and Record of the Spiritual Phenomena, Culled from the Writings of Eminent Authors, Mediums, Magazines, and Newspapers connected with the Great Spiritual Movement of My Time; With Copious Memoranda of My Own Investigations and Experiences as to the Truth of These Things* W.H. Terry, Melbourne, 1882, pp. 252–54; James Bonwick *An Octogenarian's Reminiscences* James Nichols, Anerley, 1902, pp. 251–52.
20 James S. Perkins *Adyar, The International Headquarters of The Theosophical Society* TPH, Madras, rev. edn 1975.
21 For example, 1 October 1881, p. 2070, 'The Buddhist Revival in Ceylon'; 1 February 1883, p. 2408, TS Anniversary in Bombay, reporting 'thirty-nine branches of the Society founded in Asia alone'.
22 Neff, *How Theosophy came* chs 2, 5; *Smith Papers* Sydney University Archives Biographical File 43; *Harbinger* 1 June 1882, p. 2238 and 1 August 1883, p. 2522.
23 J.L. Davidge 'Professor John Smith and Theosophy' *TinA* 23, 6, 1959, pp. 5–8, and 'Work for us in Australia!' *TinA* 19, 10, 1954, pp. 9–11; *ADB* 6.
24 *TT* 5, 3, 1883, p. 98; *Harbinger* April–May 1884, pp. 2694, 2722–23, 1 August 1886, p. 3269; F.B. Smith, Religion and Freethought in Melbourne 1870 to 1890, unpubl. MA thesis, University of Melbourne, 1960, pp. 59–61.
25 Smith, Religion and Freethought, p. 123; Campbell *Ancient Wisdom Revived* p. 32; *Harbinger* 1 December 1877, p. 1308, 1 June 1878, p. 1415 and 1 March 1879, p. 1556; *TinA*, 19, 10, 1954, p. 9.
26 Neff *How Theosophy came* appendix 3; Henry Mayer *Marx, Engels and Australia* Cheshire, Melbourne, 1964, p. 53.
27 'John Woolley' *ADB* 6; 'Notes on Seances' 14 February 1892 *Windeyer Family Papers*, ML MSS 186/12–6; R.R. Garran *Prosper the Commonwealth* Angus & Robertson, Sydney,

1958, pp. 17–19; *DNB* 22 (Suppl.). For the efforts of Maitland and Kingsford to envisage an esoteric Christianity, see E. Maitland *Anna Kingsford: Her Life, Letters, Diary and Work* vol. 2, George Redway, London, 1896. See also *Harbinger* 1 July 1884, p. 2756.

28 *TT* 1, 4, 1880, p. 108, 2, 6, 1881, p. 121, 4, 9, 1883, editorial and 11, 121, 1889, p. 55. *Harbinger* 1 July 1877, pp. 1239–40; Maitland to Deakin, 13 January 1878, Deakin Papers NLA MS 1540/ 1–1.

29 Deakin Papers Series 5: 'A Spiritual Diary, Personal and Mundane' (1880–1889), 1/8/80 (Britten), 3/2/ 82 (*The Light of Asia*), 6/10/ 83 (*Esoteric Buddhism*), NLA MS 1540/ 5/ 1453, and Swedenborg notebooks (1889), 2 vols, NLA MS 1540/ 5/ 1453 and 1173–74; La Nauze *Alfred Deakin* ch. 3.

30 *TT* 2, 9, 1881, p. 219 (Suppl.) and 7, 76, 1886, p. cvii; Ransom *Short History* p. 164; Neff *How Theosophy came* pp. 38–41; *Harbinger* 1 April 1883, p. 2446.

31 Neff *How Theosophy came* p. 40 and Appendix 3 for Hartmann in New Guinea in 1885, 1887; *Harbinger* 1 July 1882, p. 2253 (George Smith) and 1 March 1888, p. 3647 (Hartmann, obituary).

32 Hunt 'Early Days' and *AH* October 1890, p. 21; Hobart branch charter. I thank the secretary of Hobart lodge for a copy of this document.

33 *Harbinger* 1 June 1891, pp. 4421–22.

34 *AH* October 1890, p. 21.

35 Quoted Ransom *Short History* p. 214. Webb *Flight from Reason* p. 52 and Brian Inglis *Natural and Supernatural. A History of the Paranormal from Earliest Times to 1914* Abacus, London, 1979, p. 418, offer opposing views. Peter R. Best, Reason, Faith and the Founders of Psychical Research, unpubl. BA thesis, University of Queensland, 1977. I thank Raymond Evans for this reference. For Hodgson see Deakin Papers NLA MS 1540/5/ 1519, John Rickard *H.B. Higgins. The Rebel as Judge* George Allen & Unwin, Sydney, 1984, p. 58 and *ADB* 4.

36 Quoted Moncure Conway *My Pilgrimage to the Wise Men of the East* Archibald Constable, London, 1906, p. 200.

37 Meade *Madame Blavatsky*, p. 413 ff.

38 H.P. Blavatsky *The Key to Theosophy simplified* Adyar edn, 1977, p. 184 (previous quotation, p. 110).

39 ibid. pp. 239–40.

40 Ransom *Short History* Appendix, 'Objects and Rules of The Theosophical Society', pp. 545–53; *Introducing you to The Theosophical Society* The Theosophical Society in Australia, np, n.d. (c. 1978).

41 Ransom *Short History* pp. 549, 252.

Chapter 2 ~ Minds maddened by Protestantism

1 The term post-Christian society derives from A.D. Gilbert *The Making of Post-Christian Britain* Longman, London and New York, 1980, an historical analysis of secularisation. For advocacy of the merits of an alternative 'sacralisation', see Richard Ely 'Secularisation and the sacred in Australian history' *HS* 19, 77, 1981.

2 Erik Gustaf Edelfelt (18??–1895), J. Bean 'Isabelle Bean – Warrior and Pioneer' *TinA* August–September 1939 (suppl.) and *ADB* 7; Elise von Tunzelmann Pickett (18??–1906) *TinA* 16 August 1906, p. 119.

3 Nevill Drury and Gregory Tillett *Other Temples, Other Gods. The Occult in Australia* Methuen, Sydney, 1980.

4 *TT* 1, 1, 1879, p. 6.

5 Richard A. Hutch 'Helena Blavatsky Unveiled' *JRH* 11, 2, 1980.

6 A point derived from Walter Phillips *Defending 'A Christian Country'. Churchmen and Society in New South Wales in the 1880s and after* UQP, St Lucia, 1981, Index, 'insanity'. Spiritualist George Chainey in 'Nineteenth Century Miracles, or, A Rational and Scientific Basis for a Belief in Immortality', a lecture delivered in Melbourne on

7 November 1886, claimed that hospitals, asylums and gaols were filled because of 'ignorance of spiritual laws' (*Spiritualism Pamphlets*, vol. 12, p. 14 [SLVJ]; cf. 'Spiritualism and Insanity' *Harbinger* 1 June 1877, pp. 1215–17 and 1 July 1877, pp. 1236–37.

7   M.F.H. Cramble 'Chronic Delusional Insanity or Paranoia' *Medical Journal of Australia* 2, 1915, p. 167. I thank Stephen Garton for this reference. See also Samuel T. Knaggs MD *Recreations of an Australian Surgeon* W.M. Maclardy, Sydney, 1888, ch. 3, 'Spiritualism considered as an infectious mental disease' and M. Viollet *Spiritism and Insanity* Swan Sonnenschein, London, 1910.

8   For example, Andrew Garran, George Higinbotham: R.R. Garran *Prosper the Commonwealth*, Angus & Robertson, Sydney, 1958, pp. 50–52, and see my 'Challenge and Response: Religious Life in Melbourne 1876–1886' *JRH* 5, 2, 1968.

9   Susan Budd *Varieties of Unbelief. Atheists and Agnostics in English Society 1850–1900* Heinemann, London, 1977, p. 104.

10 C.M.H. Clark *A History of Australia* vol. 5 *The People Make Laws 1888–1915* MUP, 1981, p. 43.

11 Jill Roe ' "The Scope of Women's Thought is Necessarily Less": The Case of Ada Cambridge' *ALS* 5, 4, 1972.

12 Owen Chadwick *The Secularization of the European Mind in the Nineteenth Century* CUP, 1975, p. 239.

13 Owen Chadwick *The Victorian Church Part II* A. & C. Black, London, 1970, pp. 35–39.

14 Nirad C. Chaudhuri *Scholar Extraordinary. The Life of Friedrich Max Muller* Chatto & Windus, London, 1974, Orient Paperbacks edn, p. 132. J.F.C. Harrison *The Second Coming. Popular Millenarianism 1750–1850* Routledge & Kegan Paul, London, 1979, pp. 64, 82 notes an earlier response to Hinduism.

15 Edward Carpenter *From Adam's Peak to Elephanta. Sketches in Ceylon and India* Swan Sonnenschein, London, 1892, p. 152.

16 Gilbert Elliott 'Esoteric Buddhism' *Melbourne Review* 8, October 1883, p. 407. Further articles on Buddhism appeared in the colonial quarterlies, e.g. *Sydney Quarterly Magazine* September 1885–September 1886; and liberal clergymen joined the fray, e.g. Dr Jefferis 'Buddhism and Christianity' *Witness for Christ. Lectures delivered in connection with the Christian Evidence Society of New South Wales in 1884* Sydney, 1886, and J.J. Halley (ed.) *A Short Biographical Sketch of the Reverend Wm. Robey Fletcher, M.A.,* E.S. Wigg & Son, Adelaide, 1895, pp. 180–94.

17 Chadwick *Secularization of the European Mind* p. 245.

18 W.H. McNamara 'Russian Law in New South Wales' *Liberator* 26 June 1887, p. 70; Phillips *Defending 'A Christian Country'* pp. 184–85. McNamara was a founding member of the NSW Socialist League, May 1887: see Bruce E. Mansfield 'The Socialism of William Morris: England and Australia' *HSANZ* 7, 27, 1956.

19 William Lane *The Workingman's Paradise* n.p., n.d. (Sydney, 1892?), pb., p. 81.

20 ibid. p. 121.

21 Peter Bruce, 'William Lane: Personality and Politics', unpubl. BA thesis, University of Adelaide, 1970 (held History Dept, University of Queensland); *ADB* 9.

22 Charles Carrington *Rudyard Kipling. His Life and Work* Macmillan, London, 1955, pp. 362–63.

23 Moncure D. Conway *Autobiography. Memoirs and Experience of Moncure Daniel Conway* vol. 2, Cassell, London, 1904, pp. 356–57.

24 Moncure D. Conway *My Pilgrimage to the Wise Men of the East* Archibald Constable, London, 1906, p. 96.

25 C.R. Badger *The Reverend Charles Strong and the Australian Church* The Charles Strong Memorial Trust, Melbourne, 1971.

26 Conway *My Pilgrimage* pp. 90–94; *Liberal* 24 November, 1, 8, and 15 December 1883 (ML).

27 Ken Inglis 'The Colonial Religion' *Quadrant* December 1977; Deakin to Crisp, 23 August 1880, *Christopher Crisp Papers* NLA MS 743/5/269.
28 Marian Zaunbrecher 'Henry Lawson's Religion' *JRH* 11, 2, 1980, p. 311.
29 Edward Royle *Radicals, Secularists and Republicans. Popular Freethought in Britain, 1866–1915* Manchester University Press, 1980, p. x, ch. 3.
30 ibid. pp. 82–84; *Adelaide Secular & Free Discussion Society Review* 1–14 (March 1878– April l879); F.B. Smith, Religion and Freethought in Melbourne 1870 to 1890, unpubl. MA thesis, University of Melbourne, 1960, ch. 5; Peter Coleman *Obscenity Blasphemy Sedition. Censorship in Australia* Jacaranda, Brisbane, 1963, p. 76; Phillips *Defending 'A Christian Country'*; Nigel Sinnott 'William Willis, Sydney's Freethought Bookseller' *Rationalist News* July–August 1978.
31 *Freedom* (ed. W.W. Collins) 1, 10, 1889, p. 6, and 2, 1, 1890, pp. 6–7; *Freethinker* 31 January 1892, cited Royle *Radicals, Secularists and Republicans* p. 84.
32 Phillips *Defending 'A Christian Country'* p. 113; *ADB* 6 for Symes, Walker; *This World and the Next* 1894–96 (SLV, unknown to Stuart in *Nineteenth Century Australian Periodicals*, cited n. 45 below), e.g. October 1895, p. 56 and November 1895, pp. 69–72 for Miller, and February 1896, p. 119 for 'Delmer Fenton' (O'Dowd, as in Hugh Anderson *Bernard O'Dowd 1866–1953. An Annotated Bibliography* Wentworth Books, Sydney, 1963, 'Prose in Periodicals').
33 Nigel Sinnott 'Joseph Symes and the old-time sex worship' *Rationalist News* November– December 1981, pp. 4–6.
34 *Frazer Prize Essays on Agnosticism, from a moral and spiritual point of view, by Veritas Vincit and Beta* Sydney and Melbourne, 1888, p. 133 (ML, now lost).
35 Wilton Hack 'From the Baptist Pulpit to the Freethought Platform' Newcastle Hall of Science, March 1885, *Liberator* 29 March 1885, pp. 694–95 and *AT* 1, 1, 1894, p. 7 and 1, 5, 1894, p. 80. Adelaide Lodge *Register of Members* [1891 1901]. Hack circularised theosophists on his village settlement scheme at Mt Remarkable, SA: *Hobart Theosophical Society Records* minutes, 9 April and 14 May, 1894, AOT NS 851/1.
36 Zaunbrecher 'Lawson's Religion' p. 310. See also n. 52 below.
37 Manning Clark 'Faith' in Peter Coleman (ed.) *Australian Civilisation* F.W. Cheshire, Melbourne, 1962, and *Meanjin* 40, 1, 1981, Forum: 'St Petersburg or Tinsel Town? Melbourne & Sydney: Their Differing Styles & Changing Relations'. Ken Stewart in 'The Colonial Literati in Sydney and Melbourne' *New Literature Review* 6 (n.d.) discusses a shift of focus and pace from Melbourne to Sydney in the late nineteenth century.
38 Brian Inglis *Natural and Supernatural. A History of the Paranormal from Earliest Times to 1914* Hodder & Stoughton, London, 1977, ch. 22.
39 Smith, Religion and Freethought, p. 30, cf. R. Laurence Moore *In Search of White Crows* OUP, New York, p. xiv: 'In many ways spiritualism could claim to being the quintessential expression of the age of the common man.' Logie Barrow 'Socialism in Eternity. Plebeian Spiritualists 1853–1913' *History Workshop* 9, 1980.
40 Cf. Emma Hardinge Britten *The Lyceum Officer's Manual* cited in Paul Gillen, The Spiritualists. Gnosis and Ideology, unpubl. PhD thesis, Macquarie University, 1981, ch. 4; also *The Spiritual Magazine* cited in Geoffrey K. Nelson *Spiritualism and Society* Routledge & Kegan Paul, London, 1969, pp. 29–30, and *On the Road, or The Spiritual Investigator* George Robertson, Melbourne, 1878, ss. 15–17.
41 Smith, Religion and Freethought, ch. 3.
42 Emma Hardinge Britten *Nineteenth Century Miracles. Or, Spirits and their work in every country of the earth. A complete historical compendium of the great movement known as 'Modern Spiritualism'* Lovell & Co., New York, 1884, pp. 227, 230.
43 Ann-Mari Jordens *The Stenhouse Circle. Literary Life in Mid-Nineteenth Century* Sydney MUP, 1979; Garran *Prosper the Commonwealth* pp. 17–18; 'John Le Gay Brereton' (1827– 1886), *ADB* 3.

44 J.M. Peebles *Around the World; or, Travels in Polynesia, China, India, Arabia, Egypt, Syria and other 'Heathen' Countries* Colbey and Rich, Boston, 1880, 4th edn, p. 52; John Bowie Wilson (1820–1883) *Liberal* 12 May 1883, p. 4 and *ADB* 6.
45 Lurline Stuart *Nineteenth Century Australian Periodicals. An Annotated Bibliography* Hale & Iremonger, Sydney, 1979, pp. 74, 131 & 27; E. Morris Miller *Australian Literature. A Bibliography to 1938*, extended to 1950 by Frederick T. Macartney, rev. edn, Angus & Robertson, Sydney, 1956, p. 221; W.D.C. Denovan *The Evidences of Spiritualism* W.R. Terry, Melbourne, 1882, pp. 369–73.
46 Britten *Nineteenth Century Miracles* p. 260; Harbinger, March 1879, p. 1556.
47 *Liberal* 12 May 1883, p. 1; *ADB* 3 for Charles Bright.
48 Robin Walker 'Lecturers and Lecturing in Late Nineteent-Century Australia' *Australia 1888 Bulletin* 8 (September 1981).
49 For example, Sydney School of Arts, Pitt St, f. 1833, Edward Howard 'Crumbling Temples' *National Times* 27 December–10 January 1982, p. 33.
50 Smith, Religion and Freethought pp. 125–28; *Harbinger* 1 November 1883, pp. 2578, 2589–91, 1 April 1885, pp. 2945–48, 1 July 1887, p. 3494, and 1 March 1889, p. 3891; D.P. Crook, Aspects of Brisbane Society in the Eighteen-Eighties, BA thesis, History Dept, University of Queensland, 1958, p. 12; J.A. Farquharson 'Melbourne Lodge: Diamond Jubilee' *TinA* November–December 1950, pp. 12–13; H.W. Hunt 'The Early Days of the Theosophical Society in Australia' *TinA* 1 August 1919, pp. 157–58; Mary K. Neff *How Theosophy came to Australia and New Zealand TS*, Sydney, 1943, pp. 45–46.
51 *Free Thought: monthly journal of free thought, spiritualism, mesmerism and occult science* (Sydney, February–December 1880), ed. E. Cyril Haviland, 1, 3, pp. 117–18 (BL); Smith, Religion and Freethought, pp. 64–65; *Harbinger* 1 January 1884, pp. 2627–28.
52 *Free Thought* (back cover); *Cosmos. An Illustrated Australian Magazine* (Sydney, September 1894–May 1899, ed. Annie Bright) placed an 'inordinate emphasis' on theosophy: Judith McMillan, 'The Woman Question'. Images of women in selected Sydney journals 1895–1905, BA thesis, Macquarie University, 1979, p. 34, which also states that Louisa Lawson was involved with the theosophical movement (p. 36).
53 Conway *My Pilgrimage* p. 94; *Harbinger* 1 January 1883, p. 2379. See also Henry Mayer *Marx, Engels and Australia* Cheshire, Melbourne, 1964, p. 59.
54 Dorothy Scott *The Halfway House to Infidelity. A History of the Melbourne Unitarian Church 1853–1973*. Unitarian Fellowship of Australia and Melbourne Unitarian Peace Memorial Church, Melbourne, 1980; D.L. Hilliard 'Dissenters from Dissent: The Unitarians of South Australia' *Journal of the Historical Society of South Australia* 11, 1983; Eleanor Wilson *The Story of the Sydney Unitarian Church 1850–1974* Sydney, 1974. On Walter's progression see *Upahdi* March 1893 (TSL); *HVN* November 1894, pp. 1–2; and *AH* October 1898, pp. 23–24.
55 A.B. 'Freethought in Sydney. A Retrospect' *The Freethinker and New South Wales Reformer* 4 July 1886, p. 102; *Harbinger* 1 June 1881, p. 1992 and 1 January 1883, p. 2379. Harold Wilberforce Hindmarsh Stephen (1841–1889), author and editor, was the son of the astonishing George Milner Stephen, public servant and faith-healer: Miller and Macartney *Australian Literature* p. 443 and *ADB* 2. I thank Axel Clark for this point. On George Lacy and the *Liberal*, see Stuart *Nineteenth Century Australian Periodicals* p. 98 and Craufurd D. Goodwin 'Evolution Theory in Australian Social Thought' *JHI* 25, July–September 1964, p. 407.
56 Cited Britten *Nineteenth Century Miracles* p. 261. The eminent Melbourne spiritualist H. Junor Browne, Alfred Deakin's father-in-law and author of many treatises, published *The Grand Reality. Being Experiences in Spirit Life of a Celebrated Dramatist, Received through a Trance Medium* (1888) in both Sydney and Melbourne.
57 'Beta', 'A Sunday in Sydney' *Harbinger* 1 May 1887, p. 3449.
58 *AH* October 1890, p. 21; Joseph Jones *Radical Cousins. Nineteenth Century American & Australian Writers* UQP, St Lucia, 1976, pp. 73–79.

59 Information collated from the colonial and Australian censuses.
60 Richard Broome *Treasure in Earthen Vessels. Protestant Christianity in New South Wales Society 1900–1914* UQP, St Lucia, 1980, p. 111; J.D. Bollen *Protestantism and Social Reform in New South Wales*, 1890–1910 MUP, 1972.
61 This theme is developed in ch. 5.
62 Mrs Charles Bright 'The Emancipating Influence of Spiritualism' Dunedin, 1884, *Spiritualism Pamphlets*, vol. 11, p. 8 (SLY), also *A Soul's Pilgrimage* George Robertson, Melbourne, 1907; *Liberal* 11 August 1883, p. 6, 10 November 1883, pp. 6–7 and 22 December 1883, p. 7.
63 William Leach *True Love and Perfect Union. The Feminist Reform of Sex and Society* Routledge & Kegan Paul, London, 1981, p. 7. *Harbinger* 1 September 1884, p. 2805, 1 June 1885, p. 2992 and 10 October 1884, pp. 2831–32.
64 For example, Martha Webster in Melbourne, Catherine Helen Spence in Adelaide, and see Farley Kelly 'Mrs Smyth and the body politic: Health reform and birth control in Melbourne' in Margaret Bevege et al. (eds) *Worth Her Salt* Hale & Iremonger, Sydney, 1982.
65 As was the case in America: see Mary Farrell Bednarowski 'Outside the mainstream: women's religion and women religious leaders in nineteenth century America' *American Academy of Religion Journal* 48, 2, 1980. I thank Gregory Tillett for this reference.
66 For example, 'Jack', control of trance lecturer Mrs Harris, on 'Women's Influence, Rights and Mission', reported TWN July 1895, pp. 7–8. Moore, *In Search of White Crows* ch. 4, is an excellent analysis of 'The medium and her message'.
67 Besant *DNB* 1931–1940; *EB* 1962, vol. 3 (AHN); A.H. Nethercot *The First Five Lives of Annie Besant* and *The Last Four Lives of Annie Besant* Chicago University Press, Chicago, 1960 and 1963, is the authoritative biography. Bradlaugh: *DNB* 22 (suppl.).
68 Quoted Nethercot *First Five Lives* p. 286. Percival Spear (ed.) *Oxford History of India* OUP, 1958, 3rd edn, p. 732 (I thank Heather Sutherland for the point regarding the Dutch East Indies); James Webb *The Flight from Reason* Macdonald, London, pp. 155 ff., 209 ff. Michael Biddis *The Age of the Masses. Ideas and Society in Europe since 1870* Hassock, Sussex, 1970, p. 105.
69 Edward Carpenter *My Days and Dreams. Being Autobiographical Notes* George Allen & Unwin, London, 1916, p. 221.
70 Annie Besant *An Autobiography* 2nd edn, T. Fisher Unwin, 1893, p. 99, chs. 7–8.
71 Annie Besant *Why I became a Theosophist* Freethought Publishing Co., London, 1889 (1912 reprint) p. 20.
72 Theodore Besterman *A Bibliography of Annie Besant* The Theosophical Society in England, London, 1924 lists 412 books and pamphlets. Of the many biographical works on Annie Besant, in addition to those referred to in the text, Geoffrey West *The Life of Annie Besant* Howe, London, 1929 and Sri Prakasa *Annie Besant. As Woman and as Leader* TPH, Madras, 1940 (4th edn Bharatiya Vidya Bhavan, Bombay, 1969) stand out. The best recent resume is David Rubinstein, *DLB* 4.
73 Gertrude Marvin Williams *The Passionate Pilgrim. A Life of Annie Besant* Coward McCann, New York, 1931, esp. chs 1, 11, 15 (on Williams, Mary Agnes Hamilton *Remembering my Good Friends* Cape, London, 1944, pp. 198, 227, a reference I owe to Beverley Kingston); Beatrice Harraden 'Annie Besant' *The Bookman* 82, April 1932, p. 37; Carpenter *Days and Dreams* p. 222; also West *Life of Annie Besant* pp. 257, 260–62, who writes of spiritual failure, lack of imagination, and 'a woman accustomed to dominate.
74 *Our Corner. A Monthly Magazine of Fiction, Poetry, Politics, Science, Art, Literature* (1883–1888) Freethought Publishing Co., London, 12 Vols (BL). I thank Judith Godden for help here.
75 Part VI *National Reformer* 6 February 1887, p. 87.

76 E.P. Thompson *William Morris. From Romantic to Revolutionary* London, 1958 (reprinted Merlin, London, 1977) contains the most illuminating account of the many on this famous incident. For an accessible account, see Norman and Jeanne MacKenzie *The First Fabians* Weidenfeld & Nicolson, London, 1977.
77 Frederic Whyte *The Life of W.T. Stead* vol. 1 Cape, London, 1925, p. 251; *The Link* 18 February 1888, p. 1 (BL); *Our Corner* February 1888, p. 116; *Justice* 11 August 1888, pp. 4–5 (BL); *Autobiography* pp. 331–32.
78 *The Link* 18 February 1888, p. 1.
79 *Our Corner* February 1888, p. 117.
80 'Civilisation as it is and might be' *The Link* 6 October 1888, p, 2.
81 *The Link* 11 August 1888, editorial p. 1.
83 Fabian Society *Papers*, Executive Committee. Minutes vol. 3, 4 November 1890 (Nuffield College, Oxford), resignation received and secretary instructed to write 'to know that it is due to no cause they can remove'. Besant editorial contributions to *Justice* cover 1888–1890. Willard Wolfe *From Radicalism to Socialism* Yale University Press, New Haven, 1975, correctly emphasises the strategic transition effected by Besant, and the fact that she was one of the few Fabians with a working-class following.
83 Williams *The Passionate Pilgrim* pp. 191, 193; Norman and Jeanne MacKenzie (eds) *The Diary of Beatrice Webb vol. 1 1873–1892*, Virago and London School of Economics and Political Science, 1982, pp. 281, 276–77 and 223.
84 Chadwick *Secularization of the European Mind* pp. 247–48.
85 Reviews in *Pall Mall Gazette* 25 April 1889, p. 3, *National Reformer* 23 June 1889, pp. 390–91.
86 The Spread of Theosophy' *TT* 10, 119, 1889, pp. 675–76.
87 *Autobiography* p. 338.
88 Stanley Pierson *British Socialists. The Journey from Fantasy to Politics* Harvard University Press, Cambridge, Mass., 1979, p. 26.
89 Arthur Lipow *Authoritarian Socialism in America. Edward Bellamy and the Nationalist Movement* University of California Press, Berkeley and Los Angeles, 1982; Blavatsky endorsed Bellamy's vision of the future in *The Key to Theosophy* TPH, Madras, 1977, p. 36 (first publ., London 1889). Robin Gollan 'The Australian Impact' in Sylvia E. Bowman (ed.) *Edward Bellamy Abroad. An American Prophet's Influence* Twayne, New York, 1962, is not concerned with this point.
90 The contemporary term, more revealing than 'intelligentsia', then a new concept in Western society, both in theory and reality (Geoffrey Hawthorn 'The Intelligentsia' *New Society* 18 October 1976). It refers to elements of the professional middle class, an emergent and underemployed salariat, and self-educated proletarians in Lipow *Authoritarian Socialism* ch. 5.
91 *Freedom* 1, 11, 1889, p. 10; Miles Franklin *Joseph Furphy. The Legend of a Man and his Book* Angus & Robertson, Sydney, 1944, p. 110.
92 *Why I became a Theosophist* p. 19. Tom Gibbons *Rooms in the Darwin Hotel. Studies in English Literary Criticism and Ideas 1880–1920* University of Western Australia Press, Nedlands, 1973, p. 19, draws the following conclusion: 'In its attempt to reconcile the most ancient religion with the most modern science, it provides a particularly cogent example of the way in which generalised notions of evolution, extremely modern in their day, were used during the late nineteenth century as a new framework for old beliefs.'

Chapter 3 – Legends of the nineties
1 H.S. Olcott 'Our Australian Legacy: A Lesson' *TT* 12, 11, 1891; Josephine Ransom *A Short History of The Theosophical Society* TPH, Madras, 1938, pp. 246–77.

2   Mary K. Neff *How Theosophy came to Australia and New Zealand* Australian Section, TS, Sydney, 1943, pp. 48–51; M.E. Jersey 'Theosophy' *Sydney Quarterly Magazine* June 1891, pp. 110–15.
3   'Visit to Toowoomba – The Hartmann Bequest' *TinA* 19, 9, 1954, pp. 6–7; 'Queensland Theosophical Society, Brisbane, 1891' TSA Tl 5/41; Neff *How Theosophy came* p. 53.
4   Other names in category order are: G.W. Paul; Dr J.C. Ellison, Dr Geo(?) Taylor; B.L. and G.B. Barrett; A. Costella, H.L.E. Ruthning; C. Engels, E. MacDonell; Clement Wragge, Henry Tryon, J.E. Baines; R. Wishart. Information on 18 of 28: QTS *Minute Book* (1891–1900), *Roll* June–December 1891, and address lists 1891(?), 1895; *Pugh's Almanac and Directory* 1891; and D.B. Waterson *A Biographical Register of the Queensland Parliament 1860–1929* ANU Press, Canberra, 1972.
5   Minute Book 21 May 1891; Neff *How Theosophy came* p. 52; *Harbinger* 1 July 1889, p. 3975.
6   The new charter of the Queensland Theosophical Society, dated 21 January 1895, hangs on the wall of Brisbane lodge. 'Queensland Theosophical Society', TSA; Minute Book 6, 10, 24 April 1895. Subscriptions dropped from £1/10/- p.a. to 10/- in April 1895.
7   Minute Book June–December 1891, 4 August 1892, 23 June 1893. It was reported at the last-mentioned meeting that the bookcase had been forcibly opened, and books taken from it.
8   D.P. Crook, Aspects of Brisbane Society in the Eighteen Eighties, BA thesis, History Dept, University of Queensland, 1958, pp. 11, 22, 36–47 and Table 36.
9   *SMH* 8 May 1891, p. 5 and 11 May 1891, p. 4; *DT* 11 May 1991, p. 6; *Bulletin* 6 October 1894, p. 6.
10 William Turner *An Examination of Theosophy* July 1896, p. 2 (Theosophy Pamphlets, vol. 4, SLV); 'Theosophy' *AH* August 1896, pp. 177–78. *AH* August 1892, p. 213, reported the hopeful start of an Australian Church in Leichhardt by ex-Baptist minister B. Smith whose mainly working-class congregation, many of them unemployed, followed him to found 'a free church' in October 1891 (its first annual report appears in *AH* November 1892, p. 272). For attempts to establish the Australian Church in NSW in the late 1890s, see *AH* August 1897, p. 222 (Newcastle), October 1898, pp. 23–34 (Sydney), and March 1899, p. 123 (Lucknow).
11 *TT* 12, 11, 1891, p. 645; By-laws, TS-1 library, Melbourne; *SMH* 8 May 1891, p. 5.
12 Meade *Madame Blavatsky* p. 455; *SMH* 11 May 1891, p. 5; Neff *How Theosophy came* p. 55; *Harbinger* 1 June 1891 (ed.).
13 Cited Neff *How Theosophy came* p. 58; *Age* 20 May 1891, p. 6.
14 *Age* 16 May 1891, p. 8 and 18 May 1891, p. 6. See also Ambrose Pratt *David Syme. The Father of Protection in Australia* Ward Lock & Co Ltd, London and Melbourne, 1908, pp. 293–98 for the *Age* proprietor's experiences with, and attitude to, theosophy and spiritualism.
15 *Argus* 18 May 1891, p. 7; 'The Pickett Tragedy' *TT* 13, 4, 1892; *AH* August 1891, pp. 31–32; M.D. Lawson, Theosophy and Education, unpubl. MA thesis, University of Sydney, 1972, pp. 51–54.
16 'What is Theosophy?' *AH* February 1891, pp. 89–90 (reprinted *TT*) and subsequent discussion: William Gay's criticism of theosophical irrationality and redundancy (for Gay as literary and religious radical, see Joseph Jones *Radical Cousins. Nineteenth Century American & Australian Writers* UQP, St Lucia, pp. 73–79) and defence by H.W. Hunt, first secretary Melbourne lodge, *AH* April 1891, p. 116; *TinA* 6 July 1896, p. 8; Roe 'Challenge and Response'.
17 Neff *How Theosophy came* pp. 45–47 (founding members of Melbourne lodge, Mrs Elise Pickett, her son James Pickett, surveyor, Mr and Mrs H.W. Hunt of Middle Brighton, Mrs Delia Parker of Maybank, S. Yarra, and her sister Miss Minet, Mr and Mrs Patterson, Miss Jane Price). Deakin's continued interest (e.g. 'Hindu Creeds of Today'

AH October 1892, p. 245) is discussed further in ch. 4. (His name appears in *ITYB*.) *AH* February–April 1893; Theosophical Society GR 1892–97 (bound vol. TSLon)
18 *Register* 21 July 1923, p. 14; *Advertiser* 25 May 1891, p. 7 and 27 May 1891, p. 5.
19 Register 21 July 1923, p. 14; Kate Castle 'The Adelaide Theosophical Society' May 1922, TSA, T15/41/2; *Register of Members* Adelaide Lodge (1891–1901). Knox, accountant: Elizabeth Warburton *The Paddocks Beneath. A History of Burnside from the beginning* Corporation of the City of Burnside, SA, 1981, p. 36, and *ITYB* p. 216. Ernest Cooke, astronomer: *ADB* 8. Sinnett: Miller and Macartney *Australian Literature* p. 430. Gmeiner: *TinA* 17, 3, 1950, p. 12. Olifent (orginal spelling Oliphant resumed by deed-poll when he was a young man and used hereafter although *GR*s to 1925 refer to Olifent, personal communication Sir Mark Oliphant, 12 May 1981), Stewart Cockburn, David Ellyard Oliphant. *The Life and Times of Sir Mark Oliphant* Axiom Books, Adelaide, 1981, pp. 3–12, also *Adelaide Church Guardian* October 1963, p. 6 (obit.). I thank David Hilliard for references to theosophy in Adelaide.
20 Hobart Theosophical Society Records, minutes June 1891–April 1903. I understand that Dr R. Ely is presently studying these records. The quotation in the previous paragraph is from Neff *How Theosophy came* p. 61.
21 Neff *How Theosophy came* p. 61; *TT* 12, 11, August 1891, p. 647.
22 Neff *How Theosophy came* pp. 53–54; D. Izett *Health & Longevity according to the theories of the late Dr Alan Carroll* Epworth, Sydney, 1915, p. 13; Carroll file, items 1, 3, Royal Anthropological Society of Australasia records, Basser Library, Australian Academy of Science, Canberra.
23 Izett *Health & Longevity* pp. 1–39; Bryan Gandevia 'Commentary on the medical work of Dr Alan Carroll' typescript 1967, Carroll file; for information on the Child Study Association I am indebted to Carol Bacchi. On 'reform' Darwinism, see M. Freeden *The New Liberalism. An Ideology of Social Reform* Clarendon Press, Oxford, 1978.
24 *Sydney Theosophical Society President's Address* 19 June 1891, p. 15 (ML).
25 *TT* 14, 5, 1893, pp. 316–17; *TinA* 15 February 1904, pp. 164–65.
26 Lodge information from *GR* 1891–1894.
27 *Isis Unveiled* vol. 1, pp. 594–95; *The Secret Doctrine* vol. 2, Book II–Part (III), Addenda, VII, 'Scientific and Geological Proofs of the Existence of Several Submerged Continents'; James Stirling 'Lemuria, a Lost Continent, with reference to the Antiquity of Man' address to the Religious Science Club, reported *AH* November 1898, pp. 57–58.
28 *The Secret Doctrine* vol. 2 *Anthropogenesis* pp. 323–24, 402.
29 ibid pp. 196–97, 334–35, 779. On p. 194, 'we believe in races of beings other than our own in far remote geological periods; in races of ethereal, following incorporeal, "Arupa" men, with form but no solid substance, giants who preceded us pigmies; in dynasties of divine beings, those Kings and Instructors of the Third Race in arts and sciences, compared with which our little modern science stands less chance than elementary arithmetic with geometry'.
30 ibid pp. 272–73.
31 J.J. Healy 'The Lemurian Nineties' *ALS* 8, 3, 1978; Miller and Macartney *Australian Literature* pp. 384–87; Michael Sharkey 'Rosa Praed's Colonial Heroines' in Shirley Walter (ed.) *Who is She?* UQP, St Lucia, 1983, pp. 27–8.
32 *Secret Doctrine* vol. 2, p. 197.
33 *Upadhi* 2, November 1892 and 4, January 1893; *DT* 2 December 1892, p. 3; *TT* 14, 1, 1892 (suppl.), p. v; *AT* 1, 7, 1894, p. 112; *Harbinger* 1 August 1878, p. 1442.
34 *Upadhi* 1, October 1892; *TT* 14, 3, 1892 (suppl.), p. xxiv.
35 Copies of *The New Californian* (San Francisco 1891–1894) are held TSL. Robert V. Hine *California's Utopian Colonies* Huntington Library, San Marino, California, 1953, pp. 183–85.
36 *TT* 14, 7, 1893 (suppl.), p. xlviii.

37 *Theosophy in Australia*, bound vol. misc. press cuttings 1891-c.1896, MTS library, attributed to *Argus* 3 April 1893, 'A Talk with a Theosophist'; *Argus* 28 February 1893, p. 10; *Age* 28 February 1893, p. 6; *AT* 1, 1, 1894, p. 8; *SMH* 20 July 1893, p. 6; A.H. Nethercot *The First Five Lives of Annie Besant* Chicago University Press, Chicago, 1960, pp. 332–33.
38 *TTYB* p. 196; *AT* 1, 1, p. 8.
39 'A Talk with a Theosophist'; *Upadhi* 5, February 1893; *TT* 14, 7, 1893 (suppl.).
40 Press cuttings (attributed *Herald* 4 May 1893). J.F.C. Harrison *The Second Coming. Popular Millenarianism 1750–1850* Routledge & Kegan Paul, London, 1974 and Keith Thomas *Religion and the decline of magic* Penguin, 1973, both contain speculations on the survival of popular religious practices.
41 Press cuttings 'A Theosophical At Home' (no attribution); *ADB* 7 (Maybanke Anderson).
42 *SMH* 4 August 1893, p. 3; Rose Scott Papers ML MSS 38/ 33, p. 135, 26 July 1893. I thank Ann-Mari Jordens for this reference.
43 *SMH* 15 July 1893, p. 8; *TT* 15, 2, 1893, p. 128; *The Path* 8, June and December 1893, p. 92 (TSL); 13 July 1893, p. 6, 15 July 1893, p. 6 and 20 July 1893, p. 6; Radi et al. *Biographical Register* (Creed).
44 *TT* 15, 2, 1893, p. 129.
45 Press cuttings (attributed to *Herald* 4 May 1893).
46 *AT* 1, 4, p. 54, 1, 7, p. 110, 1, 8, p. 128 and 1, 1, p. 13; *Age* 28 February 1893, p. 6 and 15 March 1894, p. 6; *The Theosophical Congress, held by The Theosophical Society, at the Parliament of Religions, World's Fair of 1893, at Chicago, Illinois, September 15, 16, 17. Report of Proceedings and Documents* TS, New York, 1893, pp. 35, 192. On women at the Parliament of Religions, see ch. 5.
47 P. Serle *Dictionary of Australian Biography* vol. 2, Angus & Robertson, 1949; Nethercot *First Five Lives* p. 381; Ernest Besant-Scott 'Charles Bradlaugh. A Reminiscence' *Cosmos* 30 April 1895, pp. 426–30. Scott's editorship of the *Austral Theosophist* is unknown to Lurline Stuart (*Nineteenth Century Australian Periodicals. An Annotated Bibliography* Hale & Iremonger, Sydney, 1979, p. 22) but established firmly from biographical evidence, theosophical sources and internal inference: e.g. A.H. Nethercot *The Last Four Lives of Annie Besant* Chicago University Press, Chicago, 1963, p. 34; *TinA* 1, 2, 1895, p. 14, and Neff *How Theosophy came* p, 68; also Hobart Theosophical Society Records Minutes, 10 July 1893.
48 Because of controversy surrounding Martyn (see ch. 7) sources vary on some biographical details. This account constructed from the following principal sources: Obituary (press clipping, n.d.) TSA, T 15/41; *Dawn* 1, 19, November 1924, pp. 7–9; *Path* (Sydney) 1, 1, 1925, p. 9; J.M. Prentice 'T.H. Martyn: Fragments of forgotten (theosophical) history' *Canadian Theosophist* 40, 4, 1959; *Sands' Directories* 1890, p. 773 and 1916, p. 1517, and *Moore's Australian Almanack and Handbook*.
49 Prentice 'T.H. Martyn' p. 74; *AT* 1, 1, p. 16, 1, 7, p. 111, 1, 10, p. 159 and 2, 13, p. 14; *GR* 1894, pp. 40–41.
50 Dennis Hardy *Alternative Communities in Nineteenth Century England* Longman, London and New York, 1979, ch. 5. Compared with other movements in late nineteenth-century social thought, e.g. utopian socialism and social Darwinism, this is a neglected theme in intellectual history.
51 Axel Clark *Christopher Brennan. A Critical Biography* MUP, 1980, pp. 71–72, 98.
52 *AT* 1, 6, p. 85; F. Max Muller *Theosophy or Psychological Religion* The Gifford Lectures, Glasgow, 1893.
53 *AT* 1, 5, p. 71. A.C.H.J. 'The Single Tax, and its claim upon theosophists' *AT* 1, 3; E.G. Edelfelt 'Is Cooperation Possible?' *AT* 1, 5.
54 H.W. Hunt 'Our Third Object' *AT* 1, 9, p. 131.
55 N.A. Knox 'The Progress and Principles of Theosophy' *AT* 1, 8, p. 122.

56 Nethercot *Last Four Lives* chs. 2–3; Ransom *Short History* pp. 287–307.
57 Neff *How Theosophy came* pp. 72, 78.
58 *SMH* 21 September 1894, p. 5. The other lectures were chaired by W.C. Windeyer, Sir George Innes and Mabel Besant-Scott, after which Besant dispensed with chairpeople.
59 *Age* 1 September 1894, p. 11; *Bulletin* 15 September 1894, p. 8; *SMH* 19 September 1894, p. 6; Thyra Gebinn 'Mrs Annie Besant' *Cosmos* 1, 2, 1894; *Bulletin* 29 September 1894, p. 16 (see Sylvia Lawson *The Archibald Paradox. A Strange Case of Authorship* Allen Lane, Ringwood Vic., 1983, pp. 201–3, for 'Sapho Smith').
60 *Bulletin* 15 September 1894, p. 8; *Age* 4 September 1894, p. 8; *SMH* cited in Neff *How Theosophy came* pp. 72–73.
61 Clara Codd *So Rich a Life* Institute for Theosophical Publicity, Pretoria, 1951, pp. 39, 101, 102; D.A. Hamer 'Gladstone as Popular Orator' unpubl. paper delivered to the Australasian Modern British History Conference, Adelaide, August 1983 (I thank Michael Roberts for this reference); *Diary of Beatrice Webb* vol. 1, p. 223.
62 Personal visit April 1981 to 45 Fourth Avenue Klemzig SA, courtesy Mick Fearnside.
63 Sri Prakasa *Annie Besant. As Woman and as Leader* Bharatiya Vidya Bhavan, Bombay, 1969, 4th edn, p. 80.
64 *Age* 4 September 1894, p. 6; *Bulletin* 6 October 1894, p. 7; *SMH* 1 October 1894, p. 6.
65 *Age* 1 September 1894, p. 10, 4 September 1894, p. 8 and 8 September 1894, p. 10.
66 *Bulletin* 15 September 1894, p. 8 and 29 September 1894, pp. 6, 10, 16; *Argus* 4 September 1894, p. 6.
67 *Age* 7 September 1894, p. 8.
68 *AT* 1, 10, pp. 1–2; Neff *How Theosophy came* p. 73.
69 'Theosophical Propaganda' *AT* 1, 13, pp. 9–10 and 1, 10, p. 146; *TT* May 1895 cited Neff *How Theosophy came* p. 70. Ibis branch: *GR* 1895; *AT* 2, 14, p. 32; *TinA* 4 May 1895, p. 15. Hobart branch, whose efforts to entice Mrs Besant to Tasmania proved unavailing, studied the article: minutes, 14 January 1895.
70 *Lectures delivered in Melbourne by Mrs Annie Besant, September 1894* typescript bound vol. (TSL) p. 10.
71 Clark *History of Australia* vol. 5, p, 111; Deakin to Royce, 5 June 1892 Deakin Papers NLA MS 1540/ 1/ 159.
72 Neff *How Theosophy came* pp. 71–72 adds 'Religion and Science'; *AT* 1, 10, pp. 153–56.
73 Titles from *SMH*, passim, 21 September–1 October 1894: 'Why I became a Theosophist', 'Religion and Science', 'Civilisations, True and False', 'Spiritualism', 'The Mahatmas as Facts and Ideals', and 'Politics: What they can do and what they cannot'. The second Melbourne series added lectures on 'Necessity and Free Will' 'Death and the Life after Death' and 'Theosophy and Modern Progress' (Neff *How Theosophy came* p. 72).
74 *Lectures* p. 64.
75 *Bulletin* 15 September 1894, p. 15 and 6 October 1894, p. 6.
76 *Lectures* p. 62.
77 *SMH* 1 October 1894, p. 6.
78 *Lectures* p. 19; *SMH* 25 September 1894, p, 6.
79 J.F. Hogan *The Sister Dominions* Eyre & Spottiswoode, Sydney and Melbourne, 1896, ch. 14; *AH* October 1894, p. 5; *DT* 28 September 1894, p. 2 (letter from Frances G. Holden, nurse and reformer).
80 *SMH* 25 September 1894, p. 4; *Harbinger* 1 October 1891, p. 4513; and see ch. 4, pp. 132–34.
81 Besant to Lady Windeyer, 16 September 1894, *Windeyer Family Papers* ML MSS 186/ 14; Frank C. Forster 'The Collins Prosecution, the Windeyer Judgement and Early Publications in Australia on Birth Control' *Australia 1888 Bulletin* 10, September 1982, p, 76.

82 *Bulletin* 6 October 1894, p. 6; Hogan *Sister Dominions* p. 137; *TWN* October 1894, p. 9; 'Prominent Mediums' in William C. Hartmann (ed.) *Who's Who in Occultism, New Thought, Psychism and Spiritualism* Occult Press, Jamaica, New York, 1927, p. 138.
83 *TWN* October and December 1894; Charles W. MacCarthy 'Psychic Force' *Cosmos* 1, 1, 1894; *AT* 1, 3, p. 40, 1, 4, p. 50 and 1, 11, p. 162; *AH* October 1893, p. 4. T. Shekleton Henry, ARIBA *'Spookland!' A Record of Research and Experiment in a much-talked of realm of mystery, with a Review and Criticism of the so-called spiritualistic phenomena of Spirit Materialization, and Hints and Illustrations as to the possibility of artificially Producing the Same* n.p. (Sydney?) 1894, p. 56.
84 *'Spookland!'* Part 1; *TWN* December 1894, p, 9; 'Personal Experiences of Spiritism' (n.d.) Deakin Papers, 5/ 1175–1452 and Rose Scott Papers (seance of 24 March 1893).
85 *TWN* December 1894, p. 9; *AH* January 1895, p. 3; *AT* 1, 10, p. 163; *'Psyche' A Counterblast to Spookland; or, Glimpses of the Marvellous* W.M. Mclardy, Sydney, 1895 Petherick Collection NLA).

Chapter 4 – 'The Great Unsatisfied'

1 Mary K. Neff, *How Theosophy came to Australia and New Zealand* TS, Sydney, 1943, p. 81; *AT* 1, 12, p. 184; *GR* 1896, p. 45 and the *Theosophical Society in Australia, Seventy-fifth Anniversary Commemoration* TS, Sydney, 1970, p. 4.
2 *TinA* 5 November 1896, p. 4.
3 Ibid. 15 May 1898, p. 26.
4 The most significant of these was Rudolph Steiner's Anthroposophical Society, founded in 1913.
5 A.H. Nethercot *The Last Four Lives of Annie Besant* Chicago University Press, Chicago, 1963, chs. 2–3; Josephine Ransom *A Short History of the Theosophical Society* TPH, Madras, 1938, pp. 302–10; *TinA* 5 April 1895, p. 5.
6 *Irish Theosophist* 3, 7, 1895, pp. 122–23 (TSL, I thank John Cooper for this reference); *TinA* 5 April 1895, p. 5 and 5 May 1896, p. 4; *Hobart Theosphical Society Records* Minutes, 11 March 1895.
7 Ransom *Short History*, p. 313.
8 *First Annual Convention of the Theosophical Society in Australasia Report of Proceedings Sydney, 1895*, p. 6 (ML); *The Path* September 1895, p. 199, October 1895, p. 230, and January 1896, p. 327.
9 Katherine Tingley (1847–1929) *DAB* 3; Emmett A. Greenwalt *California Utopia: Point Loma: 1897–1942* 2nd rev. edn, Point Loma Publications, San Diego, 1978, ch. 3; Paul Kagan *New World Utopias. A Photographic History of the Search for Community* Penguin, New York, 1975, ch. 4, 'Theosophical Communes in California'.
10 *Magic* October 1896, editorial.
11 Ibid. November 1896, editorial. Cf. Greenwalt *California Utopia* p. 4 on Point Loma's guiding thesis that 'in addition to revealed wisdom and the findings of modern science, there exists a considerable deposit of occult (hidden) and esoteric (inner) wisdom by which the initiated might guide their lives aright'.
12 *Sun* 22 January 1897, p. 1; *TWN* August 1896; *TinA* 6 July 1896, pp. 1–2, 12 February 1897, p, 4 and April 1898, p. 2.
13 W.T. Willans (1849?-1942), surveyor, joined the TS in May 1889 and retired as president of the Universal Brotherhood and Theosophical Society in Australia in 1938. Obit., *Forum* September, 1942 (TS-I).
14 *Searchlight* New York, 15 October 1905, pp. 33–36. I am indebted to a Melbourne theosophist for this and other references pertaining to the early history of UBTS in Australia. Unfortunately no branch records appear to have survived and enquiries at the Theosophical University Library, Altadena, California, were unsuccessful.
15 Press cuttings MTS (attrib. *Age* 23 September 1895).
16 *TinA* 5 April 1895, p. 4 and 15 May 1897, p. 26; *GR* 1896, p. 45.

17 *GR* 1895 p. 30; Theosophical Society in Australasia (NSW) *Tracts*, 'What Theosophy Is' by John C. Staples, repr. *Bega Standard* 7 May 1896 (ML). *Hobart Theosophical Society Records* minutes, 14 and 19 June 1895.
18 A.H. Nethercot *The First Five Lives of Annie Besant* University of Chicago Press, 1960 pp. 331-32; Press cuttings; *QTS Minute Book* 1891-1900, 2 October 1895 (16 members, 40 visitors); *TinA* 4 May 1895, p. 7, and 5 August 1895, p. 4; *Hobart Theosophical Society Records* minutes, 19 and 17 January 1896.
19 *TinA* 5 September 1895, p. 1 and December 1895-July 1896; *GR* 1896, p. 7.
20 *GR* 1896, p. 45; *TinA* 5 May 1896, pp. 3-4 (there were also 39 'unattached' members in Australasia).
21 Elizabeth Preston and Christmas Humphreys (eds) *An Abridgement of the Secret Doctrine. H. P. Blavatsky TPH*, Illinois, 1966, p. 74.
22 Ann Mozley 'Evolution and the Climate of Opinion in Australia, 1840-1876' *VS* 10, 4, 1967, shows acquaintance with as well as hostility to Darwinism. See ch. 3 n. 23 on liberal, or reform, Darwinism.
23 Neff *How Theosophy came* pp. 62-63.
24 Richard White *Inventing Australia. Images and Identity 1788-1980* George Allen & Unwin, Sydney, 1981, ch. 5.
25 Correlated from *GR* 1892-1901.
26 Sharon Hayston 'Wowsers and Diggers: The Impact of Puritan Ideals upon Charters Towers, 1827-1900' *Lectures on North Queensland History* 2nd series, History Dept, James Cook University of North Queensland, 1975.
27 QTS *Minute Book* Attendance at Public Meetings, 1896-1900.
28 28 *TinA* 15 May 1898, p. 25 and 1 July 1916, pp. 86-88.
29 *TinA* 5 June 1897, p. 56 gives Edger's itinerary, followed in July-August issues by accounts of the joint tour; *Sunday Times* 20 June 1897, p. 5 reports Olcott in Sydney (I thank Chris Cunneen for this reference). *Hobart Theosophical Society Records* minutes, 10 August 1897 and 15 April 1899.
30 *TinA* 15 April 1897, p. 14, and 15 May 1897, p. 39 and 15 December 1899, p. 164; *GR* 1897-1900; Clare and Keith Thompson, A Brief History of the Perth Lodge of The Theosophical Society, 1897 to 1976, typescript (BaL). For Siebenhaar, see E. Morris Miller and Frederick T. Macartney *Australian Literature. A Bibliography to 1938* Angus & Robertson, Sydney, 1956, p. 427, *TinA* 15 March 1898, pp. 201-02 and his contribution to the short-lived Perth literary magazine *Leeuwin* 1910-11.
31 *TinA* 15 July 1903, p. 57.
32 *GR* 1896-1901. Egyptian lodge: *TinA* 15 February 1899, p. 196, 15 December 1899, p. 163 and 20 June 1900, p. 69; Newtown: *TinA* 16 July 1900, p. 92 and 19 October 1900, p. 157. H.B. Wiedersehn founded Mt Rockley branch, later was president of a revived Newtown branch (1910- 1923) and on the executive of the Independent Theosophical Society (see pp. 271 below) in 1925.
33 GR 1895, p. 86; Olcott to Deakin, 20 March 1895, *Deakin Papers* NLA MS 1540/1/2/82 and 5/3; *Victorian Post Office Directory* 1893-4, p. 720; *TinA* 5 December 1895, p. 6.
34 *AT* 1, 8, p. 123.
35 *TinA* 5 October 1895, p. 6 and July-August 1896; *Hobart Theosophical Society Records* minutes, 9 September 1895.
36 Rules of The Theosophical Society *TT* (Suppl.), 17, August 1896; *Constitution and Rules of the Australasian Section of The Theosophical Society, as amended to June 30* 1907 TSA Tl 5/41; *TinA* 5 May 1896, p. 3.
37 *TinA* 15 May 1901, p. 39. It appears from the first issue of *Theosophy in New Zealand* held ML (1917) that a separate publication was launched in 1902.
38 *ITYB* p. 223. Marques submitted only one of three section reports (see *GR* 1899-1901), being absent frequently on business. He did however contribute to *TinA* e.g. 'The Medicine of the Future' 19 October 1900, pp. 147-53, and visit (at least) Brisbane: QTS

Minute Book 1891–1900 lists lectures by Marques, 19 March 1900, 'Spiritualism and Theosophy', and 22 April 1900, 'Man's Condition after Death', both public meetings, attracting 75 and 85 people respectively

39 *TinA* 15 May 1905, p. 218; *ITYB* p. 214; *ADB* 7.
40 *TinA* 15 May 1897, p. 32, 15 May 1905, p. 224 and 16 May 1906, p. 37; Maynard Davies *Beyond My Grasp* Alpha Books, Sydney, p. 78.
41 *TinA* 15 April 1906, p. 35.
42 For biographical information see ch. 6, p. 172 and Gregory Tillett *The Elder Brother. A biography of Charles Webster Leadbeater* Routledge & Kegan Paul, London, 1892, pp. 74–75. See ch. 5, p. 156 on Edger.
43 *TinA* 15 August 1927, p. 50 (Haycraft); 15 July 1927 and *ITYB* p. 209 (Harding); for Mackay see ch. 6 p. 238. Leadbeater to Brereton, 26 May 1905, *John Le Gay Brereton Papers* correspondence ML MSS 281 9/1; Tillett *Elder Brother* p. 73 discusses Leadbeater's publications at this time.
44 *TinA* 16 May 1906, p. 35.
45 Ransom *Short History* Appendix, 'Objects and Rules of The Theosophical Society', p. 549: 1888. Objects, *re* 'A third object, pursued by a portion of the Fellows of the Society, is to investigate unexplained laws of nature and the psychic powers of man (The Fellows interested in this third object now form a distinct *private* division of the Society under the direction of the Corresponding Secretary)' (my emphasis). 'The Esoteric Section of The Theosophical Society. Preliminary Memorandum' *TT* 52, 11, 1931.
46 Ibid p. 553, 'The word "Section" changed to "National Society" ... and the term "Lodge" for "Branch" restored' The former was formally adopted in Australia in 1911 (*TinA* 1 June 1911, p. 66) though "section" remained in use to the 1970s.
47 See ch. 5 p. 196 for discussion of co-masonry. See also E.P. Thompson *The Poverty of Theory* Merlin, London, 1978 (unfortunately the absence of an index to this vast work prevented listing of page references); *TinA* 5 June 1896 (L.E. Harcus, 'Freemasonry and Theosophy') pp. 3–4.
48 Emily Lutyens *Candles in the Sun* Hart Davis, London, 1957, pp. 20–22; C.W. Leadbeater *The Masters and the Path* TPH, Madras, 1925 (11th repr. 1975); *TinA* 15 December 1905, p. 398.
49 *Harbinger* 1 September 1892, p. 4728 (White Lotus Day); 'The Lotus Circle' *TinA* 5 September 1895, p. 8; 'Is Theosophy for Children', *TinA* 20 June 1900, pp. 51–55.
50 *AT* 1, 5, p. 67 and 9, p. 128; Catherine W. Christie *Theosophy for Beginners and for the use of Lotus Circles* TPH, Madras, 6th edn, 1928 and *The Lotus Bud's Journal* 5, 6, 1915 (Auckland N Z) (ML); *TinA* 15 April 1897, p. 294, 1 June 1911, p. 64 and 2 August 1909, p. 125. See ch. 6 for further discussion of theosophy and education.
51 J. Springhall *Youth, Empire and Society* Croom Helm, London, 1977, ch. 7; M. Girouard, *The Return to Camelot. Chivalry and the English Gentleman* Yale University Press, New Haven & London, 1981, p. 254; *The Round Table. A League For Young People* booklet in Perth lodge *Minutes* 1899–1924 (BaL); *TinA* 1 May 1908, p. 32; Report on the Round Table, handwritten enclosure by Muriel Chase, dated 30 June 1913, Perth lodge Minutes; *TinA* 1 April 1919, p. 9. Also C.W. Leadbeater 'True Government of the World' *TinA* 1 September 1919.
52 M.D. Lawson, Theosophy and Education unpubl. MA thesis, University of Sydney, 1972, p. 34. *TinA* 15 May 1901, p. 41, 21. April 1903, p. 6, 1 June 1911, p. 32, and 1 May 1913, p. 43.
53 *Outline of Theosophy* pp. 58–59; *TT* 1, 7 (April 1880) pp. 187–90; a burial subcommittee was formed in 1901 (*TinA* 15 May 1901, p. 47), and agitation for appropriate ritual continued (ibid. 1 May 1909, p. 35).
54 John Morley *Death, Heaven and the Victorians* Studio Vista, London, 1971, ch. 8; Keith Dunstan *Wowsers* Cassell Australia, North Melbourne, 1968, pp. 157–63; Michael

Cannon *Life in the Cities. Australia in the Victorian Age* Vol. 3 Thomas Nelson (Australia) Melbourne, p. 132.

55 *AT* 1, 3, p. 34; *TinA* 4 May 1895, p. 2 and 11 April 1896, p. 2; *Bulletin* 12 January 1895, p. 14; 'Cremation in Australia', *AA* 3, 6, 1927, p. 277 (TSL). On the NSW Cremation Society, see *TinA* 2 November 1908, p. 185, 2 May 1910, p. 33 and 1 June 1911, p. 62. C. Williams 'Cremation: its sentimental side' *AA* 3, 2, 1927, pp. 87–89; Perth lodge *Correspondence* 1925–1926, Town Clerk to Hon. Sec. TS, 27 March 1925.

56 *TinA* 5 March 1896 p. 7 and 1 August 1907, p. 91.

57 For example, 'The Medicine of the Future' *TinA* 19 October 1900, pp. 147–53. See also ch. 8.

58 C.W. Leadbeater 'Clothes' *TinA* 1 June 1911, pp. 76–79; Annie Besant *Vegetarianism in the light of theosophy* TPH, Madras, 1932 (lecture 1894, 1st printing 1913); C.W. Leadbeater *Vegetarianism and the Occult* TPH, Madras, 1979 (1st printing 1913).

59 Julia Twigg 'Food for thought: purity and vegetarianism' *Religion* 9, 1, (Spring, 1979).

60 *Harbinger* 1 April 1888, p. 3668 (Mrs Harvie's vegetarian dining room in Little Collins St), and Izett *Health and Longevity* p. 289 (ad for 'The Ceres' Vegetarian Cafe, 65 Victoria Arcade, Castlereagh and Elizabeth Streets, Sydney, and numerous advertisements for pure foods); *TWN* August 1895, p. 24 on the Anti-Compulsory Vaccination League of Victoria, founded 1895.

61 James Turner *Reckoning with the Beast. Animals, Pain and Humanity in the Victorian Mind* Johns Hopkins University Press, Baltimore and London, 1980; Richard D. French *Antivivisection and Medical Science in Victorian Society* Princeton University Press, 1975; Twigg 'Food for Thought' p. 16. I thank Max Harcourt for guidance on this subject.

62 *TinA* 15 October 1898, p. 114 and 1 September 1907, p. 113.

63 *Macquarie Dictionary*; *ADB* 8 for Collingridge; *TinA* 1 May 1908, pp. 36–37 and 2 May 1910, p. 37. Ann-Mari Jordens, Against the Tide: the Peace Society of NSW 1907–1914, un publ. paper, Australian Historical Association Conference 1982, p. 16 refers to the Esperanto Society as part of Sydney's 'counter culture' by 1914.

64 *TinA* 1 June 1914, p. 69, 1 May 1913, p. 38, 15 May 1905, p. 217 and 1 June 1911, p. 62.

65 Besant lodge (1908–1917): *TinA* 1 May 1908, p. 33; addressed by Bernard O'Dowd, 'Science and mystery', ibid. 1 September 1908, p. 138.

66 Eastern Hill lodge (1906–1910): *TinA* 19 March 1906, p, 479 and 15 April 1907, p. 296.

67 *TinA* 1 May 1909, p. 29 and 1 June 1914, p. 69.

68 ibid. 1 May 1909, p. 29.

69 ibid. 15 May 1905, p. 224.

70 ibid. p. 225; Nethercot *Last Four Lives* p. 93ff; Tillett *Elder Brother* pp. 279–84; Ransom *Short History* pp. 356–81.

71 *TinA* 1 May 1908, p. 30.

72 ibid. 2 September 1907, p. 105.

73 ibid. p, 113.

74 *Mrs Besant's Australian Lecture Tour 1908: Press Notices* p. 91 (*Sunday Times* 5 July 1908), bound vol., TSL; all daily press notices hereafter as attributed in this collection unless otherwise indicated.

75 ibid. loose leaf insert.

76 ibid. p. 80 (*Bulletin* 18 June 1908).

77 Annie Besant *Australian Lectures 1908* George Robertson, Sydney, 1908, pp. 2–3.

78 ibid p. 23. The other five lectures were titled 'Do we live on earth again?', 'Life after death', 'The power of thought', The guardians of humanity', and 'Nature's finer forces'.

79 *Austral Light* 1 August 1908, pp. 574–82, 1 November 1908, pp. 778–88 and 1 March 1909, pp. 189–94 (I thank Patrick O'Farrell for this reference). Rev. W.H.H. Yarrington *Modern Theosophy. Being Condensed Reports of Lectures and Addresses* Sydney, 1909

repr. *Australian Churchman* (FL), and *Press Notices* p. 85 (*SMH* 1 July 1908), also Miller and Macartney *Australian Literature* p. 502; James Neil *Spiritualism and Theosophy. Twain Brothers of Anti-Christ (Founded on the First Lie, the belief of which brought Death to our Race). The Origin, Development and Destruction of These Systems, which deny the Divinity and Atonement of Jesus Christ, the only Saviour of Men*, Dunedin, n.d. (1908?)

80 *Australian Lectures* p. 3.
81 *Press Notices* p. 94 (*Star* 6 July 1908, *DT* 6 July 1908, *EN* 6 and 10 July 1908); Phillips *Defending 'A Christian Country'* pp. 185–92.
82 *Press Notices* pp. 35–44 (e.g. Annie Besant in reply to the Rev. J.C. Kirby, *Register* 11 June 1908); E.R. Norman *Anti-Catholicism in Victorian England* George Allen and Unwin, London, 1968, p. 18.
83 *Press Notices* pp. 82, 102 (*Bulletin* 25 June 1908; also *Star* 11 July 1908).
84 *Press Notices* pp. 18–19 (*Perth Daily News* 20, 24 June 1908; also *Truth* 5 July 1908.)
85 'Theosophy and the Workers' *TinA* 2 November 1908, pp. 175–79 and 1 December 1908, pp. 196–200; *Press Notices* p. 106 (*DT* 22 July 1908).
86 *Press Notices* pp. 131, 45, 106 (*Brisbane Courier* 23 July 1908, *Register* 19 June 1908, *People* 11 July 1908).
87 *Press Notices* p. 81 (unattributed).
88 ibid. p. 91 (*Sunday Times* 5 July 1908).
89 ibid. pp. 97–98, 105 (*DT* 8, 10, 14 July 1908).
90 ibid. (*Register* 6 June 1908?).
91 ibid. p. 90 ('Must be Good' *Arrow* 4 July 1908).
92 ibid. pp. 127, 82 (*Brisbane Daily M*ail 16 July 1908; *Bulletin* 25 June 1908). See also *Courier* 18 July 1908, for a sympathetic editorial.
93 *Australian Lectures* p. 120.
94 ibid. pp. 156–58.
95 *TinA* 1 September 1908, p. 137.
96 ibid. 1 July 1909, p. 96 and 1 May 1909, pp. 30, 32, probably referring to hostile articles by 'XYZ' in *Melbourne Life* July–October 1908 (*Press Notices* pp. 63–67).
97 Annie Besant *The Changing World and Lectures to Theosophical St*udents TPS, London, pp. 149–50.
98 Mary Lutyens *Krishnamurti. The Years of Awakening* Farrar, Straus and Giroux, New York, 1975.
99 Nethercot, *Last Four Lives*, ch.13.
100 *TinA* 1 June 1911, p. 71; Rall to Crisp, 12 June 1909, *Crisp Papers* NLA MS 743/8; *Deane Family Papers* NLA MS 610 98/A (on Elsie Deane, ch. 6).
101 *TinA* 1 May 1912, pp. 44–46 (first OSE conference).
102 See Appendix 2 for 'Krotona'; *TinA* 1 May 1913, p. 44; Jill Roe 'Three Visions of Sydney Heads from Balmoral Beach' in Jill Roe (ed.) *Twentieth Century Sydney. Studies in Urban & Social History* Hale & Iremonger and the Sydney History Group, Sydney, 1980.
103 *TinA* July 1908, p. 91.
104 ibid. 1 May 1913, pp. 44, 47–48. On Matthew Reid (1856–1947) see *ITYB* p. 233, Waterson *Biographical Register* p. 157 and D.J. Murphy 'Two administrators – Albert Hinchcliffe and Mat Reid' in D.J. Murphy et al (eds) *Prelude to Power. The Rise of the Labour Party in Queensland 1885–1915* Jacaranda, Milton, Qld, 1970.
105 *TinA* 1 May 1913, pp. 41, 48 (Sons and Daughters of the Empire) and 2 September 1907, p. 113 (Samurai Order).

Chapter 5 ~ To the court of the Faerie Queene

1 A.H.N. 'Annie Besant' *EB* (1962), vol. 3.
2 James Webb *The Flight from Reason* vol. 1 of *The Age of the Irrational*, Macdonald, London, 1971, ch. 6.

3   G.S.R. Kitson Clark *The Making of Victorian England* CUP, 1962, p. 145; E.P. Thompson *The Making of the English Working Class* Gollancz, London, 1963, p. 382, and J.F.C. Harrison *The Second Coming* Routledge & Kegan Paul, London, 1980, ch. 5; Barbara Taylor 'The Woman-Power. Religious heresy and feminism in early English socialism' in Susan Lipshitz (ed.) *Tearing the Veil. Essays on Femininity* Routledge & Kegan Paul, London, 1978; Olive Anderson 'The growth of Christian militarism in mid-Victorian Britain' *English Historical Review*, 338, January 1971.

4   F.K. Prochaska *Women and Philanthropy in Nineteenth Century England* OUP, 1980; Barbara Welter 'The feminization of American religion: 1800–1860' in Mary S. Hartmann and Lois Banner (eds) *Clio's Consciousness Raised* Harper & Row, New York, 1974, and (more broadly) Ann Douglas *The Feminization of American Culture* Avon, New York, 1977; J. Michael Phayer *Sexual Liberation and Religion in Nineteenth Century Europe* Croom Helm, London, 1977, pp. 95–98, and Bonnie G. Smith *Ladies of the Leisure Class. The bourgeoisie of northern France in the nineteenth century* Princeton University Press, 1981. American historians have paid most attention to women's religious experience in the nineteenth century, as in *American Quarterly* 30, 5, 1978, special issue: Women and Religion; also *Signs* 2, 2, 1976, special section: Women and Religion.

5   Elizabeth Cady Stanton *The Woman's Bible* New York, 1898, repr. *Coalition Task Force on Women and Religion*, Seattle, 1978; Joan Jacobs Brumberg 'Zenanas and girlless villages: the ethnology of American Evangelical women, 1870–1910' *J. Am. Hist.* 69, 2, 1982.

6   For example, Ada Cambridge *Thirty Years in Australia* Methuen, London, 1903; Jo Manton *Sister Dora. The life of Dora Pattison* Methuen, London, 1971; Annie Besant *An Autobiography*, 2nd edn, T. Fisher Unwin, London, 1893. Cf. Margaret H. Watt *The History of the Parson's Wife* Faber and Faber, London, 1943.

7   A fine analysis is Smith *Ladies of the Leisure Class* ch. 5.

8   Owen Chadwick *The Secularization of the European Mind in the Nineteenth Century* CUP, 1975, p. 17.

9   Dale Spender *Women of Ideas and what men have done to them. From Aphra Benn to Adrienne Rich* Routledge & Kegan Paul, London, 1982 (I thank Judith Allen for this reference). Elaine Showalter 'Florence Nightingale's feminist complaint: women, religion and *Suggestions for Thought* ' *Signs* 6, 3, 1981; William Leach *True Love and Perfect Union. The Feminist Reform of Sex and Society* Routledge & Kegan Paul, London, 1981 p. 7.

10 Rev. John Henry Barrows, DD (ed.) *The World's Parliament of Religions. An Illustrated and Popular Story of the World 's First Parliament of Religions, held in Chicago in connection with the Columbian Exposition of 1893* Chicago, Parliament Publishing Co., 1893, pp. 4, 47. The theosophical contribution is detailed in *The Theosophical Congress, held by The Theosophical Society, at the Parliament of Religions, World's Fair of 1893, Chicago Illinois, September 15, 16, 17. Report of Proceedings and Documents* TS, New York, 1893 and A.H. Nethercot, *The First Five Lives of Annie Besant* Chicago University Press, Chicago, 1960.

11 Peter F. Anson *The Call of the Cloister. Religious communities and kindred bodies in the Anglican Communion* SPCK, London, 1955; Mary Farrell Bednarowski 'Outside the mainstream: women's religion and women religious leaders in nineteenth-century America' *American Academy of Religion Journal* 48, 2, 1980.

12 Diana Burfeld 'Theosophy and feminism: some explorations in nineteenth-century biography' in Pat Holden (ed.) *Women's Religious Experience* Croom Helm, London, 1983.

13 Stanley Pierson *Marxism and the Origins of British Socialism. The struggle for a New Consciousness* Cornell University Press, 1973, ch. 6; Clara Codd *So Rich a Life* Institute for Theosophical Publicity, Pretoria, 1951 pp. 41–106 and *ITYB*, p. 195. Cf. also the experience of Beatrice Hastings, a late convert and advocate of theosophy noted in

John Carswell *Lives and Letters. A.R. Grage, Beatrice Hastings, Katherine Mansfield, John Middleton Murry, S.S. Koteliansky, 1906–1957* Faber and Faber, London 1978, p. 226.
14   Edward Carpenter *My Days and Dreams*, George Allen & Unwin, London, 1916, p. 245; Carswell *Lives and Letters* chs. 1, 3; A.R. Orage *Consciousness, Animal, Human and Superhuman* Theosophical Publishing Co., London and Benares, 1907; and for an interweaving of these influences, see Emile Delavenay *D.H. Lawrence and Edward Carpenter. A study in Edwardian transition* Heinemann, London, 1971.
15   Annie Besant *Women and Politics. The way out of the present difficulty* TPH, London, 1914.
16   Annie Besant *The Education of Indian Girls* (1904) in *The Birth of New India. A collection of speeches and writings on Indian Affairs* TPH, Madras, 1917, p. 150; 'Should Indian Girls learn English?' *TinA* 15 June 1905, pp. 279–80; A.H. Nethercot *The Last Four Lives of Annie Besant* Chicago University Press, Chicago, 1963, p. 73 on Besant's pioneering Central Hindu Girl's School.
17   Marion Meade, *Madame Blavatsky. The Woman Behind the myth* G.P. Putnam's Sons, New York, 1980 discusses background and psychology. Cf. Anne Barstow Driver 'Religion' *Signs* 2, 2 1976.
18   Raoul Mortley *Womanhood. The feminine in Ancient Hellenism, Gnosticism, Christianity, and Islam* Delacroix, Sydney, 1981, p. 24. See also Merlin Stone's instructive if methodologically naive *The Paradise Papers. The Suppression of Women's Rites*, Virago, London, 1976 on the suppression of women's rites in ancient Israel.
19   Mortley *Womanhood*, pp. 19–25; cf. Elaine Pagels *The Gnostic Gospels* Random House, New York, 1979; Asphodel 'Feminism and spirituality: a review of recent publications 1975–1981' *Women's Studies International Forum* 5, 1, 1982
20   Edna Healey *Lady Unknown. The Life of Angela Burdett-Coutts* Sidgwick & Jackson, London, 1978, p. 197.
21   Basil Crump *'The Secret Doctrine' on the Problem and Evolution of Sex* Blavatsky Pamphlets No. 2 (n.d.), p. 3 (TSL).
22   Meade Madame Blavatsky pp. 86–92, 117; Nethercot *First Five Lives* pp. 307–308; Besant *Autobiography* p. 341 on 'the mastering hand' and p. 345, the resolution of 'the dreams of childhood on the higher planes of intellectual womanhood '; Caroll Smith-Rosenberg 'The female world of love and ritual: relations between women in nineteenth-century America' *Signs*, 1, 1, 1975.
23   Angus McLaren *Birth-Control in Nineteenth century England* Croom Helm, London, 1978; *Suffrage Annual and Women's Who's Who* London, 1913; *The Awakening of Women, or Women's part in evolution* 3rd rev. edn, William Reeves, London, 1908 p. 298. On pp. 251–52 of *The Awakening of Women*, Swiney commented favourably on the progress of Australian women.
24   Frances Swiney *The Cosmic Procession* Ernest Bell, London, 1906, p. 133.
25   ibid. pp. 136–37.
26   ibid. p. 124, cf. Pagels *Gnostic Gospels.*
27   ibid. p. 48.
28   ibid. p. 42. See Anna Davin 'Imperialism and motherhood' *History Workshop* 5, 1978, for an interpretation of resurgent maternalist ideology in Edwardian England.
29   C.H. Waddington 'Biology' in C.B. Cox and A.E. Dyson (eds) *The Twentieth Century Mind. History, Ideas and Literature in Britain: vol. l, 1900–1918* OUP, 1972, p. 343: in Swiney's time the chief contributor to knowledge was August Wiesmann (1834–1914), who propounded the doctrine that 'there is an asymmetric relationship between what he called the germ and the soma. The germ, or "germ line" is the hereditary constitution which is passed on from one generation to the next by means of gametes. The germ controls the development of the gametes into the soma, that is to say the differentiated body of the adult organisms. The germ therefore influences the soma ... but the soma cannot influence the germ. The soma during its development is subject

to influences of the environment which may cause the development to take unusual or even abnormal forms, but these changes in the soma have no effect on the germ which persists within the soma quite unchanged and which can be passed on unchanged.' Waddington notes that the asymmetric relationship is dogma, and stresses that it is a radical rejection of Lamarckian (or willful) ideas of selection.

30 Mr S.T. to Marie Stopes, 21 June 1919, in Ruth Hall (ed.) *Dear Dr Stopes. Sex in the 1920s* Andre Deutsch, London, 1978, pp. 112–13.
31 Swiney *Cosmic Procession* p. 18
32 ibid. p. 177.
33 Andro Linklater *An Unhusbanded Life. Charlotte Despard, Suffragette, Socialist and Sinn Feiner* Hutchinson, London, 1980, pp. 156–57, 171.
34 ibid. pp. 158–59.
35 *Theosophy and the Woman's Movement* TPS, London, 1913, p. 2.
36 ibid. p. 49.
37 John R. Durant 'Scientific naturalism and social reform in the thought of Alfred Russel Wallace' *British Journal for the History of Science* 12, 40, 1979, p. 49.
38 *Mrs Besant's Australian Lecture Tour 1908: Press Notices* p. 80 (attrib. *Bulletin* 18 June 1908).
39 *Press Notices* p. 131 (*Brisbane Courier* 23 July 1908); also *Harbinger* October–November 1877, responses to the Bradlaugh-Besant trial.
40 *TinA* 20 April 1906, p. 17, 16 June 1903, p. 41 and 15 May 1905, p. 227.
41 W. Nichol and H. Royal 'Drs W. Sheldon and S.P. Spasshatt: two prominent New England medical practitioners of the nineteenth century' *Armidale and District Historical Association Journal* 24, 1981, pp. 67–82. On Braund see p. 177.
42 Analysis of delegates from Convention listings, *TinA* 1900–1914.
43 Leslie M. Henderson *The Goldstein Story* Stockland Press, Melbourne, 1973, p. 95 and John Rickard H.B. Higgins. *The Rebel as Judge* George Allen & Unwin, Sydney, 1984, p. 292. Feminization of the two groups is illustrated by the following table:

	Theosophy			Christian Science		
Year	Total	male	female	Total	male	female
1901	358	191	167	217	80	137
1911	781	385	396	1189	761	428
1921	1102	522	580	3015	1106	1909
1933	540	250	290	8878	3316	5562

Source: *Commonwealth of Australia Census*, 1933, p. 1023

44 Dorothy Scott *The Half way House to Infidelity. A History of the Melbourne Unitarian Church 1853–1973* Unitarian Fellowship, Melbourne, 1980, p. 41.
45 *TinA* 21 April 1903, p. 11.
46 *TinA* 6 July 1896, p. 6, 5 October 1895, p. 6, 5 April 1895, p. 7, 15 January 1897, p. 40, 15 May 1901, p. 40 and 1 August 1907, p. 91; *Hobart Theosophical Society Records* minutes, 4 October 1897. Launceston was thought to be more theosophically alive than Hobart at this time, perhaps because Northern Tasmania was still a superior seasonal spot attracting Victorian and imperial travellers.
47 *Theosophy in New Zealand* April–June 1946, pp. 50, 54–55; *ITYB* pp. 205, 207, 211 (Edger, Browning, Horne); *TinA* 5 June 1897, p. 57 and 15 January 1901, p. 224.
48 *TinA* 1 July 1908, pp. 90–93.

49 *TinA* 15 January 1898, p. 181 and 15 January 1901, p. 227; *ITYB* pp. 205, 207 (Fuller, Gmeiner). I have not found any historical study of Australian women missionaries in India, a neglected but worthwhile subject.
50 Lilian Edger 'Religion and Theosophy' (1893), *Theosophy Pamphlets* vol. 3 (SLV); *AT* 1, 2, pp. 29–30; *ITYB* p. 232 for Ransom.
51 Both listed in E. Morris Miller and Frederick T. Macartney *Australian Literature* Angus & Robertson, Sydney, 1956 where 'Sydney Partridge' is identified as Kate Margaret Partridge, Mrs H.E. Stone (p. 374).
52 *TinA* 1 October 1907, pp. 130–31. Cf. *Religion and Music. A Lecture* TPH, Madras, 1908. Ian Britain *Fabianism and Culture: A study of British Socialism and the Arts c. 1884–1918* CUP, 1982, pp. 87–93 discusses Besant's aesthetic-cum-ideological position sympathetically. Michele Lacombe 'Theosophy and the Canadian idealist tradition: a preliminary exploration' *Journal of Canadian Studies* 17, 2, 1982, provides a parallel case of cultural influence, noticing some women.
53 Mrs Leonard Matters *Australasians who count in London, and who counts in Western Australia* London, 1913, p. 51 (BaL); *TinA* 1 August 1907, p. 91; *TinA* 1 May 1913, p. 41 and *The Catholic Gnostic. Official Organ of Gnosis Lodge* 1, 1, 1912 (ML). On Mouchette and Lion see the *Critic* 17 June 1908, also 27 October 1909 where Lion's Indian inspiration is evident (I thank Dennis Davison and John Drury for Mouchette and Lion references).
54 Hawthorne to Blackmore, 31 May 1910, *Scrapbook* of Susannah Jane Earle, University of Tasmania Archive, M18/2a. I thank Marilyn Lake for this reference; and see also her 'John Earle and the Concept of the "Labor Rat"' *LH* 33, November 1977; Miller and Macartney *Australian Literature* p. 64 for Albert Robert Blackmore. On Hawthorne and the 'awakening' of Hobart lodge at this time, *TinA* 2 May 1910, p. 35 and 1 June 1911, p. 64 and *Hobart Theosophical Society Records* minutes 1908–1910.
55 Interview Elliston Campbell, Faulconbridge, 9 September 1983. A widower aged 92 at the time of interview and virtually self-sufficient still, Campbell is impressive testimony to the benefits of a theosophical life style. (For mystic poems by Phyllis Campbell, see F.C. Happold *Prayer and Meditation. Their Nature and Practice* Penguin, 1971, pp. 334–38 and notes thereon, pp. 377–78, also Miller and Macartney *Australian Literature* p. 99, which lists two volumes of poetry published by Mrs Phyllis Violet Campbell, Sydney, 1943, 1944.)
56 See n. 12; *Commonwealth of Australia Census* 1933, pp. 1076–77.
57 Biographical information too scattered to be presented in tabular form has been accumulated from various sources previously cited, e.g. *ITYB*, *TinA*, interviews. Muriel Chase appears *ADB* 7. On the Hospice, see Ray Sumner *More Historic Homes of Brisbane* National Trust, Brisbane, pp. 93–95 and see *ADB* 6 on the Wienholt pastoral empire. *AA* 3, 6, p. 285.
58 Lake 'John Earle' p. 34; Mark Finnane 'The Popular Defence of Chidley' *LH* 41, November 1981, p. 69; *TinA* 15 August 1927, p, 50 (Haycraft); personal communication, Mick Fearnside, Adelaide, August 1981 (Radcliffe); Adelaide *Register* 21 July 1923 p. 14 (Rounsevell), and *ITYB* p. 234.
59 Josephine Ransom *A Short History of the Theosophical Society* TPH, Madras, 1938 pp. 346–47; Emily Lutyens *Candles in the Sun* Hart Davis, London, 1957, p. 32; Christopher McIntosh *Eliphas Levi and the French Occult Revival* Rider, London, 1972, pp. 19ff. for the growth of French Freemasonry in the eighteenth century: 'The main appeal of Freemasonry lay in the fact that it claimed to be the sole recipient and guardian of an ancient and powerful secret handed down from antiquity.' Dudley Wright *Women and Freemasonry* Rider, London, 1922 is cited by several writers but has not been seen.
60 H.P. Blavatsky *Isis Unveiled. A Masterkey to the Mysteries of Ancient and Modern Science and Theology* Theosophical University Press, Pasadena, 1972, pp. 375–377.
61 Interview F. Hynes, North Sydney, November 1983; Ransom *Short History* p. 347; Nethercot *Last Four Lives* p. 72; Annie Besant 'The Object of Co-Masonry' *TinA*

1 November 1910, p. 208, and *EN* 7 July 1908, p. 2; C.J. Jinarajadasa *Women In Freemasonry* Sydney, 1944, pp. 8–9; Loris Ingamells *An Outline of Freemasonry. Transaction No. 1. Lodge Isis Sydney (No. 412, Universal Co-Masonry)* Publicity Press, Sydney, 1932(?), p. 16.

62 See my 'Three visions of Sydney Heads from Balmoral Beach' in Jill Roe (ed.) *Twentieth Century Sydney* Hale & Iremonger, Sydney, 1980, p. 101; Caspersz to Rischbieth, 7 May 1929, *Rischbieth Papers* NLA MS 2004/5/861 and *TinA* May–June 1950, p. 15.
63 Pers. comm., Sydney, September 1979.
64 Geoffrey Hodson 'What is Co-Freemasonry' lecture at Adyar Hall, 4 July 1938, Sydney (1938?), back page (M. Goot collection).
65 Interview, Battye Library Oral History Programme, October 1976.
66 Nethercot *Last Four Lives* p. 116; *ITYB* p. 163; 'Statement of Principles' Theosophical Order of Service, London (n. d., 1970s?). Ransom *Short History* p. 381, 'Ever since its Constitution, the Order has done an immense amount of good work in a number of deparments'.
67 *TinA* 1 September 1908, p. 13, 2 November 1908, p. 185 and 2 May 1910, p. 33.
68 Theosophical Order of Service, Brisbane *Minute Book* 21 October, 3 November 1911 and 1 March 1912 (TS, Brisbane).
69 *ITYB* p. 185 (Adair); Peter Cowan *A Unique Position. A Biography of Edith Dircksey Cowan 1861–1932* University of Western Australia Press, 1978, pp. 106, 264; records of the WA Women's Service Guild, Early Papers 1909–1914, 1949A/1 (BaL); Bessie M. Rischbieth *March of Australian Women. A Record of Fifty Years' Struggle for Equal Citizenship* Paterson Brokensha, Perth, 1964, p. 13.
70 The 'forgotten congruence' is being studied by June Ogilvie of Perth.
71 Clare and Keith Thompson, A brief history of the Perth lodge of the Theosophical Society 1897 to 1976, typescript (BaL); Rieschbieth *March of Australian Women* ch. 2; Daphne Popham (ed.) *Reflections. Profiles of 150 women who helped make Western Australia's History* Carroll's, Perth, 1978; pers. comms., Clare Thompson and Irene Greenwood, Perth, July 1980.
72 Kate White 'Bessie Rischbieth. The feminist' in Lyall Hunt (ed.) *Westralian Portraits* University of Western Australia Press, 1979.
73 Popham *Reflections* p. 127.
74 Rischbieth to Donnell y, 19 May 1913, *Rischbieth Papers* NLA MS 2004/ 1/69; ibid. 2004/ 12/ 1922; White 'Bessie Rischbieth' p. 217; executive records *Minutes* Perth lodge, 1917.
75 I thank Irene Greenwood and Lenore Layman for assistance on these points.
76 Deborah Gorham 'Flora MacDonald Denison: Canadian Feminist ' in Linda Kealey (ed.) *A Not Unreasonable Claim. Women and Reform in Canada, 1880s–1920s* Women's Press, Toronto, 1979.
77 Interview, Irene Greenwood, Perth, 12 July 1980.
78 Kate White 'Bessie Rischbieth, Jessie Street and the end of first-wave feminism in Australia' in Margaret Bevege et al. *Worth her salt* Hale & Iremonger, Sydney, 1982.

Chapter 6 ~ Men, Mars and the millennium

1 Michael McKernan *Australian Churches at War. Attitudes and Activities of the Major Churches 1914–1918* Catholic Theological Faculty and Australian War Memorial, Sydney and Canberra, 1980; *TinA* 1 September 1914, p. 150; A.H. Nethercot, *The Last Four Lives of Annie Besant* Chicago University Press, Chicago, 1963, pp. 225–26.
2 Gregory Tillett *The Elder Brother. A biography of Charles Webster Leadbeater* Routledge & Kegan Paul, London, 1982 is the most recent and authoritative biography; Brisbane lodge *Minute Book* (1913–1920) p. 56.
3 *TinA* 1 May 1915, p. 31; Tillett *Elder Brother* p. 160.

Notes

4   Marion Meade Madame Blavatsky. *The Woman Behind the Myth* G.P. Putnam's Sons, New York, 1980, pp. 323–30. Tillett's bibliography of works by Leadbeater lists 85 items.
5   Deakin Papers, NLA MS 1540/ 5/ 2; *Hobart Theosophical Society Records*, minutes 3 May 1897; *TT* 64, 5 (1923) p. 448.
6   See p. 115 above.
7   Mary Lutyens *Krishnamurti. The Years of Awakening* Farrar, Straus and Giroux, New York, 1975, p. 84.
8   C.W. Leadbeater *Australia and New Zealand as the home of a new sub-race* Sydney, 1915 [ML].
9   *TinA* 1 June 1916, p. 65 and 1 May 1917, p. 38.
10 ibid. 1 April 1916, pp. 3–15.
11 ibid. p. 14.
12 ibid. 1 June 1916, p. 66.
13 ibid. 1 April 1916, p. 15. James H. Cousins *War: A theosophical view* TPS, London, 1914 (European War Pamphlets, vol. 9, SLY), pp. 22–28 stressed the consoling and liberating effect of theosophical teaching on death.
14 *TinA* 1 May 1918, p. 34.
15 Major General the Hon. James Alexander Keith [Kenneth?] Mackay (1859–1936) is listed in *ITYB* p. 222 as 'devoted friend' of Leadbeater and several articles by Major General Kenneth Mackay appear in *TinA* in the early thirties, e.g. 'Elimination of Childhood' 15 September 1931, pp. 109–111. Major-General Sir Cyril Brudenell Bingham White (1876–1940) is reported as portrait donor to Morven Garden School *TinA* 1 March 1920, p. 632. See also C.E.W. Bean *Two Men I Knew. William Bridges and Brudenell White. Founders of the AIF* Angus & Robertson, Sydney, p. 222. The background of Lieut.-General Henry Gordon Bennett (1887–1962) is outlined by Frank Legg *The Gordon Bennett Story* Angus & Robertson, Sydney, 1956, ch. 1.
16 *J.W.B. Bean Papers* AWM 3DRL 2405, Box 8A letter 25 (S.S. 'Derfflinger', 6 April 1915). Other Bean material in AWM collections (the *Bean Collections* 3DRL 6673 and the *Dr C.E.W. Bean Personal and Family Records*, 3DRL 7447) will be referred to later. (On the Bean family see *ADB* 3 (Edwin Bean), 7 (C.E.W. Bean and Isabelle Bean). A brief biography of J.W.B. Bean appears in Watson A. Steel *The History of All Saints' College, Bathurst, 1873–1934. Compiled from Available Records and Personal Reminiscences* Angus & Robertson, Sydney, 1936, pp. 132–33; see also NSW Gazette, 11 February 1918, p. 133. I thank Michael Piggott and Matthew Higgins for assistance with AWM collections.
17 J.M. *Prentice Correspondence* AWM 3DRL 1471 (London, 27 July 1916 and Cairo, 24 February 1916). AWM File 419/82 /2 provides biographical infomation.
18 *TinA* 1 May 1918, p. 40. Braund: AWM Biography Card; C.E.W. Bean *The Official History of Australia in the War of 1914–1918* vol. 1, *The Story of Anzac* Angus & Robertson, Sydney, 1937, p. 599n; and H. Radi et al., *Biographical Register of the New South Wales Parliament 1901–1970* ANU Press, 1979, p. 25; *J. Bean Papers* letter 18 (Menai Camp, 1 March 1915); *Prentice Correspondence* (Cairo, 14 November 1915). Bean Records 52/ l 5, Military Hospital, Bulford, 22 June 1918 and Dudley McCarthy *Gallipoli to the Somme. The story of C.E.W. Bean* John Ferguson, Sydney 1983, pp. 312–13.
19 *Prentice Correspondence* (Cairo, 10 October 1915).
20 *J. Bean Papers* letter 51 (Brentwood, 7 October 1915).
21 *Prentice Correspondence* (France, 2 August 1917).
22 ibid. (Elsternwick, 9 February 1916 and Cairo, 17 February 1916). On Dr Bean's schemes, see pp. 183–185 above.
23 *J. Bean Papers* letters 69, 183 (Westminster, 26 March 1916 and Dartford, 14 August 1918).
24 *Prentice Correspondence* (Cambridge, 13 May 1916).

25 *Bean Records* 53/ 17 (Brentwood, 17 December 1896).
26 M. Girouard *Return to Camelot. Chivalry and the English Gentleman* Yale University Press, New Haven & London, 1981, ch. 18.
27 *TinA* 1 May 1918, p. 34; *The Theosophical Society in Australia Seventy-Fifth Anniversary Commemoration* TS, Sydney, 1970.
28 *TinA* 1 May 1917, p. 37.
29 ibid. 1 June 1916, p. 68 and QTS Theosophical Order of Service *Minute Book* March 1915–March 1917; *ADB* 7 (Booth).
30 *TinA* 1 April 1920, p. 7 (delivered 4 February 1917).
31 Ibid. 1 May, p. 30.
32 *Bean Records* 53/ 8/22, esp. bundle on *A.I.F. appeal re Temperance and Continence*; see also McCarthy *Gallipoli to the Somme* p. 307.
33 'The League of Active Service' *Bean Collections* 850/44/ 11.
34 ibid. (Sydney, 18 May 1919), also press cuttings n.p., n.d.
35 *TinA* 1 August 1919, p. 138.
36 J. Bean 'National Kitchens' *TinA* 1 April 1920, p. 10; also Reginald Birch 'National Restaurants' *TinA* 1 April 1920 and Bloomfield 'Central Kitchens' *TinA* 1 September 1919, pp. 173–75. Meredith Foley 'From "thrift" to "scientific spending": the Sydney Housewives' Association between the Wars' *Sydney Gazette* 6, March 1984, notes an experimental communal kitchen established in Sydney in 1920.
37 *TinA* 1 October 1919, and 1 January 1920, p. 402f.
38 *TinA* 1 August 1919, p. 139.
39 Dan Coward, The Impact of War on New South Wales. Some Aspects of Social and Political History, 1914–1917, unpubl. PhD thesis, ANU, 1974, pp. 175, 332–35 discusses the conference.
40 'Sydney Political and Economic Science League' see *TinA* 1 July 1919, p. 91; Bean to Gilmore, 7 June 1919, *Gilmore Papers*, ML MSS A3273, vol. 22 (I thank Beverley Kingston for this reference). T.H. Martyn 'The Problem of Poverty and Wealth' *TinA* 1 July 1920, pp. 102–5.
41 It is noted by Judith Brown ('India' *History Today* 32, December 1982) that 'historians' understanding of India's political history has developed markedly in the last two decades'. This account is most influenced by the following studies: Raj Kumar *Annie Besant's Rise to Power in Indian Politics 1914–1917* Concept Publishing Co., New Delhi, 1981; Joanne Stafford Mortimer 'Annie Besant and India 1913- 1917' *JCH* 18, 1983; and Hugh Owen, The leadership of the Indian National Movement, 1914–1920, unpubl. PhD thesis, ANU, 1965.
42 Cf. Tillett *Elder Brother* p. 159. *J. Bean Papers* (London, 4 July 1916); *Bean Records* 53/22 (four Home Rule pamphlets); *Prentice Correspondence* (London, 3 October 1916).
43 *TinA* 1 May 1915, pp. 39, 37; *Internment Diary of Annie Besant* cited in Kumar *Annie Besant's Rise to Power* p. 113. Annie Besant *India. A Nation. A plea for Indian Self-government* T.C. and E.C. Jack, London, Edinburgh and New York (n.d.), is one of many presentations of the case.
44 Josephine Ransom, *A Short History of the Theosophical Society* TPH, Madras, 1938, pp. 405, 409, 413–14.
45 *Bean Records* 53/8 contains an 18-page pamphlet *Mrs. Besant & India* (publ. Britain and India: An Association for the Study of their Mutual Interests, London, n.d.), with a message from Besant dated 12 June 1917 and marked KINDLY SHOW TO ALL WHO ARE INTERESTED, along with several other pamphlets, e.g. Home Rule for Indian League Leaflet No. 1, *What India Wants* (London, n.d. 1916?).
46 Ransom *Short History* pp. 420, 426.
47 Mary L. Walker, The Development of Kindergartens in Australia, unpubl. MEd thesis, University of Sydney, 1964, Sect. A; Rita Kramer *Maria Montessori. A biography* G.P. Putnam's Sons, New York, 1977, p. 341; Emmett A. Greenwalt, *California Utopia: Point*

Loma: 1897–1942 2nd rev. edn, Point Loma Publications, San Diego, 1978, ch. 8. *TinA* 1 May 1918, p. 44 states that as many as 130 members were or had been teachers.
48 Leadbeater's educational views are expounded in e.g., 'Australia and New Zealand as the home of a new sub-race', Lecture IV, where he stresses the benefits of a wholesome environment on 'the inherently good' child; also 'Child Training: the method of Love or Fear' *TinA* I February 1915, pp. 298–301. Citation here is from his *The Inner Life. Theosophical Talks at Adyar* TPH, Madras, 1917, p. 201.
49 *ADB* 7; Lutyens *Krishnamurti. The Years of Awakening*, p. 59; M.D. Lawson, Theosophy and Education, unpubl. MA thesis, University of Sydney, 1972, pp. 111–12.
50 Ransom *Short History* p. 421. *TinA* 1 May 1918, p. 45 and June–July 1937, p. 6, also October–November 1937, p. 9; On Beatrice Ensor *ITYB* p. 204 and Lawson, Theosophy and Education, pp. 378–82.
51 Interview Sydney, 5 September 1979.
52 *Rischbieth Papers* NLA MS 2004 1/69 (London, 19 May 1913); Peter Spearritt 'The Kindgergarten movement: tradition and change' in Donald E. Edgar (ed.) *Social Change in Australia: Readings in Sociology* Cheshire, Melbourne, 1974, p. 584; subsequent information from Kindergarten Union of New South Wales Inc., *Annual Reports* 1912–1926 (ML); *TinA* 1 June 1916, p. 801; *Who's Who in Australia 1929*, p. 1155.
53 Pers. comm. Mr F. Hynes, North Sydney, November 1983; *TinA* 1 June 1916, pp. 80–81; Kramer *Maria Montessori* p. 246; R.C. Petersen, Experimental schools and educational experiments in Australia, 1906–1948, unpubl. PhD thesis, University of Sydney, 1968, p. 66 (to which the following paragraphs are indebted), *TinA* 2 November 1908, p. 185 and Christopher Dowd *The Adelaide Kindergarten Teachers College. A history 1907–1974* South Australian College of Advanced Education, Adelaide, 1983, ch. 4 (I thank Brian Dickey for this reference).
54 *TinA* 1 August 1913, p. 149, 1 May 1915, p. 36 and 1 June 1916, p. 80; Petersen, Experimental schools, p. 61.
55 Petersen, Experimental schools, pp. 97–113. Regular advertisements for St Margaret's appeared in *TinA* 1920–22. With an average enrolment of 60, it offered education 'conducted on modern lines and aims at character building, musical and literary appreciation'.
56 Eurhythmics 'a system of rhythmical bodily movements, esp. with the aid of music, used with an educational object 1915' *Shorter Oxford English Dictionary* is better known as 'Greek dancing', popularised by Isadora Duncan in the 1920s.
57 Petersen, Experimental schools, p. 36; Priscilla Kennedy *Portrait of Winifred West* Sam Ure Smith, Sydney, 1976.
58 *TinA* 1 June 1916, pp. 65, 79–81, and 1 May 1917, pp. 30, 38–40.
59 Ibid. p. 51, 1 May 1918, p. 1 and 1 March 1920, p. 632.
60 ibid. 1 February 1918, p. 1 and 1 May 1918, p, 35, 43–44.
61 Petersen, Experimental schools, pp. 63–73 gives a full account of the school's work. See also *TinA* 1 April 1919, p. 26, 1 July 1919, p. 134 and 1 March 1920, p. 632.
62 Interview, Hornsby NSW, 4 November 1982.
63 Department of Education, Non-State Schools 1921–23 (AONSW: School Files 20/12886.2). Staff included a Polish composer as musical director, a sports mistress, a certified technical teacher, and a trained kindergarten teacher. Lawson, Theosophy and Education, pp. 266–67.
64 T*he Lorna Hodgkinson Sunshine Home* (Sydney, n.d. 1983?); *SMH* 22 August 1922, 18 January 1923, 3 May 1924 (I thank Chris Cunneen for these references).
65 Petersen, Experimental schools, chs. 3–4; pers. comm., Barbara Storey, Sydney, 1981; *TinA* 1 May 1922, pp. 387–98, 415 on van der Leeuw's efforts (Lawson, Theosophy and Education, p. 201 states that all the pupils were members or acolytes of the Liberal Catholic Church); *Theosophy in New Zealand* 7, 2, 1946, pp. 56–58.
66 *TinA* 1 April 1919, p. 7, 1 September 1919, p. 199 and 1 March 1920, p. 632.

67 Eric S. Taylor *The Liberal Catholic Church. What is it?* St Alban Press, London, 1966; Nethercot *Last Four Lives* p. 309; *ITYB* p. 241; 'What is the Old Catholic Church?' *TT* February 1917, pp. 495–98; Tillett *Elder Brother* ch. 16. For a full account of Arnold Mathew and churches of the Mathew succession, see Peter F. Anson *Bishops at Large* Faber and Faber, London, 1964.
68 Susannah Earle's news cuttings contain an undated report of a Wedgwood lecture, 'Telepathy and Clairvoyance' in Hobart (University of Tasmania Archives M18/1, p. 118). Perth Lodge *Minutes* 31 December 1916.
69 Tillett *Elder Brother* p. 172; *TT* 38, 1, 1916, pp. 5–6.
70 *The Australian Liberal Catholic Jubilee Issue 1916–1966*, 4, 2 (1966). I thank the editor for this and other references.
71 *TinA* 1 May 1918, p. 38.
72 *Prentice Correspondence* (London, 7 January 1918); Stanley Morrison *Some Fruits of Theosophy* Harding and More, London, 1919 (Theosophy Pamphlets, vol. 5, no. 11, SLV); Tillett *Elder Brother* p. 179.
73 'The Liberal Catholic Church' *J.H. Watson Newspaper Cuttings* vol. 2, pp. 137–38 (ML); Tillett *Elder Brother* pp. 173–76; *Liberal Catholic Jubilee Issue* p. 28. *The Liberal Catholic Church, Statement of Principles and Summary of Doctrine* 7th edn, St Alban Press, London, 1973, 15 pp., offers a full exposition of doctrine, ritual and ethics; n.b. esp. congruence with theosophy: 'Moving within the orbit of Christianity and regarding itself as a distinctively christian church it nevertheless holds that other religions are divinely inspired and that all proceed from a common source' (p. 7).
74 'The early days of our church in Sydney' *Jubilee Issue*, pp. 6–9.
75 *Deane Family Papers* NLA MS 610 / 82, Elsie Deane to J.B. McConkey, 3 May 1917, 1 May 1917 and Elsie Deane to Tyssen, 2 October 1917.
76 ibid. Isabelle John to Elsie Deane, 6 November 1918.
77 Interview, Sydney, 5 September 1979; Jubilee Issue, p. 11; Tillett *Elder Brother* p, 222.
78 The *Liberal Catholic* Vols. 1–9, October 1924–September 1929 (ML); Petersen, Experimental schools, p. 100 and *ADB* 7 (Isabelle Bean).

Chapter 7 – The height of expectancy

1 Richard White *Inventing Australia. Images and Identity 1788–1980* George Allen & Unwin, Sydney, 1981, ch. 9. For subsequent paras, H. Radi '1920–29' in F.K. Crowley (ed.) *A New History of Australia* William Heinemann, Melbourne, 1974; Ronald L. Davis (ed.) *The Social and Cultural Life of the 1920s* Holt, Rinehart and Winston, Inc., New York, 1972, and C.L. Mowat *Britain between the wars* University paperbacks, London, 1968, chs. 1, 4.
2 *TinA* 1 February 1921, pp. 314–16 for the newly formed Spiritualist Church of NSW; William C. Hartmann (ed.) *Who's Who in Occultism, New Thought, Psychism and Spiritualism* Occult Press, Jamaica, New York 1927 (twelve Australian entries for Psychic Science and Spiritualism). *Commonwealth of Australia Census* 1933, II, p. 1023.
3 'The activities of the coming half century' in *Three Great World Movements. Being the Jubilee Convention Lectures delivered at Adyar at the Fiftieth Anniversary of the Theosophical Society*, December 1925 TPH, Madras, 1926, pp. 106–7.
4 Cited Mary Lutyens *Krishnamurti. The Years of Awakening* Farrar, Straus and Giroux, New York, 1975, pp. 223–24.
5 See my 'Theosophy and the ascendancy' in Jim Davidson (ed.) *The Sydney-Melbourne Book* George Allen & Unwin, Sydney, 1986.
6 *TinA* 1 March 1921, p. 340 and 1 May 1922, p. 405; Pamphlet, 'The Theosophical Society, Sydney lodge' (1921), in NSW Attorney-General and Justice, Police enquiry into alleged immoral teachings of C.W. Leadbeater 'Bishop' of the Liberal Catholic Church, in special bundle 5/777 1.2 (AONSW), hereafter *Police enquiry*. I thank Baiba Berzins for this reference. The source has also been used, to good effect, by Gregory Tillett *The*

Elder Brother. A biography of Charles Webster Leadbeater Routledge & Kegan Paul, London, 1982, pp. 197–200.
7   C. Jinarajadasa 'E.S.T. The occult centre for the Southern Hemisphere' *Deane Family Papers* NLA MS 610/98/c; Adelaide *Register* 21 July 1923, p. 14.
8   Clara Codd *So Rich a Life* Institute for Theosophical Publicity, Pretoria, 1951 pp. 281–83; A.H. Nethercot *The Last Four Lives of Annie Besant* Chicago University Press, Chicago, 1963 p. 308.
9   *ITYB*; H. Radi et al. *Biographical Register of the New South Wales Parliament 1901–1970* ANU Press, 1979, p. 244 (Perdriau).
10 'Sydney Lodge' in *Police enquiry; Part 1*, 1 1925, p. 15; Angus McIntyre 'The Reverend Donald Fraser' *Australian and New Zealand Journal of Psychiatry* 12, 1978, pp. 109–113; Jeffrey Weeks *Sex, Politics and Society. The regulation of sexuality since 1800* Longman, London, 1981, p. 155; Mary E. Wilkinson and Arthur W. Osborn *Simple explanations of theosophical terms with an addendum containing psychological terms in current use* Hart Printing Co., Melbourne, 1924.
11 Nethercot *Last Four Lives* p. 31; Leaflet, T.H. Martyn to Annie Besant, 20 March 1921, *Police enquiry*.
12 Australian Section Records, TSA *Sydney Crisis* VI, *The Dawn. A Magazine devoted to the Promotion of Universal Brotherhood* (November 1921–November 1924), 4, 1, p. 14, and IV, item 4, T.H. Martyn 'Neutrality of the Theosophical Society', Krotona, 1919, also press cuttings 1922–1923, especially from the *Daily Telegraph*.
13 Patrick and Deirdre O'Farrell (eds) *Documents in Australian Catholic History* vol. 2, Geoffrey Chapman, London, 1969, s.5 and Patrick O'Farrell *The Catholic Church and Community in Australia. A History* Thomas Nelson (Australia), West Melbourne, 1977, esp. pp. 348–49.
14 Sydney *Crisis* IV, *Ross's Monthly* 8 July 1922, pp. 2–4.
15 David Hilliard 'Unenglish and unmanly: Anglo-Catholicism and homosexuality' *VS* 25, 2, 1982.
16 'Paedophilia', a medical term meaning sexual attraction in an adult towards children, is a less loaded term than 'paederasty', although the Greek *paiderastia*, 'love of boys', is perhaps more accurate here.
17 *Police enquiry* statements, June 1922.
18 For example, *DT* 18 May 1922, p. 5 (Köllerstrom and Medhurst in defence), *J.H. Watson's Cutting Book* (ML), three letters from Dr Rocke, Rev. Robert Firebrace and A. Norman Ingamells.
19 Bean to 'Dearest Parents & Chas & Effie', Sydney, 23 December 1921, *Bean Collections* AWM DRL 6673, 850 44/ 11.
20 Marjorie Bull and Clare Thompson, interviews September 1979 and July 1981. J. to C. Bean, 20 June 1922, Sydney, *Bean Records* AWM DRL 7447/26, 54/6; *New India* 30 May 1922, p. 3 (BL).
21 *DT* 18 and 19 May 1922, p. 5; *The Dawn* 1 January 1923, p. 4; *TinA* 1 March 1923, p. 698.
22 Marion Piddington to Marie Stopes, 30 August [1923], *Stopes Papers* BL Add. MS 58572, CXXVI. I thank Mary Murnane for this reference.
23 James Brown to Marion Piddington, 18 September 1922, ibid.
24 Fussell to NSW Minister of Justice, 1 June 1917, *Police enquiry* (also 'The Spookologist' *Truth* 18 June 1916, a reference not available for consultation NSWPL).
25 *Police enquiry* police reports 26 August 1917 and 16 and 28 December 1917.
26 ibid. 13 June and 10 August 1922. See Tillett *Elder Brother* pp. 199–200.
27 *Who's Who in Australia* 1922; Dan Morgan *The Minister for Murder* Hutchinson (Australia), Richmond, 1979. 'Our Editor's Letter', *New India* 20 June 1922, p. 3.
28 *Stopes Papers* ibid.; Finnane 'Defence of Chidley'; *DT* 23 May 1922, p. 5.
29 *Sydney Crisis* VI & VII, items 2, 23; and II, item 22.

30 ibid. VI, item 1 (Oliphant to Besant, 2 April 1923); ibid. items 17–20 and *Dawn* 3, 17, 1924; *Dawn* 3, 14, 1924, p. 2.
31 *The Path. A Magazine Devoted to The Theosophical Message of H.P. Blavatsky* 1, 1, 1925, editorial and p. 14.
32 Victor Carell & Beth Dean *On Wings of Song. Dorothy Heimrich and the Arts Council* APCOL, Sydney, 1982, p. 15; *Theosophical Forum* June 1938, September 1942 and *Path* 1, 5, 1925; *SMH* 23 April 1955 p. 6 and 29 April 1955, pp. 13, 19. (J.M. Prentice's emergence as right wing publicist in the 1940s is noted by Andrew Moore 'Send Lawyers, Guns and Money!' A study of conservative paramilitary organisations in New South Wales 1930–1932, background and sequel, 1917–1952, unpubl. PhD thesis, La Trobe University 1982, ch. 5, seen subsequent to completion of this book, courtesy the author.)
33 *Sydney Crisis* VI, items, 4, 9, Bean to Besant, 27 July 1923, 23–25 August 1923; *TinA* 1 March 1924, p. 1081, 1 June 1924, p. 30 and 15 May 1927, p. 163.
34 *TinA* 1 April 1923, p. 720 and *Bean Records* 26, 54/6 (Sydney, 17 July 1922). The following quotation, *TinA* 1 March 1924, p. 1079.
35 ibid. 1 April 1923, p. 722.
36 21 January 1923, Sydney, *Bean Records* 26, 54/6.
37 As reprinted *New India* 17 May 1922, p. 3, 20 May 1922, p. 3 and 25 May 1922, p. 3. *New India* 17 May–23 June 1922 gave detailed coverage to Besant's Australian tour, mainly in the form of attributed cuttings from the Australian press.
38 ibid. Previous press references as in ibid. 22 June 1922, p, 6, 2 June 1922, p. 3, 13 July 1922, p. 3 and 31 May 1922, p. 3.
39 ibid. 13 June 1922, p. 3.
40 *Problems of Nationality 1918–1936* OUP 1937, ch. 4, esp. pp. 50–51, 177–84.
41 'A Tribute to Mrs Besant', repr. *New India* 21 June 1922, p. 3, and 'Our Editor's Letter ', ibid. 20 June 1922, p. 3.
42 ibid. 'Our Editor's Letter'; 8 June 1922, p. 3, 20 June 1922, p. 3; *TinA* 1 March 1923, p. 698.
43 *New India* 20 and 23 June 1922, p. 3, and 6 July 1922, p. 3.
44 'Memorandum about a visit to the Prime Minister of Australia' (n.d.) and typescript, 'India and the Policy of a White Australia' TSA Tl 5/41(7).
45 *New India* 20 June 1922, p. 3.
46 *New India* 20 June 1922, p. 3 and 11 July 1922, p. 3. Sastri's Australian mission during June 1922 was covered by *New India* in the same manner as Annie Besant's tour (see n. 37 above), June–July 1922.
47 *Census* 1922, vol. I, pp. 295–97. J. Lyng *Non-Britishers in Australia* Macmillan and MUP, 1927, pp. 181–88; Marie M. de Lepervanche *Indians in a White Australia. An account of race, class and Indian immigration to eastern Australia* George Allen & Unwin, Sydney, 1984, ch. 4; *New India* 2 June 1922, p. 7 and 26 June 1922 p. 3.
48 *West Australian* 2 June 1922, p. 7; *New India* 10 July 1922, p. 3. A.T. Yarwood (ed.) *Attitudes to Non-European Immigration* Cassell Australia, Melbourne, 1968, p. 113.
49 *New India* 10 July 1922, p. 3; L.F. Fitzhardinge *The Little Digger 1917–1952. William·Morris Hughes. A Political Biography* vol. 2, Angus & Robertson, London, Sydney, 1979, p. 507.
50 *New India* 1 July 1922 (suppl.), 8 July 1922 (suppl.), 26 June 1922, p. 6 and 13 July 1922, p. 7.
51 ibid. 6 July 1922, p. 7.
52 Editorial, 15 June 1904, *TinA*; Bernard O'Dowd 'Race Prejudice' parts 1 and 2, *TinA* 2 September 1912 and 1 October 1912, also 1 February 1913; E.G. Docker *Simply Human Beings* Jacaranda, Brisbane, 1964, p. 179 (see also ch. 8, p. 270).
53 I am indebted to Noel Sanders, Sydney, for this perspective.
54 *TinA* 1 May 1919, p. 43. It may be contended with hindsight that this position contained elements of realism subsequently overlooked.

55 Nethercot *Last Four Lives* p. 319. Rukmini Arundale, founder of the Kalakshetra Classical Dance Company, was short-listed for the presidency of India by the Janata government in the late 1970s.
56 Daniel H.H. Ingalls 'The Heritage of a Fallible Saint. Annie Besant's Gifts to India' *Proc. American Philosophical Society* 109, 2, 1965, pp. 85–88.
57 Cf. Barbara Foxe *Long Journey Home. A Biography of Margaret Noble* (Nivedita) Rider, London, 1975.
58 Annie Besant *The Changing World and Lectures to Theosophical Students* TPS, London, 1909, p, 137.
59 Cited Mary Lutyens *Krishnamurti. The Years of Awakening* p. 167.
60 *TinA* 1 April 1924, p. 23.
61 *GR* 1923–1924, p. 25, p. 5.
62 *Dawn* 3, 14, 1924, p. 17; 2, 9, 1923, p. 21; 2, 10, 1923, p. 12.
63 See my 'Three Visions of Sydney Heads from Balmoral Beach' in Jill Roe (ed.) *Twentieth Century Sydney* 1980, pp. 89–104, for the story of, and local sources on, the Star Amphitheatre at Balmoral 1922–1951, to which may now be added, *per favore* Sally Kennedy, that in 1937 the building nearly became headquarters of an international lay organisation of Catholic women, the Grail (see also *Mosman Daily* 18 January 1937 on 'The Sisters of the Holy Grail'). Jack Lindsay recalls inspecting 'the temple which the theosophists had built for an Advent', *The Roaring Twenties*, Bodley Head, London, 1960 p. 179.
64 Cited Roe 'Three Visions of Sydney Heads' p. 97.
65 According to Ernest Wood the Manor became an 'occult beauty parlour' *'Is this Theosophy...?'* Rider, London, 1936, p. 288.
66 OSE membership peaked in 1928 at 75,000 (Lawson, Theosophy and Education, p. 118). I am indebted to M. Lutyens *Years of Awakening*, esp. ch. 25, 'The self-appointed Apostles', in this paragraph.
67 Cited ibid. p. 224.

Chapter 8 ~ To theosophise Australia

1 *TAT* 1 June 1926, pp. 68, 74–78.
2 *AA* 1, 1–6, 4, July 1926–April 1929 (TSL). *SMH* 24 August 1926, p. 10; Lesley Johnson '"Sing 'Em Muck, Clara". High brow versus low brow on early Australian Radio' *Meanjin* 41, 2, 1982, p. 21 1, outlines the dual system of classification before 1932. It is primarily concerned with the 1930s, and does not discuss 2GB.
3 *TAT* 1 June 1926, p. 83 and Adyar Hall, Programmes (ML).
4 *Star* 8, 1, 1926 p. 4 (ML).
5 *TAT* 15 July 1926, p. 10.
6 *Star* 8, 1, p. 5; Fellowship of Pioneers program and leaflets, *TSA* T 15/41 (also Sally McInerney 'Convict Roots out of the closet into the club' *SMH* 21 January 1984, p. 35, dating pioneer clubs in Sydney from 1910); *Advance! Australia* pamphlets Adyar Library, also NLA; *AA* 2, 6, 1927 for Arundale's policy.
7 Print run as in *AA* 1, 2, 1926, p. 49.
8 Edward A. Tiryakian 'Towards the sociology of esoteric culture' *American Journal of Sociology* 78, 3, 1972.
9 *Australasian Radio Calls* Melville Publishing Co., Melbourne, 1926; *The Theosophical Society in Australia Seventy-Fifth Anniversary Commemoration* TS, Sydney, 1970, p. 5; *ADB* 8 (Fisk).
10 'Prospectus' Theosophical Broadcasting Station Limited, TSA T 15/41 (also NLA); 'Australia. Her Purpose and Power', a talk broadcast from 4QG, Brisbane AA 1, 5, 1926, pp. 208–212; 'A.E. Bennett' *ADB* 7; Frank Legg *The Gordon Bennett Story* Angus

& Robertson, Sydney, 1956, ch. 1; pers. comm. the late R.E. Bennett, Surfers Paradise, Qld, September 1977.
11 *Wireless Weekly* 13 August 1926, p. 10, and 3 September 1926, p. 3; *SMH* 13 August 1926, p. 8. Perth lodge *Correspondence* (1925-6), Fisher to Copley, 4 May 1926; *TAT* 15 May 1927, p. 158.
12 *TAT* 15 May 1927, p. 160.
13 'Prospectus'; Balance Sheet, Theosophical Society Broadcasting Station Limited, 30 June 1931, TSA T 15/41.
14 *TAT* 15 May 1927, pp. 150, 161; also 15 January 1927, p. 31.
15 R.R. Walker *The Magic Spark. The story of the first fifty years of radio in Australia* Hawthorn Press, Melbourne, 1973, pp. 169-70; *TAT* 15 October 1926, p. 145; *SMH* 23 and 24 August 1926, p. 7 and p. 10; *TAT* 15 January 1927, pp. 30-31. For an example of early programming see *SMH* 28 August 1926, p. 12, and for developments mentioned in the next para, *TAT* 15 January 1927, pp. 30-1, and 15 September 1927, p. 99.
16 *ADB* 7; 'Tea and wireless' ABC talks pr. Margaret Evans, 20 December 1981; Walker *Magic Spark* pp. 52-53.
17 On J.L. Davidge, TS *Register* 1898-1918, Dip. 1004, *Star* 7, 3, 1925, p. 5 and *TAT* 15 September 1926, p. 93; on Pankhurst Walsh, Josie Castle 'The Australian Women's Guild of Empire' in Elizabeth Windschuttle (ed.) *Women, Class and History* Fontana Collins, Melbourne, 1980, and see p.338; Persia Campbell's letters in the Le Gay Brereton Papers (ML) hint at an interesting figure, and see Persia Campbell et al. *Studies in Australian Affairs* Macmillan, Melbourne, 1928; Bean's advocacy is in *TinA* 1 June 1924, p. 77.
18 Frank S. Greenop *History of Magazine Publishing in Australia* K.G. Murray Publishing Co., Sydney, 1947, ch. 19 emphasises the dearth of significant initiative 1915-1935.
19 Norman B.H. Keysor 'The Middle of the Industrial Road' *AA* 4, 5, 1928, p. 199.
20 J.C. Murtagh, cited Phyllis Mitchell 'Australian patriots: a study of the New Guard' *Australian Economic History Review* 9, 2, 1969, p. 156.
21 'The basic wage in New South Wales' and 'The problem of child endowment', *AA* 2, 1-2, 1927; see also 'Motherhood Endowment' *TinA* 1 December 1921, pp. 258-9.
22 Examples of *AA* contributions on diet: Bertha Crowther 'Packed Luncheons' and 'Better Breakfasts' *AA* 4, 1-2, 1928, May S. Rogers 'Vitamins' 1, 5, 1926, 'Diet for warm weather' 2, 2, 1927, Mrs Milton Powell 'How to prepare salads' 6, 2, 1929; *TAT* July 1932, p. 96; *Seventy-Fifth Anniversary Commemoration*, p. 23.
23 James Turner *Reckoning with the Beast. Animals, Pain, and Humanity in the Victorian Mind* Johns Hopkins University Press, Baltimore and London, 1980, pp. 118-19. Perth lodge *Minutes*, 1894-1924 (insert, *The Abolitionist* XLI, 6); *TinA* 1 May 1923, pp. 774-76, 1 August 1923, pp. 856-58 and 1 June 1924, p. 84; *AA* 6, 2, 1929 and 3, 5-6, 1927 for Horder and Sharpe. Society for Debating Vivisection, annual *Reports* 1929-1930 (ML), and Sealby, *AA* 2, 3, 1927, pp. 136-37. I thank Jennifer MacCulloch for referring me to SDV reports; see also her 'Animals in Sydney c. 1880-1930', *Sydney Gazette* 6, 1984.
24 *AA* 3, 5, 1927, 3, 4, 1927 and 4, 5, 1928 for Anson, Orr and Goodisson respectively; *TinA* 2 May 1921, p. 59. C.W. Leadbeater *The World-Mother as Symbol and Fact* TPH, Madras, 4th impression 1975, p. 40.
25 *AA* 4, 3 and 4, 5, 1928. 'Building for Nature' is reprinted as Appendix A, Donald Leslie Johnson *The Architecture of Walter Burley Griffin* Macmillan, Melbourne, 1977.
26 *AA* 3, 3, 1927; *Castlecrag* Sydney, n.d., p. 29; Hartmann *Who's Who in Occultism* p. 79 lists Mrs Robert Williams as Australian representative of the Anthroposophical Society (Bim Hilder of Castlecrag recalls Mr Williams as a man of independent income derived from a street-lighting invention).
27 Jill Roe 'Paradigms of the city' *Sydney Gazette* 5, 1982; Johnson *The Architecture of Walter Burley Griffin* p. 128. Rosemary Dinnage 'Benign dottiness: the world of Rudolf

Steiner' *New Society* 2 July 1981; pers. comm., Dennis Glenny, Sydney, March 1983 ('Meyerbold' is approximate spelling only).
28. Chris Cunneen '"Hands off the parks!". The provision of parks and playgrounds' in Jill Roe (ed.) *Twentieth Century Sydney* Hale & Iremonger, Sydney, 1980; T.P. Bellchambers 'Wild Life' *AA*, 5, 1928; *AA* 1, 2, 1926, p. 51.
29. Johnson *The Architecture of Walter Burley Griffin* pp. 80, 96.
30. 'The Magic of America', typescript, r. 2, S. 4, 168170 (Burnham Library, Art Institute of Chicago).
31. ibid. 393–401 and 194–201b; Illinois Society of Architects *Monthly Bulletin* 25, 2–3, 1940, pp. 1–2 (Burnham Library, Art Institute of Chicago); *ADB* 9.
32. Edward A. Vidler 'Are we barbarians?' *AA* 4, 3, 1928; also Henry A. Targent 'Cultural life in Queensland' *AA* 4, 6, June 1928.
33. James S. Perkins *An Approach to a philosophy of ART* Theosophical Press, Illinois, June 1952; Sixten Ringbom 'Art in "the Epoch of the Great Spiritual". Occult elements in the early theory of abstract painting' *Journal of the Warburg and Courtauld Institutes* 29, 1966, p. 391; Germain Bazin *The Avant-Garde in the History of Painting* Thames and Hudson, London, 1969, p. 272; Bernard Smith 'Wrestling with Modernism: McQueen's "Black Swan of Trespass'" *Meanjin* 38, 4, 1979, p. 523.
34. Cited in Gerritt Munnik 'The influence of H.P. Blavatsky on modern art' in Virginia Hanson (ed.) *H.P. Blavatsky and the Secret Doctrine* TPH, Madras, 1971.
35. 'Art, Music and Manners' *TinA* 1 October 1907, p. 130.
36. Dinnage 'Benign dottiness'. Very little has been written on the anthroposophical movement. M.D. Lawson, Theosophy and Education, unpubl. MA thesis, University of Sydney, 1972, ch. 7 on anthroposophical schools draws on Steiner's autobiography *The course of my life* Anthroposophical Publishing Company, London, 1928.
37. *Art of the Invisible* Catalogue, Bede Gallery, Jarrow, 1977, p. 54 (I thank Virginia Spate for access to this source); Ringbom 'Occult elements', p. 404; Gregory Tillett *The Elder Brother. A biography of Charles Webster Leadbeater* Routledge & Kegan Paul, London, 1982, pp. 261–62.
38. Michael Biddiss *The Age of the Masses. Ideas and Society in Europe since 1870* Hassock, Sussex, 1970 p. 170; Stephen Spender 'The glow of irreality' *New York Review* 13 August 1981; Munnik 'The influence of H.P. Blavatsky'.
39. Herbert Read *A Concise History of Modern Painting* Thames and Hudson, London, 1959, p. 175. Cf. Tom Gibbons *Rooms in the Darwin Hotel. Studies in English Literary Criticism and Ideas 1880–1920* University of Western Australia Press, Nedlands, 1973, ch. 5 on the elitism of symbolist aesthetics.
40. R.H. Croll 'Life of Tom Roberts, galley proof and letters' NLA MS 100/90–91 (I thank Humphrey McQueen for this reference). On Jane R. Price, founding member MTS, see *Janine Burke Australian Women Artists 1840–1940* Greenhouse Publications, Collingwood Victoria, 1980, p. 176, also E. Morris Miller and Frederick T. Macartney *Australian Literature. A Bibliography to 1938* Angus & Robertson, Sydney, 1956, p. 338.
41. 'Mussolini's Choice: Art or Utilitarianism' *AA* 1, 6–7, 1926–1927; Ann Galbally 'Australian Artists Abroad 1880–1914' in Ann Galbally and Margaret Plant (eds) *Studies in Australian Art* Dept. of Fine Arts, University of Melbourne, 1978, pp. 62–63; *AA* 1, 4, 1926, p. 191.
42. M.A. Turner 'The Science of Colour' *TinA* 1 May 1911; D.W.M. Burn 'Some Notes on the Bases of Art' *TinA* 1 July 1911; 'Colour Music and the Empire Spirit' *TinA* 1 January 1913; and Hilda A. Steven '"AE"-Irish Poet and Mystic' *TinA* 15 December 1929. See ch. 5, p. 158 for Gnosis lodge.
43. For example, *The Modernist* 21, August 1915 (I thank Humphrey McQueen for this reference); *TinA* 1 February 1911, p. 304, 1 May 1915, pp. 30–31; Miller and Macartney *Australian Literature* p. 387; *Mrs Besant's Australian Lecture Tour 1908: Press Notices*

pp. 131–32. On 'modernism', e.g. G.V. Portus *Happy Highways* MUP, 1953, p. 120, 'a tendency to modernism in my religious views'.
44 *TT* 38, pt. II, p. 692.
45 Gillian Naylor *The Arts and Crafts Movement, a study of its sources, ideals and influence on design theory* Studio Vista, London, 1971; Ian Britain *Fabianism and Culture: A study of British Socialism and the Arts, c. 1884–1918* CUP, 1982 pp. 87–88; J. Griffiths 'The Value of the Arts and Crafts' *TinA* 1 March 1916; 'Fellowship of Arts and Crafts' *TinA* 1 June 1923; and *TinA* 15 October 1929, p. 31. Also, *AA* 2, 3, 1927 and *Catalogue* Exhibition of Arts and Crafts by Messrs. Jas W.R. Linton and Arthur G. Cross, December 1910, Theosophical Rooms, St. George's Terrace, Perth, Royal Western Australian Historical Society, Arts and Crafts, PR 985, box 11 (I thank Tom Stannage for guiding me to this source).
46 Burke *Australian Women Artists*. On Western Australian women artists, see Clare and Keith Thompson 'Brief History of Perth lodge' and Mrs Leonard Matters *Australasians who count in London, and who counts in Western Australia* London, 1913, p. 202; *ITYB* pp. 185, 205 and *TinA* 1 September 1908, p. 136; Ethel Carrick (Mrs E. Phillips Fox) A Retrospective Exhibition Catalogue (Ruth Zubans, 'Biographical Essay') n.p., 1979 and Margaret Rich 'Ethel Carrick (Mrs E. Phillips Fox)' *Lip 1980. A feminist journal of women in the visual and performing arts* [first issue 1980, Melbourne]; Violet Teague 'Some Thoughts on Art' *AA* 3, 4, 1927.
47 Evelyn Caspersz recommended Russian expatriate Nicholas Roerich, a New York artist, *TAT* July 1933, p. 71, a figure recalled also by Frank and Margel Hinder (pers. comm. April 1984).
48 Mary Eagle 'Modernism in Sydney in the 1920s' in Galbally and Plant (eds) *Studies in Australian Art*.
49 ibid. also John Hetherington *Norman Lindsay, the embattled Olympian* OUP, Melbourne, 1973, and Renée Free *Frank & Margel Hinder 1930–1980* Art Gallery of New South Wales, 1980, pp. 3, 53 (see also n. 53 below).
50 15 October 1929, p. 2.
51 Quotations from John Henshaw (ed.) *Godfrey Miller* Sydney, 1966 (unpaginated).
52 Quoted in *Christian Waller 1895/ 1956* Catalogue, Deutscher Galleries, Melbourne, 1978. Burke *Australian Women Artists* p. 184; Tess Van Sommers *Religions in Australia* Rigby, Adelaide, 1966, pp, 69–76.
53 Nicholas Draff in *The Art of M. Napier Waller* Sun Books, Melbourne, 1978, p. 4. Perhaps there is a theosophical influence yet to be explored in the development of related arts in Australia, such as sculpture. But Sydney evidence is, at best, oblique; Bim Hilder, who worked with Marion Griffin staging plays and knew both anthroposophists and theosophists in the Castlecrag community, was not a theosophist (pers. comm.); Margel and Frank Hinder, the latter said to have been influenced by such works as Ellis's *The Dance of Life* (Geofrey Batchen, Modernism and Australian art between the Wars, Fine Arts IV thesis, Unversity of Sydney, 1981, p. 17) were not influenced specifically by theosophy (pers. comm., April 1984). Evidence for assertions that Australia's pioneering modernist sculptor Rayner Hoff was 'theosophically inspired' has not come to light.
54 Cf. Mary Normanhurst *Older than the hills* Ararat, 1929 (?), reviewed *TAT* 15 March 1929, 'a curious book by a student of the mysteries'; Paul Waldo-Schwartz *Art and the Occult* George Allen & Unwin, London, 1977.
55 Cited in Matters *Australasians who count* p. 51.
56 *EN* 25 October 1923, p. 8 and 12 November 1923, p. 9; *DT* 18 August 1924, p. 4.
57 *Mosman Daily* 14 May 1924, p. 2 and 5 November 1924, p. 1; pers. comm., Barbara Storey, Balmoral; Annette Bain '"Brighter Days"? Challenges to live theatre in the thirties' in Roe (ed.) *Twentieth Century Sydney*. The amphitheatre at work is also recalled by Mary Drake *The Trees Were Green. Memories of growing up after the Great*

War Hale & Iremonger, Sydney, 1984, p. 119, as one of Sydney's loveliest structures, but 'plagued by inclement weather'.
58 *SMH* 17 July 1982 for an obituary of that great trouper Enid Lorimer, who died aged 94 after a seventy-year career in British and Australian theatre. Trader Faulkner *Peter Finch. A Biography* Panbooks, London and Sydney, 1979, p. 42. *AA* I, 2, 1926, p. 122; 'Should the State subsidize the Theatre?' *AA* 4, 4, 1928.
59 ibid. 1, 2, 1926, p. 52, 1, 3, 1926, pp. 127–28, 2, 1, 1927, p. 4 and 2, 2, 1927, p. 95. Gala opening, the Savoy, 'Sydney's cosiest theatre' *Who's for Australia?* 11 June 1930, p. 11.
60 *Magic of America* II, S.4, 12. *TinA* 15 October 1904, p. 100, 1 January 1914, pp. 302–4 and 1 December 1917, pp. 225–26; Phyllis Campbell 'Music: Its Part in World Revolution' ibid. March 1931, p. 6; *SMH* 26 March 1983, p. 41.
61 *TinA* 1 June 1916, p. 70; LCC Jubilee p. 11; *TAT* 15 October 1926, pp. 126–7 and 15 January 1927, p. 15; N.A. Ingamells *The Hidden Significance of Music* Publicity Press, Sydney, 1924 and *Wagner's Music-Drama 'Tristan and Isolde'* Sydney, 1930, dedicated to J.I. Wedgwood.
62 Florence Harding, A sociological study of Sydney's cultural life, un publ. MA thesis, University of Sydney, 1947, p. 105. Pers. comm. Elliston Campbell, September 1983 (Mr Campbell has deposited his wife's compositions with the Music Centre of Australia). Phyllis Campbell 'Nationalism in Australian music' *AA* 5, 1, 1928; and *TAT* 15 May 1927, p. 177.
63 *SMH* 6 September 1984, p. 12 and *Harbinger* 1 September 1892, p. 4728.
64 *AA* 1, 1, 1926, pp. 15–19.
65 ibid. 1, 4, 1926, pp. 161–64 and 185; 'Vital Problems' 3, 4, 1927, p. 147.
66 'Australian women in council' *AA* I, 3, 1926, p. 119. See also Muriel Chase 'Equal status for women' *AA* 1, 4, 1926, 'A call to the women of Australia' (interview with Rischbieth) *AA* l, 6, 1926 and Bessie M. Rischbieth 'Common citizenship' *AA* 3, 1, 1927. Cf. Sabine Willis, The formation of Australian attitudes towards China: 1918–1914, unpubl. PhD thesis, University of New South Wales, 1974, pp. 307–8.
67 'Australian Motherhood' *AA* 1, 6, 1926 and 2, 2, 1927; Percy R. Meggy 'Women and politics' *AA* 3, 1, 1927 and A.G. Huie 'Women and the cost of living' *AA* 2, 6, 1927.
68 Keith Richmond 'Reaction to Radicalism: Non-Labour movements 1920–9' *JAS* 5, November 1979, p. 61; Peter Loveday 'Anti-political political thought' in Judy Mackinolty (ed.) *The Wasted Years?* George Allen & Unwin Australia, Sydney, 1981. *AA* 1, 2, 1926, pp. 92–93 and 3, 3, 1927, pp. 100 and 115.
69 'Australia First!' *AA* 3, 4, 1927, pp. 152–53 and 'Have you an Australian policy?' *AA* 2, 6, 1927, p. 243, also *AA* 3, 5, 1927, p. 229.
70 A.H. Nethercot, *The Last Four Lives of Annie Besant* Chicago University Press, Chicago, 1963, p. 422.
71 ibid. 'Dishonouring Australia: the condition of the Aborigine' *AA* 2, 6, 1927; 'The Australian Aborigines and their Allies' *AA* 3, 1, 1927; 'Our Black Brothers' *AA* 3, 4, 1927; 'Our dwindling natives; the proposed model native state' and 'Justice for the Aborigines' *AA* 4, 6, 1928. Cf. the partial claim, Frank Farrell *International Socialism & Australian Labour. The Left in Australia 1919–1939* Hale & Iremonger, Sydney 1981, p. 88 and E.G. Docker *Simply Human Beings* Jacaranda, Brisbane, 1964, p. 179.
72 *AA* 1, 4, 1926 for Dawson, Hughes; *AA* 1, 5–6, 1926 for Spurgeon Medhurst 'The new China' and response; I.M. Tokugawa 'Japan and world peace' *AA* 6, 3, 1929. Hopeful articles on the USSR appeared in theosophical journals in the early thirties, e.g. Isabelle Bean 'What Russia is doing' *TAT* July 1932, p. 93.
73 Viscount Cecil of Chelmwood 'Disarm or Perish!' *AA* 4, 4, 1928; Raymond Watt 'Disarmament: the need for a practical program' *AA* 5, 5, 1928; Persia Campbell 'Problems of the Pacific' *AA* 6, 4, 1929; Laura Bogue Luffman 'Josephine Butler' *AA* 2, 5, 1927; *Sands' Directory*, 1929.

74 Donald S. Birn 'The League of Nations Union and collective security' *JCH* 9, 3, 1974; Duncan Wilson 'The paths of internationalism' *TLS* 26 June 1981, p. 721; Willis, Formation of Australian attitudes, pp. 273–79.
75 This paragraph owes much to Freeden *The New Liberalism* (1978). See also my preliminary exploration of the shifting locale of nationalism in the 1920s, 'Annie Besant meets the magic pudding' *Nationalism and Class in Australia 1920–1980* Seminar Papers, Australian Studies Centre, University of Queensland, 1982. It was suggested to me that both Hughes and Holman were briefly members of the TS, the former before the 1920s. Confirming evidence has not been seen.
76 For example, 'Dives and Lazarus. Suggested Panaceas for Poverty' and 'Evolution or Revolution?' *AA* 6, 1, and 3, 1929; Peter Spearitt 'Mythology of the depression' in Mackinolty (ed.) *Wasted Years?* p. 3. *Who's Who of British Members of Parliament* Vols 1–3, Harvester Press and Humanities Press, Sussex and New Jersey, 1976 does not seem to contain an entry for Hamlet's father.
77 *TAT* 13 September 1927 and thereafter, May 1931, pp. 58–69 and September 1931, p. 126.
78 John L. Finlay *Social Credit. The English origins* McGill Queens University Press, Montreal and London, 1972.
79 Baiba Berzins 'Douglas Credit and the A.L.P.' in Robert Cooksey (ed.) *The Great Depression in Australia* Australian Society for the Study of Labour History, Canberra, 1970; Richard Davis 'Social Credit and the Tasmanian Labour Movement' in *Tasmanian Historical Research Association Papers and Proceedings* 25, 4, 1978.
80 Anthony W. Wright 'Guild Socialism revisited' *JCH* 9, 1, 1974.
81 Cited in Finlay *Social Credit* p. 105. Subsequent discussion begins from John L. Finlay 'The religious response to Douglasism in England' *JRH* 6, 4, 1971, also J. Oliver *The Church and the Social Order. Social thought in the Church of England 1918–1939* Mowbray, London, 1968, ch. 6.
82 Estimated from *TAT* 15 March 1927, p. 77, 15 February 1928, p. 53, 15 February 1929, p. 198 and 15 January 1929, p. 197.
83 Farrell *International Socialism*; R.A. Gollan *The Coalminers of New South Wales. A History of the Union, 1860–1960* MUP, 1963, p. 184; Keith Amos *The New Guard Movement 1931–1935* MUP, 1976, ch. 1, which also notes an estimated decline across the twenties of membership of the Communist Party from 750 (1922) to 249 (1928); Joan Rydon 'The conservative electoral ascendancy between the wars' in Cameron Hazlehurst (ed.) *Australian Conservatism. Essays in twentieth century political history* ANU Press, 1979.
84 John Lonie 'Non-Labor in South Australia' in Mackinolty (ed.) *Wasted Years?* p. 154; Josie Castle 'The Australian Women's Guild of Empire' in Windschuttle (ed.) *Women, Class and History*; Trevor Matthews 'The All For Australia League' in Cooksey (ed.) *Great Depression* p. 138.
85 Reported *AA* 4, 5, 1928, pp. 189–94.
86 *TAT* 15 April 1929, p. 8.
87 ibid. pp. 9, 32, 11.
88 F.R.E. Maulden 'The bother about coal' *AA* 6, 1, 1929 and 'The Coal Quandary. Clearing the confusion: can a Royal Commission do it?' *AA* 6, 4, 1929; Adela Pankhurst Walsh 'Foundations of industrial peace' *AA* 6, 2, 1929 and 'Is communism possible in Australia?' *AA* 6, 4, 1929. Cf. 'Labor's place in the changing social order' *TinA* 1 May 1922, p. 400.
89 'Theosophy applied to politics' *TAT* 15 October 1928.
90 *Who's for Australia?* 15 January 1930, p. 1. Miriam Dixson 'Rothbury' in Cooksey (ed.) *Great Depression* pp. 14–26.
91 *Who's for Australia?* Rules and Regulations n.d. but probably drawn up quite early as it has A.E. Bennett as presiding councillor, a title not seen later (ML).

92 *Sands' Directory* 1931; *Who's for Australia?* p. 3, 29 January 1930, 12 February 1930, p. 3, 9 April 1930, p. 3, 21 May 1930, p. 3 and 11 June 1930, pp. 3, 12.
93 *TAT* 15 April 1929, p. 32, 15 February 1930, p. 165 and 15 May 1930, p. 151. *Who's for Australia?* 9 July 1930, p. 2.
94 ibid. 29 January 1930, p. 2.
95 ibid. 25 June 1930, p. 11 and 9 July 1930, p. 5.
96 ibid. 26 February 1930, p. 2.
97 ibid. 25 June 1930, p. 3 and 9 July 1930, p. 2 for subsequent response by the ALP.
98 ibid. 29 October 1930, p. 1, 26 November 1930, p. 4 and 14 January 1931, p. 3.
99 Mitchell 'Australian patriots' p. 16.
100 George L. Mosse *The Crisis of German Ideology. Intellectual origins of the Third Reich* Weidenfeld & Nicolson, London, 1966; Bethia Foott *Dismissal of a Premier. The Philip Game Papers* Morgan Publications, Sydney, 1968, p. 56.
101 Mitchell 'Australian patriots' p. 160; also Amos *New Guard Movement* chs. 1–2; Eric Campbell *The Rallying Point. My Story of the New Guard* MUP, 1965, p. 28; Fitzhardinge *The Little Digger* pp. 591–99.
102 'Building Australia' *TAT* March 1931, p. 13. Reaction to 'altruistic organisations' by the 'Old Guard' is also noted in Moore 'Send Lawyers, Guns and Money!' p. 181 (see ch. 7, n. 32).
103 *TAT* May 1931, p. 42.
104 Matthews in Cooksey (ed.) *Great Depression* p. 146.
105 *TAT* 15 September 1927, p. 105.
106 *TinA* 1 June 1926, p. 88.
107 ibid. (supplement) 15 May 1930.
108 M. Lutyens *Krishnamurti. The Years of Awakening* pp. 301–5; Nethercot *Last Four Lives* ch. 9. *SMH* 10 March 1930, p. 10 and 8 August 1930, p. 12.
109 As recorded by the Lady Emily Lutyens *Candles in the Sun* Hart Davis, London, 1957, pp. 173–74.
110 ibid. p. 168.
111 ibid. p. 185.
112 Quoted M. Lutyens *Years of Awakening* p. 262.
113 *TAT* May 1931, p. 58.
114 ibid.

Chapter 9 ~ The end of an era
1 Presidential Address 1929 and General Secretary's Report 1933, *GR*; Emmett A. Greenwalt *California Utopia: Point Loma: 1897–1942* 2nd rev. edn., Point Loma Publications, San Diego, 1978, ch. 16; Gregory Tillett The Elder Brother: *A biography of Charles Webster Leadbeater* Routledge & Kegan Paul, London, 1982, pp. 241–42.
2 *TAT* May 1931, pp. 38, 57.
3 ibid. May 1932, p. 36, July 1932, p. 95 and September 1932, p. 115; *Notes and News* September 1934 and June–July 1935; R.R. Walker *The Magic Spark. The story of the first fifty years of radio in Australia* Hawthorn Press, Melbourne, 1973, pp. 104–105.
4 *TAT* February 1933, p. 176 and May 1933, pp. 249, 251; Australia (2GB), correspondence 4 February–30 November 1936, Adyar and the Manor, TSA T 15/41 (2); *Broadcasting Business* 21 October 1938, p. 3, 3 November 1938, pp. 22–26 and 15 December 1938, p. 8; Gavin Souter *Company of Heralds. A century and a half of publishing by John Fairfax Limited and its predecessors 1831–1981* MUP, Melbourne, 1981, pp. 116, 359–60 and *ADB* 8; pers. comm. R.E. Bennett, September 1979.
5 Adyar correspondence; *TinA* December 1936–January 1937, p. 5 and January–February 1950; Chris Cunneen '"Hands off the parks!". The provision of parks and playgrounds',

Jill Roe (ed.) *Twentieth Century Sydney* Hale & Iremonger, Sydney, 1980, p. 111. On the Chowder Head controversy, see *SMH* also *Labour Daily* February–March 1936.
6   *TinA* February–March 1937, pp. 6–8, 20, also August–September 1937.
7   C. Jinarajadasa 'E.S.T. The occult centre for the Southern Hemisphere. October 1951', *Deane Family Papers* NLA MS 610/ 98/C. Geoffrey Hodgson, 'The Manor Centre' *TinA* October–November 1938 pp. 16–18 referred to the Manor as a sacred ashram.
8   W.H. Newnham et al. *Historic Melbourne Sketchbook* Georgian House, Melbourne, 1977, p. 224.
9   Jill Roe 'Three Visions from Balmoral Beach', in Roe (ed.) *Twentieth Century Sydney* pp. 103–4.
10 M.D. Lawson, Theosophy and Education, unpubl. MA thesis, University of Sydney, 1972, pp. 140–44.
11 *Mary Lutyens Krishnamurti. The years of fulfilment* John Murray, London, 1983.
12 Marion Mahony to Walter Burley Griffin, 24 December 1935 and 23 March 1936, 'The Magic of America' S.l.
13 ibid. S.1 p. 22, S.4 p. 168, S.3 esp. pp. 132–139, 289–296, 430f. (bottom hand paginations). Louise Lightfoot 'With the Burley Griffins' *Dean Papers* NLA MS 2019/ 1 (I thank Chris Cunneen for this reference); Donald Leslie Johnson *The Architecture of Walter Burley Griffin* Macmillan, South Melbourne, 1977, pp. 84, 26; *Castlecrag* (n.d., publ. Castlecrag Infants' School Club). I thank Elizabeth Brenchley, Margaret Green and Bim Hilder for sharing their knowledge of Castlecrag with me.
14 On MMG's beliefs, see e.g. 'Man's Evolution', 'Magic of America' S.3 pp. 393–401. See also my 'Paradigms of the city' *Sydney Gazette* 5, 1982.
15 *Theosophical Forum*, April 1937, p. 143 and June 1938, pp. 180–81 ('fraternisation').

Appendix

Table 1. Progress of the Australa(as)ian Section, 1896–1914

	Membership			Branches		
	Total	Gains	Losses	Total	New branches	Losses
April 1896	267	not known	27+	10	Sydney, Dayspring (NSW); Melbourne, Ibis (Vic.); Adelaide (SA); Queensland (Brisbane); Bundaberg, Capricornia (Rockhampton); Toowoomba (Qld); Hobart (Tas.)	
1896–1900				7	Cairns 1896 (Qld); Maryborough 1896 (Qld); Perth 1897 (WA); Newtown 1900 (NSW); Fremantle 1900 (WA); Mt Rockly 1897 (NSW); Egyptian (NSW)	3	Dayspring 1899 (NSW; Mt Rockley 1898 (NSW); Egyptian 1899 (NSW)
April 1901	390	not known	not known	14		
1901–1906				6	Charters Towers 1901 (Qld); Townsville 1905 (Qld); Bendigo 1905 (Vic.); Eastern Hill 1906 (Vic.); Allansford 1906 (Vic.); Launceston 1901 (Tas.)	6	Maryborough 1902 (Qld); Bundaberg 1902 (Qld); Newtown 1903 (NSW); Rockhampton 1905 (Qld); Charters Towers 1905 (Qld); Toowoomba 1902 (Qld)
April 1906	551	169	44	14		
1907–1911				6	Besant 1908 (Vic.); Ballarat 1909 (Vic.); Bealiba 1910 (Vic.); Tweed River 1910 (NSW); Rockhampton 1910 (Qld); Stanmore 1911 (NSW)	1	Eastern Hill 1901 (Vic.)
April 1991	953	147	54	19		
				7	HPB 1911 (Newtown, NSW); Gnosis 1911–1915 (NSW); Spreyton 1912 (Tas.); Charters Towers 1914 (Qld); Toowoomba 1914 (Qld); Prahran 1914 (Vic.);	3	Allansford 1912 (Vic.); Stanmore 1912(?) (NSW); Ibis
Oct. 1914	1391	c. 277	c. 160	23		

Sources: Theosophical Society *General Reports* 1892–1914; Theosophy in Australasia (*Convention Reports*) 1896–1914

Table 2. Feminisation of theosophy in Australia: recruits

Year[1]	Membership[2]	Diplomas[3]		Recruits[4]	
		(1)	(2)	Male	Female
1898–99	392	60	57	28	29
1908–09	849	156	140	64	76
1918–19	1868	167	230	97	133
1928–29	1559	71	50	25	25

Sources: Theosophical Society *General Reports* 1899–1929; *Registers of Diplomas* 1898–1918

Notes:
1 The theosophical year from 17 November (Year 1, 1875)
2 According to *General Reports*
3 New members applied for Diplomas
   (1) Figures entered in *General Reports*;
   (2) My estimate from *Registers*, the only evidence from which male:female ratios may be calculated
4 Calculated from 3(2)

Index

A

ABC (Australian Broadcasting Commission), 251, 274
Aborigines, 67, 71, 98, 172, 237, 278, 294
  music, 274, 278
  religion, 41, 67, 78
Active Service Fund, 296–298
Adair, Alice, 158, 171, 268
Adelaide, 20, 36, 39, 43, 47, 63–65, 81–84, 97, 102, 114, 122, 124, 130, 159, 234, 295
Adelaide lodge, 57, 65, 97, 103, 107, 162, 186, 241, 279, 294, 307
  lotus circle, 111, 159, 199
Adelaide Register, 230
Advance Australia, 246, 248, 253–261, 263, 266, 268, 272–281, 283–289, 295, 296–297
Advertiser (Adelaide), 65
Advertising, 251–252, 270, 291
Adyar, 17, 24, 237, 285
Adyar Hall, 247, 273–274, 289
Adyar House, 211, 267, 242, 246, 248, 277, 279, 289, 307
'AE', 49, 267
Age (Melbourne), 64, 83, 84, 92
Agnosticism, effects of, 38–38
All for Australia League (AFAL), 285, 293–294
All-India Home Rule League, 193–194
Allman, Frederick, 124
America, 17, 29, 40, 55, 66, 76, 124, 127–128, 142, 179

Amritsar, 230
animal welfare, 112, 114, 172, 187, 254, 258–259, 306
Anson, L, 259–260
Anthropological Institute of Australasia, 67
anthropology, 21, 67–69, 98, 237
anthroposophy, 178, 260–262, 264–265, 269–270, 309
anti-clericalism, 35–36, 116, 137, 208
anti-vivisection, *see* vivisection
Argus (Melbourne), 64, 74, 85, 295
Armageddon 153, 214
Armidale lodge, 156
Armstrong, Winnifred, 164
Arnold, Sir Edwin, 15
  Light of Asia, The, 15, 33, 111, 164, 275
Arrow, 125–126
art, 101, 128, 162, 247, 254, 263–271
art and crafts movement, 134, 267, 271
  fellowship, 268, 271
Art Council, 275
Arthur, Dr Richard, 191, 254, 257, 276
Arthur-Smith, Mrs E.M. 308
Arundale, Francesca, 168
Arundale, George Sydney, 196–197, 237, 244, 245–248, 251, 257, 275, 278, 279, 281, 284, 285, 294–297, 302–303, 305–308
Arundale, Rukmini, *see* Rukmini Dewi, Shrimati
Arya Samaj, 17
Aryan race, 68, 98, 191, 271

351

Ashfield lodge, 216
Ashworth, Eleanor, 268
Astill, Miss, 296
Astor (Sydney), 236
Atkinson, Meredith, 232
Atlantis, 70, 98, 180
Auckland lodge (N.Z.), 104, 159, 199, 204
Austral Light, 122
Austral Theosophist, 76, 78–82, 86, 9, 96, 160
Australia, home of a new sub-race, 99, 133, 179, 201
Australian political parties, 275, 280, 293–294
Australia-India League, 278
Australian Church, 35, 40, 43–44, 62, 64, 103, 218, 311
Australian Federation of Women Voters, 173
Australian Herald, 63–64, 91
Australian Labor Party, 127, 280, 291, 293
Australian Legion of Ex-Service Clubs, 290, 292
Australian League of Honour, 188
Australian Party, 291, 293
Australian Reform Association (ARA), 277
Australian Theosophist, 246, 297
Australasian Secularist Association (ASA), 37, 102
Australasian Trained Nurses Association (ATNA), 191
Aveling, Edward, 53

B
Baha'i, 173
Baines, Mr, 60
Ballarat lodge, 167
Baptists, 38–39
Barnes, Mr & Mrs G.C., 225
Barton, Edmund, 62
Bavin, T.R., 275, 277, 291
Bean, C.E.W., 181, 189, 191–192, 204, 212, 221, 261, 279, 306, 312
Bean, Edwin, 184, 263
Bean, Isabelle, *see* Gater, Isabelle
Bean, John Willoughby Butler, 176, 181–185, 188–194, 212, 220, 225–228, 237, 312

Beard, E.G., 251
Beattie, J.W., 22
Beatty, Mrs Mason, 156
Bednarowski, Mary Farrell, 140
Bellamy, Edward, 89, 124
Benjamin, J., 103–104
Bennett, Alfred Edward, 246, 249–252, 277–278, 285–294, 298, 305–306
Bennett, Henry Gordon (Lt-General), 181, 249, 293
Bennett, Reginald E., 301, 308
Berger, Charles, 22
Besant, Annie, 17, 47–56, 74, 81–91, 92–93, 95–96, 99–100, 102, 107–111, 114, 119–131, 135, 137, 141–143, 146, 151, 154–155, 159–162, 164–165, 168, 170, 175, 177, 183, 202, 206, 214–215, 220–221, 228–240, 244, 247, 265–267, 277, 285, 297–298, 302–303, 304–305, 307, 311
  biographies, 50, 229
  conversion, 48–54
  India, 193–194, 229–232
  oratory, 49, 83–85
  science, 40–53
  women, 130, 142–144
  Australian Lectures, 121
  'Autobiographical sketches', 51
  Esoteric Christianity, 122
  The Changing World, 142
  'The Coming Christ', 130, 238
  The Law of Population, 90, 124
  'Theosophy and the Workers', 123
  Why I became a Theosophist, 49
Besant, Rev. Frank, 48, 86
Besant lodge, 185, 187
Besant, Mabel, 48, 60, 74, 79, 123, 183
Besant-Scott, Ernest and Mabel, *see* Besant, Mabel; Scott, Ernest
Belisario, Dr Clive, 73
Bhagavad Gita, 15, 86, 111, 275
Bibby, Joseph, 135
Birnie, Miss, 158
Birth control, 47, 48, 124, 154, 256, 259
Blackmore, Susannah, 163, 166

Blavatsky, Helena Petrovna (HPB), 8, 10–22, 24–29, 3, 33, 35, 47, 49, 53, 63–64, 70–71, 74–76, 79, 103, 109, 111, 123, 130, 144–146, 155, 157, 178–179, 194, 218, 237, 264, 269, 275, 304–305
   Isis Unveiled, 10, 12–15, 70, 144–145
   The Key to Theosophy, 26–28
   The Secret Doctrine, 25–26, 29, 33, 47, 53, 70–71, 79, 98, 144–145, 158, 271
Blavatsky lodge, 163, 227, 249, 252, 274, 295, 297
Bonwick, James, 17
Booth, Dr Mary, 187
Boult, Charles, 274
Bow, W.G., 281
Boyle, Hilda, 251
Bradlaugh, Charles, 36–37, 48, 53–54, 76
Branscombe, Edward, 247, 254, 274
Braund, Lt. Col. George Frederick, 156, 182
Brennan, Christopher, 79, 212
Brereton, Dr John Le Gay, 41
Brereton, Professor John Le Gay, 108
Bright, Annie, *see* Wright, Annie
Bright, Charles, 41–44
Brisbane lodge, 10, 20–23, 57, 59–61, 69, 100–101, 107, 111, 114, 118, 156, 159, 186, 199, 298
British American Co-operation Society, 307
British Commonwealth of Nations, 231, 235
British Empire, 18, 33, 134, 230–232, 278–279
Britten, Emma Hardinge, 10, 20, 21, 40–41
Brook, Ada, 251
Brown, James, 222
Browne, H, Junor, 46
Browning, Kate, 159–160
Bruno, Giordano, 50, 249
Buddhism, 18, 63, 80, 116, 237
Bull, Marjorie, 198, 201, 209, 211–212, 220–221, 298, 311
Bulletin (Sydney), 62, 83, 84–85, 88–90, 120, 123, 127, 154–155, 235, 255
Bulwer-Lytton, Edward, 14
Bundaberg lodge, 70, 82, 99
Burdett-Coutts, Angela, Baroness, 145

Burfield, Diana, 165
Burrows, Herbert, 52
Burt, L.W., 201, 216
Burton, Arthur, 251
Burton, Harry, 22

C

Cairns lodge, 70, 100
California, 94–95, 98
Calvinism, 138, 211
Campbell, Bruce, 13–14
Campbell, Elliston, 163, 279, 306–7
Campbell, Persia, 255, 279
Campbell, Phyllis, *see* Casperz, Phyllis
Campbell, W.D., 89, 103
Cambridge, Ada, 32
Cann, George, 277
Capital punishment, 129–130, 170
Carey, Clive, 295
Carpenter, Edward, 33, 49–50, 142
Carrick Fox, Ethel, 268
Carroll, Dr Alan, 63, 65–69, 195
Carruthers, Sir Joseph, 191
Casperz, Evelyn, 163, 169, 306–307
Casperz, Phyllis, 163, 273–274, 311
Castle, Kate, 65
Castlecrag, 260–261, 309–310
Central Hindu College, 119, 131, 142, 196
Central Hindu Girls School, 160
Chadwick, Owen, 32–33, 53, 138
Chamber of Manufacturers (New South Wales), 291
Champion, H. H., 86, 103
Chainey, Professor W.H., 42
Chappel, George H., 116, 217
Charlton, Frederick, 59, 100
Charters Towers lodge, 100, 102
Chase, Beatrice, 188
Chatswood lodge, 156, 185–186, 216, 258
Chesterton, G.K., 164
Chidgery, Victor, 186
Chidley, William, 167, 224
Child Study and Adult Health Association, 67–68

child welfare, 189, 192, 199, 254
chivalry, 185
Christian Science, 42, 114, 140, 157, 214, 257
Christian churches, 35–36, 44–45, 138–139, 176–177
   clergy, 120–122, 126–127, 133, 139
Christianity, 8, 17, 26–27, 30–32, 36, 38, 46, 49, 118, 121–123, 139–141, 211, 237
Christie, Catherine Wallace, 161, 185
Church of England, 45, 62, 123, 126, 191, 219
Clark, Axel, 79
Clarke, C.H. Manning, 32
Clarke, Marcella, 156, 159, 199, 301
class, 55–56, 62, 104, 115, 125, 141, 166, 184–185, 217–218, 224, 232, 236, 256, 261, 276, 280, 285–286, 292–294, 312
Clayton, Hope, 202
Clubbe, Dr C.P.H., 68
Codd, Clara, 83–84, 141, 307
Coleman, Peter, 37
Collingridge, George, 116
Collins, William Whitehouse, 37–38
   The Freethinker and New South Wales Reformer (1886), 37
   Freedom (1889), 37
Co-masonry, 110, 168–170, 195, 204, 206, 306–307
Communitarianism, 33, 79, 95, 216
Comparative religion, chair of, 130
conscription, 179
Conservatorium (Sydney), 202, 251, 311
Constitutional Association, 307
consumerism, 256, 276, 283, 290
Conway, Mercure, 34–35, 43, 46
Cook, Dr E. Alleyne, 117
Cooke, Professor Ernest, 102
Cooke, Mrs, 156
co-operation, 22, 26, 39
Cooper-Oakley, Isabel, 61, 69, 73–77, 79, 112, 141
Copeland, Henry, 62
Cosmos, 83, 90
'Coulomb conspiracy', 24, 81

counter-culture, 114, 312
Cowan, Edith Dircksey, 171
Creed, Dr John, 75, 90, 103, 113
cremation, 16, 79, 113–114, 130, 171, 256
crime and punishment, 124, 128, 190
Crisp, Christopher, 132
Cromer, Victor, 255
Crowther, Bertha, 256
Crowley, Aleister, 206
Crozier, Miss, 158

D

Daily Telegraph (Sydney), 62, 72, 223, 230, 250
D'Arcy, Dr Constance, 191
Darwinism, 13, 32, 68, 89, 98–99
Davidge, James Leonard, 130, 180, 246, 255, 276, 284, 289, 294–295
Davidson, Ian, 187
Davies, Lloyd, 251
Davies, Miss A.J., 160
Davies, Misses, 160
Dawn (TS Loyalty League), 218–219, 225, 242–243
Dawson, T.G., 276
Dawson, W.H., 22
Dayspring lodge, 97, 102
Deakin, Alfred, 10, 23–24, 31, 35–36, 63–64, 76, 82, 86–87, 90–91, 95, 103, 125, 178, 280, 295
Deane, Elsie, 132, 210–211, 268, 298
Deane, Henry, 210
Debney, Mr, 103
de Cairos Rego, George, 73
de Caux, L., 23
Degen, Oscar, 211
de Lissa, Lillian, 199
Denison, Flora MacDonald, 174
Denison, Sir Hugh, 306
de Norman, Beatrice, 197
Denovan W.D.C., 17
   Evidences of Spiritualism, The, 17
Denton, William, 42
de Palm, Baron, 16, 113

Depression (1890s), 37, 57
  (1930s), 261, 280
Despard, Charlotte, 147, 151–153, 173, 197
  Theosophy and the Woman's Movement, 152–3
  Women and the New Era, 152
Diggers' Parliament, 189
Dixon, Miss A.T., 159
Dobbins, Stanley, 269–270
Docker, E.G., 232
Douglas Credit, *see* Social Credit
Douglas, Major Clifford Hugh, 281–282
Douglas-Hamilton, Mrs Edith, 166
Drake, Mary, 272
drama, 264, 272
dress, 114
Driver, Mary, 147, 169, 172
Drummond, Lute, 309
Dungey, Nell, 252
Dwyer, John, 94

E
Eagle, Mary, 269
Earle, John, 163
Earle, Susannah, *see* Blackmore, Susannah
Eastern Hill lodge, 117, 162, 207
Eberle, Mr and Mrs, 225
economics, 192, 262, 282, 288, 290
Edelfelt, Erik Gustaf, 30, 59–60, 79, 99
Edelfelt, Isabelle, *see* Gater, Isabelle
education, 18, 112, 129, 143, 195–204, 233, 254
Edgar, Margaret Lillian Florence, 79, 101–102, 108, 158–161
Egyptian lodge, 102, 182
Elliott, Gilbert, 10, 20, 33
Empire Day, 134
Enmore lodge, 216
Ensor, Beatrice, *see* de Norman, Beatrice
'Entente, The', 191
environment, 172, 256, 261
esoteric Christianity, 13
esoteric culture, 249, 252, 256
Esson, Louis, 273

Esperanto, 116, 130, 279
eurhythmy, 200, 202, 271–272
eugenics, 67, 128, 190, 259
evangelicalism, 48, 53
evolution, 14, 56, 67–68, 71–72, 75, 89, 94, 98, 108, 148–149, 180, 196, (*see also* Darwinism)

F
Fabian Society, 48, 52
Far West Children's Health Scheme, 307
facism, 253, 266, 292, 312
Federation of Commercial Broadcasters, 253
Fellowship of Pioneers, 248
feminism, 46–47, 69, 89, 116, 139–141, 224, 256, 276
  Christian feminism, 139–141, 145
  theosophic feminism, 144–153, 171
'feminisation' of religion, 138
Finch, Peter, 245, 272–273
Fisher, Stanley Sprott, 201, 207, 291
Fiske, E.J., 249
Fison, Reverend Lorimer, 67
Fletcher, W., 292
Food Reform League, 246
Foott, Bethia, 293
Ford, Henry, 276, 290
Fitton, Doris, 273
Fraire, Chiaffredo Venerano, 99
Franklin, Stella Miles, 310
Fraser, Dr Donald, 218, 225–226
'fraternisation' movement, 310
Fremantle lodge, 102, 117–118, 156
freemasonry, 109
French Revolution, 36
Frensham, 200–201
Freud, Sigmund, 67, 218
Froebel, Friedrich, 111, 195
Fuller, Amy, 268
Fuller, Florence, 159, 162, 268, 271
Furner, Alice, 77, 220, 225
Furphy, Joseph, 56

G

Gage, Matilda Joslyn, 139
Gandhi, Mohandas Karamchand, 17, 173, 193, 230, 235, 238
Garden School Balmoral, 203, 272
Garran, Dr Andrew, 62
Gatchell, Mr, 89
Gater, Isabelle, (also Edelfelt, Isabelle; John, Isabelle; Bean, Isabelle), 60, 106, 120, 133, 171, 212, 217, 226
George, Henry, 78; (see also singletaxers)
George, Mrs Stella, 169
Gibson, Grace, 252
Gillot, George, 169
Gilman, Charlotte Perkins, 147, 173
Gilmore, Mary, 191–192
Given, Mrs Mary, 59, 158
Glanville-Hicks, Peggy, 273
Glenelg lodge, 156
Gmeiner, Leonora, 65, 160
Gnosis lodge, 134–135, 162, 200, 267
gnosticism, 79, 100, 145, 148
Goldstein, Vida, 147, 157
Golden Chain, 112
Goodisson, Lillie E., 259
Great White Brotherhood, 14, 110
Greek dancing, see eurythmy
Green, A.W., 191–192
Green, Dorothy, 31
Greenwood, Irene, 147, 169, 171–175
Gregory, E., 102
Greville, Edward, 41
Greville, Mrs, 191
Greig, Mrs J.E., 217, 224
Greig, Mr J.E., 224
Griffin, Marion Mahoney, 260–262, 276, 308–310
  'The Magic of America', 261
Griffin, Walter Burley, 254, 260–262, 273–274, 276, 308–310
Guild of Endless Life, 132
Guiterman, Roseen, 202
Gullett, Ivy, 191
Gullett, Dr Lucy, 202

Gurdjieff, George Ivanovich, 214

H

Hack, Wilton, 39, 79–80, 160
Haeckel, Ernst, 70
Hancock, Sir Keith, 231, 235
Harbinger of Light, 10, 18–23, 40–42, 47, 55, 58
Harcus, Lorimer E., 97
Harding, William, 108, 185, 192, 217, 297, 306
Harrison, Mr, 225
Hartmann, Carl H., 20, 22, 57
Haviland, E. Cyril, 22, 41, 44
  Free Thought (1880), 41, 44
  Rainbow, or the Sydney Progressive Lyceum News, (1883–1884), 41
  The Australian: A Monthly Magazine (1879–1881), 41
Hawkins, F.S., 114
Hawthorne, Mark, 163
Haycraft, J.H., 108
Haycraft, Miss, 112, 159, 167
Heaton, Herbert, 231
Helmrich, Dorothy, 226, 275
Heney, Helen, 163, 202–204, 211, 240
Hesselman, H.S., 210
Herald (Melbourne), 235
Hewison, F.E.S., 72, 80
Higgins, Henry Bournes, 24, 157, 232
Higgins, Ina, 157
Hill, Alfred, 274
Hilliard, Maud, 258
Hinder, Frank, 269
Hinder, Margel, 269
Hinduism, 51, 115, 123, 142, 237–238
Hobart lodge, 11, 22, 30, 57, 66, 73, 97–98, 103–105, 111, 117–118, 126
Hodgkinson, Dr Lorna K., 203, 252
Hodgson, Richard, 24–25, 63, 74, 76, 81, 123
Holman, W.A. 279–280, 284
Holmes, Edmond, 196
Hooper, Miss, 103, 158
Home, 255, 269
homosexuality, 218–220
Horder, Mrs Elsie, 258, 276–277

Horder, Monica, 251
Horne, Helen, 159
Hosking, Clement, 251
'Hospice, The', 166
hospital visiting, 103, 129, 171
HPB lodge, 185
Hughes, Billy (William Morris), 213, 233, 279–280, 284, 291, 293
Hughes, Dorothea Stanley, 202
Hugo, Victor, 52
Humanitarian Society, 246
Hunt, H.W., 15, 76, 79, 91, 117, 134, 236
Hunt, Mrs, 117, 236
Hygienic Banking Company, 255
Hynes, Lily, 199
Hynes, Samuel, 141

I
Ibis/Prahran lodge, 86, 102–103, 156, 295
immigration, 99, 277
Independent Theosophical Society, 225–226, 305, 308
India
    Australian contacts with, 18–19, 229
    'home rule', 193–194, 303
    dominion status, 235, 278
    musical influences, 273–274
    nationalism, 8, 193–194, 229
    religions, 32–33, 123, 237–238 (see also Buddhism, Hinduism, Islam, *Light of Asia*)
    women, 142–143, 161
    (see also Gandhi, New India)
Indian Mutiny, 18
Indian National Congress, 193
Ingamells, Loris, 217, 225
Ingamells, Norman, 274
Innes-Noad, Sidney Reginald, 192
insanity, 31
Institute of Public Affairs, 307
Irish Theosophist, 93
Irvine, Professor R.F., 191-2
Isambert, J.B.L., 22, 59
Isis, 12, 144–145

Islam, 80, 142–143
Ivey, Edward, 22

J
Jansenism, 31, 205
Jinarajadasa, C., 169, 230, 236, 244
John, Isabelle, *see* Gater, Isabelle
John, W.G., 60, 100, 102, 105–106, 116, 130, 132, 155, 157, 165
Johnson, Donald Leslie, 261
Johnston, Isabella, 169
Joske, Margaret, 268
Judge, William Quan, 16, 81–82, 93, 123, 184

K
Kadinsky, Wassily, 264–266, 270
Kay, Reverend, 61
Kenna, Francis, 59
Kessal, Heinrich, 97
Keysor, Norman, 285
King Arthur Home School, 204
King's Hall, 186
Kingsford, Dr Ann, 15, 61
Kingsford Smith, Charles, 258
Kindergartens, 103, 170–171, 195, 198–199, 307
Kitchens, national, 190
Knox, Nathaniel, 65, 79, 81, 103, 155
Köllerstrom, Gustav, 187, 192, 206, 223
Köllerstrom, Oscar, 244
Kormon Guild of Art Workers, 135, 267
Krishnamurti, Jiddu, 131, 164, 244, 178, 215, 238–241, 243–244, 263, 298–303
    At the feet of the Master, 183, 198
    Education as Service, 196, 200–202
Ku-ring-gai lodge, 295
Kvanka, Geza, 73

L
Labor governments, 99, 275, 287, 293
Lacey, George, 44
Lahey, Vida, 268
Lambert, George, 269
Lambrick, Amelia, 166–167

Lane, William, 33–34, 99
   Workingman's Paradise, The, 33–34
Lang, J.T., 275, 291–293
Lang, Murielle, 251
Lansbury, George, 243
Latrobe lodge, 156
Launceston lodge, 117–118, 156, 159
Lacey, George, 44
Laurie, Professor Henry, 91
Law and Liberty League, 51, 54
Lawson, Henry, 36, 58
Lawson, Louisa, 39, 46, 154
Leadbeater, Charles Webster, 95, 107–108, 112, 114, 119, 131, 133, 146, 169, 177–180, 186–187, 193, 195–196, 201–202, 206–207, 209, 218–225, 228–229, 238–240, 243–244, 245, 255, 259, 265–266, 285, 297, 302–303, 305
   'An Occult View of the War', 179–180
   The Other Side of Death, 108
   Outline of Theosophy, 108
   The Science of the Sacraments, 220
   'The Secret Life of the Lodges', 109
   Smaller Buddhist Catechism, 178
   'To Those Who Mourn', 180
   Vegetarianism and the Occult, 115
   The World-Mother as Symbol and Fact, 301
   with Annie Besant:
   Occult Chemistry, 178
   Thought-Forms, 178, 265
Leader, H.B., 64, 76
League of Active Service, 189
League of Nations Union, 232, 246, 254, 279, 295, 307
League of Sociable Service, 188
Leeson, Ida, 310
Lehmann, Rosamund, 162–163
'Lemuria', 70–73, 98
Leneva study group, 22
Leonard, Mrs, 159
Letchworth Garden School, 197
Levvy, Frances, 125
Ley, T.J., 223–224
Liberal, The, 44
Liberal Association (Sydney), 44
Liberal Catholic Church, 174, 204–212, 218–220, 245, 252, 298, 306
liberalism, 9, 21, 45, 75, 127, 134, 137, 280, 303, 311–312
Liberator, 33, 37
libraries, theosophical, 17, 76, 117, 158, 237
Lightfoot, Louise, 309
Lillingstone, W.G., 261
Lindsay, Norman, 255, 269, 312
Lion, Madamoiselle, 162
Link, The, 52
literature, 263
Lloyd Jones, Captain Russell, 202
Lorimer, Enid, 169, 254, 271
lotus circles, 111, 158, 185, 198
Lucifer, 73–4, 178
Luffman, Laura Bogue, 279
Lutyens, Lady Emily, 110, 113, 244, 300–301
Lutyens, Mary, 240, 243, 302, 308
   The Young Krishnamurti, 302
   Krishnamurti: The Years of Awakening, 240
lyceums, 37, 40–41, 113
Lyons, Mrs Rhoda, 59

M

Macaulay, Rose, 123
McCabe, Miss M.C., 190
Mac(c)ansh, Rowland, 59–60
MacCarthy, Dr Charles, 90
McConkey, John Beattie, 117, 201, 207, 210
McConkey, Sylvia, 274
Macdonald, Amelia, 171–172, 255
Macdonald, Jessie, 200, 202–203
MacKay, Major-General Kenneth, 108, 181
MacKay, John, 191, 199, 210, 217, 227, 301, 308
MacKay, Mabel, 199
Mackennel, Bertram, 266
MacKie, Professor Alexander, 232
MacKinnon, Mrs, 191
Mackenzie, Miss E.T., 158–159, 191
McLennan, Marie, 259, 267
McNeile, Ethel Rhoda, 164

Macpherson, Aimee Semple, 214
Maddox, Miss V.K., 169
Magic, 94
'Mahatma letters, the', 15, 24, 33
Maitland, Edward, 15, 2
Maitreya, Lord, 206, 208
Mallison, Mrs, 60, 158
Manly lodge, 216, 294
Manns, G.S., 20
'Manor, The', 169, 174, 216–217, 243, 246, 249–250, 272, 285, 296, 306, 307
Marks, G.W., 113
Marques, Dr A., 105
marriage, 114, 237, 259
Martyn, Thomas Hammond, 63, 77–78, 99, 104–5, 108–109, 133, 191–196, 201, 207–208, 210, 216–218, 220, 222–223, 225
Martyn, Alice, *see* Furner, Alice
Marx, Eleanor, 53
Marx, Karl, 39, 44
Maryborough lodge, 100
masters, 13–15, 19, 25, 62, 64, 79, 88–89, 93, 101, 110, 123, 187, 193
masturbation, 118–119, 219–220, 222–224
Mauldon, F.R.E., 286
Maybanke lodge, 70
Mazel, Julian Adrian, 207
Meade, Marion, 25
Medhurst, Spurgeon, 207
Melbourne lodge, 22, 30, 57, 64–65, 70, 76, 103, 107, 112, 117–118, 185, 295, 298, 307, 310
Melbourne and Sydney, 39–46
Melbourne Gnostic Society, 22, 42
Meldrum, Max, 269
Mellon, Mrs Annie, 90
mesmerism, 13, 64, 79
Mildren, Miss, 156
Miller, Godfrey, 270
Miller, Montague, 32, 102
millenarianism, 214–215, 244
Millions Club, 279
Minchen, Mr and Mrs, 93–94
Minet, Miss, 76

missionaries, 18, 24, 67, 123, 131, 160, 254
modernism, 265–271, 273–275
Mondrian, Piet, 265, 269
Montessori, Dr Maria, 195, 199
Moore, Miss E.B. Sheridan, 162, 258
Moorhouse, Bishop James, 64
Monash, Sir John, 280
Morgan, Alex, 61
Morice, Lucy Spence, 199
Morris, William, 267
Morton, Harold, 207, 285
Morven Garden School, 201–204, 226, 296
Mosley, Sir Oswald, 292
Mosman lodge, 295
Moss, Mrs, 171, 199
Moss, Olga, 202
motherhood, 147–151, 192
Mothers' Thought Guilds, 199
Mouchette, Berthe, 162
Müller, Max, 33, 80
Muncaster, Miss, 169
music, 162, 247–252, 263, 273–275
Mussolini, Benito, 266, 288, 290
Mutch, Tom, 251

N

National Council of Women of Australia (NCW), 171, 191, 254, 294, 307
National Secular Society, 48
nationalism, 235, 279, 290
Nationalist Party, 275, 277, 293
Neff, Mary, 20, 22
Neil, James, 122
Nethercot, A.H., 50, 205–246, 232
Nevill, Miss, 159
New Age, 141
New Economics Society, 307
New Education Fellowship, 197
New Guard, 292–293
New India, 193, 230, 232, 235
Neimeyer, Sir Otto, 291–292
Nityananda, Jiddu, 178, 240, 244
Noall, Hugh, 268
Noble, Gwen, 164

Noble, Margaret, 238
Noble, Miss, 156
Notes and News, 305

O
Occult tradition, 8–9, 11–14, 20, 48, 110
O'Dowd, Bernard, 37, 236
Ojai, 298, 308
Olcott, Henry Steel, 8, 11, 16–18, 25, 48, 54, 57–66, 82, 92, 108, 119
Olcott lodge, 200
Old Catholic Church, (OCC) 205–7, 209–210, 219
Oliphant, Harold George, 65, 225, 295, 311
Oliphant, Sir Mark, 65
Oliphant, Lawrence, 15
Ommen, 298, 300
O'Neill, Dr, 62
Orage, A.R., 141
Orchard, W, Arundel, 251, 276
O'Reilly, Creswell, 276
Order of the Round Table, 112, 202
Order of the Star in the East, (OSE), 112, 132, 152, 178, 182, 185, 200, 215, 240, 243, 245, 296–297
Orr, M.E., 259
Our Corner, 50–51
Outhwaite, Lillian, 200, 212
Oxenham, John, 188–189, 216, 227, 308–309

P
Pacific, 227
Paine, Thomas, 36
Palmer, Mrs, 191
Pan-Pacific Union, 255
Pankhurst, Christabel, 213
Parker, Mrs D., 156
Parkes, Henry, 33, 35, 82
Parks and Playground Movement, 306–307
'Partridge, Sydney', *see* Stone, Kate M.P.
Pascoe, Brother, 100
Patterson, Mr James and Mrs Henrietta, 101–102, 118, 156, 158
Paul, Judge, 22, 58

Peace Society, 246
Pechey, Edward Wilmot, 22, 113
Peebles, J.M., 41
Peel, George, 69, 113
Perdriau, Raymond, 217, 224
Perth lodge, 102, 107, 112, 118, 159–160, 172–174, 207, 250, 258, 281, 298
Petersen, R.C., 200
Pettigrew, Gavin, 19, 22, 59
Phillips, Dr Marion, 229
Pickett, Mrs Elise, 22, 30, 58, 64, 65–66, 70, 113, 158
Pickett, Kate, 64, 158
Piddington, A.B., 224, 232
Piddington, Marion, 222, 224, 259
Pierson, Stanley, 55
Pillars, Annie, *see* Wright, Annie
Pillars, Rev. James, 41, 43
Portus, G.V., 191
Powell, H.F., 124–125, 154
Powell, J.K., 231–232, 252
Power, Rev Manly, 59
Praed, Rosa Campbell, 72
Prakasa, Sri, 84
Prentice, John Murdoch, 177, 181–186, 187, 194, 208, 217, 220, 225, 226, 236, 305
Presbyterianism, 35
Preston, Margaret, 269
Price, Rev, Douglas, 267
Price, Jane, 266
Priest, Charlotte, 156, 258
prison reform, 103, 129, 170–171
Pritchard, Edgar, 287
prohibition, 256, 277, 286
Prohibition Society, 246
Prohibition Alliance (New South Wales), 254
Psychical Research Society (British), 24–25, 63–64
psychology, 11, 32, 53, 66–67, 86, 192, 216, 218, 252, 256
Purple Cross, 187
Pythagorean Music Society, 135, 162

Q

Quakers, 283
Queensland and the New Race, 98–100

R

Racial Hygiene Centre, 252, 258, 307
racism, 232–237
Radcliffe, Constance, 167, 209–210
Radio lodge, 306
Radio 2GB, 197, 212, 246–247, 248–253, 255, 263, 274, 277–278, 287, 289–290, 293, 296, 305–307
Railway Service Association, 292
Rall, W.R. 131–132
Ransom, Mrs Josephine Maria, 28, 156, 159, 161, 194, 245 (*see also* Davies, Misses)
Read, Herbert, 265–266
reconstruction, postwar, 189–194
Red Cross, 187, 279
Reid, Matthew, 134, 179, 221, 233, 250
Reimers, Christian, 20
reincarnation, 26, 89, 108, 121, 124, 174–175, 198
returned soldiers, 187, 284
Returned Sailors' and Soldiers' Imperial League of Australia (RSSILA), 191
Rich, Ruby, 169
Richards, Ann, 272
Richardson, Miss, 258
Richmond, Emma, 160
Riddett, Douglas, 281
Ride on Stranger, 284, 295–296
Ridgway, Ann, 170
Register (Adelaide), 230
Ringbom, Sixten, 265–266
Rischbieth, Bessie, 31, 167, 169, 171–175, 276–277, 294, 312
Rischbieth, Miss E.C., 295
Rivett, David, 160
Rivett, Edward, 260
Rivett, Eleanor, 160
Robson, Mrs, 159
Rocke, Dr Mary, 180, 242–243
Rockhampton lodge, 59, 69–70, 99
Rogers, May S., 258
Rohner, C.W., 19–20
Roinel, Victor, 116
Roman Catholic Church, 45, 62
Roseville lodge, 186
Rosicrucianism, 14, 136, 172, 269
Ross, John, 63
Ross's Monthly, 219
Rounsevell, W.B., 167, 173, 307–308
Rockley lodge, 102
Royle, Edward, 36
Royal Society for the Prevention of Cruelty to Animals (RSPCA), 172, 246, 307
Rukmini Dewi, Shrimati, 237, 244, 295, 301
Rushbrooke, E.A., 292

S

sabbatarianism, 37, 122–123
St Alban's Liberal Catholic Church, Sydney, 204–205, 209–210, 211–212, 246, 307
Theodora St John, 268
St Margaret's, Devenport, 200, 204, 212
'Sappho Smith' (Ina Wildman), 83, 85
Sastri, Sri Srinivas, 232- 235
Savoy Theatre, 289, 292, 307
Schreiner, Olive, 161, 263
'Science', 12–14, 28
Scott, Professor Ernest, 74, 76, 77, 79–81
Scott, Rose, 75, 90, 114
Scriabin, Alexander, 263, 273
Scully, Dan, 251
Sealby, Winnifred, 258–259
sectarianism, 45
secularism, 62, 9, 36–39, 267
servants, 18, 236, 277
Seventh Day Adventists, 114–115, 255
sexuality, 145–148, 192
Sharpe, Miss N.G., 259
Shaw, George Bernard, 53, 54
Siebenhaar, Wilhelm, 102
Simpson, John, 191
single-taxers, 80, 192, 261
Sinnett, A.P., 15, 65
    Esoteric Buddhism, 15, 65

Occult World, The, 15
Sinnett, Frederick. 65
Slade, Henry, 41
Sleath, Henry, 61
slums, 88–89
Smith, A.A., 93
Smith, Bernard, 264
Smith, George, 22
Smith, James, 76, 91
Smith, Professor John, 19, 20, 21, 24
Smith, Mrs Mary, 20, 158
Smythe, R.S., 42
social credit, 282–283, 288
Social Darwinism, 112, 128, 150
Social Democratic Federation, 48, 52, 141
socialism, 23, 34, 39, 48, 51, 55, 56, 78, 89, 101, 114, 124–125, 141, 147, 190, 282
  state socialism, 80, 88, 124
Society for Psychical Research (Melbourne), 90–91
sociology, 30, 129, 147
Soderberg, T., 78
Sons and Daughters of the Empire, 134–135
Southcott, Joanna, 88, 137
Spark's Fortnightly, 231–232
Spasshatt, Nina, 156
Spence, Catherine Helen, 277
Spencer, Herbert, 198
spiritualism, 8–13, 17, 20, 23, 26, 39–47, 64, 76, 88, 90–91, 101, 137, 140, 214, 311
spiritualist practitioners, 10, 26, 22, 31, 37, 40–41, 46–47, 90–91
Stanway Tapp, Mrs, 156
Star publications, 132, 241
Star Amphitheatre, 133, 241–243, 246, 258, 272, 296, 308
State Children's Relief Board (NSW), 192, 203
Stead, W.T., 51–52
Steel, Mrs, 102, 156
Steiner, Rudolph, 178, 260, 261–262, 265
Stephen, Mrs Consett, 191
Stephen, H.W.H., 44
Stirling, James, 103

Stone, Kate M.P., 161
Stopes, Marie, 149, 222, 224
Strathfield lodge, 186, 216
Street, Jessie, 175
Strong, Reverend Dr Charles, 35, 40, 43–44, 63, 76, 89, 91
Studd, S.T., 15, 181, 185–186
Sturdy, Edward Toronto, 15
Susman, Sister, 159
Swiney, Rosa Frances Emily, 147–151
  The Awakening of Women, 147
  The Bar of Isis; or The Law of the Mother, 147
  The Cosmic Procession, 147–151
Sydney lodge, 57, 63, 66, 68–69, 73, 78, 82, 93–94, 102–103, 107, 111–113, 118, 129–130, 158, 186, 198, 216–218, 225–226
Sydney Theosophic League, 75–75, 77
Sydney Morning Herald, 62, 75, 83, 88, 125, 231, 306
Symes, Joseph, 37–38, 44
Swedenborg, Emanuel, 22, 108, 137
Swedenborgians, 41, 46

T

Talbot, Dean, 183, 191
Taylor, Dr and Mrs, 60
Taylor, Thomas Griffith, 254, 278, 285
teachers, 159–160, 166, 195–202
Teague, Violet, 266, 268
Tennant, Kylie, 284, 296
Terry, W.H., 10, 19–20, 23, 40, 43, 58, 88
theosophia, 8, 11, 39, 136–137, 148, 158
Theosophical Education Trusts, 196, 201
Theosophical Fraternity in Education, 197
Theosophical Order of Service, 130, 168, 170–171
Theosophical Society (TS): founded, 8–9; beginnings in Australia, 10–11; founders, 15–16; to India, 17; headquarters, 18; objects, 27–28, 136; presidents, 11, 48, 169, 196; Esoteric Section, 28, 81, 86, 109, 117, 218, 302; Golden Jubilee, 214, 245
  in America, 8, 16, 29, 80, 93
  in Dutch East Indies, 49, 217

in England, 17, 23, 29
in Germany, 178, 260, 265
in Holland, 265
in India, 17–18, 27, 82
Theosophical Society in Australia, 57, 65, 70, 92–97, 103–104, 256, 302, 310–311
   Convention, 96, 105, 156, 185, 187
   finances, 106–107, 203, 295–298
   general secretaries, 65, 92, 95–96, 104–107, 161, 176, 245, 285
   headquarters, 65, 111, 186, 226–227 (*see also* Adyar House)
   lodges, 185–186, 216–217, 295
   membership, 96–97, 104, 133, 135, 157, 176, 215, 226, 295,305
   radio, 246–253, 305–306
   school, 195–204
   splits, 92–93, 221–222, 225, 295, 302
Theosophical Society in America (NSW Centre), 93
Theosophical Society Loyalty League, 218
Theosophist, The, 10–11, 15, 17, 19, 21–22, 25, 49, 54, 61, 67, 69, 197, 206
Theosophy in Australasia, 96, 105, 118, 161, 189, 263
This World and the Next, 90–91, 102
Thompson, Clare, 172, 221
Thompson, E. Lindsay, 292
Thompson, E.P., 110
Tillett, Gregory, 177–178, 208
Tingley, Catherine, 93, 95, 222–224, 304
Toowoomba lodge, 22, 57–58, 100–101, 308
Townsville lodge, 99
Tregear, Edward, 21
Truth, 123, 125, 222
Turner, William, 62
Tweed River lodge, 133
Tweedie, David Morton, 207
Twigg, Julia, 115
Tyerman, John, 42–43

U
Unitarianism, 39, 43–44, 46–47, 75, 159, 267, 311
United Australia Party, 293

Universal Brotherhood and Theosophical Society (UBTS), 93, 95, 222, 226, 304, 310
United Lodge of Theosophists (London), 226
United Spiritualist Church, 255
Upadhi, 73, 91, 155

V
vaccination, 103, 115, 259
van der Leeuw, J.J., 204, 207, 217, 279
van Gelder, Karel, 187, 217, 249
Vaughan, J.H., 295
Vasanta Garden School, 204
vegetarianism, 67, 79, 89, 101, 103, 114–116, 120, 257–258
venereal disease, 145, 188–190, 192, 259
Verbrugghen, Henri, 274
Victorian Association of Progressive Spiritualists (VAPS), 40, 42–43
Victorian Theosophic League, 74, 76
Vidler, Edward, 262
Vigors, Douglas, 272
vivisection, 50, 67, 79, 115, 246, 254, 256, 258–259
Vreede, Dr Adrian, 217

W
Wachtmeister, Countess, 97
Wagner, Richard, 162–163, 251, 255
Walker, Thomas, 37–38, 44
Wallace, Alfred Russel, 153
Waller, Christian, 270–271
Waller, Mervyn Napier, 271
Walsh, Adela Pankhurst, 254–255, 261, 285–286
Walters, Reverend George, 43, 90, 97, 114, 122
Wanliss, Miss, 134
Watson, W., 277
Watt, Raymond, 279
Way, Mrs Sara, 113
Webb, Beatrice, 53, 84
Wedgwood, James Ingall, 206–208, 211, 218–219, 244
Wiedersehn, H., 225

Wellington lodge (NZ), 57
West, Winnifred, 200–201
Westminster Gazette, 92, 96, 147
White Australia Policy, 123, 134, 179, 235–236
White, Sir C.B.B., 181, 204
White Lotus Day, 111
Whitlam, Gough, 213
Who's for Australia?, 289–290, 292
Who's for Australia League, 289–292, 294
Whyte, Captain Herbert, 112
Wienholt, Mary Margaret, 166
Wild Life Preservation Society, 306
Wilde, Oscar and Constance, 17
Willans, W.T., 23, 30, 63, 70, 72, 82, 93–94, 155, 226
Willans, Mrs, 158
Williams, Gertrude Marvin, 50
Willis, William *see* Collins, William Whitehouse
Wilshire, R., 161
Wilson, H.A., 60
Wilson, John Bowie, 41, 44
Windeyer, Lady Mary Elizabeth, 35, 75
Windeyer, Sir William Charles, 21, 31, 41, 44, 89–90
Windsor, A.L., 91
Winged Seed: Theosophy, 94–95

Wireless Weekly, 250
Wishart, Robert, 60, 155
Wolstenholme, Maybanke, 74, 78, 158
Women's Christian Temperance Union (WCTU), 172
Women's Service Guild, 171–172
women's suffrage, 47, 75, 142
Wood, 'Professor' Ernest, 252, 279
Woolley, Dr John, 21
Woolley, Mrs Margaret, 20, 41, 158
Workers' Educational Association (WEA), 191–192, 246, 294
World Mother, 301
World Teacher, 112, 131, 133–134, 152, 176, 178–180, 183, 195, 210, 214, 238–239, 283, 294, 301–302, 308
world university, 245
Worth, Miss, 156
Wright, Annie, (*also* Bright, Annie; Pillars, Annie) 41, 43, 46–47, 158

Y

Yarrington, Reverend W.H.H., 122
Yates, Frances, 136
Yeats, William Butler, 17, 49, 79 *Workingman's Paradise, The*, 33–34
Young, Mrs, 156
Youth work, 112

Wakefield Press is an independent publishing and
distribution company based in Adelaide, South Australia.
We love good stories and publish beautiful books.
To see our full range of books, please visit our website at
www.wakefieldpress.com.au
where all titles are available for purchase.
To keep up with our latest releases, news and events,
subscribe to our monthly newsletter.

Find us!

Facebook: www.facebook.com/wakefield.press
Twitter: www.twitter.com/wakefieldpress
Instagram: www.instagram.com/wakefieldpress

www.ingramcontent.com/pod-product-compliance
Lightning Source LLC
Chambersburg PA
CBHW021930290426
44108CB00012B/792